CHINA
into
AFRICA

CHINA
into
AFRICA

Trade, Aid, and Influence

ROBERT I. ROTBERG
Editor

BROOKINGS INSTITUTION PRESS
Washington, D.C.

Copyright © 2008
WORLD PEACE FOUNDATION
P.O. Box 382144
Cambridge, Massachusetts 02238-2144

China into Africa: Trade, Aid, and Influence may be ordered from:
Brookings Institution Press, c/o HFS, P.O. Box 50370, Baltimore, MD 21211-4370
Tel.: 800/537-5487 410/516-6956 Fax: 410/516-6998
www.brookings.edu

Library of Congress Cataloging-in-Publication data

China into Africa : trade, aid, and influence / Robert I. Rotberg, editor.
    p.   cm.
    Includes bibliographical references and index.
    Summary: "Discusses the evolving symbiosis between Africa and China and specifies its likely implications. Among the specific topics tackled here are China's interest in African oil, military and security relations, the influx and goals of Chinese aid to sub-Saharan Africa, human rights issues, and China's overall strategy in the region"—Provided by publisher.
    ISBN 978-0-8157-7561-4 (pbk. : alk. paper)
    1. China—Foreign relations—Africa. 2. Africa—Foreign relations—China. 3. China—Foreign economic relations—Africa. 4. Africa—Foreign economic relations—China. I. Rotberg, Robert II. Title.
    DS740.5.A34C45 2008
    303.48'25106—dc22   2008031155

9 8 7 6 5 4 3 2 1

The paper used in this publication meets minimum requirements of the American National Standard for Information Sciences—Permanence of Paper for Printed Library Materials: ANSI Z39.48-1992.

Typeset in Minion

Composition by Cynthia Stock
Silver Spring, Maryland

Printed by R. R. Donnelley
Harrisonburg, Virginia

Contents

Preface

Africa attracted China as early as the T'ang dynasty (A.D. 618–907); ninth century reports of the meat-eating, ivory-exporting people of Po-pa-li in the "southwestern sea" may refer to the inhabitants of what is now modern Kenya or Tanzania. By the eleventh or twelfth centuries, the city-state dwellers from Pate to Kilwa along the eastern African coast appeared to have been shipping elephant tusks, rhinoceros horn, tortoise shell, aromatic woods, incense, and myrrh directly or indirectly to southern China. During the Sung dynasty (A.D. 1127–1279), Chinese shipping was common throughout the western reaches of the Indian Ocean. Chinese objects from this period of all kinds, including specie, have been found from today's Somalia to Mozambique. Chinese references to *k'un lun*—slaves as "black as ink"—are also common from Sung times. But it is from the fifteenth century that we can date China's first certain direct involvement with Africa. Between 1417 and 1431, the Ming emperors dispatched three large expeditions to eastern Africa to collect walking proof of the celestial approval of their virtuous and harmonious reigns. Only Africa could supply a confirmation of these blessings; the arrival of unicorns from distant lands would supply the propitious signs of heaven's mandate, and only in Africa could unicorns—giraffe—be found. Hence, from Kenya or Tanzania a number of giraffe (and other animals) were strapped to the pitching decks of Chinese junks and transported across the sea to the imperial palace in distant Beijing.

China and Africa have enriched each other intellectually, culturally, and commercially ever since. But direct contact and interactive influence have been episodic. During the middle years of the twentieth century, Maoist China funded and educated sub-Saharan African anticolonial liberation movements and leaders, some of which and some of whom later emerged victorious in their national struggles for freedom; others lost out to Soviet-backed movements. China assisted the new nations of sub-Saharan Africa during the remainder of the twentieth century, especially by providing military hardware and training, but also by providing Chinese labor and capital to construct major railways and roads.

Africa and China are now immersed in their third era of heavy engagement. This one is much more transformative than the earlier iterations. Indeed, as the contributed chapters in this book make very evident, China's current thrust into sub-Saharan Africa promises to do more for economic growth and poverty alleviation there than anything attempted by Western colonialism or the massive initiatives of the international lending agencies and other donors. China's very rapaciousness—its seeming insatiable demand for liquid forms of energy, and for the raw materials that feed its widening industrial maw—responds to sub-Saharan Africa's relatively abundant supplies of unprocessed metals, diamonds, and gold. China also offers a ready market for Africa's timber, cotton, sugar, and other agricultural crops, and may also purchase light manufactures. This new symbiosis between Africa and China could—as this book demonstrates—be the making of Africa, the poorest and most troubled continent.

There are major cautions, too, which most of the chapters in this book spell out. China is no altruist. It prides itself on not meddling and on merely desiring Africa's resources. Thus it professes to care little about how individual African nations are being ruled; nor does it seek to change or improve the societies in which it is becoming a major, if not the dominant, commercial influence. China is extractive and exploitive, while simultaneously wanting friends and seeking to remove any remaining African ties to Taiwan. China also does not yet understand that, as salutary as competition might be for Africa's continuing maturation, importing Chinese labor to complete Chinese-organized infrastructural and mining projects inhibits skill transfers and reduces indigenous employment growth. Doing so also breeds resentment, as does the undercutting of local merchants and industrialists by the supply of cheaper Chinese goods or sharper Chinese entrepreneurial instincts. Africans, and Westerners certainly, further complain about China's disdain for human rights and mayhem in Africa. The fact that China may have been and may still be morally complicit in the Sudan's massacring of Darfuri civilians or the repression of Equatorial Guineans and Zimbabweans, through the supply of weapons of war to the relevant militaries and through the refusal to employ its evident economic leverage appropriately on the side of peace, weighs heavily in the balance.

China is opportunistic. The contributions to this book assess the positive and negative results of its latest move into Africa, and look at each of the salient issues in turn. Fortunately, in creating a final, mixed conclusion, the contributors do so by weighing the available evidence dispassionately and from a variety of national perspectives. This is as much an African as a Chinese analysis, with European and American inputs as well.

Harvard University's Kennedy School of Government's Program on Intrastate Conflict, the World Peace Foundation, and the Center for Global Development brought the contributors to this volume, and others, together at the Kennedy School to discuss China's impact on Africa in June 2007. Vanessa Tucker managed that process with uncommon skill. The chapters that follow mostly grew out of papers presented there; others were commissioned subsequently. Several revisions followed, all shepherded and edited ably and assiduously by Emily Wood. I am very grateful to both of them, and for the constructive comments on my first chapter by Deborah Brautigam, Harry Broadman, David Shinn, and Chandra Lekha Sriram. Along the way, Laura Rudert added important findings from her research.

This project could not have been turned into a pathbreaking book without the detailed involvement and encouragement of Todd Moss and his colleagues at the Center for Global Development, and the backing of Graham Allison, Director of the Belfer Center for Science and International Affairs at the Kennedy School, and Chairman Philip Khoury and the other always supportive trustees of the World Peace Foundation. The editor and contributors to this volume are enduringly grateful for their belief in our enterprise.

ROBERT I. ROTBERG
August 12, 2008

ROBERT I. ROTBERG

1

China's Quest for Resources, Opportunities, and Influence in Africa

China and Africa desperately need each other. China cannot easily grow without Africa. Nor can sub-Saharan Africa (a collection of forty-eight disparate countries) subsist, and now prosper, without China. Africa and China, in Auden's terms, have at last met, and their recently forged and continuously reinvigorated, mutually reinforced, interactive relationship is already tight and will for decades grow ever stronger, more thoroughly intertwined.[1] Both benefit significantly from this remarkably symbiotic relationship.

China hardly wants to colonize, but it does have immense mercantilist ambitions. It ravenously seeks raw materials—petroleum, timber, ferrochrome, cobalt, platinum, copper, diamonds, and so on. Whatever primary resources are buried beneath the soils of sub-Saharan Africa, China needs them to feed its massive industrial surge and—ultimately—America's substantial consumer demand. When the globe's largest nation-state is growing at 10 or 11 percent a year, it sucks up basic commodities from all over, including Africa. No world power, not even during the official colonial period, had an appetite equal to China's today.

Sub-Saharan Africa, in turn, welcomes such an insatiable appetite. The Chinese not only purchase Africa's unprocessed returns of the subsoil, the land, and offshore drilling, but the Chinese also invest for the long term, thus expanding Africa's permanent capacity in the mining and petroleum sectors. To service these extractive industries and manufacturing capabilities more generally, China also constructs or refurbishes roads and railways, creates export processing zones, supplies equipment, and builds up national industrial bases. Where sub-Saharan African nation-states are particularly fragile or questionably ruled, China also supplies arms and military firepower, builds barracks, provides uniforms, and offers various types of technical assistance, army to army. Never have the economies of sub-Saharan Africa grown so rapidly. Potentially, Chinese purchases and direct expenditures could lift key African countries out of poverty.

China is not interested in territorial conquest, in exporting its own surplus nationals (although the presence of Chinese nationals in Africa is growing), or, necessarily, in gaining converts for a Chinese model of development. Yet, as Chin-Hao Huang suggests in chapter 14 of this book, Chinese strategists do believe that their developmental model, and China's history, provide valuable lessons for Africa. Lifting millions of Chinese out of poverty offers a powerful guiding example, as does China's rapid achievement of political stability and international prominence. "Such a national narrative," writes Chin-Hao Huang, "resonates powerfully in Africa" (see page 298). By mid-2008, the Chinese model was looking even better, given the disarray in U.S. financial markets, the subprime mortgage crisis, and the dollar's unchecked depreciation. Moreover, China was growing, the U.S. economy stagnating. China seemed "galled" by American attitudes.[2]

China's goals are ideological as well as material. In addition to gaining sovereign control over stable supplies of primary goods, China wants to marginalize Taiwan's engagement with Africa (four African countries still recognize Taiwan; Malawi switched its allegiance to China early in 2008).

China is not necessarily in competition with the United States or Europe for Africa. Despite what Washington may believe, China is not using its engagement with Africa primarily to humble the United States or Europe, or to score political points in the ongoing battle for global hegemony. However, China is defensive, fearing that Washington may attempt to contain China's ambitious global agenda. Admittedly, China prefers and has always preferred to acquire loyal friends in Africa— friends who supported its application for a permanent seat on the Security Council, its entrance into the World Trade Organization, and its desire to host the 2008 Olympics. China has wanted friends who would now and in the future back it in international fora everywhere and always. In exchange, asserts Stephanie Rupp, "China has robust and reciprocal partnerships with African states at the highest levels of diplomacy, in contrast to Euro-American tendencies to treat African states as second-tier players."[3]

China has displaced European, American, and Japanese diplomatic and capitalistic soft power in many sub-Saharan African countries, "winning influence in countries where Western governments were conspicuous by their absence."[4] (Japan and India are pushing back, both having organized summit meetings with African leaders. In 2008, at the Tokyo International Conference on African Development, Japan pledged to double its aid to Africa to $3.4 billion by 2012, and to offer up to $4 billion in low-interest loans. Japan clearly seeks to compete on roughly equal terms with China in Africa. India held its own conference earlier in 2008, and made similar promises.)[5]

China's diplomatic offensive has been as thorough as its investment, trade, and aid advances. Unlike the less engaged West, China has established embassies in thirty-eight of sub-Saharan Africa's forty-eight countries. It has exchanged military attachés with about fourteen African nations. It has created Confucius Institutes in several national capitals and partially funds a serious think tank in South Africa. President Robert Mugabe, in Zimbabwe, decreed the mandatory teaching of Mandarin in the University of Zimbabwe. Throughout Africa, scholarships are available for study in China, and student exchanges are common. The Chinese Communist Party sponsors frequent people-to-people visits to and from Africa. Indeed, as Joshua Eisenman makes evident in chapter 11, the party's initiatives toward Africa naturally parallel and support those of the state. The party's International Department has also worked closely with China's National People's Congress to foster a range of interparliamentary exchanges with a dozen or more African legislatures. Those interactions have proved more complementary when they have been with single-party or tightly controlled African parliaments, as have the party-to-party visits. Winning and keeping friends is important and is effected through intensive party-to-party contact, vigorous wooing of African party leaders and personnel, and extensive hospitality—all in conjunction with China's developmental and trade objectives. Cementing what has become a mutually beneficial two-way relationship, President Hu Jintao of China has visited Africa five times since 2003, twice as vice president. Premier Wen Jiabao toured seven African countries in 2006. Earlier, senior leaders from the Politburo Standing Committee of the Chinese Communist Party visited most of the countries of Africa.

China has become the largest new investor, trader, buyer, and aid donor in a select number of important African countries, and a major new economic force in sub-Saharan Africa as a whole. Chinese trade with sub-Saharan Africa is growing at 50 percent a year. Already that trade has jumped in value from $10 billion in 2000 to about $50 billion in 2007. With Kenya, for example, China's trade doubled between 2005 and 2006, putting the $706 million total just below Kenya's totals in 2006 with the United States and Britain. Everywhere, China is building roads, railways, harbors, petrochemical installations, and military barracks; pumping or purchasing oil; farming; taking timber; supplying laborers; and offering physicians. A number of sub-Saharan African nations now depend critically on Chinese cash and Chinese initiatives. Of China's roughly $1.5 billion invested in Africa in 2006, about half went to resource-rich nations. The remainder of China's investments was in agroprocessing, power generation, infrastructural construction, telecommunications, and tourism in a dozen disparate African countries, such as Madagascar and Senegal. In 2008, Chinese companies were even being encouraged to purchase farmland overseas, not only in Africa. The goal was to help guarantee China's food security, especially for crops like soybeans.[6] In chapter 5, Harry Broadman asks whether Chinese investment in Africa might usefully serve to reduce Africa's dependency on the export of natural resource commodities.[7]

Growing rapidly and bursting out of its long underdeveloped cocoon to become a major world power and global economic source, China needs sources of energy and the raw materials—copper, cobalt, cadmium, manganese, platinum, nickel, zinc, tantalum, titanium, uranium, and so on—that African nations can supply. China rivals the United States for Angola's oil, controls most of the Sudan's oil, and is exploring energetically for oil onshore and up and down the coasts offshore. It is a major purchaser of timber from West Africa. About 40 percent of Africa's total exports to Asia are to China; about 30 percent of Asia's total exports to Africa are from China.

Before the 1990s, China relied for energy on abundant locally produced coal and on domestic reserves of oil. By 1993, however, it had become a net importer of petroleum; ten years later, China was the world's second-largest consumer of imported oil (now nearly 8 million barrels per day, or bbl/d) after the United States (now more than 21 million bbl/d), displacing Japan in the number two position. China now accounts for more than 13 percent of world demand for petroleum and petroleum products. As domestic demand rises in China over the next two decades, China's oil requirements will double to about 16 million bbl/d according to the International Energy Agency.[8] Two-thirds of that total will have to come from outside China. Today, China is buying crude oil on the world market, from the Middle East, Latin America, and East Asia, but because global oil supplies notoriously are volatile, it seeks secure sources over which it can exercise direct control—equity ownership. Hence, China's recent drive into sub-Saharan Africa and its unswerving focus on the Sudan. China also now explores for oil off Congo (Brazzaville), Equatorial Guinea, Gabon, Kenya, Mozambique, and Nigeria.

Angola, the Sudan, and other suppliers in sub-Saharan Africa provide 25 percent of China's crude oil imports. Almost three-quarters of that total derives from Angola alone, now Africa's largest producer, with Nigeria second. Moreover, Angola's oil is light, and thus easier to refine and much more valuable than heavier supplies from elsewhere. In order to facilitate these trade arrangements and the imports that China deems so valuable, since 2004 China has strengthened its relations with Angola, an autocratically ruled nation-state (ranked forty-two of forty-eight sub-Saharan African states on the 2007 Index of African Governance list), by being its major lender and dominating the direct construction of roads, railways, and low-income housing, and employing on those projects imported Chinese labor.[9] Large low-interest loans from China's Export-Import Bank (Eximbank), as well as other Chinese sources, are being repaid over many years by escrowed oil and various profitable concessions. In chapter 6, Henry Lee and Dan Shalmon provide many of the intricate details of this maturing relationship. One of their striking conclusions is that "by offering credit, China has been able to secure a [healthy] flow of Angolan oil for at least the next decade."[10]

Their chapter also explains China's deep involvement in the extraction and marketing of Sudanese crude oil. In the late 1990s, after American and Canadian companies abandoned the Sudan because of southern Sudanese insurgent attacks and fear of internal North American consumer and investor hostility, China saw a welcome opportunity to secure significant supplies of equity oil on favorable terms. About half of China's equity oil imports (and 10 percent of its total oil imports) now come from the Sudan. China directly runs the extractive operations in the oilfields themselves (unlike the case in Angola and elsewhere) and has constructed the 900-mile pipeline that carries the Sudan's oil from the center of the vast country to Port Sudan. China takes 40 percent of the Sudan's production. It also owns half of the country's major oil refinery and has invested heavily in the construction of a massive hydro-electric facility, in a new airport in the Sudanese capital, and in the textile industry. The Sudanese military buys its arms from Russia, Belarus, and China; allegedly, there are close ties between the Chinese military and the military junta that has ruled the Sudan since 1989. China has assisted the Sudan in developing a local arms manufacturing industry.[11] About 88 percent of the Sudan's imported small arms come from China, according to the UN. Chinese sales of small arms increased 137 times from 2001 to 2006. China also sells military aircraft to the Sudan and is training military pilots.[12]

Gathering as much African oil as possible is only a part of China's successful engagement with Africa. As Broadman says in his chapter, "Chinese businesses are pursuing international commercial strategies in Africa that increasingly are about far more than just raw natural resources."[13] Sometimes, too, these commodities have been beneficiated in country before being exported for further processing abroad. China imports timber from Gabon, the Democratic Republic of the Congo (the DRC), Equatorial Guinea, Cameroon, and Liberia; cotton from Benin, Burkina Faso, Mali, Côte d'Ivoire, and Cameroon; copper from Zambia and the DRC; ferrochrome and platinum from Zimbabwe; diamonds from South Africa; tin and tantalum from the DRC; and an increasing variety of light manufactured products, household consumer goods, and food items from several countries. Tourism is also growing. Broadman posits that "China's commercial engagement with sub-Saharan Africa could enable African businesses to build on the continent's endowment of natural resources and develop more sophisticated backward and forward integration to extract more value from processing."[14] He also points out that such positive outcomes depend on reforms in China (improved market access for African imports) and in sub-Saharan Africa (enhanced local competitiveness, improved governance, flexible labor markets, and upgraded arteries of commerce).[15]

To the aforementioned countries and others, China supplies electronic goods, machinery, motorcycles, t-shirts, other clothing, footwear, and a host of additional low-value consumer items. China's share of Africa's total trade is rising and will soon eclipse American and European annual totals. Even so, as much as China's commodities are everywhere in sub-Saharan Africa, by value more than three-quarters of China's total trade with Africa is with but four countries: the two large oil producers, already discussed, plus South Africa and Nigeria (which also has oil for sale). Angola, Equatorial Guinea, Nigeria, Congo (Brazzaville), and the Sudan provide 85 percent of all of China's imports from Africa.[16] All are oil producers. China's share of sub-Saharan Africa's total trade is about 10 percent.

China is also pioneering the establishment of Special Economic Zones, or export processing zones, throughout sub-Saharan Africa. This hitherto little noticed injection of Chinese expertise is discussed at length by Martyn Davies in chapter 7. The African goal is to attract foreign direct investment to the zones already established or contemplated in Kenya, Mauritius, Nigeria, and Zambia. In 2008, the Zambian zone was the furthest along, with construction underway. These zones, from the African and Chinese mutual view, are intended to be the new growth nodes—the drivers of the African economic forward surge that Broadman's chapter anticipates. Each zone necessarily is to be linked to transport corridors or to be in or attached to thriving harbors. In both cases, infrastructural upgrading will be necessary with anticipated Chinese assistance. Indeed, China is already working to refurbish the poorly maintained and now dilapidated Tanzam Railway from Dar es Salaam to Kapiri

Mposhi and the long-abandoned Benguela rail line from the Congolese Copperbelt to Lobito on the Atlantic Ocean in Angola. The ports of Dar es Salaam and Lobito will also require upgrading. Davies suggests that the completion of these new zones, and new railways and harbors, will have a positive impact on regional economic integration.[17] Perhaps even more important, given the neglect of arteries of commerce throughout Africa in recent decades, Chinese action in these infrastructural areas potentially could prove of enormous benefit to Africans socially, as well as economically. In Kenya, for example, the Chinese are constructing bypasses around Nairobi. Upgrading roads, railways, and harbors may also strengthen political elites and—just possibly—enrich those leaders who benefit from granting national construction contracts.

The contemplated zones follow China's own developmental model for its now fast-growing southeastern hinterland, especially the Special Economic Zones in Guangdong and Hainan Provinces. In Africa, the existing and contemplated zones presume customs duty waivers, preferential tax rates, flexible management, and access to productive labor, whether local or Chinese (the latter with work permits). They also imply technology transfer, mostly from China. Further, they are intended to enable Chinese firms to compete well with non-Chinese operations and to avoid "Made in China" labels and still accrue business and profits. Already, mostly outside of these special zones, more than 800 state-owned Chinese enterprises have set up operations in Africa. The special zones, in other words, are integral to China's grand design for Africa and for the developing world more generally. China is expanding everywhere in this manner, not only in Africa, but such Chinese initiatives potentially may uplift Africa's economic prospects and its GDP per capita faster and more completely than actions by other trading and investing partners, or by international lending organizations.

The provision of official bilateral economic and technical assistance for these and other purposes is extended increasingly to African rulers (sometimes individually) and nations so as to support China's purchasing and concession-accruing endeavors. Some of the latter include joint manufacturing ventures, but the Chinese also make zero-interest loans, offer low-interest concessional loans, and provide outright grants for ministerial office buildings, cultural centers, stadia, schools, hospitals, roads, bridges, and agricultural projects (especially for rice cultivation and vegetable growing). As Deborah Brautigam suggests in chapter 9, "China's aid is supposed to be based on equality, mutual benefit, and respect for the sovereignty of the host." Most regular loans are theoretically unconditional and interest free, with a "frank emphasis on mutual benefit" and noninterference.[18] The "mutual benefit" notion refers in large part to the careful tying of loans to the export of commodities to China, as in today's Angola and the DRC. Concessional loans are also linked but are different since they come from China's Eximbank and the Ministry of Commerce, although a few are sponsored by the China Development Bank. In chapter 10, Paul Hubbard focuses exclusively on such concessional lending—more than $1 billion worth in at least twenty-two countries.

All of these various assistance flows are managed and coordinated by China's Ministry of Commerce, and implemented by the Bureau for International Economic Cooperation within that ministry. The latter additionally supervises the Chinese firms that are sent out to realize such projects in Africa. Agricultural and fisheries endeavors (and nearly all Chinese assistance to rural Africa), however, are organized through the Ministry of Agriculture. Medical aid, another major part of China's role in Africa, is managed by the Ministry of Health. The Ministry of Education supplies scholarships to Africans studying in China and sends volunteer teachers to at least thirty African countries. In chapter 2, Li Anshan captures the breadth and depth of those far-ranging educational exchanges, which include university teaching, workshops, advanced seminars, and much more. There is a limited amount of humanitarian aid, too, and it flows through the Ministries of Commerce, Foreign Affairs, and Defense. In this regard, Chin-Hao Huang notes the recent establishment of an official International Poverty Alleviation Center in Beijing; it trains African officials and introduces them to poverty reduction projects in China's poorest provinces.[19]

As Brautigam makes clear, China provides no official figures for the amounts of its "aid." As Chin-Hao Huang remarks, "As of 2008 [there is] no systematic sharing of data by Chinese ministries with international and bilateral donors . . . or with African participants."[20] There is confusion about what constitutes Chinese official assistance, with some commentators confounding regular loans (which do not count as official developmental assistance) with concessional loans and grants (which do). Thus, Brautigam concludes that only a tiny proportion of the economic transactions between China and the developing world should qualify as what Americans call "foreign aid." The majority of those transactions, especially the larger ones, are for the purpose of facilitating exports.[21] She concludes, therefore, that China's aid budget in 2007 was about $616 million. Doubling Chinese assistance by 2009, as promised, would bring China's aid levels to more than $1 billion. Another $1 billion would account for the full amount of concessional lending by 2009. A further $6–8 billion is available as development finance (not aid). But the combined total, reports Brautigam (affirmed by Li Anshan's Beijing-based account), is still considerably lower than grant commitments to Africa from the countries of the Organization of European Cooperation and Development—which were greater than $30 billion in 2005, and even more in 2007. Whatever the precise sum of present and future Chinese assistance to Africa, much of it again puts African countries in the unenviable position of accumulating additional obligations. China's emergence as a major creditor, warns Chin-Hao Huang, has created "a wave of new debt" partially offset by the debts that China has forgiven in some African countries.[22]

Strengthening trade and aid flows include extensive Chinese activities in the security arena. Whereas China has long been worried about American and European projection of military power and security ties to and in all parts of Asia and the Pacific, its own increasingly powerful military relations with a host of African nations are propelled by resource acquisition aims. As David Shinn writes in chapter 8, these aims "translate into a strategy that encourages a desire to strengthen stability in African countries that sell or have a potential to sell China significant quantities of raw materials." That strategy is two-pronged: China supports the political status quo, whatever it is, and it supplies military hardware and other assistance to buttress existing governments, however autocratic or dubious in origin.

In the latter years of the twentieth century, China backed a variety of African anticolonial liberation movements with arms, training, and funds. Some of those ventures were successful; many were not, with more powerful opposing movements taking power despite their Soviet (and not Chinese) ties. Shinn details the ebb and flow of Chinese arms transfers during the 1960s through the 1990s. In the final years of the twentieth century, Russia and China (in that order) provided far more weapons to sub-Saharan Africa than did the United States. China constructed arms factories in the Sudan and Uganda. Its equipment fueled both sides of the Ethiopian-Eritrean war, assisted the air force of Zimbabwe, and helped the armies of another dozen sub-Saharan African countries.

In this century, China offers military assistance and training, without formal military alliances, to many of the forty-eight nations of sub-Saharan Africa. As the fifth- or sixth-largest supplier of small arms to the developing world, it sells arms (especially the Chinese version of the AK-47 assault rifle) both to cement those alliances and to make a profit from Africa. Since 2000, Angola, Benin, Botswana, Burkina Faso, Cameroon, Djibouti, Ethiopia, Ghana, Kenya, Mozambique, Niger, South Africa, the Sudan, Tanzania, Uganda, Zambia, and Zimbabwe have received such Chinese weapons in reasonable quantities. But the key bilateral military relationships have been with Angola (training, communications upgrades, and hardware); Ghana (communications upgrades, construction of military buildings, vehicles, and jet aircraft); Nigeria (military facilities, aircraft, patrol boats, and communications facilities); South Africa (formal security consultations, arms sales to China as well as from China); the Sudan (a range of military equipment, allegedly Chinese troops on the ground to protect the pipeline, jet fighters and trainers, and military trucks); Uganda (trucks, barracks, training, and the production of ammunition); Zambia (aircraft and medical experts); and Zimbabwe (jet trainers, arms, barracks, and training). In 2008, China also had 1,457 peacekeepers and observers attached to 7 UN missions in sub-Saharan Africa. It has even sent about 100 engineers to staff the peacekeeping operation in Darfur.

As Shinn observes, Chinese military and security cooperation with the countries of Africa, and China's desire to keep shipping lanes from Africa free of interference, is intended primarily to advance China's economic interests and its overwhelming concern for unfettered access to Africa's abundant raw materials. China will do whatever it can, despite criticism from the West about propping up despots and strengthening antidemocratic tendencies, in and for those prospective African partners who want assistance and possess the resources of value. Beijing will continue to call its military activities in Africa pragmatic; others, including some Africans, will label these initiatives and involvements as cynical.

All of this omnivorous activity and interaction is to the good, especially if Africa's GDP rises, new jobs are created, its primary commodities find ready markets, and its people are able to purchase inexpensive consumer items. As Rupp writes in chapter 4, "That African people are [for the first time] perceived primarily as consumers lends them a degree of economic agency that was absent previously." But Africans suspect that China sends second-tier goods to Africa; even in economically deprived Zimbabwe, hilarious posters (as Rupp shows) warn prospective purchasers against Chinese market offerings. Zimbabweans are hardly alone in decrying Chinese quality. Elsewhere, in the infrastructural arena, Africans worry that Chinese firms will cut corners on quality, ignore labor or environmental concerns, and produce shoddy results. The DRC and Gabon in 2006 and 2007 closed down several Chinese companies because of alleged environmental abuses. Even South African President Thabo Mbeki warned China that it could not "just come here and dig for raw materials and then go away and sell us manufactured goods."[23]

There are additional possible negative consequences. China's commercial success, and the sourcing of supplies from China, rather than from within Africa, has already aroused African anger and concern. There were widespread protest movements in Zambia and Lesotho in 2007 and 2008, for example.[24] A flood of cheap goods, especially textiles and apparel, has undermined and bankrupted local industries, putting hundreds of thousands of Africans out of work, especially in South Africa. China was compelled voluntarily to limit its exports of inexpensive products to South Africa. In Cameroon, market vendors of inexpensive foods face relentless competition from Chinese petty entrepreneurs. Indeed, whereas foreign merchants of earlier eras largely remained aloof from daily encounters at microlocal levels, the Chinese are there, creating anxiety and taking customers from African rivals.[25]

Nigeria seems to provide an exception to this generalization regarding hostility to the Chinese role at the market level in sub-Saharan Africa. From a small sample of traders surveyed in Lagos, Ndubisi Obiorah, Darren Kew, and Yusuf Tanko learned that the Chinese were not perceived as competitors even as their commercial acumen was respected.[26] Their goods were seen as substandard, however. Even with regard to the "catastrophic impact" of Chinese imports on the local market for Nigerian textiles, Nigerians have not demonstrated or mobilized against Chinese incursions or Chinese products.[27]

The widespread use of imported Chinese labor, rather than the hiring of local workers on infrastructural and factory projects—a common phenomenon—deprives Africans of innumerable employment opportunities. In Angola, China pays for new railways and roads but uses mostly Chinese contractors and workers, thus denying jobs to anxious Angolans. Rupp quotes a Zambian finance minister's lament about the flood of low-paid, culturally isolated, job-depriving workers from China. She also sets out the Chinese case for using their own people on critical projects; China, if the truth be known, thinks its own workers are more efficient and more trustworthy. Moreover, she reports, the communities that the Chinese create in Africa—around industries especially, but also around mines and large construction projects—are "socially thin" and often separated from contact with surrounding local Africans by barbed wire or other barriers.[28] Indeed, the opinion sampling in two markets in Lagos could not include Chinese merchants because the traders who were approached spoke English too poorly to respond.[29]

In many cases, China as an investor or as a purchaser of primary products (like oil) also implicitly or explicitly backs the harsh rule of authoritarian governments. China supports odious regimes, propping up some of them, supplying corrupt rents to many, and almost always reinforcing a regime's least participatory instincts. "China [coddles] dictators, despoil[s] poor countries and undermin[es] Western efforts to spread democracy and prosperity."[30] In the Sudan, in Zimbabwe, and elsewhere, China in numerous, specific ways is

supporting or has supported regimes sanctioned by and otherwise condemned by the United Nations (UN) and by leaders of the free and democratic developed world. "Western-style democratic theory simply isn't suited
to African conditions," the Chinese believe, and "carries with it the root of disaster," as in Kenya.[31] There is a profound Chinese disdain for Africa and
Africans, and an underlying contempt for do-gooding Western notions of
how Africa should be nurtured. For this reason, among many others, China
(as Shinn shows) supplies small arms and other weapons—sometimes aircraft—indiscriminately and in defiance of UN strictures.

Mia Farrow and Steven Spielberg—among other high-profile Hollywood
figures—writers and critics from the media, university activists and students
across dozens of campuses, committed advocates from the nongovernmental
community, and officials and politicians in Europe and the United States have
all tied China tightly to genocide in the Darfur region of the Sudan. They
accuse China of being complicit—of not preventing the government of the
Sudan from marauding in Darfur, of not using its undoubted economic (oil)
and military supply leverage to end the massacres and mayhem in Darfur. The
absence of peace, indeed the original assault of the janjaweed militias in
Darfur and the continued massive loss of life in the region, is attributed to
China's refusal to put appropriate pressure on the corrupt military junta ruling the Sudan.[32]

China's stated refusal to intervene on behalf of peace and human rights in
the Sudan, in Kenya after the disputed election at the end of 2007, and its
opposition in the UN Security Council and other fora to criticism of and
"interference" in the Sudan, in Zimbabwe, and everywhere else in the tyran-
nized nations of Africa is regarded by human rights advocates as perverse
and obstructionist. But that is China's stated posture. Otherwise world order
might critique China's actions in Xinjiang or Tibet and its harsh treatment
generally of its non-Han and religious minorities. Or, conceivably, if China
abandoned its willingness to work with repressive and nonrepressive African
and developing world regimes, it might lose access to the raw materials that
it craves. Whatever the proximate cause, China is an authoritarian regime, and
its foreign as well as its domestic policies emanate from that immutable fact.

Farrow, with empirical observations, photographic evidence, and great
eloquence, successfully attempted to embarrass China over its compromised
role in the Sudan by yoking genocide there to the summer 2008 Olympics in
Beijing. "After the Nazi Holocaust," she told a Washington audience, "we all
know the world vowed 'never again,' but how obscenely disingenuous those
fine words sound today."[33] To Farrow, and eventually to Spielberg and many

others, China's failure to act decisively for good in the Sudan fatally compromised what she and others labeled the "genocide Olympics." By late 2007 and early 2008, Farrow's actions, Spielberg's withdrawal as an artistic adviser to the Chinese Olympics in 2008, and fears regarding the Olympics themselves, plus earnest diplomatic representations from Washington, London, and Brussels, weakened China's assistance to President Robert Mugabe's Zimbabwe, pushed the government of the Sudan grudgingly to concede partial peacekeeping arrangements to the UN, and persuaded the military junta in Burma in 2007 to talk occasionally with opposition leader Aung San Suu Kyi. After Cyclone Nargis in 2008, China may also have encouraged ruling General Than Shwe of Burma to receive UN Secretary-General Ban Ki-Moon and to relax restrictions against receiving outside assistance. Early in 2008, too, China began shifting its position on Darfur, quietly pushing the Sudan to accept a large peacekeeping contingent; in March, Liu Guijin, China's special envoy to Darfur, expressed to the Sudanese government China's "grave concern about the deterioration of conditions in western Darfur."[34] Andrew S. Natsios, President Bush's former envoy to the Sudan, even called the Chinese "very cooperative"—a far cry from the words he and others had used during 2007 to depict Chinese attitudes and actions.[35] Yet, even though no observers expected China to walk away from its strong economic position in the Sudan, or to condemn or chasten the Sudanese junta openly, China seemed to have begun in 2008 to use its unique leverage to shift official Sudanese policy regarding Darfur and other issues at the margin, albeit tentatively and weakly.

By July, however, on the eve of the Olympics, China joined Russia in barring the UN Security Council from imposing sanctions on Zimbabwe's President Mugabe and his entourage for abusing the country's opposition and preventing a free and fair election in June 2008. Subsequently, in August, Mugabe publicly thanked China, his "strongest ally," for continuing to support his armed forces. He particularly cited China's procurement of uniforms for Zimbabwe's soldiers. Journalists also reported that Zimbabwe's leading generals had been flying to China with "illicit goods including ivory, gold, and diamonds," which they were converting into cash in Hong Kong and Shanghai.[36]

Moreover, Wenran Jiang, in chapter 3, reminds readers that China's new role in Africa is subject to continuous debates within Chinese policy and academic circles in Beijing. There is a growing awareness that balanced policies must accompany the thrust of Chinese commerce into Africa. By 2007, China had issued "'good corporate citizen' guidelines" to help moderate the conduct of Chinese corporations in Africa.[37] There was a growing awareness that one-sided bilateral trade imbalances were not necessarily good for specific

African countries, even South Africa. The appointment in 2007 of a special envoy to the Sudan further demonstrated China's concern for its overall image in Africa and its standing with the big powers of the world. China is hardly immune to outside criticism. Even so, despite a new awareness of the fuller dimensions of its move into Africa, China in 2008 continued to tolerate or ignore egregious human rights infractions in Angola, Equatorial Guinea, Nigeria, and a host of other African countries with which it continued to do business without compunction.

In their examination of China's culpability for human rights abuses in Africa, Stephen Brown and Chandra Lekha Sriram take a narrow view of the question: for which acts is China "legally responsible rather than just morally culpable?"[38] Legal codes, they aver, are more precise than moral codes; moral responsibility is difficult to judge, particularly when there are many compromised actors across Africa. In Equatorial Guinea, one of Africa's worst human rights abusers, for example, American petroleum companies pump oil alongside Chinese exporters.[39] It is the same in Cabinda and the rest of Angola. China is "only one among many international actors supporting the Angolan government."[40] For Zambia, they suggest that the possibility that China sponsors unsafe and inhumane conditions at the Chambishi mine should be regarded as a case of the nonapplication of domestic labor laws, not as China condoning human rights abuses. Anyway, they ask, are conditions in Chinese-run mines any worse than in mines run by others?

The two authors focus on the cases of the Sudan and Zimbabwe, where large-scale human rights abuses are presumed to exist and are accordingly measurable under international law. Some forms of support for violations, and the facilitation of infractions, would count as breaches of international law. Arms sales to states whose governments target civilians would implicate China, but general developmental assistance to those same states would not. Furthermore, Brown and Sriram conclude, when China supplies security or security services directly to a nation, or even constructs the infrastructure that permits a repressive regime to act, it also is responsible.

In the Sudan, China's extensive sales of arms and their use to target villagers in southern Sudan and in Darfur, plus the displacement of civilians along the North-South internal border and in Darfur, clearly "facilitated gross abuses" even if they did not constitute violations of international law. China has also resisted UN sanctions against supplying weapons to the Sudan. However, "evidence for the *direct* commission of human rights abuses by Chinese agents is limited."[41]

In Zimbabwe, China has invested in mining and farming, constructed roads and military facilities, and supplied equipment to the army and air force. China's own nationals are farming vast acreages taken from whites, especially in and around Banket, and working mining concessions once owned by local and foreign corporations.[42] China imports large amounts of tobacco from Zimbabwe and supplies agricultural machinery, cell phones, televisions, and radios. More than 1,000 Chinese-built buses now ply municipal streets. Three new Chinese aircraft allowed Air Zimbabwe in 2008 to operate local and regional routes. Most of all, despite official sanctions and the almost universal condemnation of Mugabe's tyranny, China has sold jet fighters, tanks, armored vehicles, artillery, riot-control gear, and radio-jamming equipment and other critical communications gear to Zimbabwe's military.

Politically, China has been supportive of Zimbabwe, shielding it from international opprobrium and binding UN sanctions. It endorsed the flawed 2005 elections and later that year backed Mugabe's brutal razing of peri-urban shantytowns because their inhabitants were thought to back the main opposition party. China has also supplied "humanitarian" food assistance. Through 2005 and perhaps into 2006, China was morally complicit in Mugabe's increasingly repressive maneuvers. Until the fatally flawed presidential election in June 2008, China has backed gingerly away, but without public criticism of Mugabe for going too far. In Zimbabwe as in the Sudan, until 2008, China failed to restrain official abuses or to exert a benign influence. China said nothing after the blatantly rigged 2008 elections. Indeed, it joined Russia in vetoing a critical UN Security Council resolution. It can be accused more of tolerating human rights excesses than of being responsible legally for aiding and abetting repression, at least in Zimbabwe.

Overall, Brown and Sriram accept that Chinese behavior and public stances legitimize human rights abuses and undemocratic practices "under the guise of state sovereignty and 'noninterference.'" Chinese policy and actions undermine human rights, good governance, transparency, and accountability as defined by the African Union, the Extractive Industries Transparency Initiative, and even the New Partnership for Africa's Development. But legal culpability could only be established in limited instances, they say.[43]

Is China a malign force—a modern colonial colossus intent on stripping Africa of its wealth without leaving behind sustainable structures? At present, there is little technology transfer, little capacity building, and little attention given to good governance and effective institutions. China's slapdash approach to safety issues, especially in mining, has also been exported to Africa, along with its refusal to take environmental concerns seriously. But is China's incursion into Africa neocolonial? Can its activity in Africa be tarred with the pejorative label "colonial?"

Because China does not regard itself as a new colonial power—it does not seek to govern subject peoples in Africa or impose a Chinese way of life and value system on indigenous inhabitants of the continent—it and its leaders repeatedly chant a noncolonial mantra. China is not attempting to "civilize" Africa. Hence, its clean-hands stance regarding the controversies of Africa and its frequently proclaimed respect for African national sovereignty, no matter the quality of the regime in question. (Respect for sovereignty, of course, permits China to deal with despots and enrich favored sovereigns in exchange for access to resources and other opportunities.) Rupp's careful and thoughtful analysis of the colonial question argues that Chinese involvement in Africa is neither colonial nor neocolonial. Instead, she writes that China "is strategically leveraging structural characteristics of African political and economic systems that advance the interests of the state—both the Chinese state and African states—often at the expense of ordinary African people. As a result of the imbalance in economic power between China and individual African states, these relations echo the dependency typical of colonial relations. Yet, significant divergences from colonialism as it was experienced in Africa—such as China's fundamental respect for the sovereignty of African states; its active nurturing of relations with African states in international fora; and its interest in African people as consumers rather than laborers—suggest that China and Africa are engaging in postcolonial relations of interdependency, however economically imbalanced these relations may be."[44]

Beneath the surface of these positive state-to-state and business-to-business interactions, however, is what Rupp perceives as tension between reciprocated regard and abhorrence. She reports that the social space between ordinary Africans and Chinese is taut; "social relations . . . are marked by a tension between mutual admiration and mutual loathing. Although Africans and Chinese alike admire the quality of strength that they observe in the other, they also share robustly negative perceptions of one another. African and Chinese people do not often or intimately interact. Chinese enterprises tend to be walled off from the surrounding landscape or neighborhood; Chinese managers tend to be aloof and hesitant to engage socially with their African counterparts, employees, or neighbors."[45] Their work ethics often seem to be different and of mutual concern. Some of these features give rise to shared suspicion, even racism. Rupp provides a nuanced account from Chinese and African sources of the underlying wariness with which Africa and China embrace each other.

China is a worthy competitor for resources and for construction projects. Additionally, its direct and indirect donor aid is now significant, overshadowing or competing for influence with the United States and Europe. Africans welcome this new heightened rivalry for their attention and partnership. They further welcome China's lack of conditionality, lack of hectoring, lack of preaching and instruction, and reduced hypocrisy; Chinese aid—including a promised $20 billion credit for worthy projects from China's Eximbank—comes without immediately obvious strings (the Taiwanese question aside).

For that reason, and because the Chinese espouse fundamentally different approaches to governance questions than does the West, the West and Africa should now encourage China to embrace sets of positive principles, mutually agreed upon, for Africa's sustained growth and prosperity. Altruistic actions now would also be in China's self-interest and, if crafted carefully, could help to unlock the potential of Africa for China. They could raise China's moral stature within and outside of Africa, and emphasize even more China's self-professed break with earlier colonial endeavors. China is a conceivable force for material and social progress in Africa; the West should help harness that potential.

Whether a new U.S. administration in 2009 and afterward will respond effectively and constructively to Chinese competition for Africa, and for Africa's hearts and minds, depends on the extent of Washington's post-Bush strategic and humanitarian interests in Africa and the overall nature of the U.S.-China détente in 2009 and beyond. Washington wisely may not wish to joust with Beijing over African influence and African resources providing that the flow of oil to the United States from Africa continues and grows, and providing that China remains helpful over North Korea and Iran and over staunching the spread of terror, remains comparatively open to American investment and trade, and refrains from attacking Taiwan. The United States needs Chinese cooperation geostrategically and economically. Therefore, Washington may be prepared (within limits) to observe and remain untroubled by an Africa more dependent than ever upon ramped up Chinese trade and aid, major military assistance, and Chinese labor.

Indeed, Chin-Hao Huang suggests that as of 2008, Washington was largely ill-prepared to assess what the Chinese really want out of Africa, and how Chinese policies are formulated and executed. Likewise, Washington has little knowledge of African opinion regarding China's new thrust into their continent. Chin-Hao Huang urges Washington to "be sensitive to the many and long-standing, positive legacies and images of the Chinese in various parts of Africa," particularly in sharp contrast to Western colonial practices.[46]

Throughout the Bush administration, top officials from Washington and Beijing talked regularly about their mutual interests in Africa. Darfur was at the apex of the agenda, but other African issues and their reverberations in the UN Security Council also tested the Bush administration's appreciation of the China-Africa nexus. Little has been done so far, however, to draw China into a multilateral discussion of positive donor assistance for sustainable African growth and the avoidance of new cascades of debt. Nor has Chinese help been sought for improving African governance generally, and for stability-building efforts in Somalia and Ethiopia, Zimbabwe, Chad, and the Niger Delta. If carefully engaged on these issues, and if China cooperates over Darfur and the Sudan and Zimbabwe after the 2008 Olympic Games, China could prove a positive partner for U.S. ameliorative initiatives in Africa.

China is transforming Africa, for good and ill. The United States and other traditional trading and aid partners of Africa need to pay closer attention than they have been, and with Africans craft bold new policies that welcome Chinese investment and trade but condemn the taking of African jobs and the destruction of African industries. Africa and the West also need to persuade China that supporting Africa's most reviled dictatorships is bad for Africa and bad for China as a world power.[47]

Africans, in turn, need to organize more effectively than they have hitherto—to meet the Chinese at least half way. Neither the African Union nor subregional organizations like the Southern African Development Community have an articulated policy regarding China and Chinese influence. Each of the forty-eight sub-Saharan countries goes its own way, responding to China and Chinese entreaties (or Taiwanese in four cases) idiosyncratically. The African petroleum producers, the African hard mineral producers, the African vulnerable industrial cases, and so on should develop specific policies toward China in new functional groupings. Africa surely needs well-articulated policies regarding the importation of Chinese laborers, special taxation privileges or not for Chinese firms (many are state owned), new tariffs tailored to increase trade, and protection or not for domestically produced goods. Without concerted African ground rules and improved governance at home, China will continue to be opportunistic, exploiting weaker nation-states in its quest for resources and asserting its own overweening economic leverage with little consideration for African values and needs. If Africans are to stand on equal footing with Chinese entrepreneurs, they need to join forces and channel Chinese energies and capital in directions that benefit Africa as much as they benefit China. Only by fashioning such a collective response can Africans throughout the continent turn China's massive and multifaceted drive into Africa to their sustainable best advantage.

Notes

1. W. H. Auden, "As I Walked Out One Evening," in *Collected Shorter Poems, 1927–1957* (London, 1966), 85.

2. Edward Wong, "Booming, China Faults U.S. Policy on the Economy," *New York Times* (17 June 2008), 1, 8.

3. Rupp, 68 in this volume.

4. "A Ravenous Dragon: A Special Report on China's Quest for Resources," *Economist* (15 March 2008), 4.

5. See "Japan and Africa," *Economist* (31 May 2008), 52; "India-Africa Summit Concluded in New Delhi," Xinhua (9 April 2008), available at http://news.xinhuanet. com/english/2008-04/09/content_7947657.htm (accessed 6 June 2008).

6. Jamil Anderlini, "China Eyes Overseas Land in Food Push," *Financial Times* (8 May 2008).

7. See also Harry Broadman, *Africa's Silk Road: China and India's New Economic Frontier* (Washington, D.C., 2007). To some extent Li Anshan echoes this question in chapter 2 of this volume.

8. See Wenran Jiang, 53 in this volume.

9. See Robert I. Rotberg and Rachel M. Gisselquist, *Strengthening African Governance: Ibrahim Index of African Governance, Results and Rankings 2007* (Cambridge, MA, 2007), 9 ff.

10. See Lee and Shalmon, 122. See also Rupp, 74; Lucy Corkin, "All's Fair in Loans and War: The Development of China-Angola Relations," in Kweku Ampiah and Sanusha Naidu (eds.), *Crouching Tiger, Hidden Dragon: Africa and China* (Scottsville, South Africa, 2008), 108–123.

11. See Chris Alden, *China in Africa* (New York, 2007), 62. See also David Shinn, 170–171 in this volume; Sharath Srinivasan, "A Marriage Less Convenient: China, Sudan and Darfur," in Ampiah and Naidu, *Crouching Tiger*, 55–85.

12. Nicholas D. Kristof, "Prosecuting Genocide," *New York Times*, 17 July 2008.

13. See Broadman, 88 in this volume.

14. Ibid. See also Harry Broadman, "China and India Go to Africa," *Foreign Affairs*, LXXXVII (2008), 96.

15. Broadman, *Africa's Silk Road*, 41–58.

16. Broadman, "China and India," 97.

17. See Davies, 137 in this volume.

18. Brautigam, 200 in this volume.

19. See Chin-Hao Huang, 300.

20. Ibid. However, China's Eximbank and the World Bank have an agreement to share some information.

21. See Brautigam, 209.

22. See Huang, 302.

23. Quoted in "Ravenous Dragon," 17.

24. See Ndubisi Obiorah, Darren Kew, and Yusuf Tanko, 272 in this volume. For more on Zambia, see Muna Ndulo, "Chinese Investments in Africa: A Case Study of Zambia," in Ampiah and Naidu, *Crouching Tiger*, 124–137.

25. See also Ampiah and Naidu, "The Sino-African Relationship: Towards an Evolving Partnership?" in Ampiah and Naidu, *Crouching Tiger*, 335.

26. See Obiorah, Kew, and Tanko, 286 in this volume.

27. Ibid.

28. Rupp, 76.

29. Obiorah, Kew, and Tanko, 281.

30. "Ravenous Dragon," 13.

31. *People's Daily* (14 January 2008).

32. For a different, Chinese perspective, see Li Anshan, chapter 2.

33. Statement at the National Press Club, Washington, D.C., February 2008, quoted in Phyllis Spiegel, "WWS and The Economist Co-Host D.C. Panel, 'The Dilemma of Darfur,'" *WWS News*, XXXI (2008), 9.

34. Quoted in Jim Yardley, "China Defends Sudan Policy and Criticizes Olympics Tie-In," *New York Times* (8 March 2008), available at www.nytimes.com/2008/03/08/world/asia/08darfur.html?_r=1&oref=slogin (accessed 6 June 2008). This article also quotes Spielberg and includes a Chinese rebuttal. See also "Blowback: How China Torpedoes Its Investments," *Enough* (7 August 2008).

35. Quoted in Lydia Polgreen, "China, in New Role, Uses Ties to Press Sudan on Troubled Darfur," *New York Times* (23 February 2008), available at www.nytimes.com/2008/02/23/world/africa/23darfur.html (accessed 6 June 2008).

36. Wayne Mafaro, "Mugabe Rewards Political Violence Architects," *Zimonline* (12 August 2008); Russell Skelton, "Exposed: Mugabe's Secret Flights," *The Age* (Melbourne) (22 July 2008).

37. Broadman, "China and India," 100.

38. See Stephen Brown and Chandra Lekha Sriram, 251 in this volume.

39. For the abuses, see John R. Heilbrunn, "Equatorial Guinea and Togo: What Price Repression?" in Robert I. Rotberg (ed.), *Worst of the Worst: Dealing with Repressive and Rogue Nations* (Washington, D.C., 2007), 223–249. See Richard Behar, "Special Report: China in Africa (Part 5). Equatorial Guinea: A Strongman Turns East," available at www.fast-company.com (accessed 13 August 2008).

40. Brown and Sriram, 252.

41. Ibid. Brown and Sriram's italics.

42. Information in regard to farming in Zimbabwe comes from Eddie Cross (private communication, 16 March 2008).

43. See Brown and Sriram, 252.

44. See Rupp, 66.

45. Ibid.

46. See Huang, 305.

47. Ampiah and Naidu, from Africa, urge a stronger stance by Africa. "Beijing's bankrolling of a state such as Sudan . . . should be condemned and exposed." They sensibly want African civil society to monitor the Chinese-African engagement in order to compel African governments to become "more transparent" in their engagement with China and to "expose" the impact of China's economic penetration at the microlevel. They further decry the problems posed by Chinese exports to Africa. See Ampiah and Naidu, "The Sino-African Relationship: Towards an Evolving Partnership?" in Ampiah and Naidu, *Crouching Tiger*, 335.

LI ANSHAN

2

China's New Policy toward Africa

As a dynamic part of China's grand foreign policy, elements of China's African policy have remained constant while others have changed. In 1992, Segal concluded that "there may be grounds for believing that as China grows strong, it will grow somewhat more important for Africans. But in the Chinese perspective, it seems that while Africa will attract attention from the writers of official policy statements, the continent will remain the least important area for Chinese foreign policy, whether of an expanding or a withdrawing kind."[1]

What is happening today obviously challenges Segal's prophecy. In recent years, China's rapid economic growth and impressive role in the international arena have sparked concerns about China's engagement in Africa.[2]

China and Africa's mutual dependence on one another is evident in the Beijing Summit of the Forum on China-Africa Cooperation (FOCAC) held every third year. In 2006, it included the heads of state, government officials, and representatives from forty-eight African countries. Former Chinese President Jiang Zemin visited Africa four times, while, as of 2007, President Hu Jintao had paid five visits to the continent (twice as vice president, three times as president). The *intention* of China's involvement in Africa, though, has

This chapter was originally presented as a paper at the International Workshop "China-Africa Links" held at Hong Kong University of Science and Technology, 11–12 November 2006. The revised version was presented at an off-the-record meeting, "China in Africa: Geopolitical and Geoeconomic Considerations," held at the John F. Kennedy School of Government, Harvard University, 31 May–2 June 2007. I am grateful to the conference organizers, David Zweig and Robert Rotberg, respectively, and would like to thank participants for their comments.

been greatly questioned, especially by Western powers. China's policy toward Africa is clearly shown in "China's African Policy," a 2006 document.[3] But how has this policy come into being? And how does this policy fit into China's grand strategy?

Through the analysis of three transformations in China's African policy, this chapter draws a conclusion different from most analysts' claim that China's policy has changed in recent years owing to its thirst for Africa's oil and other natural resources.[4] It is argued here that changes in China's African policy are closely linked to China's transformation of its grand strategy to open up Africa. Various misunderstandings and accusations are addressed, and new challenges related to Chinese-African relations and possibilities for bilateral and multilateral cooperation are pointed out and discussed.

Ideology: From Emphasis to Neutrality

China's African policy can be divided into three periods: a period of normal development (1949–1977), a transitional period (1978–1994), and a period of rapid development (1995 to present).[5] With the end of the Cultural Revolution and the change of the Chinese leadership, there was a gradual shift in China's policy toward economic development. The relation between diplomacy and economy was reversed, for example, "economy serving diplomacy" was changed to "diplomacy serving economy."[6] This shift was followed by a new foreign policy of independence, peace, and development.

The first change in China's African policy lies in its move *from* a posture of forming an alliance in international politics for the purpose of fighting against super powers *to* strengthening exchange and dialogue with Africa on the basis of seeking common ground while also reserving differences.

After the founding of the People's Republic of China (PRC), China's foreign policy was greatly circumscribed by international politics. In the 1950s, China first adopted a pro-U.S.S.R. and anti-U.S. policy, which was termed *"yi-bian-dao"* (one-sided policy). In the 1960s, China adopted the policy of anti-imperialism and antirevisionism. The 1970s witnessed China's policy of reconciliation with the United States and opposition to the U.S.S.R.[7] The focus of China's policy toward Africa was that of anticolonialism, anti-imperialism, and antirevisionism.[8] This stance derived from the unfavorable international situation after the founding of the PRC. The hostile policy of Western countries and later of the U.S.S.R. forced China to seek more "diplomatic room" to survive as a sovereign state.

The link between China's foreign policy and its ideology hindered diplomacy between China and Africa. The Communist Party of China (CPC) had contact with communist parties only in South Africa and Reunion. Later, due to the conflict between China and the U.S.S.R., the CPC discontinued its friendly relations with the parties in those two African countries. Early in the Cultural Revolution, China's ultraleftist policy had some impact on its foreign policy, and Chinese diplomats began to "export revolution" to Africa.[9]

In 1967–1969, the CPC discontinued its contact with the African Party for the Independence of Guinea-Bissau and Cape Verde. The Parti Congolais du Travail (the Congolese Labor Party) wanted to establish interparty relations to promote cooperation with the CPC, yet its offer was refused because it was not a communist party. The Partido Frelimo had been in contact with the CPC, yet the proposal to establish formal relations between the two parties was refused as well. Later, Partido Frelimo invited the CPC to attend its Third National Congress, without success. The two parties did not establish formal relations until 1981.

The new radical policy was rectified under the leadership of Premier Zhou Enlai. Starting in May 1969, China began to send its ambassadors to all countries with which it had diplomatic relations. However, the real change in China's policy did not come until the late 1970s.[10]

In July 1977, after CPC Chairman Hua Guofeng met with a Mozambique delegation, he asked the International Department of the CPC and the Ministry of Foreign Affairs to study the relations between Chinese and African parties. In November 1977, two ministries received instructions regarding nationalist parties in sub-Saharan Africa that wanted to establish relationships with the CPC. On 20 December 1977, the Political Bureau of the CPC made a positive decision, and, in 1978, the International Department of the CPC began to receive those African party delegations.[11] This was a breakthrough in the CPC's history of foreign affairs and greatly improved the development of Chinese-African relations because the move signaled that the CPC was no longer limited to contact with only communist parties. Since 1978, the CPC's relations with African parties have developed rapidly.[12]

The CPC's Twelfth Assembly in 1982 defined the new principle of its party relations—"Independence, Complete Equality, Mutual Respect, Noninterference in Others' Internal Affairs"—and proposed to establish relations with progressive parties and organizations.[13] China's contacts with parties of developing countries have greatly increased since the 1982 assembly.[14] From 1978 to 1990, more than 230 delegations from parties in sub-Saharan countries visited

Table 2-1. *CPC and African Parties' Visits, 2002–2006*

	2002	2003	2004	2005	2006	Total for period
African parties' visits to China	16	13	16	24	21	90
CPC's visits to Africa	17	8	20	19	14	78

Sources: *People's Daily, Observer,* various issues, 2002–2006.

China. At the same time, the CPC sent out fifty-six delegations to visit ruling parties of thirty-nine sub-Saharan countries.[15]

As of 2002, the CPC had established relations with more than sixty political parties in more than forty sub-Saharan countries. More than thirty were ruling parties.[16] In 2006, twenty-one African parties sent their delegations to China, while fourteen CPC delegations visited Africa (see table 2-1). During these visits, both sides discussed a wide range of topics, such as politics, the economy, culture, and military relations. In addition to the contact between parties, China and Africa also increased exchanges between their congresses and parliaments.[17]

In conclusion, the CPC no longer uses ideology as a standard of practice. The *principle* of contact is no longer ideological. The CPC cooperates, not only with socialist or communist parties but also with other parties that adhere to different ideologies. *Partnership* is not confined to ruling parties but includes also nonruling parties. The *content* of this contact is not limited to party politics but extends to economic cooperation and cultural exchange. For example, in 2000 Jia Qinglin, then secretary of CPC Beijing, visited Uganda and promoted cooperation in the coffee trade. Former Secretary of CPC Shandong Wu Guanzheng, Secretary of CPC Guangdong Zhang Dejiang, and Secretary of CPC Hubei Yu Zhengsheng visited Africa in 2001, 2004, and 2005, respectively, and their large economic and trade delegations signed cooperation agreements with African countries.[18]

Due to China's transition, the political relationship between China and Africa has deepened. High-level visits have been frequent, especially since the 1990s. Vice Premier Zhu Rongji paid his first visit to Africa in 1995, which kicked off the new "African boom" in China. President Jiang visited Africa four times and in 1996 put forward five suggestions for the strengthening of Chinese-African relations.[19] President Hu Jintao visited Africa five times, and in 2004 he noted that China and Africa should help each other economically and support each other in international and regional affairs.[20] The opening up of political relations with various African parties indicated that there was no longer any political criterion attached to relations with Africa. The CPC could exchange ideas with various African parties or political organizations of different ideologies and discuss various subjects, such as politics, governance, ethnicity, economy, and education. The change has greatly promoted Chinese-African cooperation and has become an important component in China's African policy. China has but one political demand for Africa: no political relations with Taiwan.[21]

Bilateral Exchange: From Unilateral Character to Multiple Channels

The second change in China's African policy was a switch from an emphasis on political contact to exchanges through multiple channels.

During 1949–1977, China's African policy concentrated on three aspects: supporting African people in their drive for national independence; uniting African countries in the struggle against colonialism, imperialism, and hegemony; and helping African countries with economic development. In the political arena, China tried its best to assist African independence movements; it also offered military assistance, such as training of military and political personnel.[22] After Africa's nations achieved independence, China began to seek Africa as an ally in its fight against imperialism and hegemonism. Despite internal pressure as China's economy suffered, its assistance to Africa continued.

Chinese-African economic cooperation comprised bilateral trade and economic assistance. The total sum of bilateral trade in 1977 only reached $720 million.[23] Between 1956 and 1977, China provided $2.476 billion in economic assistance to 36 African countries, about 58 percent of China's total foreign aid ($4.276 billion), according to an external source.[24] During the 1970s, although the U.S.S.R. was the biggest arms trader in Africa, its economic aid to Africa lagged far behind China's, which totaled $1.8 billion—double the amount of Soviet aid.[25]

The end of the Cultural Revolution witnessed a short period of decline in Chinese-African relations. First, the assistance to Africa decreased: China's assistance to Africa during 1976–1980 was estimated at $94 million.[26] The bulk of this assistance was given between 1976 and 1978.[27] Second, trade between China and Africa declined. Trade volume decreased after 1980 (1982 was an exception) and did not pick up until 1986 (see table 2-2). Third, the number of Chinese medical teams and doctors sent to Africa also decreased. China did not send doctors to Africa in 1979 or 1980, and between 1978 and

Table 2-2. *China-Africa Trade Statistics, 1980–1987*
Millions of dollars

Year	1980	1981	1982	1983	1984	1985	1986	1987
Export	747	798	978	675	623	418	638	854
Import	384	299	212	244	252	207	216	154
Total[a]	1,131	1,097	1,190	920	876	626	854	1,008

Source: *Almanac of China's Foreign Economic Relations and Trade*, years 1984–1988.
a. Sums may not total due to rounding.

1983, the number of doctors and medical teams sent to Africa were at their lowest (table 2-3).

The decline in Chinese-African relations was due to several factors. First, during the Cultural Revolution, China's economy struggled, and even with the end of the Cultural Revolution, there was little money to be spent on foreign aid. Second, in order to recover, China's economy needed funding and technology. With the cooling of relations with the West, the Chinese government's attention naturally turned toward developing countries. Third, relations with Albania and Vietnam, two major Chinese aid recipients, deteriorated, suggesting the limitations of China's foreign aid. Of course, the change in China's leadership also had some impact on continuity in foreign aid policy.[28] A new thinking was needed to establish better relations between China and Africa.

Three months after the Twelfth CPC Party Assembly in 1982, Premier Zhao Ziyang first visited Africa. Beforehand, he declared that his visit showed China's diplomatic focus on Africa, as well as on other developing countries; his visit was intended to establish a mutual understanding and friendship, and to strengthen the two sides' cooperation. During his visit to eleven African countries, Zhao announced "Four Principles on Sino-African Economic and Technical Cooperation"—including equality, bilateralism, effectiveness, and co-development.[29] Zhao's "Four Principles" were a supplement to Zhou Enlai's "Eight Principles of Economic and Technical Aid" put forward during his visit to Africa during December 1963–January 1964.

Zhou Enlai's "Eight Principles" were:

—Aid should not be considered as a unilateral grant, but as mutual help.

—Neither conditions nor privileges should be attached to the aid.

—To reduce the burden of the recipient countries, the repayment period could be extended for no-interest or low-interest loans.

—The purpose of aid is to help recipient countries develop *independently*.

—To increase the income of recipient countries, Chinese programs should produce faster results with less investment.

Table 2-3. *China's Medical Teams and Doctors in Africa, 1963–1983*

Time range	Countries with Chinese medical teams	Number of clinics	Number of doctors
1963–1967	Algeria, Tanzania, Somali, Congo	17	326
1968–1972	Mali, Tanzania, Mauritania, Guinea-Bissau, the Sudan, Equatorial Guinea	18	197
1973–1977	Sierra Leone, Tunisia, Zaire, Togo, Senegal, Madagascar, Morocco, Niger, São Tomé and Príncipe, Upper Volta, Guinea-Bissau, Gabon, the Gambia	23	300
1978–1983[a]	Benin, Zambia, Central Africa, Botswana, Djibouti, Mozambique, Rwanda, Uganda, Libya	13	173
Total (1963–1983)	...	71	996

Source: *Almanac of China's Foreign Economic Relations and Trade: 1984,* IV–219.
a. During 1979–1980, no new medical teams were sent to Africa.

—China will provide the best equipment and materials for the recipient countries, and promises to replace them if the quality is not what was stipulated in the agreement.

—Guarantee that technicians in recipient countries will master relevant technology when technical assistance is provided.

—Experts from China should never enjoy any privileges and should receive the same treatment as the local experts in recipient countries.[30]

Those principles were more a declaration of China's framework and self-restraint regarding assistance, which provided favorable conditions for the recipient country.

While the "Eight Principles" were concerned with China's assistance to Africa, Zhao's "Four Principles" focused on mutual economic and technological cooperation. The former policy guaranteed that China would provide the most favored assistance to Africa, with additional restraints on Chinese aid personnel. The latter stressed bilateral cooperation and co-development. The newer policy was noticed by the international community.[31]

In more recent years, the international community's popular perception is that the recent, rapid developments in the Sino-African relationship have arisen after a long, dormant period, revealing new and potentially unsettling Chinese ambitions in Africa. For example, a Center for Strategic and International Studies report stated: "After remaining dormant for thirty years, China's contemporary engagement in Africa reflects the emergence of a new and ambitious vision."[32] This view does not hold water. During the transitional period

(1978–1994), China continued to promote cooperation with Africa in various fields. African presidents or heads of state paid thirty-three visits to China in the 1970s and fifty-one visits in the 1980s.[33] Chinese leaders such as Chen Muhua, Geng Biao, Ulanfu, Ji Pengfei, and Li Xianlian visited thirty-three African countries from 1978 to 1980. Premier Zhao Ziyang visited eleven African countries after the Twelfth CPC Assembly and visited Tunisia in 1986. Other high officials—Li Xianlian (1986), Li Peng (1986, 1991), Wu Xueqian (1987, 1990), and Qian Qichen (1989)—also visited many African countries to promote bilateral relations.

Studying Chinese projects from the 1980s and 1990s, Brautigam notes that China continued its aid to Africa after the Cultural Revolution, although the emphasis differed from earlier periods: "Chinese projects in the 1980s and [19]90s stress economic results, efficiency, and profits," and they were deeply affected by China's domestic political contexts, values, and ideologies.[34] Brautigam drew a different conclusion than most other Western Africanists: "Although marginalized in the foreign policy calculations of current and former superpowers, sub-Saharan Africa does still figure in[to] Chinese global geopolitics."[35]

After the Tiananmen Square incident in 1989, Western countries enforced sanctions against China, while African countries helped China. Foreign Minister Qian visited eight African countries (Lesotho, Botswana, Zimbabwe, Angola, Zambia, Mozambique, Egypt, and Tunisia) that year. The next year, he visited Morocco, Algeria, and Egypt. Beginning in 1991, he visited a group of African countries after 1 January; visiting Africa after the New Year has become a tradition for Chinese foreign ministers.[36] Though Chinese diplomacy has increased in Africa, educational exchange and economic cooperation between the two sides have developed even more rapidly.

Educational Exchange

Between 1949 and 1977, China sent volunteer teachers to nine African countries, including Algeria, Egypt, Togo, Congo (Brazzaville), Guinea-Bissau, Mali, Somali, Tanzania, and Tunisia, with the first group sent to Egypt in 1954. The period 1978–1995 witnessed an increase, with teachers sent to twenty-one countries.[37] In 2003, there were 238 teachers in more than 30 African countries. Until recently, Chinese teachers in Africa have taught at the undergraduate through Ph.D. levels.[38] Since the late 1980s, China has tried through various means to help African countries build their own educational systems.

In June 2004, the first Confucius Institute in Africa was planned for the University of Nairobi.[39] Since then Confucius Institutes have been founded

Table 2-4. *African Students with Chinese Scholarships, 1950s–1990s*

Decade	Number of students
1950s	24
1960s	164
1970s	648
1980s	2,245
1990s	5,569

Source: Center for African Studies of Peking University (ed.), *China-Africa Education Cooperation* (Beijing, 2005), 12–22.

in Kenya, Nigeria, Zimbabwe, and South Africa. As of 2007, fifteen Chinese volunteers were in Zimbabwe, four of them Chinese language teachers, and two were at the Confucius Institute at the University of Zimbabwe. In South Africa, a Confucius Institute has been established at the University of Stellenbosch.[40]

Likewise, the number of African students in China has increased greatly since the 1950s (table 2-4). In 2000, at the time of the first FOCAC in Beijing, there were 1,388 African students in China; in 2005 the number was 2,757. Aside from the enrollment of African university students, China has held seminars, training courses, and symposia that concentrated on fields such as management capabilities, engineering skills, and school administration. By the end of 2003, China had established forty-three educational and research programs in areas such as agriculture, Chinese medicine, long-distance education, and computer technology, in addition to setting up twenty-one research laboratories.[41]

China's Ministry of Education (MOE) has supported courses at local universities for African teachers, engineers, and professionals. From 2002 to 2006, Jilin University trained 225 Africans in long-distance education. Northeastern Normal University also set up a base for training Africans. Since 2002 it has run 9 seminars for over 200 administrators from more than 30 African countries. China Agricultural University also managed 10 seminars from 2001 to 2006, training 206 experts, scholars, and officials from Africa.[42] Zhejiang Normal University started cooperation with Cameroon in 1996 by setting up its Chinese Language Training Center in Cameroon.

With the help of the MOE, in 2003, Zhejiang Normal University set up the first Center for African Education Studies in China. Since 2002, the University has run thirteen seminars for African teachers and administrators. Although the seminars focus on higher education and include African university presidents and high-level administrators, they also cover the administration of middle school and elementary education. The university cooperates with more than twenty universities in twelve African countries. In October 2006, Zhejiang Normal University held the first "China-Africa University President Forum," with a focus on "capacity building of higher education institutions in developing countries," "reform on management system in higher education institutions," and "international cooperation and partnership." Participants included more than thirty presidents and education officials from fourteen African countries.[43]

Tianjin University of Technology and Education was designated in 2003 as another MOE assistance base for vocational education training programs. As an answer to the call from the "Forum on China-Africa Cooperation—Addis Ababa Action Plan," in 2005 the university set up the Center for African Vocational Education Studies to train midrange engineering professionals from Africa. It has trained more than 200 students from Africa, and sent out 84 teachers in recent years to facilitate vocational education in African countries.[44]

In 2005, the MOE entrusted eleven universities to run twelve seminars and training courses on higher education management, long-distance education, and vocational technical education. Participants were from forty-one countries, most of them African.[45] In November 2005, the first "China-African Ministers of Education Forum" was held in Beijing, where State Councilor Chen promised cooperation regarding educational assistance and exchange.[46]

Every year the MOE holds a workshop on educational assistance in developing countries, with an emphasis on Africa. In March 2006, the MOE, together with the Ministries of Commerce and Foreign Affairs, held the "Fourth Seminar on the Exchange of Experience on the Training of Educational Personnel from Developing Countries," and more than seventy participants from different universities exchanged their ideas and experience.[47] In December 2006, the Center for African Studies at Peking University held a "National Universities' Workshop on Africa: Teaching, Study and Assistance." Officials from the Ministries of Education, Commerce, and Foreign Affairs attended the workshop along with participants from universities. All contributed their opinions on teaching and research in Africa, assistance to African education, and how the ministries could make the best use of their resources in universities. In May 2007, the fifth workshop was held in Chengdu, with more than fifty participants from the Ministries of Education, Commerce, and Foreign Affairs, as well as participants from more than twenty Chinese universities.

Economic and Trade Cooperation

New developments in economic cooperation include the engagement of state-run companies and private companies with various funding (some are funded by foreign investment). Such private companies are developing quickly. Statistics for January to October 2005 indicate that the export of state-run, private, and funded enterprises (Sino-foreign joint ventures, Sino-foreign cooperative enterprises, and foreign-invested enterprises) to Africa reached $559 million, $511 million, and $286 million, respectively, with a corresponding increase of 23, 59.6, and 52.7 percent, respectively.[48]

Trade commodities also reflect the cooperation between Africa and China. In 2004, the top four commodities exported from China to Africa were electrical equipment and machinery (41 percent), textiles (18 percent), garments (11 percent), and new technology (8 percent), such as electronic and information facilities, software, and aviation and aerospace equipment.

These numbers demonstrate that production machinery, everyday goods (instead of luxury goods), and high-tech commodities constituted a large percentage of China's exports. The top commodities imported to China from Africa were crude oil (64 percent), iron ore (5 percent), cotton (4 percent), iron or steel (3 percent), diamonds (3 percent), and lumber (3 percent).[49]

Economic cooperation can be seen not only in trade but likewise in areas such as investments, contract business, labor service, and consultant services, all of which show rapid progress. By the end of 2004, approximately 715 non-financial projects in Africa were approved by the PRC's Ministry of Commerce.[50] By the end of 2005, the number of Chinese firms reached 813, and they had invested $1.18 billion in Africa in areas such as infrastructure, natural resources, transportation, and agriculture.[51] Chinese-contracted construction projects have greatly increased as well. In 2005, the contracted projects of labor service totaled $8.61 billion.[52]

The Chinese government has tried to provide various services to encourage businesses to invest in Africa; they set up eleven centers for the promotion of investment, regularized bilateral economic trade with African countries, and announced business opportunities and trade regulations with Africa.[53] In addition, the Ministry of Commerce publishes timely information regarding the trade policies of African countries, shortages of commodities, and reports of the market situation.

In summary, there have been changes in Chinese-African economic cooperation. Unitary state-managed trade has split into two parts (state-owned and private companies). Trade volumes have greatly increased, and aid-type has become cooperative. "Gone are the days when cooperation between China and Africa concentrated mainly on state-to-state cooperation, political support in international affairs, and economic assistance."[54]

China has signed bilateral agreements regarding promotion and protection of investments with twenty-six African countries, and trade and cultural agreements with more than forty African countries. A Chinese-African multilateral cooperation system is gradually emerging, and the forms of cooperation have become multifactorial.[55] China has likewise established a diplomatic consultative system in twenty-eight African countries. This exchange covers the economy and trade, culture and education, medicine and sanitation, military, and civil administration.[56]

Field of Cooperation: from Unilateral Aid to a Win-Win Strategy

After the adjustment of China's African policy, emphasis was put on cooperation, bilateralism, and a win-win strategy, followed by a change in China's aid pattern, from unitary aid to multiple forms of aid, such as government deducted-interest loans, aid combined with co-investment, and grants. Naturally, China's African policy has its own strategic aim, yet one of its starting points was to help African countries eliminate poverty and consolidate their independence. In other words, co-development was the most important principle, and Chinese-African cooperation clearly follows this principle.

From the early 1980s to the mid-1990s, Africa experienced a process of marginalization, expressed as a decrease in investment and an increase in debts. From 1980 to 1990, although Africa was undergoing structural adjustments due to Western pressure, 43 of 139 British companies withdrew from Africa.[57] Japan also held a pessimistic view of Africa, and the number of its companies in Kenya dropped from fifteen to two in the 1980s. The total debt of sub-Saharan Africa was $6 billion in 1970; that figure grew to $84.3 billion in 1980. After the Cold War and the dismemberment of the Soviet Union, the importance of Africa's strategic position greatly decreased, contributing to its further marginalization. African debt reached $200.4 billion in 1993 and $210.7 billion in 1994, equal to 82.8 percent of its GNP in 1994, as well as 254.5 percent of its export earnings. According to a 1995 World Bank report, the debt-export ratio of 28 African countries was over 200 to 1 at the end of 1994.[58]

Change in Aid

At the Tokyo International Conference on African Development held in 1993, African countries suggested that foreign investment based on development and production was more effective than traditional aid.[59] China's early grant assistance accrued a significant return from its African counterparts: China became a member of the United Nations (UN).[60] Grants, however, hardly changed the reality of poverty. As Hu Yaobang pointed out in 1982, "As for economic assistance, the method of sheer gift is disadvantageous to both sides, judging from historical experience."[61] Therefore, during the late 1980s and early 1990s, China underwent a foreign trade and aid reform.

In 1987, a Togo sugar plant assisted by the Chinese had a shortage of technicians and experienced managers. Chinese experts took over, and the plant began to run effectively. The Togolese government praised the remarkable increase in enterprise.[62] This combination of China's assistance and joint-investment cooperation gradually spread to other China-aided enterprises. In 1991, the Malian government decided to privatize the Segu Textile Plant, a Chinese aid project. After negotiation, however, the Malian government transferred 80 percent of its shares to a Chinese company with the condition that the company pay its debts. Since then the company has been running smoothly, valued in 1996 at 7.6 billion African francs.[63] In 2003, China cancelled Mali's debt of 37 billion African francs.[64]

In late 1995, after three years of experimentation, the Chinese government put into effect its interest-deducted loan scheme.[65] Vice Premier Zhu and Vice Premier Li visited thirteen African countries during that year to explain China's new foreign aid policy. A year later, China signed agreements to give low-interest loans to sixteen African countries.[66] The new form of aid was gradually accepted. In 2000, the FOCAC implemented a new stage of bilateral relations; in response, China promised to relieve African debt. In 2002, China signed agreements with 31 African countries to relieve 156 debts, the sum reaching RMB 1.05 billion ($145 million).[67] As of the end of 2007, the figure had increased to RMB 10.9 billion.[68] According to the PRC's Ministry of Commerce, as of March 2008 China had forgiven the debt of thirty-two African countries, honoring pledges made at the FOCAC Beijing summit in 2006.

Exchange of Development Experience

Providing seminars is another way China helps African countries train their professionals. For example, the "Seminar on Economic Reform and Development Strategies" was held in 2003; participants included twenty-two administrators from different economic or financial units in sixteen African countries, together with seven officials from the African Development Bank. Both sides exchanged ideas on development, and African participants learned more about China's ongoing reform.

Nigerian historian Femi Akomolafe recognizes that "China's rapid economic transformation holds special lessons for those in Africa. Whilst the Chinese opted for an indigenous solution to their economic backwardness... China's economic performance is nothing short of a miracle. It shows what a people with confidence, determination and vision can achieve."[69]

The Chinese government has also frequently invited African diplomats to visit China. The "Understanding China Symposium" was first designed in 1996 specifically for young African diplomats. The China Foreign Affairs University ran the symposium for 9 years (1996–2004) for participants from more than 130 countries and 9 international organizations. One-hundred sixty-one diplomats from African countries having diplomatic relations with China attended nine symposia; ten African regional organizations also participated. The symposia included lectures on Chinese history, culture, and arts, and a tour of both rich and poor regions. From 2001 on, Peking University also ran various seminars and training courses for African diplomats and economic administrators. The School of Government at Peking University has run several symposia for African diplomats from English-, French-, and Arabic-speaking countries; a recent one was held from August to October 2007, with thirty-five participants from fourteen French-speaking countries. The Chinese government also holds seminars to train African professionals. In the first half of 2007, the Chinese government held 93 such training seminars, with 2,241 trainees from 49 African countries. According to its action plan, China will have trained 15,000 Africans between 2007 and 2009.[70]

This approach has been praised by African governments such as Nigeria, Mozambique, Uganda, Madagascar, Ethiopia, South Africa, and Zambia. For example, in 2005, Sudanese officials expressed their thanks for China's training program for Sudanese administrators in economic management, which was attended by senior officials from the Sudanese Ministry of Foreign Affairs and the Ministry of Finance and International Cooperation. About forty Sudanese went to China for training in their respective fields.[71]

Co-development and Bilateralism

The most impressive demonstrations of Chinese-African economic cooperation have been China's tariff relief for African exports, leading to increased trade between China and Africa. Vice Minister of Commerce Wei Jianguo said in November 2007, "From January to September, 2007, Chinese-African trade volume was 52.3 billion US dollars and the figure for the whole year is expected to reach 70 billion US dollars. Under the zero-tariff category, by the first half of 2007, China had imported commodities worth 440 million US dollars from Africa."[72] These increases indicate the positive impact of the

Chinese policy of promoting African exports to China. The original 199 zero-tariff African goods have increased to 454 types of goods from 26 of the least developed countries in Africa. In 2005, about 12,400 African businessmen came to the 97th Guangzhou Trade Fair, where the volume of business transactions totaled $1.7 billion. From January to September 2005, thirty African countries' trade with China totaled more than $100 million, while nine other countries' trade with China reached more than $1 billion.[73]

In 2000, Chinese-African trade volumes exceeded $10 billion ($10.598 billion), and China's imports from Africa surpassed its exports to Africa ($5.5 billion versus 5.04 billion).[74] Chinese-African trade reached about $30 billion in 2004, and China's imports from Africa were again more than its exports to the continent ($15.6 billion versus $13.8 billion).[75] This trade reached $39.75 billion in 2005, with imports again exceeding exports.[76] In 2006, Chinese-African trade reached $55.46 billion, an increase of 39.6 percent. Imports from Africa ($28.77 billion) again surpassed Chinese exports to Africa ($26.69 billion).[77] According to Ministry of Commerce statistics, it took twenty years for Chinese-African trade to increase from $100 million to $1 billion, and another twenty years to reach $10 billion, but only six years to reach $55.5 billion. From January to September 2007, Chinese-African trade volume was $52.3 billion, and the figure for the whole year was expected to reach $70 billion.[78]

With such trade increases, Chinese export goods have become better suited to Africa. Sales of machines, electronics, and new high-tech goods have grown rapidly, totaling more than half of the value of China's exports to Africa. China's aid emphasizes the combination of technical and economic support and the transfer of technology with commodities.[79] For example, China has provided much of the technology necessary for space launches and in-orbit services and has even trained Nigerian command and control operators. While Nigeria acquired satellite technology, China also gained from the collaboration by burnishing its credentials as a reliable player in the international commercial satellite market.[80] China also sent oil expert and engineer Wang Qiming of Daqin to the Sudan to provide African engineers with new technology that assists with the best pumping practices for seemingly exhausted oilfields.[81] This framework for China's aid—based on the principles of sustainability and mutual benefit rather than charity—has proven beneficial to African development.[82]

Characteristics

Chinese-African relations are characterized by summit diplomacy, equality, co-development, and cooperation.[83] Such summit diplomacy cannot be seen in Africa's relations with any other country, or in the relationship between

China and other continents. Although the principle of equality has been advocated among individuals in modern times, there is no mention of it in international relations. The equality in Chinese-African relations is a model for international relations. Equality means respect for sovereignty, mutual benefit, discussion, and coordination. A unique feature of China's foreign policy is the principle of noninterference in the internal affairs of other countries. Mutual benefit and co-development are likewise features in Chinese-African relations, their purpose being to improve Africa's ability to self-develop. The most impressive characteristic of the Chinese-African relationship is the standardized mechanism of cooperation, for example, FOCAC and its follow-up actions.

Criticism, Suspicion, and Explanation

China's African policy has become the focus of the international community, especially the Western powers. Western countries still regard Africa as being in their "sphere of influence," and China, with other developing countries, is usually considered an "external player" in Africa.[84] Western powers may fear that Chinese engagement will harm their interests in Africa, and thus they voice various criticisms and suspicions. Some of the criticisms are caused by misunderstanding, some by bias.

"New Colonialism"

There are accusations that China is developing relations with Africa solely to secure oil and other natural resources and that, in Africa, China is engaging in "new colonialism" or acting as "new economic imperialists."[85] This view has become popular in Western media. However, in its dealings with African states, China views them as equals, respecting their sovereignty.[86] In addition, China's trade activities in Africa, especially its imports of oil and other natural resources, have turned Africa's potential wealth into real wealth. Chinese involvement has greatly contributed to Africa's economic development and to Africa's 5 percent growth rate for the past twelve years. China's engagement has brought hope to Africa, a continent neglected by the outside for decades. Its positive impact on the continent has been demonstrated in terms of economic development and technology transfer. For example, the Sudan has changed from an oil importer to an oil exporter, with a whole system of exploration, production, refining, and exportation. With China's help, Nigeria launched its first communication satellite. As a Nigerian journalist points out, "The Chinese have effectively ended the Western dominance of one of Africa's most powerful countries, and their presence has resulted in a change in Nigeria's global relations."[87]

Chinese-African relations were established long before China's need for raw materials in the mid-1990s. At present, while China imports oil from Africa, it exports electronic, mechanical, and high-tech products that satisfy critical needs in Africa, creating a rough equilibrium in the economic and trade relations between the two countries. The oil drilling and exploration rights that China has obtained have been secured through international bidding mechanisms in accordance with international market practices, posing no "threat" to any particular country. Rights to oilfields in the Sudan and Nigeria were purchased by Chinese companies after the withdrawal of competitors.[88]

Human Rights Issue

Linked with the accusation of "neocolonialism" is the criticism that China, in order to gain raw materials, supports corrupt authoritarian regimes at the expense of "human rights."[89] The limits and norms of the international system only allow China to deal with sovereign states through their governments. The European Union constantly criticizes China's human rights record, yet Britain, France, and Germany are trying to promote trade with China. The United States and China have issued human rights reports criticizing each other for several years, yet such criticism by no means hinders the exchange of goods and ideas, and both sides endeavor to increase their economic trade. With state behavior based on Western ideals, China does not necessarily accept the naming and shaming of certain African regimes as corrupt.[90]

Zimbabwe and Darfur

Zimbabwe and Darfur have been picked out as two important cases among the accusations leveled against China's engagement in Africa.[91] China's position of noninterference with regard to Zimbabwe is in accord with that of the African Union (AU). In 2005, when Robert Mugabe demolished urban dwellings in an attempt to crack down on illegal shantytowns in Harare, Britain and the United States called on the AU to act. However, the AU felt that it was not its role to start running the internal affairs of member states and gave Mugabe its blessing to resist sanctions imposed by the West.[92] During March 2007, Britain and the United States criticized Mugabe for taking strong measures against Zimbabwe's political opposition. However, the leaders of southern African governments held a special meeting on Zimbabwe; all supported Mugabe unanimously and asked Western countries to give up their sanctions on Zimbabwe.[93]

Darfur is a very complicated case, with historical origins, national integration, religious conflict, refugee migration, and poverty all playing a role. First, the crisis in Darfur is mainly caused by environmental degradation, as pointed out by the UN Environment Program report issued in 2007: "Environmental degradation, as well as regional climate instability and change, are major underlying causes of food insecurity and conflict in Darfur—and potential catalysts for future conflict throughout central and eastern Sudan and other countries in the Sahel belt."[94] Second, Darfur is a regional tragedy that affects many people and disastrously impacts the region. However, except for the United States, neither the UN, regional organizations, nor other counties use "genocide" to describe the situation in Darfur.[95] Third, the crisis in Darfur is related to development and can only be solved through development. Fourth, the Darfur crisis is expressed as a conflict between different Sudanese peoples. Nation-building is a difficult process for all countries. Consider the U.S. Civil War: after more than 80 years of independence, the United States undertook a war to prevent part of the country from seceding, resulting in 600,000 deaths. The international community should give the Sudanese people time to solve this problem.

China has used its ties to the Sudan to persuade the Sudanese government to cooperate with the UN.[96] Since there is mutual respect and trust, China can work with the Sudanese government to find a solution agreeable to all parties to alleviate the suffering of the Sudanese people. Recently, the Sudanese government has accepted a "hybrid peacekeeping force" in Darfur.[97]

There is an accusation from the media that "China takes Sudan under its wing."[98] Some scholars echo this view.[99] In refutation, one could look at China's reaction after the Canadian oil firm Talisman decided to sell its interest in a Sudan consortium that also involved Chinese and Malaysian firms. The China National Petroleum Corporation wanted to purchase the interest, but Khartoum turned down the Chinese offer and awarded the shares to an Indian firm instead.[100] This shows that China and the Sudan are equal partners, and they each make decisions to guard their national interests independently.

China has constantly supported the Sudanese people with humanitarian aid. Aside from offering help to the Sudan to build its oil industry and infrastructure, China recently sent its fourth shipment of humanitarian aid, including tents, blankets, and medical and agricultural equipment. As of this writing, the Chinese government has sent humanitarian aid valued at RMB 80 million.[101]

Observation of the current international situation indicates that foreign intervention, especially by force, brings no solution but rather more trouble, as demonstrated by events in Afghanistan and Iraq, for example. Peaceful settlement is the best solution for all parties.

Transparency in China's Aid to Africa

There is a suspicion that China hides the amount of its aid to Africa. It is true that there are no accurate figures available for China's aid to Africa from official sources in Chinese. This lack may be due to China's sensitivity about the aid figure, domestic politics, or Chinese culture. First, although China has been providing support to Africa for more than a half century and there is a strong belief that China has provided large sums to Africa, the amount of Chinese aid to Africa is still rather small compared with that of Western countries.[102] Second, China is a developing country, with more than 20 million people below the poverty line. With a large number of poor people, it is not wise for the Chinese leadership to publicize the amount of China's aid to Africa. Third, according to Chinese tradition, it is improper and even immoral to reveal one's assistance to others. A Chinese saying goes, "Do not forget how others have helped you, and do forget how you have helped others." It is not only a matter of saving face, but also a matter of sovereignty.

Opportunity, Challenge, and Cooperation

It is not surprising that China's engagement in Africa has benefited African countries and the world as a whole. China's demand for raw materials and energy enables the rich resources of Africa to be utilized fully, benefiting both Chinese purchasers and African suppliers. Chinese demand has stimulated raw material prices, increasing the income of resource-rich countries in Africa, and has accelerated African development, turning potential wealth into real wealth. For example, Nigeria has paid off its outstanding loans, and the Sudan has gone from being a net oil importer to an oil exporter. In return, China has greatly increased its oil imports from Africa, which counted for 30 percent of its annual oil imports in 2005.[103] The investment of Chinese enterprises has promoted African industries and is breaking the longstanding hold that the West has had over trade in commodities between Africa and the rest of the world.[104] China, together with other new emerging countries, has entered Africa as an investor, has promoted African industries, and has "fueled the revival of a global interest in Africa because of high commodity prices."[105] Such investment is also enhancing the autonomy of African countries in production, sales, and investment. Chinese-African trade has the potential to help Africa win greater and truer independence. China's engagement also provides African countries with more choices for business partnerships, for export markets, and for pricing their commodities.

China's investment flow is usually accompanied by infrastructural construction, which can enable Africa to attract more investment. South African scholars have acknowledged China's role in helping African economies to achieve long-term growth through the principle of mutual benefit.[106] One particularly poignant analysis explains, "Unlike Belgium, which built roads solely for the extraction of resources in the Democratic Republic of [the] Congo, China is constructing or improving roads that are suitable not only for the transport of resources but which citizens can also use to travel."[107]

China's involvement in Africa faces five major contradictions or challenges. There are incongruities between China's interests and Africa's interests in market and labor; conflicts between China's national interests and Chinese enterprises' interests; disagreements between China's interests and the Western powers' vested interests; challenges regarding China's need for natural resources and Africa's need for sustainable development; and, finally, conflict between temporary interests and long-term interests, an issue not only for the Chinese but also for other international businesses and their African partners.[108]

Vines points out that China's engagement in Africa "has worried Western and Japanese governments and businesses."[109] Berger says that "The emergence of external players such as China and India poses a challenge to the European strategy."[110] Therefore, all countries involved must pursue confidence-building measures. Through mutual confidence, a win-win strategy can be achieved. To reach bilateralism, countries must consider their partners' interests, sustain bilateral and multilateral initiatives, and ensure cooperation. All countries involved should coordinate short- and long-term interests in order to guarantee the vitality of the cooperation and to strengthen African partners' capacity for both self-reliance and equal cooperation with the international community. With mutual confidence, cooperation in Africa can address areas such as research on the treatment of diseases (such as malaria and AIDS), research and development of new resources (such as solar and nuclear energy and biofuels), and assistance (such as humanitarian).

In conclusion, China's African policy has retained its principles while adapting to changing domestic and international conditions. This approach is closely linked with the transformation of China's grand strategy, as well as its outlook on world development. China's engagement in Africa is changing Africa and the world, providing more opportunities and creating more challenges. Despite such challenges, Chinese-African cooperation demonstrates what equality and co-development in international relations can produce.

Notes

1. Gerald Segal, "China and Africa," *Annals of the American Academy of Political and Social Science*, DXIX (1992), 126.

2. There are negative and positive interpretations of China's development. The negative is expressed by two views, collapse and threat. For the collapse theory, see Gordon G. Chang, *The Coming Collapse of China* (New York, 2001). Minxin Pei also draws a gloomy picture of China's reform, which has stalled with problems such as corruption, declining state power and credibility, and increasing inequality. See Minxin Pei, *China's Trapped Transition* (Cambridge, MA, 2006). For the threat theory, see Michael D. Swaine and Ashley J. Tellis, *Interpreting China's Grand Strategy* (Santa Monica, 2000); Bill Gertz, *The China Threat: How the People's Republic Targets America* (Washington, D.C., 2000); Zbigniew Brzezinski and John J. Mearsheimer, "Clash of the Titans," *Foreign Policy*, CXLVI (2005), 46–50; John J. Mearsheimer, "China's Unpeaceful Rise," *Current History*, CV (2006), 160–162. The positive is expressed in two views as well: gradualism and optimism. For the first, see Edward Friedman, "Why China Matters," *Journal of International Affairs*, XLIX (1996), 302–308. For the second, see Bruce Gilley, *China's Democratic Future* (New York, 2004); Zheng Bijian, *China's Peaceful Rise: Speeches of Zheng Bijian, 1997–2005* (Washington, D.C., 2005).

Since the end of 2005, there have been international conferences, seminars, workshops, and expert roundtable meetings on Chinese-African relations in Johannesburg, Beijing, London, Cambridge, Hong Kong, Tokyo, Berlin, and Shanghai; and special journal issues, such as *China Brief*, V (2005); *Southern African Journal of International Affairs*, XIII (2006); *International Politics Quarterly*, Issue 4 (2006); *West Asia and Africa*, Issue 8 (2006).

3. "China's African Policy," *People's Daily* (13 January 2006).

4. For example, "CSIS Prospectus: Opening a Sino-U.S. Dialogue on Africa, 2003" as quoted in Domingos Jardo Muekalia, "Africa and China's Strategic Partnership," *African Security Review*, XIII (2004), 8; Joshua Eisenman and Joshua Kurlantzick, "China's African Strategy," *Current History*, CV (2006), 219–224.

5. Li Anshan, "China-African Relations in the Discourse on China's Rise," *Journal of World Economics and Politics*, Issue 11 (2006), 7–14.

6. Qu Xing, *The Forty Years of China's Diplomacy* (Nanjing, 2000), 440–441.

7. Ibid., 375–376; Robert Ross (ed.), *China, the United States, and the Soviet Union: Tripolarity and Policy Making in the Cold War* (New York, 1993), 11–61.

8. See Ministry of Foreign Affairs of the People's Republic of China and Documentation Office of CPC Central Committee (ed.), *Mao Zedong on Diplomacy* (Beijing, 1994), 403–413, 416–420, 463–467, 490–492, 497–502, 526–528, 587–588, 600–601.

9. For an excellent study on the period, see Alaba Ogunsanwo, *China's Policy in Africa, 1958–71* (London, 1974), 180–257.

10. Long Xiangyang, "Sino-Africa Relationships between 1966 and 1969," in Center for African Studies of Peking University (ed.), *China and Africa* (Beijing, 2000),

72–86. China's foreign policy during the Cultural Revolution was also mentioned in Barbara Barnouin and Yu Changgen, *Chinese Foreign Policy during the Cultural Revolution* (London, 1998), 75–78.

11. Jiang Guanghua, *Records on Visits to Foreign Parties* (Beijing, 1997), 191, 451, 667; Ai Ping, "Chinese Communist Party's Contacts with African Political Parties," in Chen Gongyuan (ed.), *Strategic Reports on the Development of Sino-African Relationship in the 21st Century* (Beijing, 2000), 12–13.

12. Li Liqing, "Chinese Communist Party's Contacts with African Political Parties: History and Present," *West Asia and Africa*, Issue 3 (2006), 16–19.

13. Collection of Documents of the Twelfth Assembly of the Communist Party of China (Beijing, 1982), 50.

14. China hosted the Third Asian Parties International Conference in 2004. See also Huang Wendeng, "Deng Xiaoping Theory and Sino-Latin American Party Relations," *Journal of Latin American Studies*, Issue 6 (1998), 1–7.

15. Jiang, *Records on Visits to Foreign Parties*, 670–671. As the vice minister of the International Department of the CPC, Jiang recorded his eleven visits to sub-Saharan African countries in the book.

16. Li, "Chinese Communist Party's Contacts," 16–19; "Furthering the Development of Sino-Africa Relationship: Reports on 5th African Parties' Seminar," *Contemporary World*, Issue 6 (2002), 18–19; Zhong Weiyun, "The Contemporary Situation of Parties in Sub-Saharan Africa and Sino-African Parties Relationship," in Center for African Studies of Peking University (ed.), *China and Africa*, 129–142.

17. Zeng Jianhui, *Parliamentarian Diplomacy: Communication and Contention— Dialogues with Foreign Congressmen and Politicos* (Beijing, 2006), 101–103, 184–186.

18. Li, "Chinese Communist Party's Contacts," 18.

19. Shi Zongxing and Wang Xiangqing, "Jiang Zemin Met with OAU General Secretary Salim and Highly Appraised OAU and African Countries' Important Role in International Affairs," *People's Daily* (14 May 1996), 1.

20. Wang Tian, "Hu Jintao Had a Talk with Gabonese President Bongo," *People's Daily* (3 February 2004), 1.

21. Brian Smith, "Western Concern at China's Growing Involvement in Africa," available at www.wsws.org/articles/2006/apr2006/afri-a10.shtml (accessed 26 May 2008).

22. Jiang, *Records on Visits to Foreign Parties*, 130, 303–305, 442–443, 621–622. China trained 2,675 military personnel for Africa from 1955 to 1977. Warren Weinstein and Thomas H. Henriksen (eds.), *Soviet and Chinese Aid to African Nations* (New York, 1980), 102–111.

23. Ministry of Foreign Trade and Economic Cooperation, *Almanac of China's Foreign Economic Relations and Trade: 1984* (Beijing, 1984), 5–30.

24. Weinstein and Henriksen, *Soviet and Chinese Aid*, 117, 121.

25. Naomi Chazan and others, *Politics and Society in Contemporary Africa* (Boulder, 1992), 410.

26. Samuel Kim, "The Third World in Chinese World Policy," Center for International Studies Occasional Paper 19 (Princeton, 1989), 38.

27. After the PRC returned to the UN in 1971, China's foreign aid increased rapidly. Yan Yiwu, "The Work of China's Foreign Aid in 1989," in Ministry of Foreign Trade and Economic Cooperation, *Almanac of China's Foreign Economic Relations and Trade: 1990* (Beijing, 1990), 55.

28. However, China established 181 foreign aid programs from 1979 to 1983, 90 percent of which were carried out in Africa. See "China's Foreign Aid Programs Accomplished from 1979 to 1983," in Ministry of Foreign Trade, *Almanac 1984*, table IV, 217–218.

29. "Premier Zhao Said His Visits to Ten African Countries Had Reached the Expected Purpose at the Dar Salaam Press Conference," *People's Daily* (15 January 1983), 1.

30. "Premier Zhou Answered Questions of the News Reporter of Ghana News Agency Stating a New Independent Powerful Africa Will Appear in the World and China Will Support the Newly Rising Countries Develop Their Independent National Economy Strictly According to the Eight Principles," *People's Daily* (18 January 1964), 4. For an analysis of the Eight Principles, see Li Anshan, "Africa in the Perspective of Globalization: Development, Assistance and Cooperation," *West Asia and Africa*, Issue 7 (2007), 5–14.

31. Lillian Craig Harris and Robert L. Worden (eds.), *China and the Third World: Champion or Challenger?* (Dover, MA, 1986), 100–119.

32. From "CSIS Prospectus," as quoted in Muekalia, "Africa and China's Strategic Partnership," 8.

33. Wang Taiping (ed.), *Fifty Years' Diplomacy of New China* (Beijing, 1999), 699.

34. Deborah Brautigam, "Foreign Assistance and the Export of Ideas: Chinese Development Aid in the Gambia and Sierra Leone," *Journal of Commonwealth and Comparative Politics*, XXXII (1994), 340.

35. Deborah Brautigam, *Chinese Aid and African Development: Exporting Green Revolution* (New York, 1998), 43.

36. Qian Qichen, *Ten Notes on Diplomacy* (Beijing, 2003), 256–257.

37. Center for African Studies of Peking University (ed.), *China-Africa Education Cooperation* (Beijing, 2005), 24–25. See also Sandra Gillespie, *South-South Transfer: A Study of Sino-African Exchanges* (New York, 2001).

38. Deputy Minister Zhang Xinsheng's speech at the "Fifth Workshop on the Exchange of Experience on the Training of Educational Personnel from Developing Countries" (Chengdu, 24 May 2007).

39. In March 2004, Cao Guoxing, director of the Department of International Cooperation and Exchanges in the Ministry of Education (MOE), led an Africa assistance working group to Kenya. Guo Chongli, Chinese ambassador to Kenya, proposed to establish a Confucius Institute in the University of Nairobi. In June 2004, Minister of Education Zhou Ji visited Kenya and signed the Memorandum of

Understanding with George Saitoti, Kenyan minister of education, science and technology, to establish a Confucius Institute in Nairobi. MOE, "Typical Cases Introduction about China-Africa Cooperation in Education," Sino-African Education Minister Forum, Department of International Cooperation and Exchanges (Beijing, 21 November 2005).

40. Zhao Zuojun, Yuan Ye, and Liang Shanggang, "Chinese Teachers Entered African Continent with Confucian School," *Reference News* (7 June 2007).

41. *China-Africa Education Cooperation*, 3–5; Zhang Xiuqin, "Educational Exchanges and Cooperation between China and African Countries," *West Asia and Africa*, Issue 3 (2004), 24–28.

42. Department of International Cooperation and Exchanges, Ministry of Education, "Collection of Materials of Fifth Workshop on the Exchange of Experience on the Training of Educational Personnel from Developing Countries" (Chengdu, 2007).

43. Li Xu, "Zhejiang Normal University Holds Seminars for University Presidents of African English-Speaking Countries," *West Asia and Africa*, Issue 6 (2004), 69. See also Zhejiang Normal University, *ZNU's Educational Endeavor in Africa: A Retrospection (1996–2007)* (Jinhua, 2007).

44. Wang Yuhua, "Center for African Vocational Education Studies Established in Tianjin University of Technology and Education," *West Asia and Africa*, Issue 4 (2005), 20.

45. MOE, PRC, "Typical Cases Introduction about China-Africa Cooperation in Education," Department of International Cooperation and Exchanges (Beijing, 2005); International Education Section of MOE of the PRC, "Reports of the Fourth Seminar on the Exchange of Experience on the Training of Educational Personnel from Developing Countries" (Kunming, 2006).

46. Chen Zhili, speech at the Sino-African Education Minister Forum.

47. "Working Materials of the Fourth Seminar on the Exchange of Experience on the Training of Educational Personnel from Developing Countries" (Yunnan, 2006).

48. Zhou Jianqing, "Sino-African Economic and Trade Cooperation Develops Steadily—Survey of 2005 and Prospects for 2006," *West Asia and Africa*, Issue 1 (2006), 16.

49. Division of Coordination, Department of West Asia and Africa, Ministry of Commerce, "The Economic and Trade Relations between China and African Countries in 2004," in *China Commerce Yearbook 2005* (Beijing, 2005), 182–183.

50. Ibid., 183.

51. See also Martyn Davies, 141 in this volume.

52. *China Commerce Yearbook 2006* (Beijing, 2006), 725. China will also provide $3 billion in preferential loans and $2 billion of export credits over the next three years and establish a special fund of $5 billion to encourage Chinese investment in Africa. Ministry of Commerce, "China-Africa Trade Expected to Top 100 bln USD by 2010," available at http://english.mofcom.gov.cn/aarticle/subject/focac/lanmud/200611/20061103631550.html (accessed 20 December 2007).

53. Zhou, "Sino-African Economic and Trade Cooperation," 16.

54. Mahamat Adam, "Africa Starting to Rise in Partnership with China," *China Daily* (13 January 2006).

55. Zong He, "Sino-African Friendship, Cooperation and Common Development," *West Asia and Africa*, Issue 2 (2005), 59.

56. Drew Thompson, "China's Soft Power in Africa: From the 'Beijing Consensus' to Health Diplomacy," *China Brief*, V (2005), 1-4; Department of Health of Hubei Province (ed.), *Famous Doctors in North Africa* (Beijing, 1993); Xu Chunfu, "Chinese Medical Workers Building Bridges of Friendship with Africa," *West Asia and Africa*, Issue 5 (2003), 73–75; Zhan Shiming, "African Students from University of National Defense Have Informal Discussion at IWAAS," *West Asia and Africa*, Issue 3 (2004), 23.

57. "UK Companies Sell African Investments," *Financial Times* (28 June 1990), 4.

58. World Bank figures cited in April A. Gordon and Donald L. Gordon (eds.), *Understanding Contemporary Africa* (Boulder, 1996), 116. The deterioration of African political situations also worsened the food crisis. See Peter Lawrence (ed.), *World Recession and the Food Crisis in Africa* (Boulder, 1986).

59. Zhang Zhixin, "Carrying Out New Principles of Foreign Aid to Open Up a New Phase," in Ministry of Foreign Trade and Economic Cooperation, *Almanac of China's Foreign Economic Relations and Trade 1994/95* (Beijing, 1995), 62.

60. Weng Ming, "Appointing Just before Leaving—'Milord Qiao Leading Delegation to General Assembly of UN for the First Time,'" in Fu Hao and Li Tongcheng (eds.), *Great Talents and Their Great Achievement—Diplomats in UN* (Beijing, 1995), 9.

61. Documentation Office of CPC Central Committee (ed.), *Collection of Important Documents since the Third Plenary Session of the 12th Central Committee of the CPC* (Beijing, 1982), 1127–1128.

62. Yan, "Work of China's Foreign Aid in 1989," 55.

63. He Xiaowei, "Continuing Reforms of Foreign Aid Approach, Carrying Out Contracts of Foreign Aid," in Ministry of Foreign Trade and Economic Cooperation, *Almanac of China's Foreign Economic Relations and Trade 1997/98* (Beijing, 1997), 75.

64. Zhang Zhongxiang, *Mali* (Beijing, 2006), 215.

65. This low-interest loan is provided by Chinese banks, which are encouraged to do so by favorable government policies that offer subsidies to cover the difference between the low-interest and the standard loan rates. The low-interest loans are mainly used in programs that benefit the economic development of developing countries, as well as improve their infrastructures.

66. He, "Continuing Reforms of Foreign Aid," 75.

67. Qiu Deya, "China's Foreign Aid in 2002," in Ministry of Foreign Trade and Economic Cooperation, *Almanac of China's Foreign Economic Relations and Trade 2003* (Beijing, 2003), 91.

68. "China's Relief of Debt of RMB 10.9 billion of 31 African Countries," Xinhua, available at http://news.163.com/06/1029/12/2UJOAR4D.html (accessed 21 December 2007).

69. Femi Akomolafe, "No One Is Laughing at the Asians Anymore," *New African,* CDLII (2006), 48–50.

70. "Focus: China and Africa Are in Win-Win Cooperation," available at http://news.cctv.com/world/20070820/115321.shtml (accessed 20 December 2007).

71. Speaking at the symposium, a representative of the Sudanese Ministry of International Cooperation expressed his thanks to the Chinese embassy for arranging the training program. Xinhua (27 July 2005).

72. Ministry of Commerce, PRC, "Speech at the Progress Briefing on the Implementation of the 8 Africa-Targeting Measures of the Beijing Summit of the Forum on China-Africa Cooperation," available at http://english.mofcom.gov.cn/aarticle/speech/200711/20071105246103.html (accessed 20 December 2007).

73. Zhou, "Sino-African Economic and Trade Cooperation," 15–18.

74. Ministry of Foreign Trade and Economic Cooperation, *Almanac of China's Foreign Economic Relations and Trade: 2001* (Beijing, 2001), 503.

75. *China Commerce Yearbook 2005,* 182.

76. *China Commerce Yearbook 2006,* 724.

77. Ministry of Commerce, PRC, available at http://zhs.mofcom.gov.cn/aarticle/Nocategory/200702/20070204346971.html (accessed 20 December 2007).

78. Ministry of Commerce, "Speech at the Progress Briefing." See also Robert I. Rotberg, 3, and Harry Broadman, chapter 5, both in this volume.

79. See Deborah Brautigam, chapter 9 in this volume.

80. "China Launched Satellite for Nigeria," Xinhua (14 May 2007).

81. "Wang Qimin Is Welcomed by Sudanese," *China Petroleum Daily* (June 26, 2007), available at www.oilnews.com.cn/xinan/system/2007/06/25/001105577.shtml (accessed 26 May 2008); Li Anshan, "China and Africa: Policy and Challenges," *China Security,* III (2007), 69–93.

82. Premier Wen Jiabao recently pointed out three focuses during his visit to Africa. China is going to try every means to increase imports from Africa; to combine closely technological export and economic cooperation, with a special emphasis on strengthening the African capacity for self-development; and to help African countries train African technicians and management personnel. See Li Xinfeng, "Wen Jiabao Held a Press Conference in Egypt," *People's Daily* (19 June 2006), 1; He Wenping, "The Balancing Act of China's Africa Policy," *China Security,* III (2007), 23–40.

83. For a detailed analysis, see Li, "China and Africa."

84. Bernt Berger, "China's Engagement in Africa: Can the EU Sit Back?" and Princeton Lyman, "China's Involvement in Africa: A View from the US," *South African Journal of International Affairs,* VIII (2006), 115–127 and 129–138, respectively.

85. See Princeton Lyman, "China's Rising Role in Africa," available at www.cfr.org/publication/8436/ (accessed 24 June 2008); Lindsey Hilsum, "China's Offer to Africa: Pure Capitalism," *New Statesman* (3 July 2006), 23–24.

86. As the Nigerian general consul in Hong Kong claimed, "We Nigerians just want

to do business with China, because we respect each other, can sit there and talk to each other equally." Speech at the International Conference "China-Africa Links," Hong Kong University of Science and Technology (12 November 2006).

87. Dulue Mbachu, "Nigerian Resources: Changing the Playing Field," *South African Journal of International Affairs,* XIII (2006), 82.

88. "Nigeria Gives China Oil Exploration Licences after Auction," Agence France-Presse (19 May 2006). See also Stephanie Rupp, 81 in this volume.

89. Gideon Mailer, "China in Africa: Economic Gains, Democratic Problems," available at www.henryjacksonsociety.org/stories.asp?id=220 (accessed 26 May 2008).

90. At an international symposium on 25 February 2004 in Tokyo (Center for Asia Pacific Partnership, Osaka University of Economics and Law), a scholar from American University in Washington, D.C., told me that the American government is the most corrupt regime because it is an "institutionalized corruption." "Just think of Cheney, our vice president!" he exclaimed.

91. Joshua Eisenman, "Zimbabwe: China's African Ally," *China Brief,* V (5 July 2005), 9–11; Yitzhak Shichor, "Sudan: China's Outpost in Africa," *China Brief,* V (13 October 2005), 9–11.

92. Ewen MacAskill, Vikram Dodd, and Eric Allison, "African Union Defends Mugabe," *Guardian* (25 January 2005), available at www.guardian.co.uk/world/2005/jun/25/zimbabwe.ericallison (accessed 26 May, 2008).

93. Rob Crilly and Jan Raath, "Africa Gives Mugabe Its Blessing to Fight West's Sanctions," *The Times* (30 March 2007), available at www.timesonline.co.uk/tol/news/world/africa/article1588679.ece (accessed 26 May 2008).

94. United Nations Environment Program, *Sudan Post-Conflict Environmental Assessment, 2007* (June 2007), 329. See also the program's Post-Conflict and Disaster Management Branch website at http://postconflict.unep.ch. This view on the role of environmental degradation is not new but has been neglected by the outside world. For a similar perspective, see Adam Mohammed, "The Rezaigat Camel Nomads of the Darfur Region of Western Sudan: From Cooperation to Confrontation," *Nomadic Peoples,* VIII (2004), 230–240. The Sudanese ambassador to the United States provided the same explanation in his speech at the National Press Club in Washington, D.C., on 30 May 2007, when addressing the Bush administration's new sanctions on the Sudan.

95. It is noteworthy that a much more serious disaster in the neighboring Democratic Republic of the Congo did not elicit as much attention from the United States. See Séverine Autesserre, "Local Violence, International Indifference? Post-Conflict 'Settlement' in the Eastern D.R. Congo (2003–2005)," Ph.D. thesis (New York University, 2006). Exaggerated figures on the deaths in Darfur may have contributed to misunderstanding the situation. See Peter Apps, "Watch Your Facts, UK Ad Watchdog Warns Campaigners" (14 August 2007), available at www.alertnet.org/thenews/newsdesk/L14822855.htm (accessed 20 December 2007).

96. "What Kind of Issue Darfur Is: A Special Interview with the Special Representative of the Chinese Government," *Chutian Metropolis Daily* (8 July 2007), available at www.cnhubei.com/200707/ca1379834.htm (accessed 26 May 2008).

97. "Sudan Government Deals with Darfur Issue with a Light Pack," Xinhua, available at http://news.xinhuanet.com/world/2007-07/15/content_6377969.htm (accessed 15 July 2007).

98. David Blair, "Oil-Hungry China Takes Sudan under Its Wing," *Telegraph* (23 April 2005), available at www.telegraph.co.uk/news/main.jhtml?xml=/news/2005/04/23/wsud23.xml&sSheet=/ news/2005/04/23/ixworld.html (accessed 20 December 2007).

99. Shichor, "Sudan: China's Outpost in Africa," 9–11.

100. Barry Sautman and Yan Hairong, "Wind from the East: China and Africa's Development," paper presented at a conference on "China's New Role in Africa and the South" (Shanghai, 16–17 May 2007). For analysis of India's entry into the oil enterprise in the Sudan and its impact, see Raja Mohan, "Sakhalin to Sudan: India's Energy Diplomacy," *The Hindu* (24 June 2002), available at www.hinduonnet.com/thehindu/2002/06/24/stories/2002062404201100.htm (accessed 20 December 2007).

101. Since 2004 China has sent five shipments of material for humanitarian aid to Darfur. The fourth shipment, worth RMB 20 million ($2.6 million), left for the Sudan on 16 August 2007, and included pumps, tents, and blankets to help residents in the Darfur region improve their living conditions. FOCAC, "Humanitarian Aid from China Leaves for Sudan's Darfur" (20 August 2007), available at www.focac.org/eng/zxxx/t353371.htm (accessed 20 December 2007). The fifth batch of aid material, valued at RMB 40 million, was shipped on 25 August 2007 and included dormitories for at least 120 schools, generators, vehicles, and pumps. See http://news.enorth.com.cn/system/2007/08/24/001839261.shtml (accessed 20 December 2007).

102. According to a Chinese source, over the past fifty years, China has provided a total of RMB 44.4 billion in aid to Africa and assisted with about 900 infrastructural and social welfare projects. See Zhang Hongming, "China Policy of Assistance Enjoys Popular Support," People's Daily Online (23 June 2006), available at http://english.people.com.cn/200606/23/eng20060623_276714.html (accessed 20 December 2007).

103. Zha Daojiong, "China's Oil Interest in Africa: An International Political Agenda," *International Politics Quarterly*, IV (2006), 55.

104. Sanusha Naidu and Martyn Davies, "China Fuels Its Future with Africa's Riches," *South African Journal of International Affairs*, XIII (2006), 69–83.

105. Alex Vines, "The Scramble for Resources: African Case Studies," *South African Journal of International Affairs*, XIII (2006), 63. Chris Alden also analyzed Africa's interests in China in his article "China in Africa," *Survival*, XLVII (2005), 153–156.

106. Martyn Davies and Lucy Corkin, "China's Market Entry into Africa's Construction Sector: The Case of Angola," paper presented at the international symposium "China-Africa Shared Development" (Beijing, 19 December 2006).

107. Toya Marks, "What's China's Investment in Africa?" *Black Enterprise* (1 March 2007), available at www.thefreelibrary.com/What's+China's+investment+in+Africa %3F+Many+ African+nations+provide...-a0160105455 (accessed 20 December 2007).

108. Li, "China and Africa," 80–86.

109. Alex Vines, "China in Africa: a Mixed Blessing?" *Current History,* CVI (2007), 215.

110. Berger, "China's Engagement in Africa," 124–125.

WENRAN JIANG

3

China's Emerging Strategic Partnerships in Africa

Chinese President Hu Jintao wrapped up his eight-country, twelve-day African tour in February 2007 in the midst of controversy regarding China's role on the continent. Government officials from the countries that received China's leader expressed gratitude for their guest's generous offers of aid, cancellations of debt, and promises of trade and investment. Critics, however, charge that China's actions in Africa are no less than neocolonialism, as China seizes a new sphere of influence, grabs oil and other resources, props up repressive regimes, and leaves individual African countries on the losing end. Beijing has refuted such characterizations by identifying itself with the developing world, stressing the reciprocal nature of its interactions with Africa and promising a new paradigm of China-Africa partnership based on the traditional friendship.[1]

This chapter reviews China's growing presence in Africa and how its traditional ties to the continent have been translated into a commercial relationship. It then examines energy as China's new focus in Africa and explores the challenges facing China's expansion on the African continent. This is followed by a comparison of China's relations with Africa and Latin America, and a number of questions are raised for developing countries' engagement with China. In concluding, the chapter briefly touches upon Africa's strategic future in great power politics.

The author would like to thank Simin Yu and Nong Hong for their research assistance and Emily Wood for her editorial assistance.

Beijing's Intensive Engagement with Africa

The international attention to China's relations with Africa is in part a result of the Chinese leadership's decision to make the resource-rich continent one of its foreign policy priorities. Hu's trip to Africa was his second within a year, the third as China's president, and the fifth since he became a member of the Politburo in the early 1990s.

In the summer of 2006, Chinese Premier Wen Jiabao toured seven African countries. The seven countries on his itinerary—Angola, Egypt, Congo, Ghana, South Africa, Tanzania, and Uganda—had a combined trade volume of over $38 billion with China, or 52.2 percent of total Chinese-African trade in 2007.[2] Since 2004, six senior Chinese leaders from the nine-member Politburo Standing Committee of the Chinese Communist Party have visited Africa, covering most of the countries on the continent.[3] The Chinese foreign minister's decision to select an African country as his first foreign trip of each year since 1991 indicates the extensive focus that Chinese leaders have placed upon Africa and, in doing so, reveals the importance that Beijing has attached to that part of the world.[4]

Such high-profile visits, a recurring practice of the past few years, have aroused speculation that Beijing's pursuit of great power status may include a new strategic plan for Africa. After all, top Chinese leaders have similarly toured Latin America since President Hu first visited Brazil, Argentina, Chile, and Cuba in 2004. But China's ties to African countries can be traced back to the 1960s when one after another African state was declared independent. Throughout the 1960s and 1970s, China developed close relations with many of those states, primarily based on a shared ideological belief and political identity: anticolonialism, national independence, economic self-reliance, and developing world cooperation. Beijing provided substantial aid and other assistance to struggling African states in order to show that China was fully on the side of the developing world.

But priorities have changed since the 1970s. China's economic reforms have gradually moved China away from its radical revolutionary worldview. Beijing's open-door policy—mainly designed to attract foreign trade, investment, and joint-venture opportunities from Western countries—and China's entry into the World Trade Organization (WTO) have moved China much closer to a market economy where profits, not political agendas, drive most of the economic and trade activities. In this process, China's relations with African and other developing countries have also been restructured from being anticolonial brothers-in-arms to economic and trade partners based on market principles.

Many things, though, have remained the same. Beijing continues annually to pay and train young African diplomats at the prestigious Foreign Affairs University, which it has been doing for many years. China continues to present itself as a member of the developing world. Beijing even named 2006 the "Year of Africa."[5]

Most of China's foreign aid, totaling RMB 7.5 billion ($950 million) in 2005, goes to more than fifty African countries.[6] In fact, Wen claimed that China has offered Africa more than $44 billion in aid over the past 50 years to finance 900 infrastructural projects. "There's more pragmatism, more business focus in how China engages in foreign policy. I wouldn't say China's interest in Africa is newfound, but an old set of relationships wearing a new jacket," summarized Kobus van der Wath, founder and managing director of the Beijing Axis.[7] Meanwhile, all signs indicate that Chinese-African relations have entered upon a new phase centered on energy and raw materials.[8]

The watershed event in Sino-African relations was the elaborate Forum on China-Africa Cooperation (FOCAC) summit held in Beijing in November 2006. As a part of China's 2006 "Year of Africa" and in commemoration of the fiftieth anniversary of China's diplomatic relationship with Africa, forty-eight of the fifty-three African countries sent their leaders to Beijing for a gathering that no other country in the world has yet been able to assemble. Beijing's streets and subways were filled with celebratory signs; President Hu, standing at the Great Hall of the People, received all forty-eight African leaders, most of them presidents or prime ministers, and over the course of the following days promised a long list of future initiatives of cooperation bundled together with generous financial incentives:

—A "new type of China-Africa strategic partnership," characterized by "political equality and mutual trust, economic win-win cooperation and cultural exchanges," was announced as an overall framework of bilateral relations.

—Additional high-level bilateral visits were proposed in order to maintain the positive momentum of Sino-African relations. The foreign ministers of China and the African countries "would hold political consultations in New York on the sideline of the UN General Assembly to exchange views on major issues of common interest."

—China and Africa would work to more than double the current trade volumes by 2010, reaching $100 billion in bilateral trade.

—China would encourage investment in Africa by setting up a China-Africa development fund amounting to $5 billion and establishing Special Economic Zones in Africa.

—Beijing would provide African countries with $3 billion in preferential loans over three years, while also canceling $1 billion of debt from African countries.

—Trade deals signed between Chinese and African corporations during the summit totaled $1.9 billion.

—In addition to providing a $37.5 million grant for antimalarial drugs over three years, Beijing would assist African countries to build thirty hospitals and thirty demonstration centers for the prevention and treatment of malaria.

—China would build 100 rural schools in Africa over the next 3 years and double the number of current scholarships given to African students to study in China from 2,000 to 4,000 by 2009.[9]

Energy as the New Focus of Beijing's African Strategy

China's relentless pursuit of economic development turned the country from a petroleum exporter to an importer by 1993. Beijing's new target is to quadruple its economy again by 2020, as it did from the late 1970s to the mid-1990s. To achieve this goal, China must rely more and more on an external energy supply. In 2007, the middle kingdom was burning 7.8 million bbl/d.[10] Although still far behind the United States, which consumes 20.7 million bbl/d , Chinese consumption is projected to reach a daily level of 16 million barrels within the next two decades, according to International Energy Bureau Agency estimates.[11]

This quest for energy and other resources has swiftly directed China's attention to Africa. From 2001 to 2007, China's trade with Africa increased 681 percent, only slightly slower than the growth of China's trade with Latin America in the same period (687 percent) and faster than China's trade growth with the Middle East (546 percent), the Association of South East Asian Nations (487 percent), the European Union (415 percent), and North America (378 percent).[12] In 2007, China's trade with the seven African countries on Premier Wen's June 2006 touring list was $38.4 billion, a surge of 130 percent from the previous year.[13]

It is not surprising that in such a broad economic context, Africa has turned into a major energy supplier for China. In 2003, both President Hu and Premier Wen, along with Chinese energy company executives, visited several oil-producing African states, and, since then, China has been involved in increasing the number of energy deals on the continent. By the end of 2006, Africa supplied nearly 30 percent of China's total oil imports; the same was true in 2007.[14]

The Chinese-African energy deals share a number of characteristics. First, Beijing is willing to move into the "troubled zones" with bold investment and aid packages in exchange for energy. When Angola ended its twenty-seven-year civil war in 2002, few foreign countries were willing to go there, but China arranged a $3 billion oil-backed credit line to rebuild the country's shattered infrastructure. Angola soon became the second-largest supplier of crude to the Chinese market after Saudi Arabia, and during the first 10 months of 2006 it became the largest supplier of oil to China, losing out by just 0.42 million tons to Saudi Arabia by year's end. Angola replaced Saudi Arabia as the top supplier of crude oil to China in the first half of 2008, by 0.47 million tons.[15] Beijing also made Angola its largest foreign aid destination, adding another $2 billion in aid to Angola during Premier Wen's 2007 two-day visit.[16] As of 2007, Angola produced 1.4 million bbl/d, second only to Nigeria in sub-Saharan Africa—and one-third of that total went to China, making up 13 percent of total Chinese imports. Similar arrangements have been made in Nigeria and other countries. In April 2008, Angola topped Nigeria for the first time, producing 1.87 million bbl/d, compared to Nigeria's 1.81 million.[17]

Second, Chinese energy companies are committing large amount of funds and labor for exploration and development rights in resource-rich countries. A project in the Sudan, for example, is one of the earliest and largest overseas energy projects conducted by China's major energy companies. Chinese operations in the Sudan include investment, development, pipeline building, a large Chinese labor deployment, and continuous operations. China has a $4 billion investment in the country. The China National Petroleum Corporation (CNPC) has a 40 percent controlling stake in Greater Nile Petroleum, which dominates the Sudan's oilfields. In 2006, China purchased more than half of the Sudan's oil exports. Early in 2007, China National Offshore Oil Corporation (CNOOC) bought a 45 percent stake in a Nigerian oil and gas field for $2.27 billion and also purchased 35 percent of an exploration license in the Niger Delta for $60 million. Chinese companies have made similar investments in Angola and other countries.[18]

Third, Chinese energy majors enter into joint ventures with national governments, state-controlled energy companies, and individual enterprises to establish a long-term, local presence. It appears that Chinese companies often outbid their competitors in major contracts awarded by governments of African countries because their concerns are not just short term but strategically oriented so as to position themselves for the future.[19] After the U.S. Congress effectively blocked the $18.5 billion bid by CNOOC for the U.S. energy firm Unocal Corporation in 2005, Chinese energy companies' investments in other parts of the world intensified. "If you can't do it somewhere, then you can always do it somewhere else," Fu Chengyu, chairman of CNOOC, said in an interview in Beijing. "We're looking at opportunities in Africa as a whole."[20]

Fourth, China's selection of energy cooperation partners does not mirror the particular preferences of the United States or other Western countries. The Sudan is a case long known in the international community.[21] As of 2007, China accounted for 65 percent of Sudanese total exports.[22] In addition, in 2004 China and Zimbabwe reached an energy and mining deal worth $1.3 billion.[23] In exchange for building three coal-fired thermal power stations, among others, Zimbabwe is likely to repay the Chinese investment with rich deposits of platinum, gold, coal, nickel, and diamonds.[24]

A New Model of Cooperation or a Return to the Past?

In the past few years, the demands from China, India, and other developing economies for more oil, natural gas, and other resources are major factors, although not the only ones, that have driven up world energy and other commodity prices. Chinese energy companies' extensive search for oil and gas assets in Africa, Latin America, the Middle East, and Central Asia has created some anxiety about the world's future supplies of energy.

Beijing's extensive engagement and its ascending status in Africa also raise important questions about the nature of China's involvement on the continent, who gets what, and how. Critics charge that China has pursued mercantilist policies in the region for pure economic benefit without concern for human or environmental impacts. Due to China's support, they argue, the Sudanese government continues its genocide in the Darfur region, and the Mugabe regime can survive and carry on its human rights abuses in Zimbabwe.[25]

Officially, Beijing has rejected such criticism, stressing noninterference in domestic affairs. As Premier Wen put it, "We believe that people in different regions and countries, including those in Africa, have their right and ability to handle their own issues."[26] Beijing emphasizes that China's involvement in Africa is different from the old or new colonialism of the past, and that an affluent China is now putting money back into local African economies. As Chinese leaders like to say, it is a win-win situation. Many African countries tend to agree that China's growing presence has helped the continent economically; thanks to China many African countries are experiencing good development outcomes.

Nevertheless, with China's rapidly expanding activities in Africa, international concerns over Chinese behavior are deepening, and calls for Beijing to be a more responsible world power are strengthening. There are also indications that Chinese policymakers, academics, nongovernmental organizations, and even enterprises are reflecting on China's role. Indeed, China's newly acquired status in Africa is subject to continuous debate within Chinese policy and academic circles. While some celebrate Beijing's achievements, others caution that balanced policies must accompany the rapid expansion of Chinese commerce.

President Hu's much publicized African trip early in 2007 was clearly a strategic follow-up to the FOCAC summit. To carry out Beijing's promise of enhanced cooperation, Hu delivered offers and initiatives at every stop of his eight-country tour. Three particular countries on Hu's itinerary, however, generated more headlines than the others: the Sudan, Zambia, and South Africa. Each country represents a specific challenge for Beijing's African diplomacy.

Of the three countries, China has the most significant energy interests in the Sudan, and its oil companies have been operating there since the departure of the Western oil majors in the mid-1990s.[27] The state-owned CNPC has the largest overseas production in the Sudan, and other Chinese firms have also invested heavily in refineries, pipelines, and other infrastructural projects. Bilateral trade reached $5.7 billion in the first eleven months of 2007.[28] China is the Sudan's largest trading partner, while the Sudan is China's third-largest trading partner in Africa.[29] In recent years, Beijing has been facing increased international criticism for its unwillingness to use its significant economic leverage to persuade the Sudanese government to cease its sponsorship of atrocities in Darfur. In what seemed to be a response to the criticism and possibly a departure from China's traditional policy of noninterference, Hu supported a United Nations peacekeeping mission to Darfur.[30]

The appointment of a special envoy to the Sudan demonstrates Beijing's desire to avoid criticism and craft an image of working actively to end the Darfur crisis. But it is too early to conclude that Beijing has changed its foreign policy approach. Wherever and whenever possible, China avoids getting involved in domestic politics and rather tends to focus on economics. Deep in Chinese foreign policy philosophy there is a strong belief that conflict resolution is primarily realized through domestic dynamics, and that foreign interventions are less decisive, do not really work, and are often counterproductive.

In Zambia, the rapid influx of Chinese businessmen and investment into the country's rich copper and other commodity sectors has brought accusations that Chinese owners have exploited the local workers. Not long ago, the opposition leader in Zambia's presidential election ran on an anti-China platform, and though he lost the election, accusations of low wages and other mistreatment in Chinese-owned mines linger. Hu's stop in Zambia was marked by efforts from both sides to defuse criticisms, with Beijing offering Zambia

$800 million in special loans and canceling $350 million in debts that Zambia owed to China. The two governments also announced the establishment of a Special Economic Zone.[31] While Hu emphatically rejected the view that China was simply interested in extracting Africa's resources for its own economic benefit—in effect, replacing the old colonial powers—China's own record of labor protection during the past three decades is a troubling one; extraordinary efforts will be required if fair labor laws are to be enforced abroad.

China's presence in South Africa is likewise being questioned, though the debate has centered upon the extent to which the bilateral economic ties between the two countries are competitive or complementary. South Africa is China's largest trading partner on the continent, with bilateral trade totaling $14 billion in 2007, up 42.4 percent from 2006.[32] As the most advanced economy in Africa, South Africa's domestic economy has received serious challenges from the arrival of Chinese products. There are significant concerns that Chinese imports are resulting in the loss of manufacturing jobs in South Africa. Facing concerns that South Africa may end up in a neocolonial relationship, exporting resources to China and receiving more expensive value-added manufacturing goods in return—a familiar pattern that characterizes Africa's past colonial trade relations with Europe—Hu pledged to address the trade imbalances between China and South Africa, which are heavily in China's favor.[33]

What Determines China's Behavior in Africa?

Much has been debated about China's growing influence in Africa and around the world. To understand better China's rapidly expanding relations with Africa, it is useful to compare its presence and policies in Africa with those in Latin America. China's rapidly developing ties to these two continents in recent years are a result of the following combined factors. (Any changes in these factors may also have a potentially negative impact on China's engagement with the two continents.)

High Economic Growth Rate

China's high economic growth rate of over 9 percent annually has been sustained for nearly three decades. China is the world leader in this regard, outperforming all other major economies; it is now the fourth-largest economy in terms of US dollars and the second-largest in terms of purchasing power parity. Its economic development has been accompanied by an even higher growth rate in its foreign trade, contributing more to a global trade increase than any other major economy since the 1990s. China is now the third-largest trading nation after Germany and the United States in terms of export volumes. Trade volumes between China and Africa and between China and Latin America are the fastest growing among China's regional partners around the world.

Any slowdown or collapse of such a growth regime will have an impact on China's trade partners, especially in the developing world. The more interdependence there is between China and other developing countries in terms of trade and other economic activities, the more serious the impact will be from a Chinese economy that falters.

Membership in the WTO and Trade Practices

China's entry into the WTO in 2002 further opened the door for trade with and investment in the Chinese market, while making Chinese goods more available and Chinese investment abroad easier, especially given a phased tariff liberalization process. With the easing of rules, a high savings rate, and accumulating capital, more Chinese companies, public and private, are investing abroad. Africa and Latin America, with their huge potential and cheap labor force, have become major destinations for Chinese overseas expansion, with about 50 percent of China's total foreign direct investment going to Latin America in 2004.

China has also been the subject of the greatest number of antidumping cases during its short history in the WTO, and most of the cases brought to the WTO came from developing countries. The greater the number of cases and complaints against Chinese trade practices, the more likely it is that China will be seen as copying the West's historical exploitation of developing countries.

Growing Energy Needs

China is attempting to quadruple its economy again by 2020, a goal that will require substantial energy and resources supplied from abroad. In order to solve its energy shortage problems, Beijing has encouraged its state-owned and private companies to "go out" in search of energy and other resources. Latin America is also endowed with resources and energy deposits, and its share of China's oil imports is still small but growing fast.

A slowdown in Chinese economic growth or energy demand or a combination thereof will have a direct impact on the African and Latin American countries that primarily base their economic interactions with China on energy and resource exports. The more a developing country depends on energy export to China, the more vulnerable it will be if China's demand for energy falls off.

Positive Views of China

Many developing countries in both Africa and Latin America are eager to translate China's booming prosperity into opportunities for their own development, in hopes that their experiences with China will be more positive than their past experiences with European powers and the United States. Worldwide surveys have shown that most countries in the world, especially developing countries, see China's economic rise as an opportunity rather than a threat. After many decades of "underdevelopment" and being unable to benefit from the globalization process, many African countries are looking for new partners and new economic relations beyond their historic ties to Europe and the United States. In Latin America, there is growing resentment over how the United States has handled its relations with its southern neighbors, and from this perspective, China is viewed as a new market and a potential alternative to the traditional U.S. dominance in the hemisphere.

Yet, a rapid shift by African and Latin American countries from traditional economic partners to China may not necessarily serve the particular developmental goals of a given state on either continent. China may be a source of opportunity, but it should not be regarded as the new savior for a developing country's own problems. The more a developing country diversifies its economic partners, the better leverage it has in serving its own national interests.

Decreasing Western Influence

Over time, European influence on the African continent has declined, and the United States has paid less attention to Latin America due to its preoccupation with the Middle East and the Iraq war. It is clear that the EU countries have neither the power nor the will to continue to claim Africa as their backyard, and that is an important reason for the rapid rise of Chinese influence on the continent. The high-profile China-Africa summit indicates that Beijing sees Africa as available. There are few constraining forces that could stop China from asserting its influence. In contrast, the United States can and still will claim Latin America as its traditional sphere of influence, and it has explicitly warned Beijing that China's presence in the Western hemisphere should not harm U.S. interests. This may partially explain the "low-key" style and nonpolitical nature of China's involvement in Latin America.

Regardless, the United States and other Western powers are increasingly worried about China's presence in Africa and Latin America. The more these major powers perceive their relations with Africa and Latin America as a zero-sum game, the more detrimental it will be to the developing countries on the two continents.

Caveats

In considering the aforementioned factors, it is important to avoid drawing overly simplistic conclusions regarding China's policies in either Africa or Latin America.

First, China's economic presence on the two continents, as fast as it has been growing in recent years, is still relatively new and small in scale. Thus, the research agenda is wide open, many issues are yet to be explored, and patterned behavior has yet to be established. Beijing is also in search of its own policy directions and will continue to make changes and adjustments.

Second, it is important to bear in mind that China's "go out" strategy is driven primarily by the need to meet energy and resource demands for its own economic development rather than by a predatory and well-planned agenda for taking over the world, one step at a time.

Third, just as a pan-African or a pan–Latin American approach to China is not possible, there also is no single, linear Chinese policy for all of Africa or Latin America. Beijing may have some overall strategic thinking to do about its role in Africa and Latin America, but China is not a monolithic polity. Debates go on inside China's policymaking circles all the time. The Chinese leadership may want certain outcomes from China's engagement in Africa and Latin America, but it may not be able to control a rapidly expanding network of state and private actors who have entered these markets based on the logic of globalization and profit maximization.

Domestic Developmental Dynamics

It is not sufficient to study Africa's or Latin America's or any individual country's relations with China from a narrow bilateral perspective. Nor is it complete to focus on a particular theme, such as energy, human rights, or strategic ambitions. China's domestic developmental dynamics will have a decisive impact on how the Chinese government and Chinese firms behave abroad. These domestic developmental dynamics have a lot more to do with the ever-increasing assertive forces of the market in the past two decades than does the one-party state, upon which many studies of Chinese-African relations are focused. Strategic thinking and even some good intentions to do well in managing China's relations with Africa are exhibited at the higher levels of government, but policy formation and implementation have serious constraints and limitations. These constraints and limitations primarily come from the current stage in China's own domestic development, which is characterized by

—a brutal, cutthroat capitalist market economy (or as some call it, a primitive accumulation process in its classical Marxist sense);

—severe exploitation of labor forces;

—a lack of protection for workers and the collapse of the welfare and health care system;

—greedy forces of profit maximization;

—widespread corruption in both political and economic areas;

—the worsening of environmental and ecological conditions;

—a lack of corporate responsibility and transparency; and

—no experience or expertise with democratic governance.

All of these market-driven developments will not just stay within Chinese borders; they will move to the rest of the world as China expands into Africa and other parts of the globe. Many of China's operational difficulties, challenges, and problems in Africa are the externalization of China's domestic developmental difficulties, challenges, and problems. The Chinese leadership may want to promote good will by sending more aid, setting up more hospitals, constructing more schools, giving more scholarships, canceling more debts, and educating its entrepreneurs to behave better. But there are market-oriented structural forces driving things in other directions. When the ruthless competition for profits is very much the rule of the game in China's current development stage, how can one expect Chinese enterprises to operate differently abroad? Chinese firms pay their labor forces very little and have them work long hours; how can one expect them to behave differently overseas? With 6,700 Chinese coal miners dying from accidents every year (17 a day) since 2001, how can one expect Chinese ventures to do better in other parts of the world? When corruption is rampant in China, how can Chinese firms do better in terms of governance and transparency in Africa? China has severely damaged its own ecological system during its rapid modernization process; how can one expect it consciously to implement Western-style environmentally friendly measures elsewhere? When China has difficulties reforming its own political system, how can it possibly require democratic reforms in other countries? The Chinese central government has difficulties controlling market-oriented misbehaviors at home; how can one expect it to effectively moderate Chinese firms operating in other parts of the world?

Unless we pay close attention to China's domestic developments, we will not be able to understand China's external behavior. Answers to Chinese foreign policy issues in Africa may lie inside, rather than outside, China. The narrow focus on state behavior or foreign policy is inadequate. Unless fundamental changes occur in China's own reform process, many of the issues we encounter in China's external behavior will not easily be modified.

Great Powers in Africa: A Zero-Sum Game?

The prospects of further Chinese-African cooperation and the issues raised during Hu's trip to Africa will almost certainly resurface again. Economic interests in the continent, as well as global aspirations, guarantee that China will not be disengaging from Africa in the near future. In fact, China's policymakers and academics will pay even closer attention to these contentious issues, and Beijing is likely to continue to adjust its policies toward Africa, both to advance its relations with the continent and to fend off international criticism.

Such resolve may only be reinforced, rather than weakened, by the decision of the United States to create an Africa Command.[34] That the announcement of the command coincided with President Hu's tour of Africa may lead China to believe that the United States intends to compete with it for both geopolitical influence and resources on the African continent. Yet, such a move is likely to reinforce Beijing's awareness of the current limitations of its global reach, and could strengthen the voices inside China's military and policymaking circles that call for the development of even greater power projection capabilities.

The irony is that both China and the United States have similar interests in gaining access to Africa's vast energy and raw material resources, and both require a stable geopolitical environment on the continent in order for them to achieve their objectives. The two major powers could also work together to tackle many of the development problems facing African countries. It is therefore in Beijing's interests to forge a truly "win-win" situation in its relations with Africa, while exploring a cooperative framework with the United States and the EU countries to ensure that the major powers do not engage in hostile policies that harm not only the people of Africa but China as well.

Notes

1. See Stephanie Rupp, 83 in this volume.

2. According to data from the Chinese Ministry of Commerce (MOFCOM); raw data available (in Chinese) at http://zhs.mofcom.gov.cn/tongji.shtml (accessed 30 June 2008). See also Gabriel Rozenberg, Jonathan Clayton, and Gary Duncan, "Thirst for Oil Fuels China's Grand Safari in Africa," *The Times* (1 July 2006), available at http://business.timesonline.co.uk/tol/business/markets/china/article681487.ece (accessed 6 June 2008).

3. Data assembled by the author through the special report on Hu Jintao's Africa trip, available at http://politics.people.com.cn/GB/1024/5388818.html (accessed 6 June 2008).

4. See Li Anshan, 28, and Stephanie Rupp, chapter 4, in this volume.

5. For more details, see Jonathan Katzenellenbogen, "Behind the Chinese 'Year of Africa,'" *Business Day* (21 June 2006).

6. Li Xiaoyun, "China's Foreign Aid and Aid to Africa: Overview," data from the Organization for Economic Cooperation and Development, available at www.oecd.org/dataoecd/27/7/40378067.pdf (accessed 30 June 2008).

7. Andrew Pasek, "Growing China-Africa Investment Targets Energy, Raw Materials," Xinhua (24 July 2006).

8. See Harry Broadman, 88, 89, and Henry Lee and Dan Shalmon, 110, 116, in this volume.

9. FOCAC, "Action Plan Adopted at China-Africa Summit, Mapping Cooperation Course," available at http://english.focacsummit.org/2006-11/05/content_5167.htm. See also www.focacsummit.org/zxbd/2006-11/05/content_5186.htm (both accessed 14 August 2008).

10. Michael Klare, "The U.S. and China Are over a Barrel," *Los Angeles Times* (28 April 2008), available at www.latimes.com/news/opinion/commentary/la-oe-klare28apr28,0,1651403.story (accessed 30 June 2008).

11. Energy Information Administration, "Short-Term Energy Outlook," released May 2008, available at www.eia.doe.gov/steo (accessed 30 June 2008); see also Christopher Flavin, "State of the World 2005 Global Security Brief 1: Oil Price Surge Threatens Economic Stability and National Security" (Washington, D.C., 2004), available at www.worldwatch.org/node/75 (accessed 30 June 2008). See also Robert I. Rotberg, 4 in this volume.

12. Author's calculations based on data from China Customs; raw data available (in Chinese) at MOFCOM, http://zhs.mofcom.gov.cn/tongji.shtml (accessed 30 June 2008).

13. The seven nations are Egypt, Ghana, the Republic of Congo, Angola, South Africa, Tanzania, and Uganda. Statistics from China Customs are available (in Chinese) from the MOFOM website at http://zhs.mofcom.gov.cn/tongji.shtml (accessed 30 June 2008).

14. David H. Shinn and Joshua Eisenman, "Building a Foundation of Trust: U.S.-China Cooperation in Africa," *Environmental News Network* (29 April 2008), available at www.enn.com/business/article/35511 (accessed 30 June 2008); "China Oil Import from Middle East Down," *China Daily* (17 January 2008), available at www.china.org.cn/english/business/239753.htm (accessed 30 June 2008).

15. "Table of China December Crude Oil Imports, Exports," *Dow Jones Energy Service* (26 January 2007); Tu Lei, "Angola, China's Biggest Oil Supplier," *China Daily* (21 December 2006). For 2008 see "China June Crude Oil Imports and Exports," Reuters (21 July 2008).

16. "China Gives Angola $2 bln in Fresh Credit," Reuters (21 June 2006); see also Rupp, 74, and Lee and Shalmon, 119, in this volume.

17. Carmen Gentile, "Analysis: Angolan Oil Output Tops Nigeria," United Press International (5 June 2008), available at www.upi.com/Emerging_Threats/2008/06/05/Analysis_Angolan_oil_output_tops_Nigeria/UPI-41081212676432/ (accessed 9 June 2008).

18. More data on China's energy relations with Africa and other regions is available from the China Institute at the University of Alberta; see www.china.ualberta.ca.

19. For an example, see "Sinopec Beats ONGC, Gets Angola Block," *Financial Express* (14 July 2006), available at www.financialexpress.com/old/fe_full_story.php? content_id=134075 (accessed 6 June 2008).

20. "CNOOC Seeks Expansion in Africa," *People's Daily* (20 July 2006).

21. See Carmen J. Gentile, "Sudan Bolsters Refining with China's Help," UPI (16 July 2006).

22. See Gavin Stamp, "China Defends Its African Relations," BBC (26 June 2006), available at http://news.bbc.co.uk/2/hi/business/5114980.stm (accessed 30 June 2008).

23. Isaac Idun-Arkhurst and James Laing, "The Impact of the Chinese Presence in Africa," *Africa Practice* (2007), available at www.davidandassociates.co.uk/davidand blog/newwork/China_in_Africa_5.pdf (accessed 30 June 2008).

24. Andrew Meldrum and Jonathan Watts, "China Gives Zimbabwe Economic Lifeline," *Guardian* (16 June 2006). See also Dumisani Muleya, "Zimbabwe Signs Mining and Power Deals with China," Bloomberg (15 June 2006).

25. See "China Denies It Ignores Human Rights Abuse in Pursuit of Oil," Agence France-Presse (26 April 2006); see also Stephen Brown and Chandra Lekha Sriram, chapter 12 in this volume, for a discussion of China's *legal* responsibility for human rights abuses in the Sudan and Zimbabwe, and Rotberg, 11–12 in this volume.

26. "Premier Wen defends African oil deals. Reiterating policy of non-interference, he says nations can handle own issues," *South China Morning Post* (19 June 2006).

27. See Lee and Shalmon, 124.

28. Calculation based on data released by China Customs, raw data available on http://zhs.mofcom.gov.cn/tongji.shtml (in Chinese) (accessed 30 June 2008).

29. "Sudan Ambassador: International society should help Darfur people as China has," Xinhua (20 March 2008), available at http://news.xinhuanet.com/english/2008-03/20/content_7829151.htm (accessed 9 June 2008); Lindsay Beck, "Sudan in focus for China's Hu on Africa tour," Reuters (24 January 2007).

30. "Chinese president puts forward four-point principle on solving Darfur issue," *People's Daily* (3 February 2007). See also "China urges support to deployment of peacekeeping troop in Darfur," Xinhua (16 June 2007).

31. Bivan Saluseki and Brighton Phiri, "Zambian Leader 'Hu Invites KK,'" *The Post* (Zambia) (5 February 2007). See also Rupp, 72, 76, and for further discussion of Chinese Special Economic Zones in Africa, see Martyn Davies, chapter 7 in this volume.

32. Calculation based on data released by China Customs; raw data available (in Chinese) at http://zhs.mofcom.gov.cn/tongji.shtml.

33. For an extensive discussion of this, see Broadman, chapter 5.

34. The United States Africa Command (US AFRICOM) was established 1 October 2007. More information is available at www.africom.mil/AboutAFRICOM.asp (accessed 6 June 2008).

STEPHANIE RUPP

4

Africa and China: Engaging Postcolonial Interdependencies

The alignment of Africa's natural resource endowments with China's core economic interests has placed Africa at the center of emerging geopolitical tensions. In the first decade of the twenty-first century, China is likely to succeed in securing economic and political ties to African nations that rival if not displace relations that Euro-American nations have dominated over 150 years of colonial rule and neocolonial influence.

This chapter analyzes the nature of relations between China and Africa, unpacking the frequent characterization of China's recent activities in Africa as "colonial" or "neocolonial" and asking if there might be an alternative framework for making sense of Africa's contemporary position vis-à-vis China. Supporters of China's recent surge in activities perceive these efforts as fundamentally positive engagements, representing these relations as "pragmatic cooperation for mutual benefit"—cooperation that advances Africa's socioeconomic development and secures China's access to vital resources. Detractors of Chinese investment in Africa—both within the continent and in Europe and the United States—perceive and portray Chinese activities as economically predatory: profiting the Chinese state and its commercial interests, displacing African industries and markets, and embedding the continent in relations of dependency that resemble colonialism.

While some analysts dismiss this debate as spurious and exaggerated, the frequency of this characterization in African public discourse highlights fundamental anxieties about the recent surge in Chinese activities in Africa.[1] African experiences with colonialism reordered social, political, and economic structures and provided foundations—however problematic—for contemporary African life. Understanding the roots of the comparison

65

between contemporary Chinese and colonial European activities illuminates the fundamental disquiet that shapes African perceptions of and behaviors toward Chinese engagement in Africa, an unease that influences the successes and failures of Chinese ventures on the continent. In December 2006, South African President Thabo Mbeki warned fellow African leaders to "guard against sinking into a 'colonial relationship' with China as Beijing expands its push for raw materials across the continent."[2] Indeed, the widespread anxieties about China's actions in Africa underline several basic congruencies between current Chinese activities and European colonial relations in Africa. These congruencies are both contextual and behavioral, and warrant systematic comparison beyond the common, but often superficial, alarmism of public discourse. This comparison also reveals divergences between contemporary Chinese interventions and colonial European activities in Africa that are politically, economically, and socially significant.

This chapter argues that Chinese involvement in Africa is neither colonial nor neocolonial. Instead, China is strategically leveraging structural characteristics of African political and economic systems that advance the interests of the state—both the Chinese state and African states—often at the expense of ordinary African people. As a result of the imbalance in economic power between China and individual African states, these relations echo the dependency typical of colonial relations. Yet, significant divergences from colonialism as it was experienced in Africa—such as China's fundamental respect for the sovereignty of African states; its active nurturing of relations with African states in international fora; and its interest in African people as consumers rather than laborers—suggest that China and Africa are engaging in postcolonial relations of interdependency, however economically imbalanced these relations may be.

A Chinese "Scramble for Africa?" Geopolitical and Macroeconomic Factors

Referring to China's investments and involvement in Africa from 1996 to 2006 as China's "Scramble for Africa," critical observers draw a clear comparison between China and European colonial powers of the nineteenth and twentieth centuries.[3] Several macroeconomic and geopolitical factors that propelled the European "scramble" for Africa also appear to be at work in China's recent engagement on the continent.

During the European colonial era, as during the past decade of Chinese activity, the objective of external powers in Africa was to gain economic and political advantage for the interventionist power.[4] This overriding reality offers preliminary evidence that China's current engagement with Africa is (neo)colonial: in this basic analysis, China uses its power to influence relatively weaker African economic and political systems in its own interest. More specifically, however, two central factors that drove the colonial scramble—surging demand for natural resources and international competition to secure monopolistic access to these resources—are also evident in the current dynamics of China's engagement in Africa. During the colonial and contemporary periods alike, rival powers have vied to secure access to resources that are vital to their domestic economies. European colonial powers competed for access to Africa's timber, ivory, rubber, tin, palm oil, and cotton; China, the United States, and the European Union (EU) now struggle to secure access to Africa's mineral wealth, in particular crude oil and natural gas.[5] The prevailing climate of booming commodity prices, disposable capital, and swelling domestic revenues that characterized the late colonial period similarly shape the dynamics of current Chinese investments in Africa.[6] As other chapters in this volume make clear, China is in a strong economic position to make long-term investments in premium African resources, given its capital reserves and the strength of its domestic economy.

In both eras, economic contests to secure access to African resources involve distinct political dimensions. European colonial powers and contemporary states alike have used the African continent as a staging ground for the expression and expansion of their international political positions. Just as European powers jockeyed for prominence using Africa as a terrain to delineate their relative positions, China expands its interests in Africa at the expense of the United States and the EU, eliciting reactions in Washington and in European capitals that reflect this potential displacement. Just as colonial powers such as Portugal and Germany redoubled their efforts to secure African territories and markets in the face of mounting expansion by Britain and France, today the United States and the EU accelerate their attempts to secure access to African resources and markets.

Euro-American powers simultaneously seek to promote their visions of socioeconomic development, through frameworks such as the United States Africa Command and the decisions of the December 2007 EU-Africa Summit. While the United States and the EU downplay the degree to which these intensified initiatives represent concerted responses to China's robust economic and diplomatic engagement on the continent, it is clear that China, Europe, and the United States are engaged in a triangular competition for influence in Africa.[7]

Yet, in the arena of international politics, China engages with African nations on a fundamentally different level, and in a substantially distinct manner, from the ways European powers behaved toward their African colonies. African colonial states remained peripheral players on the international stage, participating as junior partners at best.[8] In contrast, China actively cultivates and strengthens its diplomatic relationships with African states in bilateral as well as multilateral relations, taking great care to emphasize that African nations are political equals. In the contexts of international bodies such as the United Nations (UN), the World Trade Organization (WTO), and even the International Olympics Committee, China has emphasized and nurtured its relations with African member states, recognizing that as a regional voting bloc, the African continent has the preponderance to affect the outcomes of significant issues. Building on its legacy of political solidarity with African nations that dates from the Non-Aligned Movement of the 1950s, China actively nurtures mutually supportive diplomatic relations with African states.

In an initial display of the continent's diplomatic support of China, African nations played a vital role in China's accession to the UN General Assembly and the Security Council in 1972. China's pragmatic recognition of the steadfast international support offered by African nations came as the Chinese leadership was reeling from its international isolation in the wake of its crackdown in Tiananmen Square in 1989. In contrast to the critical condemnation of Euro-American nations, African leaders stepped forward publicly to support Beijing's strong stance against pro-democracy protestors.[9] Support provided by African nations also played a pivotal role in securing China's membership in the WTO (2001) and in China's successful bid to host the 2008 Olympics. In return, Beijing has sought to counterbalance international pressure against African states, especially those states in which it has vested interests, as China's shielding of the Sudanese government from UN sanctions has demonstrated. This pattern of international engagement indicates that China engages in robust and reciprocal partnerships with African states at the highest levels of diplomacy, in contrast to Euro-American tendencies to treat African states as second-tier players.

Markets: Goods, Consumers, Industries, and Labor

In addition to seeking natural resources, China is keen to find outlets for its manufactured goods in African markets, as were European colonial powers. Chinese entrepreneurs receive tax benefits and subsidies—provided by both African and Chinese states—to facilitate the entry of Chinese goods into

Figure 4-1. *Zimbabwean Bumper Sticker, 2005*[a]

Source: "This Is Zimbabwe," available at www.sokwanele.com/thisiszimbabwe/archives/223.
a. Translation from Ndebele: "The people say no. Do not buy izhing-zhong."

African markets. From luxury items such as chandeliers and vases to electronic gadgets such as cell phones and DVD players, from durable goods such
as refrigerators and cooking ranges to consumable household items such as
batteries, bed sheets, and buckets, Chinese goods proliferate in marketplaces
throughout the continent. For some consumers, the availability of Chinese
goods gives them access to items that they never before could afford. In a
coastal town of Cameroon, an elderly man expressed this sentiment: "I have
worked as a warder with the government of Cameroon for over forty-three
years, but my meager salary could not allow me to buy a television set. Today,
with my pension allowance, I have bought a cheap Chinese-made television,
which if I handle well will serve me for some time."[10]
    For others, however, Chinese goods represent an economic malignancy
spreading through African markets, displacing African-made goods and, in
the process, destabilizing African industries. It is in the marketplace that
African anxieties and anger about Chinese "colonialism" are most often and
most vigorously expressed. In Zimbabwean markets, Chinese goods are called
"zhing zhong," a derogatory, racialized epithet that mimics Chinese speech
and highlights deep dissatisfaction with the quality of Chinese goods and
with their propensity to undercut African-made products. A Zimbabwean
bumper sticker that circulated in 2005 warns (in Ndebele), "The people say
no. Do not buy izhing-zhong" (Figure 4-1). As analyzed by a high-profile civil
society organization in Zimbabwe, "the image of 'China' giving two fingers to
Zimbabweans while nonchalantly crushing the Zimbabwean bird says it all:
this is a Zimbabwean protest against Chinese 'colonisation.'"[11] Because of the
relatively limited interaction between ordinary African and Chinese people,
many Africans experience China's engagement through the cheap Chinese

products that flood their marketplaces. As a result, much of the racialized and anxious discourse about China's involvement in Africa is directed at Chinese "things," and the escalating sense that Chinese goods are colonizing African markets.

At the same time that African consumers express frustration and resentment about the commercial success of Chinese products in African markets, the very existence of such an array of Chinese goods highlights another basic difference between the colonial European and contemporary Chinese approaches to doing business in Africa. For the Chinese state as well as private entrepreneurs, African people are not primarily reservoirs of labor for procuring African natural resources or for producing agricultural commodities for overseas industries. Instead, Chinese investors view African people as a substantial, undersupplied market for their manufactured goods. Chinese manufacturers take aggressive advantage of this opportunity to supply the African market, bringing in massive quantities of low-quality, inexpensive goods. African consumers note with bitterness the substandard quality of Chinese goods imported into Africa versus those produced for Euro-American markets, and intuit their position as second-class consumers.[12] While African consumers may resent the quality of Chinese goods, that African people are perceived primarily as consumers lends them a degree of economic agency that was absent previously.

While the availability of Chinese goods elevates Africans to the level of consumers, this supply of goods simultaneously undercuts African industries that produce competing products. Although many of the items imported to Africa from China have no African-made equivalents (there are no African manufacturers that produce DVD players and cell phones, for example), some industries with important domestic African bases, such as textile and leather industries, have been severely undermined by competition with Chinese factories. For example, during the mid-1990s, 80 percent of the t-shirts imported into South Africa came from China.[13] During the same period, employment in the textile industry declined steadily; by 2002, 75,000 jobs in South Africa's apparel industry had been cut, beginning a steep and steady slide in Africa's textile and manufacturing industries in South Africa, Lesotho, Swaziland, Madagascar, Mauritius, Ghana, and Kenya. With the end of the Multi-Fiber Agreement in 2005, the stringent and long-standing U.S. quota limiting the import of Chinese textiles and apparel was lifted. African producers that had established burgeoning industries in textiles and apparel, buoyed by the preferential terms of trade established by the African Growth and Opportunity Act, were rapidly swamped by Chinese competition. African factories have closed and employees have been laid off, affecting tens of thousands of workers and hundreds of thousands of individuals in families and communities that were supported by workers' wages. In tiny, landlocked Lesotho, six textile factories closed in 2005 alone, and over 10,000 workers lost their jobs, affecting tens of thousands of these workers' dependents.[14]

When the government of South Africa expressed its concerns about the imbalances in economic competitiveness and the subsequent displacement of the South African textile industry, the Chinese state initially reacted with an air of defensive pride. China's economic and commercial counselor in South Africa, Ling Guiru, expressed China's frustration with cries of foul play by African states and protectionism for African industries. China's success in expanding its textile industries was based on

> its positive response and timely readjustment in the face of difficulties, instead of flinching and resorting to self-protection. . . . This (effort) entailed the readjustment of the industrial policy, renovation and restructuring of the textile and clothing sector, as well as the optimization of sectoral structure. Thanks to the arduous efforts over the years, the Chinese textiles and clothing industry managed to sharpen its international competitive edge and gained the comparative advantages it now enjoys. . . . [U]nfair and discriminative restrictions will never be accepted by China.[15]

After several months of further negotiations, however, China voluntarily agreed to restrict its apparel exports to the South African market, to give South African businesses time to reorganize and relaunch after their precipitous collapse. This willingness to find middle ground with their African counterparts, indeed making concessions to support African industries that compete directly with Chinese investments, marks a significant departure from classic relations of dependency. In an ironic twist, as soon as China systematically withdrew its imports from the South African textile and apparel markets, the void was filled not by rejuvenated South African products but by cheap imports from Bangladesh and Vietnam, suggesting that in the twenty-first century Africa is being buffeted by the broader challenges of globalization, rather than by specific competition from China.[16]

Utilization of the African labor force marks another significant difference between China's contemporary investment and European colonial activities in Africa. During the colonial period, European states leaned heavily on African peasant labor for the extraction of colonial wealth. By means of ruthless campaigns of forced and poorly paid labor, colonial states throughout the continent coerced able-bodied adults to undertake arduous work to fill the colonial coffers. The cardinal rule of colonial economics was that each colony had to pay for itself; colonial officials were systematic in collecting taxes from African producers to underwrite their subjugation. Hut and capitation taxes necessitated the procurement or production of resources that could be sold for hard (always European) currency. In many regions of Africa, European colonial officials applied notoriously brutal measures to ensure the collection of taxes.

In contrast to the use of the adult African population to support colonial economic enterprises, China makes limited use of African labor. Even where Africans *desire* opportunities to work, employment is often unavailable. Because China has an abundant supply of its own inexpensive labor, Africans watch as even menial labor, much less managerial or technical work, is performed by Chinese. African frustration with China's lack of engagement of African workers is expressed by Dipak Patel, Zambia's minister of commerce, trade, and industry, who argues that China is "displacing local people and causing a lot of friction. You have Chinese laborers here moving wheelbarrows. That's not the kind of investment we need. I understand they have 1.2 billion people, but they don't have to send them to Africa."[17] Indignant over the opportunities lost, ordinary African workers complain that they should be the ones to benefit, through employment and wages, from the extraction of the continent's resources. Chinese commercial bosses and state officials counter that the cultural commonalities among Chinese—shared language and common cultural expectations of work and discipline—mean that Chinese workers are more efficient and effective than their African equivalents, allowing Chinese investments to be maximally beneficial for Chinese and African partners alike. By employing Chinese labor, Chinese companies sidestep African regulations of labor conditions and wages even as they maintain tight reins over their workers with implicit and actual threats of deportation for poor performance or resistance to company policies.[18] Defending China's labor policies, Sun Baohong of the Chinese embassy in Washington, D.C., explains, "We take advantage of our low cost, cheap materials, technology and cheap labor to maximize our efficiency of aid (to Africa)."[19] Although some Chinese enterprises have made an effort to employ Africans, African dissatisfaction with the limited job opportunities provided by Chinese investment continues to simmer.

At the same time that African workers resent the lack of employment offered by Chinese enterprises, African merchants also fear the inroads that Chinese entrepreneurs have carved into traditional African markets. Chinese entrepreneurs demonstrate a relentless competitive spirit that African business people both fear and admire. In Cameroon, for example, Chinese business-people have emerged as prominent competitors in many sectors of petty trade. But what Cameroonians find fundamentally alarming is the success that Chinese vendors have had selling "beignets Chinoises"—round, fried dough-nuts—on street corners in towns throughout western Cameroon, displacing Cameroonian makers and sellers of ordinary beignets. Women interviewed in the market in Bamenda expressed a collective anxiety about the lengths that Chinese businesspeople will go to in order to make a profit, fearing that Chinese entrepreneurs will soon join them by the roadside, selling roasted plan-tains to passersby.[20] To a greater degree than European colonial business ventures in Africa, Chinese entrepreneurs have been willing to extend them-selves into traditional African markets and apply their creative energies to generate competitive advantages over small-scale African entrepreneurs.

Development Projects: Infrastructural and Socioeconomic Programs

States that invest in Africa typically offer development projects, both infra-structural and socioeconomic, as inducements for African participation in bilateral partnerships. These "trade and aid" packages accomplish several strategic tasks. From the perspective of Africa's external partners, offering development initiatives lubricates their economic negotiations with African political leaders, allowing external partners to claim that their engagement with African states is mutually beneficial and certainly not predatory, because ordinary African people stand to benefit by the provision of basic services. Aid packages that target the refurbishment, reconstruction, or outright develop-ment of infrastructure such as roads, ports, and airports benefit local African communities for whom these axes of transportation are often insufficient. China's efforts to rebuild African infrastructure is a centrally important con-tribution to the betterment of the lives of African communities. In contrast, refurbishment and extension of infrastructure were sorely neglected through-out the continent during the final decades of the twentieth century, when trade and aid to Africa were dominated by Euro-American partners.

Investment in projects that (re)construct basic infrastructure is also essen-tial to transport African resources to ports of exit efficiently. In this respect, Chinese (re)development of roads, railroads, ports, and airports mirrors the self-interested construction of these facilities during the European colonial era. For example, the cartography of colonial railroads along the West African coast illustrates that, rather than serving the purpose of connecting African markets and communities within the continent, the rail lines were constructed to transport resources from the interior of the continent to coastal port cities, where European-owned vessels brought them directly to European industries and markets. To take but one example, the colonial construction and contemporary Chinese reconstruction of the Benguela rail line in Angola, which runs from the Angolan coast directly eastwards toward the rich mining zones of the Democratic Republic of the Congo and Zambia, illustrate that such large-scale projects are designed primarily with overseas commercial interests, rather than domestic African interests, in mind. Yet, it is important to emphasize that despite the clear necessity of infrastructural networks to the economic objectives of external partners, their current revitalization—in large measure by China—is simultaneously of vital importance to the economies of African states and their citizens.

The link between trade and aid is unambiguous; packages of aid to African partners have proven influential in securing trade deals for external partners. As part of its massive effort to redevelop Angolan infrastructure that was devastated by the decades-long civil war, in 2004 China extended $2 billion in soft loans to Angola in exchange for Angola's promise of unrestricted flows of crude oil to China. This agreement in turn paved the way for China to secure a monopoly on access to deepwater oil sources, outbidding both European investors backed by the International Monetary Fund (IMF) and Indian enterprises. Bilateral trade between Angola and China reached $5 billion in 2006; Angola is now China's second-largest African trading partner, supplying China with 15 percent of its oil imports and surpassing Saudi Arabia's oil flows to China.[21] Yet, the details of China's trade and aid deals with Angola remain murky, despite—or perhaps because of—their enormity. Estimates of China's loans and aid to Angola range from $2 billion to $9 billion; neither China nor Angola has been forthcoming with even the most general information. Similarly, estimates of Chinese laborers in Angola range from 10,000 to 80,000; accurate figures are elusive.[22] This obscurity serves the interests of the Chinese and Angolan states simultaneously, as neither international observers nor domestic civil society groups are easily able to challenge Angola's use of the enormous receipts it has gained from China.

In addition to the clear potential for corrupt arrangements that benefit African leaders, Chinese efforts to overhaul Africa's crumbling infrastructure also serve the political interests of African elites. On the watch of many African leaders, transportation and communication networks throughout the continent have fallen into disrepair. African leaders now stand to benefit from the

Chinese assistance in refurbishing these national necessities; Africa's political elite leverage on the improvement of infrastructure, taking political credit for having negotiated these important deals with the Chinese state and its economic subsidiaries. High-profile construction projects, such as building resplendent stadia to house national football teams, have proven effective in sweetening popular perceptions of both the Chinese economic presence in Africa and the African leadership that has midwifed Chinese involvement in African economies. In this sense, the cementing of relations between Africa and China may lead to entrenchment of current African political regimes, which take credit for having negotiated China's contributions to national development—the same efforts that some African leaders have been unable or unwilling to undertake on their own.

That African observers express ambivalence regarding Chinese-built infrastructure reflects deeper concerns about the long-term trade-offs of Chinese involvement in the continent's development. On the one hand, China quickly builds infrastructure that is desperately needed. African elite note the lack of planning meetings, environmental impact reports, and other bureaucratic hurdles that typify projects by Euro-American nations and international lending organizations such as the World Bank and the IMF. They view the Chinese approach as a refreshingly efficient change. Senegalese President Abdoulaye Wade publicly expressed his sense of relief that African nations have a newfound power to choose *not* to accept funding from traditional Euro-American partners, a sense of power so fresh that he—and Senegalese elite in attendance at a recent public forum—seemed giddy at the prospect of embracing Chinese efficiency and snubbing former overbearing development partners.[23] But African civil society organizations and communities in areas that have seen Chinese developments unfold are keenly aware of the potential negative repercussions on African social and natural environments as a result of this expedited approach. Many African commentators note with trepidation the environmental degradation of China's own landscapes and resources, and express serious concerns about uncritical acceptance of Chinese development initiatives in Africa. Africans' uncertainty about China's support for their national leadership reflects deeper ambivalence toward the current state of political affairs in many nations where China seeks increased ties. While Africans may appreciate their new national stadia, they perceive unalloyed Chinese support of their often despotic leaders—through the building and renovation of presidential palaces and the funding of their militaries—to be detrimental to serious African efforts to achieve political reform in their own nations.

In addition to providing the hardware for national development, China has stepped forward to establish socioeconomic programs to improve the daily lives of ordinary Africans. While China trumpets its contributions to the socioeconomic welfare of Africa, its contributions in this area remain relatively modest: the provision of 100 Chinese agricultural experts to staff 10 agricultural technology demonstration centers; the building of 30 hospitals and 30 malaria treatment and prevention centers, including a grant to supply Chinese-made arteminisin to malaria patients; the construction of 100 rural schools; and the dispatching of 300 Chinese youth volunteers.[24]

Contributions in the area of education are more significant: China has pledged to train 15,000 African professionals (although details of this training, and in what professional areas, are not readily available) and has committed to sponsor 4,000 African students at Chinese universities.[25] These initiatives have tremendous potential to advance Africa's class of technicians, professionals, and managers, enhancing African self-reliance and future stability.

Ironically, China's efforts to improve the socioeconomic conditions in African communities remain divorced from China's direct economic activities. Communities that are located in regions where China undertakes its extractive, industrial, or commercial pursuits often do not see direct benefits from the Chinese presence. Unlike large extractive industries during the late colonial era, which often included housing for tens of thousands of workers and their families, as well as dispensaries, schools, training facilities, and other social amenities, Chinese industrial investments in Africa tend to be "socially thin."[26] Industries such as mining and petroleum extraction, activities enthusiastically undertaken by Chinese state-owned enterprises in many regions of the continent, require high levels of capital investment but tolerate low levels of social investment in surrounding communities. Particularly where these industries employ primarily Chinese labor, the extractive installations may be barricaded physically from neighboring African communities by means of razor wire and armed security forces, leading to the isolation of the Chinese enterprise, its management, and its workers, thus arousing suspicion and resentment among African neighbors. African workers who do succeed in landing employment with Chinese extractive firms have found wages, benefits, and basic safety measures to be lacking, igniting vitriolic and even violent protests against the Chinese industries' presence, as in Zambia's Chambishi mining zone during 2006. Thus, while the Chinese government has made a concerted effort to extend a degree of socioeconomic assistance as part of its partnership with African nations, its state-centered approach has resulted in a fundamental decoupling of these programs from the often rural communities that would most benefit from them, and the people whose lives are directly affected by the presence of Chinese extractive industries.

In the Cultural Arena

China's cultural approach to engaging Africa diverges from the European colonial model of cultural paternalism. Fundamentally, China is not driven by a "civilizing mission" to reform and save African individuals from their perceived primitivity. Unlike attempts by French colonial authorities to create "Frenchmen" from their African subjects by imparting French language, etiquette, and habits, Chinese authorities have no interest in transforming Africans into "Chinamen." European colonial attitudes were paradoxical: paternalistic attempts to bring "civilized" ways of life to African subjects were debasing, even as this cultural engagement signaled the shared essence of humanity and *fraternité*. That the Chinese engagement with Africa is culturally value free may be liberating for African partners, even as this approach may underline the cultural assumption that Africans never *could* become "Chinamen," as there is no place for Africans in the Chinese cultural sphere.

Social relations between ordinary Africans and Chinese are marked by a tension between mutual admiration and mutual loathing. Although Africans and Chinese alike admire the quality of strength that they observe in the other, they also share robustly negative perceptions of one another. African and Chinese people do not often or intimately interact. Chinese enterprises tend to be walled off from the surrounding landscape or neighborhood; Chinese managers tend to be aloof and hesitant to engage socially with their African counterparts, employees, or neighbors.

Despite this separation, Chinese and Africans have a shared admiration for one another. As illustrated in public displays throughout Beijing during the Forum on China-Africa Cooperation (FOCAC) summit in 2006, Chinese audiences marvel at the majesty of African animals and landscape and celebrate the historical endurance and cultural authenticity of its people. In Africa youths embrace Chinese martial artists as emblems of individual tenacity and potential; throughout the continent in urban and rural areas alike, martial arts clubs have sprung up, as young African men (in particular) memorize and mimic the moves of their Chinese martial arts heroes.

African commentators have also noted with appreciation the simple lifestyle and disciplined work ethic of Chinese entrepreneurs and managers in Africa. Chinese state directives consistently exhort the Chinese in Africa to live in a manner that reflects the living conditions of Africans. As opposed to the luxurious living standards enjoyed by European colonists, even project managers live in simple accommodations, with several men sharing a single room and facilities. Africans respect this Chinese restraint, even as they recognize that because of the disciplined austerity of Chinese businesspeople, their disposable income does not enter local African economies through the purchase of either goods or services. Similarly, Africans observe the disciplined work ethic of Chinese managers and laborers; the Chinese task-oriented approach differs from both the European colonial management style, which generally involved plentiful breaks for tea among the managers, and from the African approach to work, which is typically relaxed and social. Some Africans strive to emulate the Chinese ability to focus on practical goals and to complete tasks efficiently. In the words of Sierra Leone's information minister, "The Chinese don't seem to rest. We could learn from that."[27]

Despite these favorable cultural perceptions, both Chinese and Africans simultaneously view each other with suspicion. Public discourse—both among African and Chinese observers—often tends toward potently racist extremes. Many Africans seem suspicious of Chinese intentions, an unease reinforced by their perceptions of Chinese wealth, stinginess, and social distance. An online response to a BBC article about Chinese investment in Africa captures this racialized anxiety: "Asian invasion. They are everywhere. Infiltrating like a colony of ants. I'm telling you . . . they have the numbers and the money to be successful. Because they've run out of space in their country. They are everywhere, people . . . and they are deadly. They hate other races and they are ruthless. Watch out for them."[28]

Similarly, Chinese stereotypes of Africans that circulate in public discourse tend to be negative. Indeed, the Chinese characters for Africa, *fei zhou* 非洲 , translate literally as "negative continent."

In recognition and support of its expanding presence in Africa, and in an attempt to lay foundations for positive social engagements between Africans and Chinese, China has actively supported the expansion of Chinese-language education and media throughout the continent. The government-sponsored Office of Chinese Language Council International organizes Confucius Institutes throughout the world to offer public courses in Mandarin Chinese. In 2005, the first Confucius Institute in Africa opened at the University of Nairobi, offering classes in Mandarin Chinese to fifteen students. Since then, two Confucius Institutes have opened in South Africa (the Universities of Stellenbosch and Pretoria), and one each in Rwanda (Kigali) and Zimbabwe (Harare). Enrollments have swelled. Enthusiasm for learning Chinese has been high, as Africans with knowledge of Mandarin have found steady employment as facilitators for Chinese business and tourist ventures. Private language schools in Nairobi and other African capital cities have also begun to offer courses in Mandarin. African students enrolled in Mandarin classes point to the necessity of speaking Chinese to take advantage of the economic opportunities offered by recent "look East" policies promoted by African governments and the resulting surge in Chinese involvement on the continent.[29] Yet others in Africa resent the "necessity" of learning another foreign language after Africans had mastered the prevailing colonial European languages of the twentieth century.[30]

Africa and China: Postcolonial Interdependencies

Fundamentally, relations between China and Africa are neither colonial nor neocolonial. China respects the national sovereignty of African states; China does not seek political or economic hegemony over African nations, nor does it seek to perpetuate its political and economic advantage in Africa in the capacity of a former colonial power. China's current engagement in Africa is taking place in a postcolonial world order; nations in today's global context do not tolerate the naked ambitions of hegemonic domination that characterized the European colonization of Africa. However, several features of the postcolonial African state—features that have contributed to the continent's precipitous economic decline and political decay—are structurally compatible with Chinese penetration and partnership. China is not encumbered by the patronizing (and often hypocritical) moral platitudes of Euro-American nations that decree democracy and transparency as preconditions to economic engagement. As a result, China is uniquely positioned to take advantage of its structural alignment with postcolonial African states whose leaders have developed and deepened colonial institutions of governance that exploit African producers, markets, and resources for the benefit of the state, or at least its "sovereigns."

Building on colonial administrative architectures, African leaders tended in the first decades after independence to tighten the state's hegemonic dominance of extractive industries and to consolidate their control over territorial, economic, and judicial administration; principles of authoritarian rule became entrenched.[31] In the process, leaders of newly independent African states positioned themselves as undisputed masters of their nations' resources, with unlimited control of the state apparatus. African leaders promoted ambitious development initiatives, leading to bulging ranks of government employees, swelling needs for revenue, and increasingly onerous taxes on

African producers. African governments turned to grants from former colonial powers and, particularly during the 1980s, loans from international financial institutions to meet increasing demands for paychecks and payouts in the short run, even as massive development initiatives stagnated and foreign debt escalated. This "integral state" required suppression of civil society through squelching the liberties of speech, press, and organization, and has been characterized by autocratic forms of presidential leadership.[32] Increasingly, African states seized control of assets deemed vital to national security, creating parastatal companies to manage energy and mineral resources, communications, and transportation in the interests of the state, often at the expense of its citizens. The colonial state had suppressed autonomous African capitalism; the predatory politics of independent African states ensured that African entrepreneurs remained paralyzed.[33]

With economies in decline, bloated governments demanding soaring compensation, ineffectual development projects stagnating, and foreign debts spiraling, many African states were in utter disrepair and hostage to incompetent leadership by the late 1980s. Developmental assistance tied to "structural adjustment programs" was intended to replace the most pernicious of Africa's governance structures with reformed, neoliberal institutions, but ultimately failed to improve economic conditions on the continent.[34] Political and social upheaval, in the midst of economic ruin, characterized many regions of Africa in the 1990s. Many Africans distrusted their own governments, at the same time that they were disillusioned by the failure of structural "fixes" imposed by the United States, former European colonial powers, and lending institutions.

China began its decade of intensifying forays into Africa in the mid-1990s, entering the African scene with a radical approach that offered partnership to African states without preconditions. It put lucrative packages of investment and development on the table in exchange for continuous flows of African resources. China thus offered welcome relief to beleaguered African governments, extending much-needed trade and aid while also enabling them to sidestep the moralistic demands that Euro-American partners and financial institutions set as preconditions to economic engagement. With its policies of "no strings attached" aid, "noninterference" in domestic politics, and promises of "mutual development," China provided many African leaders with an unsurpassed opportunity to stabilize their national economies and develop crucial infrastructure, even as those leaders consolidated their hold on political office. With China's sudden arrival as an enticing alternative, African states now began to have political and economic leverage to negotiate more aggressively with former colonial powers. Some African states, such as Angola and Zimbabwe, have since used Chinese support as a cover for rebuffing their former Euro-American partners.

In its efficient and effective courtship of African states, China has successfully engaged with many independent African states in ways that Euro-American (neo)colonial powers never did and perhaps never could. The very structures of postcolonial African states that Euro-American partners have sought to redress—illiberal economies and undemocratic governments—offer opportunities for China to build mutually supportive partnerships. African countries that control resources that are central to China's security concerns, primarily oil and other petroleum products, are also countries that score the lowest in measurements of democracy, civil liberty, and liberal economic structure. But because China neither exemplifies nor promotes these qualities, China is absolved from considering these factors in negotiating partnerships with countries such as Angola, Equatorial Guinea, the Democratic Republic of the Congo, Gabon, and the Sudan. China, itself a one-party state since 1949, does not hesitate to negotiate with one-party regimes in Africa to secure access to resources vital to China's continuing economic surge. Both China and African states are familiar and comfortable with tight connections between state and economic interests. With China's network of state-owned enterprises running parallel to the parastatal industries that typify many African economies, the Chinese state is able to negotiate smoothly for contracts to develop resources and redevelop infrastructure such as roads, ports, and telecommunications networks, simultaneously paving the way for its own extractive activities.

What makes African observers anxious about the strengthening of relations between China and Africa is China's uniquely successful ability to interface with the structures of African political realities and economic systems that bear resemblances to—and have roots in—the most insidious elements of colonial domination. While China's activities in Africa are neither colonial nor neocolonial, China exploits features of postcolonial Africa that provide benefits to the state, often at the expense of ordinary Africans' basic well-being. Rather than replicating a colonial model in creating its partnerships with African nations, however, China is successfully making use of structural similarities that it shares with postcolonial, independent African states. The irony is that the structures of political and economic domination that are most amenable to China's exploitation of Africa's natural resources are the very same structures that African governments inherited from European colonial powers and subsequently nurtured and deepened in their quest to maintain power during the decades after independence.

The basic principles that guide China's engagement with Africa—respect for sovereignty and mutual economic benefit—indicate that China is committed to engaging political and economic equals. This emerging "Beijing Consensus" underlines a clear divergence between China's current activities in Africa and the political agenda of the colonial era in which European states overtly pursued policies of territorial, political, and economic dominance. Nowhere in colonial agendas was there room to acknowledge African sovereignty on equal political terms. Furthermore, not until the final decades of the colonial era did the notion of "economic benefit" to African people enter the picture.[35]

In the context of contemporary Africa, however, these principles leave substantial room for the expansion of economic advantage to African elites, as well as to Chinese investors and entrepreneurs, at the expense of ordinary African people. In principle, China's fundamental pillar—"respect for sovereignty"—allows China to proclaim its embrace and maintenance of the highest virtue of the international arena: the recognition of political equality among nations. However, in the reality of African postcolonial politics, respect for sovereignty allows China to cut deals with leaders of African states, who may or may not represent the interests of the nation, civil society, or the vast majority of ordinary citizens. Under the mantle of respect for sovereignty, China engages despotic African leaders to secure rights to exploit African resources. Many of these deals certainly benefit the sovereigns of Africa and China, in particular rewarding African political elites who control national patrimony as a personal inheritance while ensuring China's monopolistic access to strategic resources such as oil and petroleum derivatives. Despite China's unscrupulous relationship with Africa's autocratic political class, if there is to be any interaction with such nations at all, is there any alternative to engagement that respects their sovereignty, as unrepresentative of the citizenry as particular sovereigns may be? While some nations may prefer a policy of economic boycotting to deal with rogue leaders who pursue interests at variance with Euro-American goals and ideals, that China is willing to engage with such countries—and exert preponderant influence—does not indicate that China is or seeks to be a colonial power in twenty-first-century Africa.

Bolstering its principle of respect for sovereignty, China engages African nations for "mutual economic benefit," arguing that it brings to Africa investments in basic infrastructure and in other entities that are necessary for socioeconomic development such as schools, clinics, and training institutes. What goes unsaid in China's policy of mutual benefit is that the benefits that accrue to China (state benefits as well as benefits to private Chinese entre-preneurs) and the benefits that accrue to Africa (benefits to African political elites as well as benefits to ordinary African people) are not equal, either between or within states. As Tanzanian President Julius Nyerere famously noted during an earlier generation of Chinese involvement in Africa, China and Africa are "most unequal equals."[36] Despite the reality that the mutual benefits are not equal, Chinese investment in Africa is coupled with the kind of development in financial, commercial, infrastructural, and socioeconomic sectors that is urgently needed for Africa's longer-term growth and eventual self-sufficiency—development efforts that were neglected during the post-colonial decades of the twentieth century.

Relations between African states and China can be best characterized as postcolonial interdependency. Rather than one side seeking coercive political and economic domination over the other, on both sides of the postcolonial relationship between Africa and China the basic objective is making economic progress and securing or developing the resources necessary for future eco-nomic growth and political stability. Given the constraints that both China and African nations have encountered in their relations with Euro-American nations and institutions that require neoliberal political and economic struc-tures, relations between China and African nations offer a complementary partnership. While relations between individual African states and China are not balanced because of China's sheer demographic and economic weight, relations are increasingly intertwined and interdependent.

African states can and should do more to ensure that relations with China work to their advantage. The onus is on African leaders to evaluate critically their countries' engagement with China and to use this unprecedented oppor-tunity of influence to secure real advantages for their citizens. The challenge in ensuring that relations between China and Africa benefit African *citizens* lies in establishing mechanisms that bring Chinese contributions to the provincial, regional, and local levels. In partnership with China, African lead-ers should insist on developing the growth of an economic middle class, sti-fled during the colonial era and first half-century of independent rule, by providing robust and widespread training opportunities for African entre-preneurs and managers. At the same time, African leaders could insist on preferential trading conditions to be extended to the tens of thousands of African entrepreneurs that currently live and do business in China. Stimulat-ing the growth of Africa's atrophied economic bourgeoisie would make essen-tial and lasting contributions to the economic well-being of Africans throughout the continent. African leaders would also be wise to examine

China's treatment of the environment in its own context and insist on environmental measures and controls to safeguard the resources that its citizens—and its economy—will require for future economic stability and growth. The burden of envisioning, planning, and implementing partnerships with China that ensure advantages for Africa lies squarely with African leaders.

Notes

1. Chris Alden, *China in Africa* (New York, 2007).
2. Thabo Mbeki, speech delivered at the Fourteenth National Congress of the South African Students Congress (9–14 December 2006).
3. A small sample of international newspapers, magazines, and journals that have published articles on China's contemporary "scramble" in Africa include *Economist*; *Financial Times*; Reuters news agency; *Independent*; *Guardian*; *African Affairs,* an academic journal of African studies; *China Brief,* a publication of the Jamestown Foundation; *afrol News* (African News Agency). This issue also has been covered by an array of blogs and online commentaries.
4. Crawford Young, *The African Colonial State in Comparative Perspective* (New Haven, 1994), 97.
5. As a gauge of Africa's increasing importance as a source of oil, in 2006 China imported more of its oil from Angola than from Saudi Arabia, while the United States imported more of its oil from African countries along the Atlantic coast (especially Angola, Gabon, and Nigeria) than from Saudi Arabia.
6. Young, *African Colonial State,* 212.
7. During the time that this chapter was written, President George W. Bush was on the second African tour of his presidency (February 2008). During his five-nation visit, Bush highlighted American efforts to reduce poverty and fight disease, and extended hundreds of millions of dollars in trade and aid to these African partners, particularly for antimalarial and anti-AIDS programs. On his trip, Bush highlighted the fact that U.S. assistance to Africa had doubled during his presidency and would double again to $8.7 billion by 2010. Concurrently with Bush's tour, U.S. Secretary of State Condoleezza Rice was in Kenya to assist in brokering a peace agreement between the government of Kenyan President Mwai Kibaki and his opposition rival Raila Odinga. Rather than imposing sanctions or penalties, the United States offered to increase significantly aid and trade packages to Kenya, which already receives more than $500 million in aid annually from the United States.
8. Young, *African Colonial State,* 195.
9. For discussion of African leaders' support for the Chinese Communist Party's crackdown against pro-democracy demonstrators at Tiananmen Square in June 1989, see (among others) Ian Taylor, "China's Foreign Policy towards Africa in the 1990s," *Journal of Modern African Studies,* XXXVI (1998), 443–460.

10. See Ivo Ngome, "Cameroonian Perceptions of the Chinese Invasion," *Africa Files*, available at www.africafiles.org/atissueezine.asp?issue=issue6#art3 (accessed 2 October 2007).

11. See "This Is Zimbabwe," available at www.sokwanele.com/thisiszimbabwe/archives/223 (accessed 13 November 2007).

12. See discussions among African participants in online fora such as "Should Africa Embrace China" (4 March 2005), hosted by the BBC. According to one commenter, Ripon from Maputo, Mozambique, "Chinese products have two versions—a good quality one for western market and a poor quality (one) for Africa." See http://news.bbc.co.uk/2/hi/africa/4318379.stm (accessed 8 February 2008).

13. Amos Safo, "South Africa: The Textile Saga: Workers Turn the Heat on Government," *Public Agenda* (27 June 2005), available at allafrica.com/stories/200506271442.html (accessed 21 February 2008).

14. Ibid.; see also Princeton Lyman, "China's Rising Role in Africa: Presentation to the US-China Commission" (21 July 2005), available at www.cfr.org/publication/8436 (accessed 29 May 2008).

15. As quoted in Safo, "South Africa: The Textile Saga."

16. Chris Alden, unpublished remarks at the "Africa-China Roundtable: Perspectives on Political Economy" (Cambridge, MA, 8 November 2007).

17. As quoted in Chris McGreal, "Chinese Influx Revives Colonial Fears," *Guardian Weekly*, available at www.guardian.co.uk/guardianweekly/story/0,,2007803,00.html (accessed 19 February 2008).

18. See also Stephen Brown and Chandra Lekha Sriram, 252 in this volume.

19. As quoted in Darren Taylor, "Chinese Aid Flows into Africa," *Voice of America News* (8 May 2007), available at www.voanews.com/english/archive/2007-05/Chinese-Aid-Flows-into-Africa.cfm?CFID=18527730&CFTOKEN=37889563 (accessed 21 February 2008).

20. Ngome, "Cameroonian Perceptions."

21. Loro Horta, "China and Angola Strengthen Bilateral Relationship," *Power and Interest News Report* (23 June 2006), available at www.pinr.com/report.php?ac=view_printable&report_id=516&language_id=1 (accessed 8 February 2008).

22. Paul Hare, "China in Angola: An Emerging Energy Partnership," *China Brief*, VI (8 November 2006), available at www.jamestown.org/news_details.php?news_id=205 (accessed 15 February 2008). See also Henry Lee and Dan Shalmon, 122 in this volume.

23. Remarks by Abdoulaye Wade at the Forum, Kennedy School of Government, Harvard University (Cambridge, MA, 27 September 2007).

24. *China's African Policy* (Beijing, 2006), available at www.gov.cn/misc/2006-01/12/content_156490.htm (accessed 29 May 2008); see also Deborah Brautigam, 207 in this volume.

25. Ibid.

26. James Ferguson, *Global Shadows: Africa in the Neoliberal World Order* (Durham, NC, 2006).

27. Septimus Kaikai, quoted in Lindsey Hilsum, "We Love China," *Granta 92: A View from Africa* (15 January 2006), available at www.granta.com/extracts/2616 (accessed 2 April 2007).

28. Passage from the Readers' Comments on "Trading One Master for Another," BBC (3 October 2007), available at www.bbc.co.uk (accessed 17 November 2007).

29. Mu Xuequan, "Kenyan Confucius Institute Sees First Group of Graduates," *China View* (10 May 2006), available at http://news.xinhuanet.com/english/2006-10/05/content_5169459.htm (accessed 18 February 2008).

30. Adama Gaye, remarks at roundtable panel "China and Africa," Fiftieth Annual Meeting of the African Studies Association (New York, 15 October 2007).

31. Young, *African Colonial State*, 286–87; Achille Mbembe, *Afriques indociles: Christianisme, pouvoir et état en société postcoloniale* (Paris, 1988).

32. Young, *African Colonial State*, 287–290.

33. Ibid., 291.

34. Ferguson, *Global Shadows*.

35. Young, *African Colonial State*, 242.

36. As quoted in Martin Bailey, "Tanzania and China," *African Affairs*, LXXIV (1975), 50.

HARRY G. BROADMAN

5

Chinese-African Trade and Investment: The Vanguard of South-South Commerce in the Twenty-First Century

The recent explosion of commerce between China and the countries of sub-Saharan Africa is a striking hallmark of the new trend in South-South trade and investment. Indeed, this acceleration in exchange among developing countries is one of the most significant features of the current global economy. For decades, world trade has been dominated by commerce both among developed countries—the North—and between the North and the developing countries of the South. Today, South-South trade accounts for about 11 percent of global trade and is growing at about 10 percent a year; 43 percent of the South's trade is with other developing countries.[1]

Press accounts give the impression that China's commercial relations with Africa are a recent development, beginning in just the last few years. In fact, they actually date back several decades, with most of China's early investments being made in Africa's infrastructural sectors, such as railways, at the start of the continent's postcolonial era. What is true is that the current scale and pace of China's trade and investment flows with Africa are unprecedented. Since 2000 there has been a massive increase in those flows between Africa and Asia. Asia now receives about the same share of Africa's exports as do the United States and the European Union (EU)—Africa's traditional trading partners. Asia's imports from Africa also are growing rapidly. Foreign direct investment (FDI) between Asia and Africa is much more modest than trade, but it is likewise increasing. While the United States and the EU, Africa's

This chapter draws from the author's book *Africa's Silk Road: China and India's New Economic Frontier*, published by the World Bank in 2007. The author wishes to acknowledge the contributions provided by Xiao Ye and Yutaka Yoshino.

traditional foreign investors, still account for the overwhelming stock of investment on the continent, the recent growth rate of African-Asian FDI flows is remarkably high, especially China's FDI flows into Africa.

News headlines regarding Chinese-African commerce also create the perception that only oil and minerals are at play. But deeper and systemic analysis indicates that Chinese businesses are pursuing international commercial strategies in Africa that increasingly are about far more than just raw natural resources.[2] China's emergence as an economic giant in Asia, with rapidly modernizing industries and an expanding middle class with rising incomes and purchasing power, is resulting in growing demand not only for Africa's traditional exports of extractive and raw agricultural commodities but also for the continent's nontraditional exports, such as processed commodities, light manufactured products, household consumer goods, food, and tourism. By virtue of its low-cost, labor-intensive productive capacity, African firms have the potential to export these nontraditional goods and services competitively to the average Chinese consumer and firm. To take advantage of this demand, African policymakers, businesses, workers, and other stakeholders on the continent need to be proactive in implementing domestic reforms that both foster the international competitiveness of African firms and leverage China's commercial interest in Africa consistent with achieving the same goal.[3]

Against this backdrop, policymakers and businesses in both Africa and Asia, as well as international development partners, have shown intense interest in better understanding the evolution and character of Chinese-African trade and investment relations. Despite the sizable—and rapidly escalating— attention devoted to this topic, especially by some of the world's most senior officials, there is a paucity of systematic data available on the nature of Chinese-African commerce.

A Heterogeneous, Growing, yet Risky Continent: How the Chinese See Africa

How do the Chinese see the African continent? Sub-Saharan Africa is a highly heterogeneous group of forty-seven countries, each having different-sized economies, populations, and surface areas (see table 5-1).[4] There are also vast differentials in levels of income—with GDP per capita ranging from less than $200 to $7,000—and of industrial development. It is also highly fragmented geographically, with extremely inconvenient and costly transportation links contributing to its small role in global trade and investment. One-third of the world's resource-dependent economies are in Africa. This engenders a high degree of dependence on resource rent and, concomitantly, opportunities for corruption. Partly as a result, the continent is characterized by a high degree of income inequality and is prone to conflict.

At the aggregate level, after years of growth spurts followed by downturns, the African continent now appears to have broken that cycle and seems to be growing at a sustainable rate. Over the past decade, Africa grew at an average rate of 5.4 percent, on par with the rest of the world (see figure 5-1).

The heterogeneity of the continent is especially evident in its economic growth. Indeed, the record shows clearly that Africa has become increasingly diverse over the last decade (see figure 5-2). In this sense, Africa's development pattern resembles other regions of the world. While the rise in the world price of oil is certainly a major factor at play for some African countries, these data show that non–oil-rich countries also have had sound economic growth. Indeed, since the mid-1990s, 34 percent of the African population resided in the non–oil-rich countries, where the average annual GDP grew at least 4.5 percent in the decade beginning in 1996. This portrait of a "growing Africa," where there are emerging economic success stories—especially outside of the oil economies—runs counter to conventional wisdom. Yet it is an Africa that Chinese businesses increasingly perceive as presenting important commercial opportunities.

Despite the fact that many countries in Africa have been making significant progress in economic development over the last decade, the continent's overall trade performance in the global marketplace has been disappointing. World trade accounted for 16 percent of global output in 1991, and this figure rose to 20 percent in 2004. The trade flows of African economies on the whole, however, have yet to be favorably affected. In fact, Africa's export market shares have continuously fallen over the last six decades (see figure 5-3). Making African firms more competitive and thus increasing the volume of exports are clear priorities for Africa. It is through this prism that Chinese investment and trade on the African continent is being viewed by African policymakers, businesspersons, workers, and the international community. As such, issues are being raised about the extent to which Chinese commerce is displacing domestic production capacity or enhancing its competitiveness, as well as having analogous impacts on job creation, social systems, and the environment.[5]

It is not only the volume of Africa's exports that matters; it is also their composition. African exports are largely undiversified and heavily oriented toward raw materials. In fact, only in the Middle East and North Africa do raw materials constitute a higher share of total exports (see figure 5-4). Although

Table 5-1. *Heterogeneity of the Sub-Saharan African Continent*
Units as indicated

| | GDP growth, 1996–2005 | GDP per capita, 2000 (US dollars) | Sectors as percent of GDP | | | | Oil producers | Land locked | Number of borders | Conflict affected | Population (millions) | Surface area (thousands of sq. km.) | Population density (number of people/ sq. km.) | Export diversification index |
			Agriculture	Industry	Manufacturing	Services								
Angola	7.9	799	9	59	4	32	✓		3	✓	14.5	1,247	12	1.1
Benin	4.8	324	35	14	9	50			4		7.1	113	63	2.1
Botswana	5.7	3,671	2	44	4	43		✓	2		1.7	582	3	
Burkina Faso	4.6	248	31	20	14	49		✓	6		12.7	274	46	2.2
Burundi	1.2	107	49	19	n.a.	27		✓	3	✓	7.5	28	269	1.6
Cameroon	4.5	737	43	15	8	40			6		16.7	475	35	4.4
Cape Verde	6.5	1,292	7	20	1	73			0		0.5	4	122	9.2
Central African Republic	0.9	225	56	22	n.a.	22		✓	5	✓	4.0	623	6	3.4
Chad	7.8	261	59	8	6	29	✓	✓	5	✓	9.1	1,284	7	2.6
Comoros	2.0	378	41	12	4	47			0		0.6	2	282	1.2
Congo, Democratic Republic of	0.0	88	59	12	5	n.a.			9	✓	56.4	2,345	24	3.0
Congo, Republic of	3.5	940	6	56	6	38	✓		4	✓	3.9	342	12	
Côte d'Ivoire	1.5	574	26	18	15	56			5	✓	17.4	322	54	4.0
Equatorial Guinea	20.9	4,101	5	60	n.a.	3	✓		2		0.5	28	18	1.2
Eritrea	2.2	174	14	22	10	55			3	✓	4.6	118	39	5.2
Ethiopia	5.5	132	41	9	n.a.	39		✓	5	✓	71.3	1,104	65	4.0
Gabon	1.7	3,860	9	68	5	22	✓		3		1.4	268	5	1.6
Gambia, the	4.5	327	28	13	5	48			1		1.5	11	130	5.2
Ghana	4.7	275	35	25	9	40			3		21.4	239	90	4.0
Guinea	3.6	381	24	35	4	37			6		8.2	246	34	4.2

Guinea-Bissau	0.6	134	61	12	9	25		2		1.6	36	44	4.8
Kenya	2.8	427	13	16	11	52		5	✓	32.9	580	57	16.0
Lesotho	2.7	543	16	36	18	38		1		1.8	30	61	
Liberia		130	61	9	8	30	✓	3		3.5	111	32	2.0
Madagascar	3.3	229	26	15	13	50		0		17.7	587	30	8.1
Malawi	3.2	154	36	14	10	40	✓	3	✓	11.4	118	96	3.0
Mali	5.7	237	33	24	3	35	✓	7	✓	12.2	1,240	10	1.3
Mauritania	4.9	437	17	27	8	46		4		3.0	1,026	3	3.8
Mauritius	4.9	4,223	5	26	19	56		0		1.2	2	612	11.7
Mozambique	8.4	276	23	32	14	36		5	✓	19.5	802	24	2.0
Namibia	4.0	2,035	10	23	11	57		3		2.0	824	2	
Niger	3.5	155	40	17	7	43	✓	7		12.4	1267	10	1.9
Nigeria	4.0	402	26	48	4	24		3		143.3	924	155	1.3
Rwanda	7.5	250	40	21	10	38	✓	4		8.4	26	320	2.4
São Tomé and Principe	3.1	354	17	16	4	67	✓	0		0.2	1	171	1.5
Senegal	4.6	461	17	21	13	62		5		10.6	197	54	12.2
Seychelles	2.0	6,688	3	28	16	70		0		0.1	0ᵃ	189	2.7
Sierra Leone	1.1	170	n.a.	n.a.	n.a.	n.a.		2	✓	5.5	72	77	3.8
Somalia		n.a.	n.a.	n.a.	n.a.	n.a.	✓	3	✓	10.3	638	16	6.1
South Africa	3.1	3,346	3	29	18	59	✓	6	✓	45.3	1,219	37	
Sudan, the	6.4	439	28	27	7	39	✓	8	✓	35.2	2,506	14	1.6
Swaziland	2.8	1,358	n.a.	n.a.	n.a.	n.a.	✓	1		1.1	17	65	
Tanzania	5.4	314	41	15	7	35		7		37.2	945	39	21.7
Togo	3.3	244	41	23	9	36		3		5.1	57	89	5.3
Uganda	6.1	262	29	19	8	43	✓	5		27.2	241	113	7.3
Zambia	3.6	339	19	33	11	38		7	✓	10.9	753	15	5.0
Zimbabwe	-2.4	457	16	21	13	42		4		13.1	391	34	8.1

Source: Harry Broadman, *Africa's Silk Road* (Washington, D.C., 2007).
a. Surface area of Seychelles is 450 square kilometers.

Figure 5-1. *Per Capita Incomes of Africa Increasing in Tandem with Other Developing Countries*

Annual change in real per capita GDP (percent)

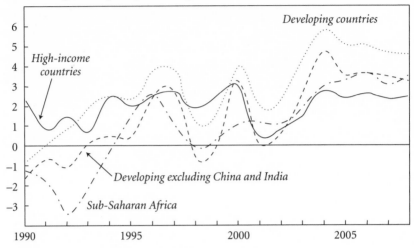

Source: World Bank staff.

Africa made progress in reducing its dependency on raw materials in the late 1980s, it has not made much progress since. This disappointing performance means that Africa has not taken full advantage of international trade to leverage growth. This point will surely take on new importance as China's businesses assume a greater commercial presence in Africa. A prominent debate, receiving increasing amounts of attention, is whether Chinese investments in Africa will serve to exacerbate or to help reduce the continent's export dependency on natural resource commodities.

Africa is, to be sure, a difficult place to do business relative to other regions of the world. This is a fact appreciated not only by the traditional investors in Africa but also by (the relative) newcomers such as the Chinese, Indians, and Russians. (This reality is also understood by African entrepreneurs, as well as the diaspora, who have voted with their feet in terms of the overseas locations of their investments.) Underdeveloped market institutions, constraints on business competition, and weak governance—compounded by the geographical fragmentation and poorly developed infrastructure—make trade and investment in Africa costly. Since 1990 FDI flows to all developing countries have increased rapidly, including to Africa and China.[6] Indeed, in recent

Figure 5-2. *Economic Growth across Africa, 1996–2005*

Percent of total African population

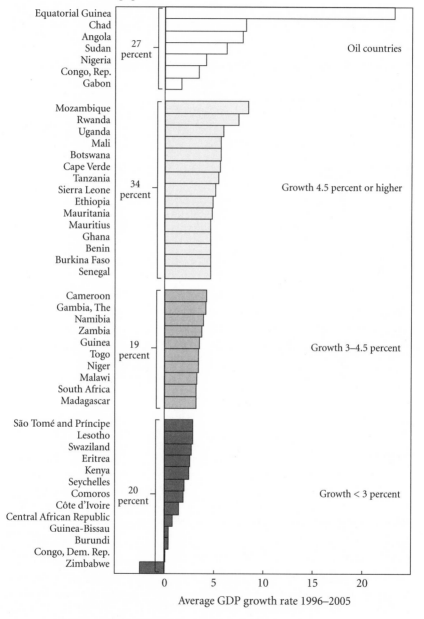

Average GDP growth rate 1996–2005

Source: Broadman, *Africa's Silk Road.*

Figure 5-3. *Decline in Africa's Share of World Exports, 1948–2004*

Percent

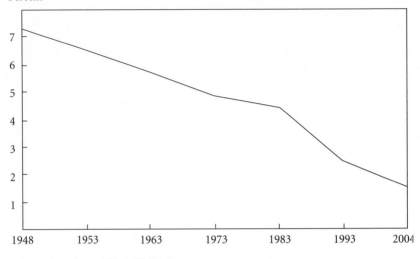

Source: Broadman, *Africa's Silk Road.*

Figure 5-4. *Africa's Exports Are Concentrated in Raw Materials*[a]

Raw materials as percentage of total exports

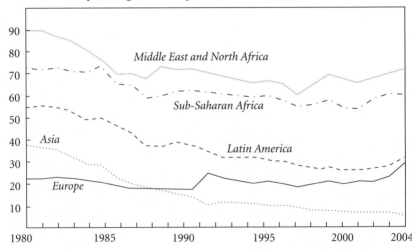

Source: Broadman, *Africa's Silk Road.*
a. Raw materials include agricultural raw materials, crude petroleum, ores, and coal. Asia excludes Japan, Republic of Korea, and Singapore. All other regions are restricted to low- and middle-income countries only.

years, the average annual growth rate of FDI flows to Africa was 17 percent, comparable to the 20 percent growth rates in China. Still, in spite of Africa's rapid growth in FDI, the continent accounts for only 1.7 percent of global net FDI flows. But, once again, there is great variation on the continent. Earnest reform of various facets of the business environment has been underway, with notable achievements made by some countries such as Burkina Faso, Ghana, Madagascar, Mauritius, and Mozambique.[7]

The Pattern of Africa's Merchandise Trade with China

There are several dimensions along which the pattern of Africa's trade flows with China can be usefully assessed. It is helpful first to nest the analysis within the broader context of African-Asian trade, and then to examine how these flows differ in terms of volume, product composition, and geographical concentration.

African-Asian Trade Flows

The volume of African exports to Asia is growing at an accelerated rate: while exports from Africa to Asia grew annually by 14 percent between 1990 and 1994, they grew by 19 percent between 2000 and 2004 (see table 5-2). Asia is now a major trading partner with African countries. Asia accounts for 27 percent of Africa's exports, an amount that is almost equivalent to the EU and U.S. shares of Africa's exports, 32 and 29 percent, respectively. However, despite this growth, Africa's exports still remain relatively small from the Asian perspective: Africa's exports to Asia account for only 1.6 percent of Asian global imports.

African imports from Asia are also increasing (see table 5-3). Over the last five years, they have grown at an 18 percent annual rate, higher than that of any other region, including the EU. These imports are largely manufactured goods, which have surged into African markets. Some of them are intermediate inputs for products assembled in Africa and shipped out to third markets, such as the EU and United States, or capital goods (machinery and equipment) for African manufacturing sectors themselves. At the same time, there are also a sizable number of African imports of consumer nondurables from Asia, which compete against Africa's domestically produced products.

Volume of African-Chinese Trade

The recent growth of African countries' exports to Asia largely reflects a sharp upturn in Africa's exports to China (as well as to India, the other emerging economic giant of the South).[8] While Japan and South Korea, in the early

Table 5-2. *Composition of African Exports to Asia,*
Ranked by Annual Growth, 1999 and 2004
Units as indicated

	1999		2004		
Exports	Value of exports (millions of US$)	Share (percent)	Value of exports (millions of US$)	Share (percent)	Annual growth (percent)
Machinery and transportation equipment	435	2.3	1,383	3.7	26
Ores	804	4.2	2,377	6.4	24
Petroleum products	158	0.8	401	1.1	20
Electronics	19	0.1	47	0.1	20
Crude petroleum	7,136	37.2	17,113	46.1	19
Pharmaceuticals	5	0	12	0	19
Electronic machineries	36	0.2	71	0.2	15
Other manufactured goods, such as paper, pulp, furniture	490	2.6	904	2.4	13
Nonpharmaceutical chemicals	520	2.7	955	2.6	13
Basic manufactured metals	4,880	25.5	8,201	22.1	11
Cotton, textile fibers, and yarns	848	4.4	1,423	3.8	11
Manufacturing of non-oil minerals	2	0	3	0	8
Agricultural raw materials, nonedibles	1,525	8.0	1,970	5.3	5
Processed food and beverages	271	1.4	342	0.9	5
Agricultural raw food edibles	1,437	7.5	1,777	4.8	4
Apparel and footwear	30	0.2	25	0.1	−4
Manufacturing of nonminerals	11	0.1	4	0	−18
Coal	554	2.9	132	0.4	−25
Total	19,159	100.0	37,141	100.0	14

Source: Broadman, *Africa's Silk Road.*

1990s, were the most important markets for Africa's exports, China alone accounts for 40 percent of Africa's total exports to Asia today.

African exports to China have risen dramatically over the past fifteen years (see figure 5-5). China doubled its annual growth rate of export purchases from Africa between 1990 and 1994; during the period from 1999 to 2004, exports from the continent to China grew by 48 percent annually. It is significant that while the growth rate of Africa's exports to China is high, the volume of sub-Saharan exports going to China accounts for only 10 percent of

Table 5-3. *African Imports from Asia, Commodity Group, 1999 and 2004*
Units as indicated

	1999		2004		
Imports	Value of imports (millions of US$)	Share (percent)	Value of imports (millions of US$)	Share (percent)	Annual growth (percent)
Machinery and transportation equipment	5,241	28.2	12,336	32.3	19
Agricultural raw food edibles	2,075	11.2	3,947	10.3	14
Processed food and beverages	1,426	7.7	2,997	7.8	16
Pharmaceuticals	1,851	10	3,529	9.2	14
Electronics	1,457	7.8	2,607	6.8	12
Coal	1,220	6.6	2,586	6.8	16
Cotton, textile fibers and yarns	1,228	6.6	2,283	6.0	13
Apparel and footwear	1,165	6.3	2,087	5.5	12
Agricultural raw materials, nonedibles	1,110	6	2,204	5.8	15
Manufacturing of non-minerals	917	4.9	1,525	4.0	11
Basic manufactured metals	286	1.5	559	1.5	14
Petroleum products	269	1.4	825	2.2	25
Other manufactured goods, paper, pulp, furniture	181	1	324	0.8	12
Nonpharmaceutical chemicals	102	0.5	210	0.5	16
Ores	35	0.2	78	0.2	17

Source: Broadman, *Africa's Silk Road.*

the continent's total exports worldwide. This is a far smaller level of exports than generally believed.

The leading role of China in African-Asian trade relations is not limited only to Africa's exports. On the import side as well, China has become a major trading partner for African countries (see figure 5-6). Japan used to be the largest supplier of products that Africa imported from Asia. However, China has taken over the leading position, accounting for more than one-third of Asia's total imports to Africa.

Product Composition of Africa's Trade with China

The increase in African exports to China is largely driven by unmet domestic demand for natural resources, reflecting rising consumption by households and businesses in China. At present, petroleum is the leading commodity,

Figure 5-5. *Growth in Africa's Exports to China versus India and the Rest of Asia, 1990–2004*

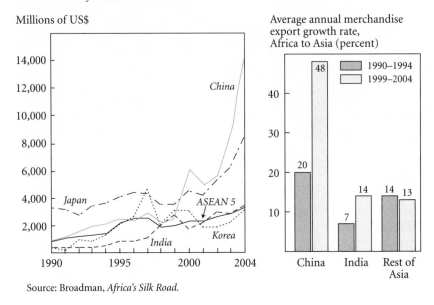

Source: Broadman, *Africa's Silk Road*.

Figure 5-6. *Growth in Africa's Imports from China, 1990–2004*[a]

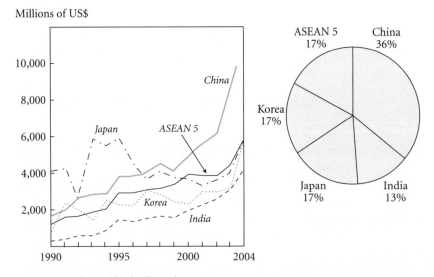

Source: Broadman, *Africa's Silk Road*.
a. Imports are based on partner's export data, except for 2002 Thailand data, which were based on Africa's export data.

Figure 5-7. *Product Distribution of Africa's Trade with China, 2004*

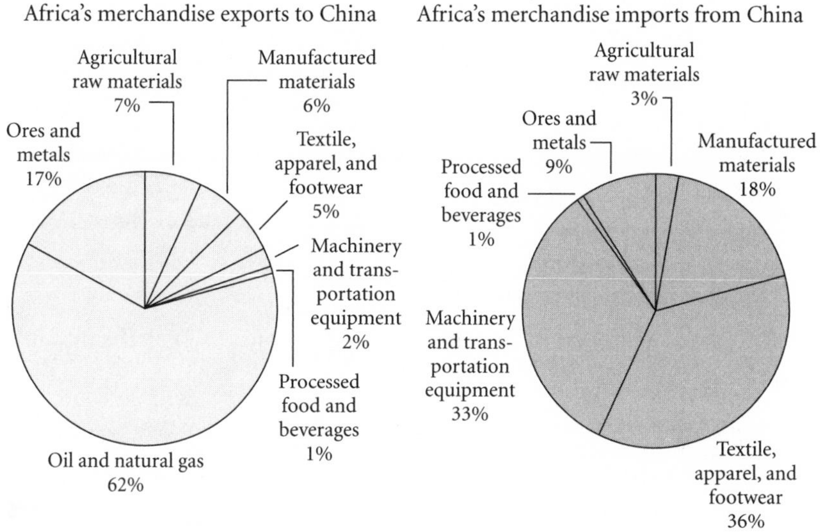

Africa's merchandise exports to China

Agricultural raw materials 7%
Manufactured materials 6%
Ores and metals 17%
Textile, apparel, and footwear 5%
Machinery and transportation equipment 2%
Processed food and beverages 1%
Oil and natural gas 62%

Africa's merchandise imports from China

Agricultural raw materials 3%
Ores and metals 9%
Manufactured materials 18%
Processed food and beverages 1%
Machinery and transportation equipment 33%
Textile, apparel, and footwear 36%

Source: Broadman, *Africa's Silk Road.*

followed by ores and metals. Indeed, oil and natural gas account for 62 percent of total African exports to China, and ores and metals account for 17 percent (see figure 5-7).

That natural resources currently dominate Africa's exports to China is part of the larger profile of Africa's export pattern to Asia and globally. Coupled with the 7 percent share of exports comprising agricultural raw materials, it is clear that the majority of products Africa is currently selling to Chinese markets are unprocessed. Still, Africa's rapidly growing exports to China are not limited to fuels and other mineral and metal products. As discussed below, labor-intensive, raw, or semiprocessed agricultural commodities for industrial use (timber, cotton) or consumer use (food products) are also increasingly being exported to China.

If Africa's present exports to China tend to be dominated by natural resources or raw agricultural commodities, its imports from China are typically value-added products (see figure 5-7). Out of all imports from China, 87 percent are machinery and equipment, textiles and apparel, and other manufactured products. In fact, African imports from China are more broadly based than African exports to China. Table 5-4 indicates, on a statistical basis, the dramatic difference in the level of product concentration between Africa's

Table 5-4. *Product and Geographic Concentration of Africa's Trade with China, 2002–2004 averaged*[a]
Herfindahl-Hirschman index

	Exports to China	Imports from China
Product concentration	0.40 (+0.25)	0.02 (+0.01)
Geographic concentration	0.17 (+0.09)	0.09 (+0.05)

Source: Broadman, *Africa's Silk Road*.
a. The higher the value of the index, the greater the level of concentration. Figures in parentheses are the difference in index figures from those based on Africa's trade with the world.

exports to and imports from China using the conventional Herfindahl-Hirschman Index.

Geographical Concentration of Africa's Trade with China

There are also significant differences in the geographical patterns of Africa's exports to and imports from China. Geographically, Africa's exports are highly concentrated in a few countries, most of which, except for South Africa, are oil-producing states (see figure 5-8). This is not surprising, of course, given the dominance of oil and natural resources in the continent's exports to China. By contrast, there is considerably greater diversity among the largest African importers of Chinese goods, although, again, oil-producing countries play a pronounced role. This pattern is confirmed statistically by the Herfindahl-Hirschman Index figures presented in table 5-4.

Coupling Product and Geographical Concentration

The concentrated trade patterns of the product side and the geographical side are intensified when the two are combined. Thus, for example, Angola supplies 50 percent of African oil exports to China, followed by the Sudan (19 percent), Republic of the Congo (Congo [Brazzaville], 16 percent), Equatorial Guinea (10 percent), and Nigeria (4 percent). South Africa is almost the exclusive supplier of ore and diamonds to China. However, logs and cotton, the two leading agricultural raw materials for industrial use in China, are supplied by a range of countries concentrated in West Africa: Gabon, Republic of the Congo (Congo [Brazzaville]), Equatorial Guinea, Cameroon, and Liberia for logs; Benin, Burkina Faso, Mali, Côte d'Ivoire, and Cameroon for cotton.

On the import side, West African countries such as Niger, Nigeria, Ghana, Togo, Benin, and the Gambia; and East African countries such as Kenya and Tanzania are the major buyers of Chinese cotton fabric exports. China also

Figure 5-8. *Leading African Trade Partners with China*
Percent of export or import values in importing country

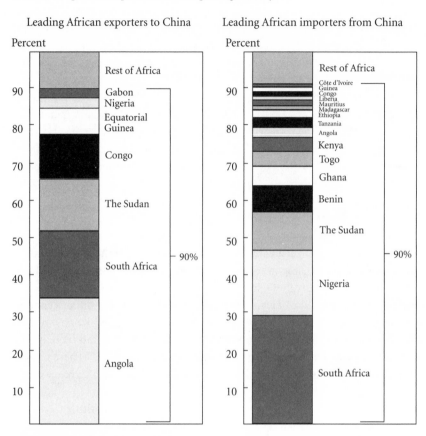

Source: Broadman, *Africa's Silk Road.*

exports synthetic fibers to African countries with relatively more developed light industries, such as South Africa, Mauritius, and Nigeria.

Is Africa's Trade With China an Opportunity to Diversify?

Although African exports to Asia as a whole do not exhibit a significant pattern of product diversification, intersectoral complementarities between Africa and Asia do exist, and in particular between Africa and China. This is true in a general context, where Africa is a large supplier of raw materials to China, including energy resources, and China is a supplier of manufactured products to African countries. This is largely driven by factor endowments. The rich resource endowment in Africa provides a natural comparative advantage based on raw materials and resource-based products. China, on the other hand, has a rich stock of skilled labor compared to Africa and, thus, has a comparative advantage in manufactured products.[9]

The endowment-based theory of comparative advantage provides a simple, but intuitive, framework to understand the trade patterns of African countries. In light of Africa's relative scarcity in highly skilled human capital but rich natural resource base, the theory would suggest that it is not economically efficient for African countries to push for manufactured exports. At the same time, there is a belief that with greater trade between Africa and an emerging economic power like China, Africa's concentration on primary commodity exports will increase, undoing any African efforts to promote manufactured exports. However, the data show that, if anything, manufactured exports from Africa to China, like other parts of Asia, are beginning to increase significantly, as shown in table 5-2.

These data raise the critical issue of the extent to which there are beneficial complementarities arising in commerce between African countries and China. New evidence suggests that China's commercial engagement with sub-Saharan Africa could enable African businesses to build on the continent's endowment of natural resources and develop more sophisticated backward and forward integration to extract more value from processing and increase the participation of local firms in modern global network trade.[10] These opportunities stem from linkages between China's flows of FDI to Africa and exports generated from such investments, particularly when the sectors in which they occur allow for dividing the production chain into its constituent components across international markets.

Foreign Direct Investment between Africa and China

Flows of FDI between sub-Saharan Africa and China are part of the broader trend of South-South investment that has been expanding significantly in recent years. While the bulk of these flows runs from China to Africa, there is an increasing emergence of African investors in China.

Africa's Inward FDI: The Global Context

European countries (primarily the UK and France) and North American countries (primarily the United States and Canada) have long been the dominant foreign investors in sub-Saharan Africa, accounting for 68 percent and

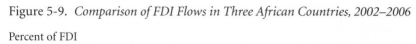

Figure 5-9. *Comparison of FDI Flows in Three African Countries, 2002–2006*

Percent of FDI

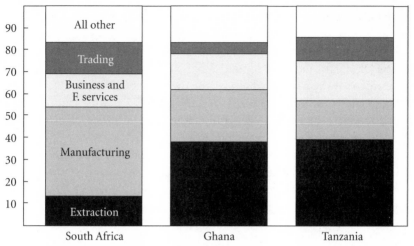

Source: Broadman, *Africa's Silk Road.*

22 percent of the FDI stock, respectively. But as the volume of FDI to Africa increases, it is becoming more diversified, with more investors from different countries. In particular, FDI in Africa from developing countries has increased substantially, particularly from China, India, Malaysia, and Brazil, as well as from South Africa (which stands out as the major intraregional FDI source country on the continent).

Just as the sources of FDI flows to Africa are broadening, so too is the sectoral distribution. Although data on global sectoral FDI flows to Africa are incomplete, by looking at FDI destinations in Africa, one can conclude that a large proportion of FDI still goes to the oil sector. For the last 15 years, 70 percent of FDI has been invested in 5 out of the 7 African oil-exporting countries, as well as in South Africa. In fact, South Africa has been able to attract the most dynamic FDI among African countries, including in the financial sector after its mid-1990s liberalization reforms.

Indeed, it would be a mistake to conclude that Africa is host to FDI only in the oil or natural resources sectors. While in most African countries about 50–80 percent of FDI goes to natural resource exploitation, increasingly African countries are able to attract FDI into the financial, telecom, electricity, retail trade, light manufacturing (apparel, footwear), and transportation equipment sectors (see figure 5-9).

Chinese FDI in Africa

Like trade, African-Asian flows of FDI are growing rapidly, but the volume of such flows is more modest than that of trade. While there is some African FDI in China (see below), Chinese FDI in Africa predominates. As of year-end 2005 (the latest year for which complete data are available), the stock of Chinese FDI in Africa amounted to $1.3 billion, a comparatively small level of investment. Indeed, as noted above, the overwhelming bulk of FDI on the African continent today still originates from the EU and the United States. Thus, as with trade, what is noteworthy about Chinese FDI in Africa is not the level of investment, but its rate of growth.

As in the broader global setting, the vast majority of FDI inflows from China to Africa over the past decade have been largely concentrated in the extractive industries. Historically, Chinese FDI went primarily to other Asian countries, mostly to Hong Kong. However, Chinese FDI has been targeting Africa—among several other regions of the world—where natural resources are abundant. In other words, China's FDI in Africa's oil resources needs to be considered in the broader strategic context of China's global search for fuel inputs.

At the same time, while China has been investing largely in oil production facilities in Africa, Chinese firms have begun to diversify their investment on the continent into many other sectors, including apparel, agroprocessing, power generation, road construction, tourism, and telecommunications, among others. Moreover, Chinese FDI in Africa has also become more diversified geographically; figure 5-10 shows the 2004 country distribution of Chinese FDI flows to Africa.

It is also important to recognize that for China, FDI in Africa represents a small proportion of its global FDI portfolio (see figure 5-11). Survey work in China indicates that Africa is perceived by Chinese investors as a risky environment and that a major incentive for making investments on the continent stems from government support.[11] China established its economic and political ties to the African continent during the Cold War-era, but the motivation for Chinese FDI has changed significantly since the end of the Cold War. During its earlier involvement in Africa, China participated in various major infrastructural projects throughout Africa and is still very active in this area. In fact, globally, 75 percent of China's FDI is in the tertiary sector, including construction and business activities. In 2002, the Chinese authorities approved about 500 Chinese enterprises to invest in Africa; today it is estimated that there are over 800 such firms.[12]

Figure 5-10. *China's FDI outflows to Africa, by Country, 2004*

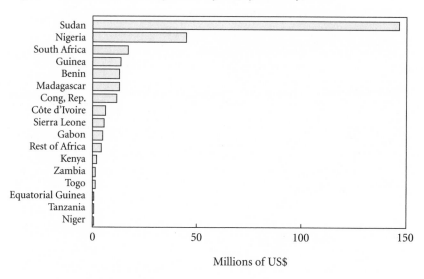

Millions of US$

Source: Broadman, *Africa's Silk Road.*

Figure 5-11. *Chinese Outward FDI Stock and Flows by Region, 2004*

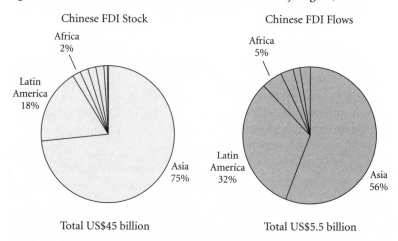

Source: Broadman, *Africa's Silk Road.*

Emerging African FDI to China

Based on statistics from the Chinese authorities, African FDI flows to China reached $776 million in 2004 versus $565 million in 2002, posting a 17 percent annual compounded growth rate over two years. Mauritius accounted for more than three-quarters of such FDI in 2004.[13] Clearly, a large proportion of that FDI is pass-through, unlikely to have originated solely from Africa. Worth noting is that South Africa has been actively investing in China. In 2004, FDI from South Africa to China increased significantly to $109 million from $26 million in 2002. In 2005, SABMiller, the giant South African food and beverage company, announced plans to invest about $15 million in China. Nigeria is another emerging African investor in China, having more than doubled its FDI to China between 2002 and 2004.

Conclusions and Policy Implications

Africa's commerce with China is growing rapidly in both directions. To date, this has largely been based on high demand for natural resources by China and its industrial advantage in manufactured products over African countries. Is this a sign of complementarities between African countries and China based on factor endowments of natural resources in Africa versus skilled labor in China?

There may be three aspects that suggest positive shifts in complementarities between Africa and China. The first concerns the prospects for resource-based, value-added manufacturing exports. In fact, there is already evidence of Chinese imports of resource-based, manufactured products from Africa. African countries could increase their manufactured exports to China based on the existing exports of raw materials. However, there is a limit to growth based on horizontal diversification. African countries will want to avoid being trapped as a "resource basket" for a rapidly modernizing economy, such as China, and to realize their own dynamic efficiency gains by extracting value from their own endowed resources. Natural resources provide a quick launching base for African countries to generate value-added activities. Although still limited to a few countries, such as South Africa and Nigeria, resource-based, manufactured products, such as aluminum, could become a viable export to China.

The second aspect relates to the prospects for broader participation in global value chains. There are growing vertical complementarities along value chains between Africa and China. Among the top African exports to and imports from China, there are clear complementarities in the cotton-textile-garment value chain. Raw material (cotton) is supplied by West African countries to

China, and intermediate materials (fabrics) are supplied by China to apparel producers in South Africa, Mauritius, Nigeria, and other countries in sub-Saharan Africa. Prospects thus exist for African producers to participate in global network trade in the apparel sector.

The third aspect concerns the heterogeneity among African countries and the potential benefits from regional integration. Just as African-Asian trade relations encompass various dynamics due to rich variability among Asian countries—from high-income Japan to low-income but dynamically developing economies such as Vietnam—as emphasized at the outset, Africa is hardly a homogenous region. Particularly South Africa has evolved into a regional hub of industrial and commercial development in sub-Saharan Africa and beyond. The technological complementarities between South Africa and China exist at a higher level than those between China and other African countries. This reality provides scope for more intra-industry (that is, network) trade between South Africa and China. Through regional integration, the emerging complementarities between such industrial leaders in Africa and China could lead to wider benefits at the subregional markets through further forward and backward linkages, and thus create more value-added production on the continent.

Clearly, increasing exports to China presents both opportunities and challenges to Africa. Africa could benefit from rapidly growing markets in China to achieve broader based economic development, or Africa could become merely a resource base for Asia's growing economies, with little benefit to its domestic economic development. While the boom of natural resource exports to China is providing short-term gains, African countries need long-term strategies to leverage China's commercial interest and create opportunities for enduring economic competitiveness among African firms. This will require the implementation of reforms that foster scale economies, export diversification, and climbing the value chain. Going forward, African countries should focus on engaging the Chinese to work with African firms to enhance value-added production, both in natural resources to create backward and forward linkages domestically and in other (non–natural resource related) sectors to enable Africa to participate more effectively in global supply chains.

Notes

1. Puri Lakshmi, "A Silent Revolution in South-South Trade," World Trade Organization (Geneva, 2004), available at www.wto.org/english/tratop_e/dda_e/symp04_paper7_e.doc (accessed 25 February 2008).

2. Harry G. Broadman, *Africa's Silk Road: China and India's New Economic Frontier* (Washington, D.C., 2007).

3. The full analysis of this point is elaborated in Broadman, *Africa's Silk Road*, 41–58.

4. Throughout this chapter, "Africa" refers to forty-seven countries of sub-Saharan Africa as defined by the World Bank, which does not include Djibouti.

5. See Stephanie Rupp, 70 in this volume.

6. United Nations Conference on Trade and Development, "Prospects for Foreign Direct Investment and the Strategies for Transnational Corporations 2005–2008" (Geneva, 2008).

7. See World Bank, *Doing Business 2007* (Washington, D.C., 2007).

8. For a discussion of India's trade with and investment role in Africa, see Broadman, *Africa's Silk Road*.

9. For a comparison of Africa's endowments with those of other regions, see Adrian Wood and Kersti Berge, "Exporting Manufactures: Human Resources, Natural Resources, and Trade Policy," *Journal of Development Studies*, XXXIV (1997), 35–59; Adrian Wood and Jörg Mayer, "Africa's Export Structure in a Comparative Perspective," *Cambridge Journal of Economics*, XXV (2001), 369–394. Countries higher up along the spectrum of the skills-resource endowment ratio export more manufactured products relative to processed or primary goods, and a larger proportion of higher-technology manufactured products. This seems to be a compelling story of trade relations between Africa and China.

10. See Broadman, *Africa's Silk Road*, 289–357.

11. Ibid., 235–287.

12. See Li Anshan, 31, and Martyn Davies, 141, in this volume.

13. Since Mauritius is a major offshore financial center, it is difficult to determine the actual FDI source country, particularly because of pass-through investments.

HENRY LEE AND DAN SHALMON

6

Searching for Oil:
China's Oil Strategies in Africa

Pressured by skyrocketing demand, Chinese oil companies have branched out across the globe seeking new oil supplies to feed the country's economic growth. By 2006, China had made oil investments in almost every part of the world, including Africa. These initiatives have not been without controversy. From the commercial perspective, Western companies complain that China's ability to link its oil investments to government-to-government financial assistance gives its companies an unfair advantage. From the political perspective, Western nongovernmental organizations have accused China of using its investments to support some of the more abusive, corrupt, and violent governments in the world. The poster child for this argument has been China's support for the Sudanese government and its unwillingness to condemn publicly the genocidal practices of the janjaweed militias operating in Darfur.

China's repeated contention that it does not get involved in domestic politics and that its relationships with African governments is strictly commercial is perceived by many as hollow. Critics argue that without China's investments and tacit support, African governments, such as the Sudan's, would be forced to amend their behavior.

This chapter looks at the validity of these arguments and how they are manifested on the African continent. It focuses on China's activities in the Sudan and Angola, not only because they are the largest measured, both in terms of dollar value and scope, but because they incorporate features that characterize Chinese efforts to secure incremental oil supplies from African countries.

China's Need for Imported Oil

China is the world's most populous country, with a population of 1.4 billion people. Its economy has grown at a pace unprecedented in modern history: more than 9 percent a year between 1978 and 2005. Energy is critical to service this growth. Despite building almost 200,000 megawatts of new electric generating plants over the last five years, increasing its coal consumption by 21 percent over the same period, and initiating one of the world's most aggressive campaigns to increase energy productivity, China continues to be plagued by localized energy shortages.[1] A dramatic increase in motor vehicle sales and modal shifts in the movement of freight from railroads to trucks have increased oil demand beyond China's limited domestic supply, forcing China to rely on an ever-growing volume of imported oil.[2] Overall, China's reliance on imported oil as a percent of total energy remains low (approximately 8 percent), but as China becomes more urbanized and its demand for transportation services continues to grow, oil will increase in importance.[3] Between 2000 and 2006, China's oil consumption increased from 4.7 million bbl/d to almost 7.4 million bbl/d, 47 percent of which was derived from imports.[4] In 2006, China's annual growth in oil demand approached 500,000 bbl/d, accounting for one-third of the world's incremental increase and 70 percent of the growth in the Asia-Pacific region.

Despite its vastness, China has never discovered large oil reserves. Its traditional fields in and around Daqing and Shengli are old, and their production is either flat or declining, while its newer discoveries in the Junggar and Tarim basins are modest on a global scale and are far from China's population centers on the coast. There is no evidence to suggest that China's domestic oil reserves will double or triple in the next decade, and thus a significant proportion of its incremental consumption will have to be met by imports. Most Chinese officials agree that the country has no choice but to venture aggressively into the global oil market. In fact, the International Energy Agency predicts that China's oil imports will grow from 1.5 million bbl/d in 2000 to approximately 10.9 million bbl/d in 2030, at which time China will be importing about 77 percent of its crude oil, with more than half of its imports coming from the Gulf States.[5]

Recognizing that its demand was outstripping its domestic supply, in 1997 China concluded that it must obtain significant oil supplies from outside its borders. It understood that doing so would not be easy. The Western multinational companies had a fifty-year head start in developing and nurturing relationships with most of the major producing countries. There were very few unexplored regions left in the world. China would have to convince countries that had historically sold oil to the United States, Europe, and Japan that they should include China among their major trading partners. More important, China was determined to ensure that its interests would not be discarded if supplies became tight. Shen Dingli captured the dilemma in his oft-quoted question, "If world oil stocks were exceeded by growth, who will provide energy to China?"[6] If supplies are scarce, are the United States and Japan likely to share their oil?

Private oil companies in Western countries not only had strong relationships with officials from producing countries, but they also had access to substantial capital through their own earnings, and through commercial banks and other sources of private funding. What were China's comparative advantages, and how could it exploit them?

Moreover, because China's oil industry consists of state-owned companies, its strategies for building relationships with oil-producing countries had to be synchronized with its foreign policies, both economic and diplomatic. This could be both a benefit and a constraint.

Given these goals, China's global oil strategy has three basic elements:
—Differentiate Chinese initiatives from those offered by the Western governments and their oil companies.
—Leverage China's comparative advantages while downplaying its disadvantages.
—Focus on those countries in which there was a high probability that oil reserves would grow and where China could negotiate arrangements that catered to its long-term interests.

Differentiating from the West

Often oil-producing nations perceive Western governments as solely focused on oil, ignoring their country's long-term economic and social interests. China realized that if it could offer a package of benefits that went beyond oil, it would be able to develop partnerships as opposed to commercial relationships based on one commodity. Its efforts would be in stark contrast to those of its Western competitors. The ensuing bonds would grow to the point that China might receive the type of preferential treatment historically given to Western companies.

There were two elements to this strategy. First, in addition to purchasing oil supplies or investing in oil production, China would invest in the economies of African oil producers and would help the host governments meet their immediate infrastructural or commercial needs. For example, in Africa, China is rebuilding Angola's transportation network, is constructing a large hydroelectric dam in the Sudan, and has opened up hundreds of commercial enterprises throughout the continent, doing over $11.7 billion of business in forty-nine African countries.[7]

The thrust of China's strategy is to create a level of interdependence that will lead to greater trade and build stronger bonds, while securing a flow of oil to China in an increasingly insecure market.

In an ideal world (from the Chinese perspective), China would be able to gain equity ownership of oil supplies through concessions. However, this outcome is difficult to achieve. Most countries have assumed ownership of their own oil and sell it on the open market through their state oil companies. Often the private oil companies are limited to managing and operating production and processing facilities, while ownership of the assets remains with the host country. China realizes that a majority of its future oil supplies will be purchased in the marketplace and subject to substantial price fluctuations. Hence, the value of equity oil has increased dramatically. China has been willing to make significant investments to capture that value. Certainly this ability is one of the principal reasons that China has been willing to commit billions of dollars in the form of aid and new investment to the Sudan.

The second element in China's strategy is its policy of noninvolvement in the domestic affairs of host governments. China steadfastly refuses to pass judgment on the behavior of other countries with which it trades. Nor does it link its commercial relationships to any standards of conduct.

Some argue that this position is an outgrowth of China's fierce protection of its own rights and sovereignty, and its resentment of foreign interference in its domestic affairs. The involvement of Western traders, the Boxer Rebellion, and the general humiliation at the hands of Western interests in the nineteenth century have not been forgotten. In a revealing moment, Zhou Enlai told an audience in Khartoum in 1964 that China was grateful to the Sudanese for killing British General Charles Gordon in 1885. Evidently, Gordon had supervised the burning of the old Beijing Summer Palace in 1860, twenty-five years earlier. More than a century later, Beijing still considered Gordon's activities an insult to the Chinese people.[8] This resentment of outside interference has colored Sino-Russian relations since Nikita Khrushchev and Mao Zedong split in the mid-1950s, and it certainly characterizes China's response to U.S. criticism of alleged human rights violations. Therefore, China's respect for a country's sovereignty leads it to pursue more subtle and less public forms of persuasion and diplomacy.

Others argue that China's unwillingness to criticize domestic behavior stems from more cynical and commercial goals. By continuing to aid rogue and repressive states, China obtains a competitive advantage, gaining access to significant oil supplies that are off-limits to most other oil companies. These critics point out that China's policy of domestic neutrality is nothing of the kind. They argue that without China's financial aid, repressive governments would not survive and almost certainly would be unable to pursue their abusive behavior. Their primary example is the Sudan, where China's support of the Sudanese government has enabled Khartoum to purchase arms to use against the rebels in the South and to supply the janjaweed militias in Darfur, enabling them to slaughter thousands of civilians.

China's Institutional Advantages and Disadvantages

By the mid-1990s, China realized that the dream of energy self-sufficiency was not realistic and that it needed to build a capacity to compete in the international marketplace. The country's "going abroad" strategy was adopted in 1997.[9] In response, China restructured its preexisting state oil and gas enterprises into two major companies: the China National Petroleum Corporation (CNPC) and the Chinese National Petrochemical Corporation (Sinopec). Both companies produce, import, trade, and process oil. While there are exceptions, CNPC has a stronger presence in the North and the West of China, and Sinopec is more visible in the South and the East.[10] Sinopec owns more refining capacity and thus is a major buyer of foreign oil, while CNPC is more likely to enter into exploration and production contracts, both within and outside of China. The China National Offshore Oil Corporation (CNOOC), a smaller company, as its name suggests, focuses on offshore investments.

In the 1980s and early 1990s, one could think of Sinopec and CNPC as arms of the state. But in 1998, as China's economic policies became more market oriented, the companies and associated ministries were reorganized to respond to commercial, more than social, goals. These changes, however, only went so far. The result is a mixture of decisions, some exclusively driven by commercial opportunity and others evidencing strong governmental intervention. It is not always clear which of these motives is operational, since there is little transparency. Furthermore, China's oil companies are becoming increasingly competitive with each other as each strives to gain commercial advantages. Erica Downs, a leading U.S. expert on Chinese oil policy, argues that investment decisions often have been generated from the bottom up and have not been highly coordinated with the relevant government agencies. She points out that the more high-quality assets a company acquired, the more likely it was to obtain diplomatic and financial support from the Beijing government for its subsequent investments.[11]

China's government may very well leave the management of its state-owned oil companies and many of its investment decisions to the professional executives, but clearly it has the legal means to intervene, if it so decides. Further, the boards of all of its oil companies consist of senior officials, many of whom hope to be promoted to higher government posts. Their ambition makes its difficult for them to ignore "requests" made by the central government since failure to respond could decrease the probability of future promotions. However, this balance is delicate, and tensions between managers of the oil companies and their boards are increasingly common. As these companies grow and the complexities of the industry increase, the senior managers of Sinopec, CNPC, and CNOOC will become more focused on commercial goals.

China's forays into African countries have been a team effort, involving Chinese oil companies, the country's export-import bank, its economic and trade agencies, and key trading companies, many of which are still state run. This combination gives China the ability to offer access to significant low-cost financing and to invest in a variety of complementary economic ventures, from infrastructural projects to textile plants to department stores.

China's oil companies are now an unusual agglomeration of modern entrepreneurial talent striving for earnings growth and ever-greater profitability, while at the same time remaining arms of a government increasingly focused on China's long-term energy needs.

Oil Reserves and China's Existing Infrastructure

In assessing its energy needs, China is aware of its existing energy infrastructure, which has relied on conventional coal-fired electricity facilities, older refineries, and very little in the way of a natural gas distribution system. China realizes that it needs to upgrade and modernize its energy infrastructure, but doing so will not occur overnight. Hence, a premium is placed on those energy resources that can be utilized by the present system.

Nowhere is this more apparent than with oil. China's oil refineries tend to be old and relatively simple. When gasoline demand is low, simplicity is not a problem since many of the heavier oil products can be produced in local refineries. However, in recent years, there has been a large increase in the sale of passenger cars and thus in the consumption of gasoline. To meet this growing demand, China has three choices: import gasoline, build new refineries to maximize gasoline production, or purchase light crudes that will result in greater gasoline yields from older refineries.

China would rather not import more gasoline. It is pursuing joint ventures with Middle Eastern state oil companies to build several new refineries in China; despite this increased capacity, Chinese demand for gasoline may quickly outstrip these additions. Thus, access to light crude oil becomes extremely valuable (crudes with lighter viscosities are easier to refine into products such as gasoline, and aviation and diesel fuel). Unfortunately, the availability of light crude as compared to heavy crude is declining, and this trend is forecast to continue. The exceptions are the new discoveries in Africa, especially in the Gulf of Guinea and off the southern African coast, where most of the oil has been light. Oil from places such as Angola and Nigeria is becoming increasingly valuable in today's market, and China is willing to go to great lengths to access it.

Furthermore, there are few areas in the world in which there are high probabilities of significant new oil and gas discoveries. Angola, Libya, Nigeria, and the Sudan are four exceptions. Obtaining a favored status within each of these countries could prove to be very valuable. Therefore, it is not surprising that China has aggressively pursued the Sudan and Angola and is attempting to gain entry into Nigeria. The one exception has been Libya, where China's involvement to date has been limited to bidding for one or two production-sharing agreements. Oil from Libya would have to be taken out through the Mediterranean Sea, which lies within the European sphere of influence. In addition, China does not have the same levers in dealing with Libyan strongman Muammar el-Qadaffi as it has in countries that are strapped for capital and investment. In fact, Libya employs a transparent bidding process for new oil and gas licenses, which does not favor China. Hence, if security of supply is a national priority, Libyan oil is probably less valuable than supplies from the Sudan or Angola or even Mauritania or Kenya.[12]

Nigeria presents a different set of problems. China and Nigeria have signed multiple trade agreements. Their presidents have exchanged visits, and both have committed to building close economic ties between the two countries. Nigeria sits on significant reserves of light crude oil and forecasts a doubling of production by 2025.[13] China would like to capture a portion of this additional oil, and Nigeria is eager to sell it. However, continued attacks by militant insurgents have delayed investments and have forced Nigeria to cut back its existing production. Nigeria had no incremental oil to sell in 2007 and in fact has had to reduce existing sales to China. In January 2006, CNOOC agreed to pay $2.27 billion for a 45 percent working interest in a portion of the undeveloped Akpo field. The Nigerian National Petroleum Company would own 50 percent of this concession.[14] In 2008, it was uncertain whether the projected dates for production start-up would be met.

Why Is China Interested in Africa?

There is a view in the West that China is an insular country that has traditionally embraced a posture of isolationism. This view stems largely from images of China from the nineteenth century and the first half of the twentieth century. However, on a longer time scale, China can be seen as one of the greatest trading nations in the world. The Mongol Empire stretched halfway around the globe, and the Silk Road was one of the great trading routes. In the early fifteenth century, Emperor Zhu Di ordered the construction of what might have been the most impressive shipping fleet in the world. Commanded by Zheng He, Chinese ships reached Africa and established trading posts on the continent, decades before the Portuguese.[15] For much of the last millennium China was a major global trader.

Kirby declares that "a defining characteristic of modern China is its incorporation into the global system."[16] After the decade of the Cultural Revolution, during which China turned inward, it aggressively sought to expand its economic reach beyond its borders. Western countries have found China's entry into the world economy disconcerting, if not threatening. This reaction is magnified when China pursues strategies and arrangements different from those followed by Western governments and corporations. Nowhere has this been truer than in China's efforts to obtain access to raw materials—especially oil.

In the eighteenth century, Africa was part of the huge European colonial empire in which countries were divided up and exploited for their potential mineral wealth. Even after the end of colonialism in the 1960s, there was little competition from non-European foreign countries. This is no longer the case. Beginning in the late 1980s, Chinese firms and state-owned enterprises have spread throughout the African continent. To a lesser degree this is also true of companies from Malaysia, Japan, and India. Furthermore, the United States, which did not have a large presence in the nineteenth century, is now the dominant foreign power on the continent.

African governments now look at foreign investments as a net benefit to their economies. The image of the exploitive foreign power ravaging their resources has been tempered. President Festus Mogae of Botswana made the point that all African countries have benefited from China's investments, which bid up the prices of raw materials, providing African countries with more revenue to invest in national priorities.[17] China has been instrumental in funding infrastructural development, including 6,000 kilometers of road, 3,000 kilometers of railroad, and 8 electric power plants.[18] The Chinese are welcome not only because they provide up-front capital for needed projects, but they also serve as a balance to European and United States interests. Host countries are no longer exclusively reliant on Western interests and are in a stronger position from which to negotiate the conditions for new investments.

As Downs points out, the value of Chinese oil companies' investments in Africa is just 8 percent of the combined commercial value of the private multinational investments.[19] This figure will increase as oil from the Angolan and Nigerian fields begins to flow. In fact, over the next two decades, China will likely purchase more oil from African state oil companies than it produces from its own concessions. However, under almost any scenario, Chinese companies will be some of several major oil-producing companies operating in Africa and will not have control over a significant portion of the continent's oil production.

To understand what motivates China's participation in Africa, it is useful to look at its activities in two countries: Angola and the Sudan. Despite the rhetoric in foreign newspapers, there are many subtle and important differences regarding how those relationships have evolved. However, in both cases, China has used two instruments to leverage its influence: a promise of greater trade across a wider range of investments other than oil, and access to cheap capital through its unregulated and government-controlled financial institutions.

Angola

The history of Angola is one of intrigue, corruption, and exploitation on a massive scale. Portugal established two settlements in the sixteenth and early seventeenth centuries and used them to facilitate one of the largest slave-trading enterprises in history, transporting over 3 million slaves to work large farming plantations in Brazil. In the nineteenth century, Angola's coastal settlements, especially Luanda, were major shipping ports, exporting cotton, bananas, and coffee, as well as minerals from what is now Angola, Congo (Brazzaville), and Zambia.

Fighting between non-Portuguese Angolans and the colonial government in Lisbon broke out in April 1966 and raged for nine years before independence was granted in 1975. Peace was short lived as civil war broke out between the Movement for the Liberation of Angola (MPLA) and the National Union for the Total Independence of Angola (UNITA). The former was heavily supported by the Russian and Cuban governments. In the late 1970s, approximately 37,000 Cuban "technical assistants" were sent to assist the MPLA. UNITA was supported by the United States, South Africa, and, for a period of time, China. To complicate matters, UNITA obtained money to buy arms through both illicit aid from the United States and by transporting diamonds, while the MLPA bought its arms through the revenue from its Cabinda oilfields, operated primarily by U.S. multinationals. To an extent, the United States, either directly or indirectly, provided both sides with the financial capability to wage the civil war, resulting in thousands of casualties. It is important to put this chapter in Angola's history into perspective as the world expresses outrage over China's recent activities in the Sudan.

The civil war waxed and waned over three decades before UNITA leader Jonas Savimbi died and a final settlement was reached in 2002. The MLPA agreed to give UNITA followers blanket amnesty and to allow them full rights to participate in the government.[20]

Western multinationals have had a presence in Angola for over forty years. However, until the 1990s, total production remained small, and the oil companies were primarily located in enclaves. The largest of these enclaves was in Cabinda, which is territorially separated from Angola proper by a small sliver of the Democratic Republic of the Congo.

In 1986, Angola's oil production was about 280,000 bbl/d, but by 2005 daily production had risen to 1.25 million barrels; daily production is predicted to exceed 2 million by the end of 2008 and 2.6 million by the end of 2011.[21] Proven oil reserves have tripled in the last seven years. By 2007, Angola was the second-largest oil producer in sub-Saharan Africa, behind Nigeria, and in January 2007, it became the twelfth member of OPEC.[22]

The oil and gas sectors account for 40 percent of Angola's GDP and have attracted many of the world's largest multinational corporations. Exxon Mobil, BP, Eni, Agip, Total, and Chevron all have major investments in Angola, and all have historical relationships with the government of Jose Eduardo dos Santos, president since 1979. Angola's role in the world's oil market is significant since there are few countries in which oil reserve estimates are increasing rapidly and that produce light oil. Most oil companies understand the value of forging a relationship with the Angolan government and gaining access to its growing supply of crude. The competition is intense.

China's task was daunting. It had to create a relationship with a government that it had actively opposed, at least through the end of the Cold War. Between 1990 and 2004, China's involvement in Angola consisted of little more than isolated technical assistance projects, primarily focused on agriculture. Yet, two years later, Angola supplied 47 percent of the oil that China bought from African countries or about 15 percent of China's total imports.[23] In addition, Angola has become China's second-largest African trading partner. How did this situation turn around so rapidly?

When its civil war ended, Angola's infrastructure lay in ruins. The government's financial resources had been poured into the war instead of being directed toward its transportation, power, and economic infrastructure. The country needed capital, and the only feasible option was to appeal to the International Monetary Fund (IMF), which agreed to provide a substantial loan, conditioned on Angola committing to both transparency reforms and to the IMF stabilization program, aimed at reducing inflation as opposed to increasing capital expenditures. The IMF was particularly concerned that oil revenues were being siphoned away and were not being adequately used to support the country's social needs. According to the IMF, over $8.5 billion in public money was unaccounted for between 1997 and 2001.[24] It demanded that Angola open its books so that the financial records of Sonangol, the country's national oil company, could be compared with actual oil revenues, treasury transactions, and deposits in the national bank. Since Angola ranked near the bottom of Transparency International's Corruption Perceptions Index, this was not seen as an unreasonable request by most neutral observers. Angola, though, was reluctant to make such reforms, but it saw no alternative since it was desperate for capital to renovate its infrastructure. Enter China.

In 2004, Angola suddenly broke off negotiations with the IMF, characterizing its conditions as "humiliating" and announced that China's Eximbank had agreed to give Angola a $2 billion line of credit to be repaid over twelve years with an interest rate based on the London Inter-Bank Offered Rate (LIBOR) plus 1.5 percent. Starting in year 5, Angola agreed to repay the loan by setting aside approximately 15,000 bbl/d. This figure would increase to 40,000 bbl/d until the loan was repaid. The Chinese pay market price for the oil, the funds go into an escrow account from which the annual debt repayments are made to the China Eximbank, and the remainder goes to the government of Angola. The loan has to be used for infrastructural projects, including roads, low-income housing, and an upgrade to Angola's railroad. Not surprising, all of these infrastructural concessions as of mid-2007 have been awarded to Chinese companies.[25]

This arrangement is basically a forward contract with the payments backloaded into the later years. China provides money in year one and receives substantial oil supplies in the future.

These negotiations occurred simultaneously with the discussions around the sale of Shell's oil share (50 percent) of Block 18, a major offshore concession. Shell proposed that it be allowed to sell its share to ONCC Videsh, one of India's state-owned companies. Allegedly, the Indian firm offered $620 million for a 50 percent stake in the field that was scheduled to produce 240,000 bbl/d by 2007.[26] In addition, India offered $200 million to rebuild Angola's railroad. The Angolan government, through Sonangol, exercised its preferential rights under the operating agreement to match the offer. Sonangol then sold the concession to a consortium of Sinopec (75 percent) and Sonangol (25 percent). This new consortium went by the name Sinopec-Sonangol International (SSI).

The connection between the $2 billion line of credit and the sale of the 50 percent share of Block 18 is not explicit, but there is a strong suggestion that they were directly linked. The coincidence is too great.

SSI gained a second concession in October 2004, when the Angolan government decided not to renew Total's share of the oil concession for Block 3-80, which, at the time, was producing 80,000 bbl/d. To make the concession more attractive, the government also included several additional medium-size fields.

In 2006, Angola put up for sale several deepwater blocks. The response was unprecedented. Over $3 billion was bid in up-front fees or signature bonuses. An analyst at Wood Mackenzie in Scotland claimed that these bids were the "highest ever offered for exploration acreage anywhere in the world."[27] Sinopec and Sonangol together bid a total of $2.2 billion for three tracts, in contrast to bids that were twenty times lower from Exxon Mobil and BP for the same tracts. In the end, SSI was awarded 60 percent of Block 18-06 (operated by the Brazilian national oil company Petrobras), 67.8 percent of Block 17-06 (operated by the French company Total), and 35 percent of Block 15 (operated by the Italian firm Eni).

During this same period, Angola tried to persuade Sinopec to build a 240,000 bbl/d refinery in Lobito. However, these negotiations collapsed over differences about the target market. Sinopec wanted most of the oil products to go to China, and Angola wanted the products to be sold in Africa.[28] Sinopec claimed that under the conditions sought by the Angolan government, the refinery was not likely to be profitable. Furthermore, China would much rather import crude and build refineries in China than build them in Angola and import product.

In June 2006, Chinese Prime Minister Wen Jiabao visited Luanda. While in Angola, he announced an additional $2 billion line of credit as a supplement to the existing loans. Additional loans have been made by international banks in partnership with Chinese banks.[29] Most of these take the form of traditional project finance loans and are given to Sonangol for projects related to offshore oil production. These have been offered at commercial rates, and Unipec—the trading subsidiary of Sinopec—is designated to receive the oil set aside to pay back these loans.

Are China's Efforts in Angola Sustainable?

Angola's goal has been to sell its oil in the ground, using the funds for domestic improvements, and, if possible, find financial organizations willing to securitize a small portion of its future oil revenues. Under this arrangement, Angola obtains the capital to rebuild its infrastructure, and the lenders obtain a future flow of high-quality oil, which they can consume or sell. This arrangement is not substantially different from the project finance loans supplied by European banks to Sonangol.[30] To guarantee all of the loans from Chinese banks, Sonangol has agreed to set aside more than 80,000 bbl/d.[31] This figure will increase to 120,000 bbl/d over the next 10 years. Given that Angola's oil production is forecast to exceed 2 million bbl/d, commitments of 80,000–120,000 bbl/d (4–6 percent of total production) do not seem an unreasonable "amortization" payment schedule from Angola's perspective, especially when its present need for capital is so pressing.

While there is enormous uncertainty surrounding the numbers, China is "buying" about 80,000 bbl/d of light crude oil through loans to the government, which was about 10 percent of its total purchases in 2006. Equity oil (oil to which Sinopec has ownership rights) will increase, if the 2006 offshore concessions prove to be as productive as forecast, but they will not come online for a few years. Furthermore, as China's demand for oil continues to grow, the proportions of oil that China will obtain from forward sales, equity oil, and direct sales will not appreciably change. The last will continue to account for a majority of China's imports from Angola.

Is China gaining competitive advantages through its arrangements with the Angolan government? This depends on whether the available data are correct. There is always the chance that the public numbers are not accurate, especially when one is examining a series of arrangements between a government that repudiates transparency and several state-owned enterprises that rarely report the particulars of their financial transactions. But if the public numbers are correct, Sinopec and China have successfully used their ability to offer significant amounts of low-interest financial credit to gain access to moderate amounts of Angolan oil. This is not the first time this has been done, and, in fact, British and French interests are doing the same through their large commercial banks. Without providing financial assistance to the government, China would probably not have been able to receive either the Block 18 concession or a percentage of Total's concession. Therefore, by offering credit, China has been able to secure a flow of Angolan oil for at least the next decade.

Unlike in the Sudan, China does not have a dominant position in the Angolan oil production market, and it is unlikely to seek or be granted such a position. Western companies continue to be well represented. From Angola's perspective, China's involvement only creates greater competition, increasing its power to leverage higher prices and gain greater access to cheap credit.

There are, however, several problems that may become more troublesome in the future. First, Sinopec does not have the significant technical knowledge required for construction and production operations in deep water. Therefore it relies on other partners to operate the concessions in which it participates. BP operates Block 18, and Petrobras, Total, and Eni operate the other offshore concessions in which Sinopec has a majority interest. One might argue that one of the indirect benefits of China's investment in oil properties is the opportunity to gain experience in deepwater production technologies.

Second, China is reluctant to hire local workers, both for management and for unskilled jobs. Therefore most of the people who work in Chinese enterprises in Angola, as well as in other parts of Africa, are Chinese nationals. They live in their own enclaves, do not learn the local language, go to Chinese schools, and stand apart from the native population. The Chinese defend these practices by arguing that they allow them to ensure discipline within their labor force, increase productivity through better communication, improve morale within the workforce, and ensure quality control. It is not surprising that these practices also lead to resentment in the local populations, as witnessed by the demonstrations against the Chinese in Zambia and Namibia.[32] It is ironic that China, a country insistent on local content requirements and the hiring of local labor in contracts with foreign firms doing business in China, ignores this issue outside of its borders.

Bolon contrasts these hiring practices with those of Chevron, which employs 2,500 Angolans—88 percent of the company's workforce.[33] Chevron has also aggressively provided assistance to enhance local school systems, reaching more than 8,500 students. Finally, it has worked closely with health authorities to reduce the spread of HIV in the country. Total has an equally impressive record of building local capacity to construct and operate its Angolan facilities. These agendas are very different from that of the Chinese, and while they may not significantly change the views of the central government, they certainly are enhancing the image of Chevron and Total at the local level. Whether China's current hiring practices will be sustainable in Angola and other regions of Africa is an open question.

Third, many experts believe China is overpaying for its access to oil. Perhaps such high payments are required to knock down the barriers to entry, and perhaps they buy security benefits sufficient to make the high prices reasonable. To some extent, Japan pursued a similar strategy after the 1973 embargo, arguing that cost premiums served the role of insurance. This rationale seemed logical at the time, but eventually the cost of those premiums became a fiscal drain. When Japan entered its prolonged recession in the 1990s, it decided to pay less and avoid redundant or overpriced contracts.

As China moves away from its quest to lock up a flow of imported oil to fuel its growing demand and trusts the marketplace, it is likely to follow in Japan's footsteps. Given China's continual struggles with its domestic fiscal policies and its growing confidence in its state oil companies, at some point its leaders will decide that they can effectively compete in the international marketplace with Western countries without paying above-market prices for access to oil supplies.

Fourth, Western governments have accused the Chinese of undercutting their efforts to force the Angolan government to institute reforms, specifically those related to transparency. Angola continues to rank among the most corrupt countries in the world. An implication is that this corruption is diverting massive amounts of money from the people to the pockets of a select few Angolans.[34] China's intervention—and subsequent alternative to the IMF's 2004 loan—is seen as undercutting the West's efforts to reform the dos Santos government. In addition, U.S. firms must abide by the Foreign Corrupt Practices Act whereas Chinese firms face no similar constraints. Some believe that in ignoring transparency concerns, China gains a significant competitive advantage in a jurisdiction with a perceived high level of corruption.

Finally, there is a fear that Chinese initiatives in countries, such as Angola, will undermine efforts by multilateral organizations, such as the IMF and World Bank, to promote collective efforts throughout the region.[35] This criticism is probably less valid since there are many other issues inhibiting African collective initiatives. However, if it had a choice, China would clearly prefer to continue to pursue deals in the context of bilateral, as opposed to multilateral, arrangements.

Are Chinese investments and trade arrangements undermining Western efforts to promote progressive leadership throughout sub-Saharan Africa? For the answer to be clearly "yes," one would have to believe that if the Chinese had not offered the 2004 loan, the IMF would have been successful in persuading the dos Santos government to accept Western transparency requirements and that the Angolan government would have aggressively enforced those requirements. One would also have to conclude that despite its enormous growth in oil production, Angola would have been solely dependent on the IMF, or other multilateral banks, for debt relief and capital. That Angola has raised capital from European banks, as well as from Chinese banks (and more recently Indian institutions), suggests that access to capital might not have been as restrictive an obstacle going forward. If this is the case, Angola's unwillingness to make the reforms sought by the IMF might not have appreciably changed. Furthermore, in 2003 and 2004, the IMF was insisting that Angola delay the rebuilding of its public infrastructure until its fiscal condition improved and its currency inflation reduced. It is not self-evident that this course of action would have been superior to a strategy of investing up front in its energy, transportation, and communications infrastructure through obligating a small portion if its future oil revenues.

Have China's actions in Angola made reform efforts more difficult? At the margin, they probably have, but placed in the governance context of Angola in 2008, it is difficult to conclude that Chinese actions determine Angola's position on governance reforms. Furthermore, Sinopec's (and China's) influence in Angola is tempered by the reality that it is one of a number of oil companies doing business there. Angola has been very careful to sustain relationships with many companies, gaining bargaining leverage through maintaining a portfolio of investors.

The Sudan

While China is criticized in some circles for its activities in Angola, it is its conduct in the Sudan that has garnered the most attention and provoked the greatest controversy. Like Angola, the Sudan's oil reserve estimates are growing significantly; many areas remain unexplored. But unlike in Angola, CNPC, the Chinese oil company in the Sudan, faces very little competition from Western multinationals, which left the country because of the West's unwillingness to abide by the conduct of the government in Khartoum. The Sudan represents a unique opportunity to gain secure access to significant amounts of oil—particularly equity oil. Yet, those benefits have come with a high price tag in terms of international opinion and may not prove to be as beneficial in the long run as the Chinese believed at the time that they made their initial commitments.

As much as 52 percent of China's equity oil came from the Sudan in 2005.[36] While the Sudan is clearly of major importance to China, the reverse is also true. China is of critical importance to the Sudan, since more than half of its exports go to China.[37] The number of Chinese workers in the Sudan has tripled since the early 1990s and reached 24,000 in 2006.[38] Chinese non-oil investments are significant and include a major hydroelectric facility, a new airport in Khartoum, and several textile plants. China also operates the vast bulk of the Sudan's oil production and has a 50 percent stake in the nation's only major refinery in Khartoum.

To understand the factors that induced China to make these commitments, it is helpful to put them in a historical context. Chevron USA began exploring for oil in 1974 in the Muglad Basin. But when civil war broke out for the second time in the mid 1980s, Chevron abandoned more than $1 billion of private investments and sold its interests to a Canadian firm, which formed the Greater Nile Petroleum Operating Company (GNPOC). In 1997, GNPOC sold a 40 percent share to China's largest oil company, CNPC. The goal of the newly formed company was to develop the Sudan's oilfields in the south-central part of the country and build a 1,500-kilometer (about 930-mile) pipeline to a coastal port facility at Marsa al-Bashair, near Port Sudan.[39]

Despite the fact that oil was first discovered in the early 1970s, it was not until 1999 that the Sudan actually exported a barrel of oil. Thus, when China initiated its negotiations with the Sudan, its petroleum resources were undeveloped and most of its territory was unexplored. It was one of the few areas in the world that geologists felt might still hold large unexploited resources. While proven reserves still remain low, some geologists estimate that investment in exploration and development could allow the Sudan to produce more than 600,000 bbl/d in the near future.[40]

Hence from China's perspective, the Sudan had enormous upside potential. Furthermore, U.S. and European companies had left the region, ensuring virtually no competition for access to the country's oil resources.

By 1997, the Sudan was in desperate financial straits. Its debt was 250 percent of GDP, interest payments were $4.5 million a day, and each day the civil war was draining another $1 million from its treasury. Rural areas were devastated, undermining the Sudan's agricultural economy. GDP was in a free fall. The only escape from this financial death spiral was to increase oil revenues. Western companies had left, and China was the only country prepared to fill this vacuum. The Sudan agreed to sell (or arranged to sell) oil concessions to China on generous terms. For example, there are no restrictions on profit reparations, and the Sudanese government exempts CNPC from all domestic taxes on exported oil (although CNPC does pay royalties). In addition, the concession acreage is significantly larger than that awarded to other countries. Thus, from a purely commercial basis, investments in the Sudan were almost too good to refuse, especially given China's perception that most other producing regions were tied to U.S., European, or Japanese interests, and might be less receptive to Chinese overtures.

The Sudan has been wracked by civil wars since the 1950s. While there are multiple factions, the basic split has been between the South, which is primarily Christian with close cultural links to its African heritage, and the much more populous North, which embraces a traditional Islamic culture. Northern factions have controlled the government for the last half century. In 1989, Colonel Omar Hassan al-Bashir, backed by the National Islamist Front, overthrew the elected government and escalated military actions against the Sudan People's Liberation Army/Movement (SPLA/M) in the South. By the time the civil war ended, more than 2 million people had died and 4 million were displaced.

Oil and the North-South Civil War

While a campaign to convert the southern population to Islam was the public issue that split the two sides (in the 1970s, the national government initiated an effort to convert all Sudanese to Islam), oil played a significant, if not dominant, role. The Sudan's oil reserves are located in the South and central parts of the country, primarily in Unity and Abyei provinces, which are close to the border with the northern part of the Sudan. Initially all oil revenues went to the autonomous southern government, but this was during a period in which reserve estimates were quite small. When it became clear that the Sudan might be sitting on major supplies, the North reasserted control. It created a new province—Benitiu—that primarily consisted of the existing oilfields. Concerned about security of supply, the Sudanese government decided to locate the country's only refinery near Khartoum, over 1,000 kilometers away, and build a pipeline from the oilfields to the refinery. This investment allowed the North to control the oil revenues, a portion of which was captured by the government and used to fund the army and various militia groups. China supplied the technical expertise and helped to make the financial investments to develop these reserves. It also provided the workers to expand, construct, and operate the oilfields, pipeline, and refinery. In other words, China agreed to serve as a total turnkey contractor.

Given that oil revenues were essential to the North's ability to fight the war, rebel forces from the South targeted the oil facilities. In turn, the government spent considerable resources defending the infrastructure. China was caught in a difficult position: with thousands of its citizens at risk, it was under pressure to protect its workers and the facilities that they had built. China had three choices: withdraw from the Sudan and leave its investments behind, send security personnel to protect its managers and workers, or provide technical assistance and equipment to the Sudanese army so that it could protect the Chinese workers. While the details remain sketchy, it is clear that the Chinese chose some combination of the second and third options.[41] Although there is no hard evidence that Chinese troops were ever present in the Sudan, from the perspective of the rebel forces in the South, the Chinese had clearly sided with the North and the military government in Khartoum.

After years of bitter fighting, the two sides finally signed the Comprehensive Peace Agreement (CPA) in 2005. Under its terms, the South is well into a six-year period of autonomous self-rule, which will be followed by a vote scheduled for 2011 on whether or not to secede from the Sudan.[42]

In the interim period, the two sides agreed to honor all existing contracts and share the net revenue from oil resources located in southern Sudan.[43] A National Petroleum Commission (NPC) was established, with its membership divided between the North and the South. Three nonpermanent members from oil-producing provinces were added. Thus, control of the NPC board will depend in part on whether those provinces are determined to be located in the North or the South. Since the NPC approves all new oil contracts, this determination is critically important.

To set the stage for the 2011 secession vote, the CPA established several tribunals to demarcate borders between the provinces, especially the disputed areas separating southern Sudan from the North. A particular source of controversy is the future of Abyei, an area along the North-South border that also lies near Unity province. Unity and Abyei together contain a substantial portion of the Sudan's known oil reserves.

There are several issues bearing on the future of this region that remain outstanding. First, under the CPA, the citizens of Abyei can vote on whether they would like to be affiliated with the North or the South. Second, the government of the Sudan has refused to accept the border delineations promulgated by the Abyei Boundary Commission (ABC) on the grounds that the commission did not protect the rights of the Misseriya Arabs, some of whom live in the lands that would fall within the jurisdiction of the South.[44] Finally, the ABC placed the Heglig oilfields, previously considered to be in Unity, in Abyei. In other words, not only is the future of Abyei in play, but also its boundaries are changing in such a way that the economic stakes are much higher.

Douglas Johnson, chairman of the ABC, stated that the issue surrounding the future of Abyei is "who will own the oil."[45] In the fall of 2007, both Vice President Salva Kiir Mayardit and President al-Bashir ratcheted up their rhetoric on the future of Abyei, and military forces positioned themselves closer to the oilfields.[46]

In October 2007, the South recalled all its ministers, deputies, and advisers because the North had not fulfilled its obligations under the CPA. Specifically, the North continued to allocate only half of the oil monies that the South claimed was owed to it, refused to withdraw its troops north of the border, and reshuffled the ministries without consulting the South.[47] In December 2007, President al-Bashir negotiated a settlement, giving the South more representation in the cabinet and, at least temporarily, persuaded the southern officials to return to the government. In May 2008, fighting broke out between Northern and Southern troops in Abyei. While peace was temporarily restored, the relationship between the Southern and Northern governments continued to deteriorate.

Whether a new civil war will eventually erupt over the issue of oil is uncertain. Despite South Sudan President Kiir's efforts to dampen cross-border tensions, unless the two sides are able to negotiate their differences and begin to develop a greater sense of trust, the potential for renewed civil war will remain, leaving the Chinese and their investments in an uncomfortable position.[48]

Darfur

While the threat of civil war looms on the horizon, it is the conflict in Darfur that has drawn the attention of the world community. It has also placed China's relationship with the Khartoum government in the crosshairs of human rights groups.

At first glance, one might question how Darfur is linked to China's oil investments since no one has discovered significant amounts of oil in Darfur, nor are Chinese advisors active in the region. However, the janjaweed militias are heavily funded and supported by the Khartoum government, which in turn is heavily funded and supported by Chinese state corporations.

In 2006, a series of UN investigators found that a majority of the small arms used in Darfur were manufactured by the Chinese, despite an international ban on arms sales in the region. In addition, Amnesty International reported that China provided hundreds of military trucks to the Sudan and that those showed up in the possession of Arab militias.[49]

China's response was that many countries sell arms and that most of the equipment and arms cited in the UN's report were sold to the Khartoum government during the North-South civil war. How they ended up in the hands of the Darfur militia groups was outside China's control. It further asserted that the arms embargo did not restrict sales to Khartoum; it banned the transfer of weapons into Darfur itself.

These arguments may be technically correct, but they do little to blunt the searing images of the massacre of women and children with Chinese weapons. China emphasizes that it does not get involved in a country's domestic politics and that it does not judge the conduct of other governments. Its involvement is always purely commercial. Thus, for several years it refused to support UN resolutions calling for the deployment of a peacekeeping force in Darfur because the Sudanese government was "not ready to accept peacekeepers on its soil."[50] This argument is not convincing to most observers. They point out that if China left the Sudan, the Sudanese government would lose its principal source of revenue.

Since at least the fall of 2006, China's posture has changed significantly. Using the three-phase plan for deployment outlined by then UN Secretary-General Kofi Annan and endorsed by both the high-level dialogue in Addis Ababa and the African Union (AU) Peace and Security Council's summit in Abuja, Nigeria, China began to lobby al-Bashir to accept the plan and adopt measures to relieve the crisis. In February 2007, President Hu Jintao visited the Sudan and enunciated five principles: respecting the Sudan's sovereignty, insisting on dialogue and consultation on an equal basis, allowing the AU and UN to play a constructive role in peacekeeping, promoting stability in the region, and improving the living conditions of local people.[51]

In 2007, China's ambassador to the Sudan expressed the hope that the Sudan would "show more flexibility to improve the situation in Darfur."[52] In April 2007, Khartoum accepted a significant portion of the Annan plan, and, in May, the Chinese government appointed a special representative for African affairs, whose near-term mandate is the Darfur issue.

In June 2007, *Qiushi*, the magazine of the Chinese Communist Party, stated, "Efforts made by China on the Darfur issue reflect the distinctive features of China's diplomacy in advancing with the times. China has always advocated the proper handling of relevant conflicts by political means through dialogue and consultation. Only through dialogue and consultation among the parties and respect for an accommodation of reasonable concerns can differences be reconciled and the directions of joint efforts be identified. China has prodded the Sudanese government to adhere to the broad direction of Annan's plan."[53]

The statement ended with the following words, "China's policy [in the Sudan] is characterized by its policy of non-interference in each other's internal affairs and non-attachment of any conditions."[54] Yet it is clear that China did modify its prior position and has prodded the Sudanese government to amend its position on the Darfur issue. As Andrew Natsios, former U.S. special envoy to the Sudan, said in his testimony to the Senate Foreign Relations Committee: "We have evidence at this point that the Chinese are now taking a more aggressive role than in the past. . . . I think the Chinese actually may be the critical factor that led to the Sudanese reversing their position on the Kofi Annan plan. . . . If every country behaved the way we [the United States] did, I am not sure we could always get done what we need to get done. Sometimes more subtle approaches need to supplement what we are doing. And my sense is that the Chinese are taking a more subtle approach and that is really affecting the behavior of the Sudanese government."[55]

Did world criticism of its prior position and the threat of a boycotted Olympics cause China to change its policies? The answer will probably never be known since China contends that its policy of noninterference remains. But clearly China's willingness aggressively to push the Sudanese government was far greater in late 2006 and in 2007 than in earlier periods. By the spring of 2007, the differences between China and the West on the Darfur question were tactical, not strategic or substantive.[56]

Our conclusion is that China's interpretation of its noninterference doctrine is changing to fit its status as a superpower. A complete "hands-off" strategy is unsustainable, conceptually and practically. Yet, it would be equally unrealistic to expect China to substitute public and dogmatic tactics for the more subtle and private style of diplomacy. The former is often pursued to appeal to audiences back home. China's need to appease domestic interests or opposing political interests on the home front remains weak, and thus its audience is often governments in other developing countries with whom China is building diplomatic and trade relations.

Remaining North-South Tensions

Will China be willing to use its powers of persuasion to influence the actions of the Sudanese government to reduce the prospect of a renewed North-South civil war? In this case, China's energy investments could be directly affected. Moreover, China has put billions of dollars into the Sudan with the expectation that over the next two decades it will reap tangible economic benefits: a continuing flow of imported oil, mineral rights, and commercial returns on its infrastructural projects. A new civil war would put all of these at risk. Yet, these same investments limit China's flexibility to change course without paying a very high economic penalty.

When asked about this predicament, Ambassador Liu Guijin, China's special representative for Africa, said, "As with any investor, in any country, it is logical that the investor hopes to have a more stable and more peaceful situation."[57] Unfortunately, "hope" by itself is unlikely to be sufficient to head off a new conflict, and China's diplomatic skills are sure to be tested.

In the longer term, China's experience in the Sudan exposes the risk of overinvesting in states characterized by autocratic rule and civil instability. Inevitably, such rulers will be challenged, either by external or internal sources. More often than not, the government will eventually fall since it rests on the shoulders of a small clique. Partnerships forged with the old regime will no longer be favored by the new one, and what looked like a beneficial relationship could quickly become unsustainable.

Furthermore, countries that lack stable institutions, predictable processes of governance, and popular support are subject to more volatile economic cycles, greater civil unrest, and the continual threat of hostilities, either from internal or external sources. Such an environment does not augur well for either sustainable investments or strategic partnerships.

China has used all of its diplomatic skills to persuade the Sudanese government to accept a peacekeeping force in Darfur. Even with this success, China has not recovered the credibility and trust of much of the world community, which continues to criticize it for having been slow to pressure the Sudanese government. Whether this criticism is fair or deserved is another question. There is no doubt that it exists and that China has paid and will continue to pay a price in the currency of popular opinion.

The threat of a renewed civil war between the North and South may not grip the world's collective attention in the same way as genocide in Darfur, but it directly threatens the future of China's oil investments. Furthermore, the issues that divide the stakeholders are even more complex and intractable than those in Darfur.

China realizes that it is in a vulnerable position and has begun to mend its relations with the South Sudanese government. It has aggressively sought to invest in new businesses and in 2007 and 2008 was constructing buildings throughout Juba, the capital of southern Sudan. The perception in many circles within SPLA/M is that the United States may promise assistance and investments, but the Chinese actually deliver; this is a far different attitude than would have been found in the South two years ago. But what is more interesting is that the Chinese are working with the Kenya Pipeline Corporation to explore the possibility of building a $1.4 billion pipeline connecting the oilfields in Unity province with the port of Lamu in Kenya, which the Chinese likewise hope to develop.[58] At the moment, the only way to export oil from the Sudan is through the port of Masra al Bashair in the North. Thus, if the South gained control of a portion of the oilfields, it would have to ship the oil to a northern port, which could prove politically untenable. The Kenyan pipeline is only in the discussion stage, but if pursued, it would significantly change the dynamic of future oil negotiations.

While China's actions with the SPLA/M may cause some consternation in Khartoum, China is attempting to buy a political hedge to protect its investments and its future access to oil. Whether it will be successful, only time will tell, but its ability to adjust its diplomatic and economic strategy and to do so quickly and effectively is impressive.

China has made a major commitment to reach out to Africa and to develop a long-term strategy to ensure a flow of oil to meet its growing demand for energy. What has happened and what will happen over the next five years in the Sudan will represent the most complex and difficult challenge to China's energy initiatives on the African continent. There is a danger that for all its attractiveness as a source of oil, the Sudan may end up a political and economic quagmire that will extract an uncomfortably high strategic price for years to come.

Conclusion

When China initially decided to make major investments in African energy supplies, it did so with the hope of acquiring secure flows of oil. Equity oil (oil owned by Chinese companies) would be the most secure. The early success in the Sudan in acquiring such oil may have wetted the appetite of the Chinese companies, but it has become clear that equity oil in the form of concessional agreements granted to foreign oil companies are a rarity. In today's marketplace, most oil is owned by the country in which it is found, and the closest a nondomestic oil company can come to owning equity oil is either through amortization payments in the form of oil, such as those arranged in Angola, or oil from production-sharing agreements. Neither of these are technically equity oil.

A portion of China's limited supply of equity oil is sold on the international market and not shipped to China. This is not surprising since the oil is technically owned by one of China's state oil companies, which can either sell the oil at international prices in the world market or sell it in China at prices that are regulated by the government.

China's enormous financial investments in the Sudan have proven to be riskier and carry with them more negative political spillovers than China realized when it made its initial commitments. Yet, while China's investments in

Africa may not have yielded all the benefits that their designers hoped, there is no question that China has benefited overall. Most African governments see China as a reliable partner and one that allows them to offset the influence of the private multinational oil companies. The more players bidding for oil concessions and other economic investments, the greater the leverage African countries will have as they develop their resources and attempt to build their economies.

China is a player in every oil-producing region on the African continent, save Libya, and as its companies develop more technical expertise and become more experienced in the nuances of the economic marketplace, their capacity to compete for business will improve. Furthermore, China's strategy of aggressively offering economic investment packages and trade opportunities is working, improving its ability to gain opportunities either to purchase additional oil supplies or to develop partnerships with state oil companies.

China's oil industry has demonstrated that it can learn from its mistakes and adjust rapidly. Unless there are major shifts in political and economic conditions, China's involvement in Africa's oil development will be even greater a decade from now. However, in almost every case it will not be a dominant player. African governments will ensure that they, themselves, are the dominant players.

Notes

1. British Petroleum, *BP Statistical Review of World Energy* (London, 2006), 35.

2. In the first months of 2006, 5.8 million cars were sold in China, an increase of 26 percent over the same period in 2005. "The Fast and the Furious: Carmaking in China," *Economist* (29 November 2006), available at www.economist.com/business/displaystory.cfm?story_id=8319382 (accessed 7 January 2008).

3. Zhang Guobao, "How Can Energy Shortage Be Blamed on China," *People's Daily* (21 September 2005), available at http://english.people.com.cn/200509/21/eng20050921_209937.html (accessed 7 January 2008).

4. British Petroleum, *BP Statistical Review of World Energy* (London, 2007),11.

5. International Energy Agency, *2006 World Energy Outlook* (Paris, 2006), 34, 145. In addition to crude oil imports, product imports are increasing, especially aviation fuels.

6. Quoted in Peter Goldman, "Big Shift in China's Oil Policy," *Washington Post* (13 July 2005), D10.

7. Song Yen Ling, "In the African Firing Line," *Energy Compass* (25 May 2007).

8. Jay Matthews and Linda Matthews, *One Billion: A China Chronicle* (New York, 1983), 10.

9. James A. Baker III Institute for Public Policy, "The Changing Role of National Oil Companies in International Energy Markets: Implications for the Middle East" (Houston, April 2007), 9.

10. International Energy Agency, *2006 World Energy Outlook*, 36.

11. Erica Downs, "The Fact and Fiction of Sino-African Energy Relations," *China Security*, III (2007), 49, 50.

12. Kenya presently produces no oil, but geologists believe that several offshore areas may hold large deposits of oil. CNOOC has signed six production-sharing contracts with Kenya.

13. Energy Information Administration, U.S. Department of Energy (EIA-USDOE), "World Total Liquids Production by Region and Country Reference Case 1990–2030," table G1, in *2007 International Energy Outlook* (2007), available at www.eia.doe.gov/oiaf/ieo/excel/ieopoltab_1.xls (accessed 7 September 2007).

14. "Chinese Investors Offer $2bn for Nigerian Oil Field," *African Oil Journal* (9 January 2006), available at www.africanoiljournal.com/1-9-2006%20chinese_investors_offer%20$2bn%20for%20Nigerian%20Oil%20field.htm (accessed 7 September 2007).

15. See Preface, vii in this volume.

16. William Kirby, "China's Internationalization in the Early People's Republic: Dreams of a Socialist World Economy," *China Quarterly*, CLXXXVIII (2006), 870.

17. Festus Mogae, speech at John F. Kennedy School of Government (5 May 2007).

18. Song, "In the African Firing Line," 1

19. Downs, "Fact and Fiction," 44.

20. In 1999, UNITA signed the Lusaka Peace Agreement and was included in the government. However, it soon splintered into two groups. One stayed with the government, and the other, led by Savimbi, went back to war. Hence, there was some UNITA participation in the government as early as 1999.

21. Jad Mouawad, "Nowadays, Angola Is Oil's Topic A," *New York Times* (20 March 2007), available at www.nytimes.com/2007/03/20/business/worldbusiness/20angola.html?_r=1&oref=slogin (accessed 5 June 2008).

22. In April 2008, Angola produced more oil than Nigeria for the first time. See Wenran Jiang, 54 in this volume.

23. In 2006, the United States imported the greatest amount of Angola's oil, with South Korea second and China third.

24. John Reed, "Angolan Oil Loan Likely to Raise Transparency Issues," *Financial Times* (11 October 2005), 13.

25. Interview between the authors and Carlos Aires da Fonseca Panzo, Angolan finance minister (19 July 2007).

26. Indrajit Basu, "India Discreet, China Bold in Oil Hunt," *Asia Times Online* (29 September 2005), available at www.atimes.com/atimes/South_Asia/GI29Df01.html (accessed 7 January 2008).

27. "Going Off the Deep End for Oil," *Business Week* (26 June 2006), available at www.businessweek.com/magazine/content/06_26/b3990080.htm (accessed 7 January 2008).

28. Lucy Corkin, "Angola: Country Flexes Newfound Muscle," *Business Day* (23 March 2007), available at www.resourceinvestor.com/pebble.asp?relid=30121 (accessed 7 January 2008).

29. Energy Intelligence, "Angola to Raise Another $2 Billion Oil-Backed Loan," *Energy Compass* (14 October 2005). The total value of all the loans is estimated to be between $10 billion and $12 billion, but the authors could find no public documents to confirm these numbers.

30. Ibid. Standard Chartered Bank (Britain) and BNP Paribas (France) have loaned over $3.45 billion to Angola.

31. Ibid.

32. Chinese oil operations in the Sudan are a notable exception to this hiring pattern. In 2007, 93 percent of those who worked for Chinese oil operations were native Sudanese—all of whom were trained by the CNPC. See also Stephanie Rupp, 76 in this volume.

33. Emily Bolon, "Chinese Energy Investments in Angola: Strategic Implications for Western Multinationals," independent student research paper (Boston, 2007).

34. UN Integrated Regional Information Networks, "Angola: China Entrenches Position in Booming Economy" (17 April 2006), available at www.irinnews.org/report.aspx?reportid=58756, citing Transparency International's 2005 Corruption Perceptions Index, available at www.transparency.org/policy_research/surveys_indices/cpi/2005 (accessed 7 January 2008).

35. Bolon, "Chinese Energy Investments in Angola," 8.

36. "China's CNPC Targets Overseas Integration Deals," *Petroleum Intelligence Weekly* (23 January 2006).

37. EIA-USDOE, "Sudan Energy Data, Statistics and Analysis" (2006), available at www.eia.doe.gov/emeu/cabs/Sudan/Full.html (accessed 7 January 2008).

38. "Friend or Forager? How China is Winning the Resources and the Loyalties of Africa," *Financial Times* (23 February 2006), 15.

39. Henry Lee and Dan Shalmon, "Searching for Oil: China's Oil Initiatives in the Middle East," discussion paper (Cambridge, MA, January 2007), 24–25.

40. EIA-USDOE, "Sudan Energy Data, Statistics and Analysis."

41. China built several munitions factories for the Sudanese government, in part to avoid being accused of exporting arms to the Sudan.

42. Stuart Price, "Sudan's New Peace," *Middle East,* Issue 353 (February 2005), 353.

43. See "Agreement on Wealth Sharing during the Pre-Interim and Interim Period," signed 7 January 2004, available at www.sudantribune.com/spip.php?article1425 (accessed 17 April 2008).

44. John Young, "Emerging North-South Tensions and Prospects for a Return to War," report for the Small Arms Survey (Geneva, 2007), 31, available at www.smallarmssurvey.org/files/portal/spotlight/sudan/Sudan_pdf/SWP%207%20North-South%20tensions.pdf (accessed 7 January 2008).

45. Ibid., 32.

46. Salva Kiir Mayardit is vice president of the entire country and president of the autonomous South Sudan.

47. Benjamin Myer, Benson Mayen, and Bedru Mulumba, "South May Recall MPs from Khartoum," *Citizen* (1 November 2007), 1.

48. *Sudan Mirror* 4 (22 October–4 November, 2007).

49. Ian Taylor, "China's Oil Diplomacy in Africa," *International Affairs,* LXXXII (2006), 950.

50. "Responsible China?" *Washington Post* (6 September 2006), A14.

51. "Diplomat Views China's Role on Darfur Issue, Stresses Even-Handedness," *Qiushi Magazine* (1 June 2007), as reported by *BBC Monitoring International Reports* (2 June 2007).

52. Ibid.

53. Ibid.

54. Ibid.

55. Andrew Natsios, "Darfur: A Plan B to Stop Genocide," testimony before Senate Foreign Relations Committee (11 April 2007).

56. But see Robert I. Rotberg, 13 in this volume, for 2008.

57. Quoted in Alec Russell and William Wallis, "Beijing Puts Quiet Pressure on Sudan," *Financial Times* (19 June 2007), 6.

58. Global Insight, "Woodside Spuds Offshore Well; Kenya's Oil Future to Be Determined in 2007," available at www.globalinsight.com/SDA/SDADetail7703.htm (accessed 7 January 2008).

MARTYN J. DAVIES

7

Special Economic Zones:
China's Developmental
Model Comes to Africa

A new developmental model is in the process of being rolled out in key African countries—Special Economic Zones (SEZs). They provide liberalized investment environments focused on strategic industries to attract foreign companies. The model of dedicated geographical zones where investing companies enjoy preferential economic policies is by no means unique. Numerous African governments have established or are establishing such zones in their countries in an attempt to attract foreign direct investment (FDI), especially in labor-intensive manufacturing industries. Kenya, Egypt, and Mauritius are the most proactive on the continent in establishing such zones.

What makes this new developmental model unique is that it has been initiated on the African continent by the government of the People's Republic of China (PRC). Rather than being initiators of this process, African governments are the recipients. China is carving out designated SEZs across the continent. These zones are positioned to become Africa's new economic growth nodes.

Chinese-initiated SEZs in Africa require large amounts of investment in infrastructure, both within the zones and linking them to ports and the regional markets. If completed as envisioned, the infrastructural corridors will provide the essential linkages between fragmented African markets and will have a positive impact upon regional economic integration.

The Chinese SEZs originated at the Forum on China-Africa Cooperation (FOCAC) summit held in Beijing in November 2006, which was attended by over forty African heads of state. At this summit, the Chinese government made a number of commitments to the continent, including one to establish three to five preferential trade and economic zones in Africa. These commitments are to be met before the next FOCAC summit, to be hosted by the Egyptian government in Cairo in November 2009.

The terms of these zones are being negotiated between Beijing and targeted African governments that are willing to offer the required policy concessions in order to receive committed Chinese investment. Decisions made in Beijing and implemented by Chinese state-aligned firms in Africa will have a significant impact upon the growth trajectory of specific sub-Saharan African countries and regions.

The SEZ Developmental Model

After the political change and resultant dramatic shift in economic policy that occurred in China in the late 1970s, the leadership of the Communist Party of China created dedicated geographic zones on the eastern seaboard of the country that would serve as experiments for market liberalization to attract Chinese diaspora and foreign capital.

Four SEZs were introduced two years after the party's Eleventh National Congress in December 1978. The conference recognized the need for the country to implement economic reform, promoting a market-led policy to encourage higher levels of foreign capital, trade, technology, and growth in an economy that had until then been insular and based on the premise of self-sufficiency.

The new "open door policy" and the SEZs were mechanisms to open the country's economy gradually to the rest of the world. SEZs in Shenzhen, Zhuhai, and Shantou in Guangdong Province and in Xiamen—including Xiamen Island and Gulangyu Islet—in Fujian Province were announced in 1980.

A fifth zone in Hainan Province was created in 1988, after the passage of a resolution to establish Hainan Province and Hainan SEZ. The Hainan SEZ was the largest of the zones, including 6 cities and 13 counties with a total population of 7.4 million.[1]

Several other areas were targeted to attract foreign investment and joint ventures. In 1984, fourteen coastal cities were opened to outside investment, and in 1985 the same was done for coastal areas extending the economic zones of the Yangtze River Delta, Pearl River Delta, and South Fujian Triangle Delta.

The designated SEZs had previously contributed less than 1 percent of China's GDP, with a labor force engaged primarily in the agricultural sector.

In 1980, Shenzhen's GDP was RMB 270 million; Xiamen's, RMB 375 million; and Shantou's, RMB 889 million. In 1987, the GDP in Xiamen was RMB 640 million, and it was RMB 5.6 billion in Hainan.[2] However, these areas played a limited role in the country's economic development: the provinces of Guangdong, Fujian, and Hainan covered 0.35 percent of the country's land and had a population of 9.79 million—just 0.8 percent of the country's population.[3]

Above all, the zones were located along China's east coast, taking advantage of potential links between Shenzhen and its neighbor Hong Kong, Zhuhai and nearby Macao, Xiamen, and Taiwan, while also providing easier access to foreign markets. Most important, they were positioned to attract capital from the Chinese diaspora. As manufacturing costs were rising in Hong Kong and Taiwan, industry shifted to the mainland in search of low-cost labor and preferential tax rates.

Chinese and foreign investment was sought through preferential tax holidays, low tariffs, preferential fees on land use, access to a cheap but trained labor force, and flexible business management.[4] Furthermore, encouraging foreign investment, capital growth, and technology transfer potentially could help develop not only the SEZs but also the wider domestic Chinese market beyond the zones.[5]

Attraction of investment, accumulation of capital, employment creation, technology transfer, and export success could be used as yardsticks to measure the success of the SEZs.

Infrastructural development became a priority during the initial implementation of the SEZs, as it was required to lure potential foreign investors to an environment conducive to export promotion in areas that until then lacked even basic facilities. FDI remained limited in the first few years, with central and provincial governments funding the majority of the construction in the zones. State funding is estimated to have been 48 percent of fixed capital investment in Shenzhen alone in 1979, decreasing to 24 percent in 1980.[6] The state acted as the primary funding agency of the SEZs in their initial growth stages.

An estimated 90 percent of FDI to Shenzhen originated from Hong Kong, while China's own emerging business sector moved into the SEZs to take advantage of the incentives offered.[7]

The SEZs started to appeal to the market in the early 1990s, and the zones saw an increase in FDI. For example, in Shenzhen FDI increased from $23.4 million in 1980 to more than $672 million in 1993. In addition, joint ventures between the PRC and foreign firms increased dramatically, from $2.5 million in 1980 to more than $670 million in 1993.[8] Shantou and Xiamen became comprehensive zones, as was the case with Shenzhen and Zhuhai, moving beyond their initial mandate to deal primarily with processing exported goods. Thus, the SEZs all came to encompass primary, secondary, and tertiary sector industries mainly geared toward foreign trade.

Employment levels within the zones increased dramatically by an average of 30 percent annually between 1980 and 1993. The state-owned businesses in the SEZ were, however, the greatest source of employment, providing approximately one-third of the employment in all the zones.[9]

The SEZs were very successful in fast-tracking China's commitment to reform. The attraction of diaspora Chinese capital from Hong Kong and Taiwan led to the integration of these economies with the mainland, despite the political separation and differences between the respective governments in Beijing, Hong Kong, and Taipei.

SEZs also served as the model for market liberalization across China. This process of rapid liberalization continues to be introduced across western, southwestern, and northeastern China. The success of the SEZs gave credibility to Deng Xiaoping's reform program and laid the foundation for the commitment to liberal market forces that the PRC continues to pursue to this day.

China's SEZ Model Moves Offshore

It is nearly three decades since the inception of SEZs, and China is currently establishing SEZs in targeted foreign economies. Adapted from China's own domestic experience in running preferential economic zones, the PRC's Ministry of Commerce (MOFCOM) is encouraging Chinese enterprises to "go global" by locating their foreign operations in designated Chinese SEZs in the global economy. This strategy forms an integral part of the PRC's Eleventh Five-Year Plan (2006–2010).

These designated zones are being set up in an array of very diverse countries that include Cambodia, Egypt, Mauritius, Nigeria, Pakistan, Russia, Tanzania, Thailand, and Zambia. China's MOFCOM is coordinating the planning of these zones in conjunction with host governments that have already initiated domestic development zones. Thus, the PRC's strategy is to align the introduction of Chinese SEZs with similar processes occurring in the global economy.

The strategic intent behind these SEZs is to

—offset the risk of protectionist trade practices against "Made in China" products by moving production offshore to foreign economies,

—assist Chinese enterprises to permeate untouched markets and regions in the international economy better,

—minimize the extent of risk for Chinese firms when investing abroad by offering them a degree of state protection through government-to-government agreements, and

—promote industrial competitiveness through clustering of enterprises within common industries.

Combined, these approaches will result in dedicated zones, established in key strategic international economies, that will act as "safe havens" for Chinese capital. Chinese firms located in these foreign zones will enjoy tax and investment incentives, customs duty waivers, work permit approvals for Chinese expatriate labor, and discounted land and services. Chinese business has a tendency to cluster in foreign markets; the SEZ model reinforces this socioeconomic trend, giving it state support.

China's Foreign Commercial Policy in Africa

African governments have welcomed Chinese investment, with energy-endowed economies receiving the largest inflows. The nature of Africa's economies—commodity rich, heavy on state intervention, and characterized by weak commercial laws and shaky public sector institutions—lends itself to rapid market entry, and Chinese firms have been able to gain market traction quickly.

Chinese firms are acquiring mineral assets across the continent. There are now over 800 Chinese state-owned enterprises present in Africa, mostly in the extractive industries. Considering all the merger and acquisition activity among China's leading state-owned firms, this number may have peaked. The same firms that are active on the continent will remain but will begin to integrate their businesses better with their previous Chinese competitors on the continent. This is evident in the construction sector. For example, in December 2005, two of China's largest construction firms, namely China Road and Bridge Corporation and China Harbour Engineering Company, merged to form China Harbour Engineering Co. Ltd. Over time, this integration is likely to improve further the competitive positions of Chinese firms on the continent. However, these firms still face the great challenge of infrastructural shortcomings.

By establishing close commercial ties to African states, China also discourages them from recognizing Taiwan as an independent country. China's assertive commercial drive into Africa signals the end of Taiwan's relations on the continent. Currently, Taiwan only has diplomatic ties to four small African states, and this number could diminish further in coming years.

FOCAC Commitments

To cement further the political, commercial, and cultural relationship between China and Africa, the FOCAC was established in 2000, with the first ministerial meeting taking place in Beijing the same year. Since then there have been two more FOCAC summits—2003 in Addis Ababa and 2006 in Beijing. FOCAC was designed as a vehicle to conceptualize, strategize, and project Chinese foreign policy interests into Africa.

The first head of state conference was held in Beijing in October 2000; it was attended by four African heads of state, ministers from forty-four African countries, and representatives from seventeen international and regional organizations. The conference passed the Beijing Declaration of the Forum on China-Africa Cooperation and the Programme for China-Africa Cooperation in Economic and Social Development.[10]

The 2003 meeting went on to pass the Addis Ababa Action Plan (2004–2006) and consolidate trade relations, with the PRC announcing the Special Preferential Tariff Treatment program, which removed import tariffs on 190 different items from 25 African countries. It was implemented in January 2005 and has resulted in a substantial boost in Chinese-African trade.

The November 2006 Beijing summit adopted the Beijing Action Plan (BAP), which covered 2007 to the end of 2009. This multibillion-dollar development package included a number of commitments from the PRC.[11] Chinese President Hu also pledged at the summit that China would forgive all interest-free loans that matured at the end of 2006 and were owed by the most heavily indebted and underdeveloped African nations.

China's pragmatic policy focus on economic concerns is reflected in the drive behind its diplomatic relations, particularly with African countries. Increased diplomatic activity has laid the foundation for the market entry of Chinese state-owned, as well as private, companies into Africa's economies.[12]

Under the BAP, the PRC also announced its intention to develop between three and five SEZs on the African continent to serve as enclaves for Chinese investment in key African states. There has been no formal announcement as to where these SEZs would be located. Point 3.2.6 of the FOCAC BAP reads: "China is ready to encourage, in the next three years, well-established Chinese companies to set up three to five overseas economic and trade cooperation zones in African countries where conditions permit."[13] The SEZs will complement the China-Africa Development Fund, established out of the same action plan, with a value of $5 billion set aside for this purpose.

Ordinarily, the SEZs are initiated by the host governments, but in mid-2008, the PRC approached various African states to seek investment and labor concessions for the SEZs. Within these SEZs, it is anticipated that China will negotiate bilaterally with African host governments for Chinese companies to operate free from the tax and labor law restrictions that normally apply to commercial operations in other parts of the country, thus offering an improved investment climate. In return, such preferential policies are expected to attract FDI and stimulate regional economic activity. This arrangement leaves Chinese companies operating inside a SEZ with a decided advantage over other market competitors.

China's SEZ Model Transplanted to Africa

China's reform program began in the late 1970s with the creation of SEZs. China embraced globalization almost a generation ahead of most other developing nations. The SEZs were so successful they were rolled out across the country. China's capitalist experiments became the model for the country and have underwritten China's phenomenal growth over the last twenty-five years.

Beijing has strategically selected some key African economies in which it will apply its SEZ model. These designated countries reflect China's commercial priorities in Africa, are geographically dispersed across the continent, and have had long-term and close political relations with the PRC.

Zambian Mining Hub

In February 2007, President Hu paid an official visit to Zambia—the fourth leg of his eight-nation Africa tour.[14] Hu remained in Zambia for three days, his longest stay in any state during his African visit. This was interpreted by many observers as a clear indication of the importance China attributed to its relations with Zambia. During his visit, Hu announced a package of measures designed to further boost bilateral relations, including debt relief, an expansion of Zambian tariff-free exports to China, and the establishment of China's first special economic and trade zone, in the Chambishi mining area.[15] Zambia, in turn, promised to continue to back the one-China policy and to oppose "Taiwanese independence" in any form.[16]

Behind the usual rhetoric, the most important announcement was the establishment of the SEZs in Chambishi, the heart of Zambia's Copperbelt region. The Copperbelt is a commodity-rich, strategic center of the African mining industry. Not only does China seek to secure a supply line of copper from the SEZ, but other commodities are also plentiful in the region, including cobalt, diamonds, tin, and uranium. Increased Chinese investment in the hard extractive industries is to be expected in the medium term.

An initial amount of $800 million in investment credit was committed into which Chinese firms could tap. Firms located in the zone enjoy import duty waivers and tax incentives. According to the terms of the SEZ agreement, the Zambian government has set aside forty-five square kilometers of land for the zone, with construction being carried out by Chinese companies.

The zone's anchor investment will be a $250 million copper smelter. It was forecast by both governments that up to 60,000 jobs—occupied by both local residents and Chinese—would be created in the SEZ. This figure may be exaggerated; the basis upon which it is calculated has not been specified.

There appears to be some policy uncertainty between the PRC and the Zambian government over which firms are permitted to invest in the zone and qualify for the investment incentives. According to the Office of the President of Zambia, all firms—local, foreign, and Chinese—can establish operations in the zone.[17] However, the author was told by China's MOFCOM that investment in the zone was exclusively for Chinese firms—even Sino-Zambian joint ventures are excluded.[18] This lack of clarity over policy from both governments is of concern and needs to be addressed in order to maximize the local developmental benefits that the SEZ will offer to the African private sector.

Indian Ocean Rim Trading Hub

The second official SEZ was announced in July 2007 and will be located in Mauritius. That country provides a strategic destination for Chinese investment: it is well situated on the Indian Ocean rim; it is an offshore financial center with attractive investment laws; Mauritian firms are well integrated into the economies of South Asia; it is a member of the Southern African Development Community and of the Common Market for Eastern and Southern Africa, and thus enjoys preferential market access to the African region; and the country has a sizable ethnic Chinese community that trades with China.

All of these factors have led to the PRC deciding to announce a SEZ in Mauritius. One of the PRC's leading policy banks, the China Development Bank (CDB), will be the main financier of the project and is also set to open an office in Mauritius, its first within Africa.

The $500 million manufacturing zone will host up to 40 Chinese companies, with a forecast of 5,000 jobs for locals and 8,000 for Chinese contractors. Construction on the 210-hectare zone's infrastructure began in late 2007 and is slated for completion within 5 years. Key infrastructural projects include the construction of a fishing port, a dam, a road project from Verdun to Terre Rouge near Port Louis, as well as a new town development at Highlands.

The majority of Chinese firms will have their financial backing from the Chinese provincial economy of Shanxi. One of the zone's main investors, Shanxi Tianli Enterprises Group, is a diversified, state-influenced industrial group with its roots in Shanxi Province. A number of its member companies will set up shop in the SEZ. At present, the first wave of investment in the Chinese SEZs in Africa will come from state-owned firms.

Investment will be in manufacturing, with specific sectors targeted including light industrial goods, medicine production, textiles, and electrical products. It is also forecast that exports from the zones will earn the Mauritian fisc more than $200 million a year. Manufacturing firms in the zone will enjoy import duty waivers for raw material inputs. The SEZ will constitute the largest investment in the country.

According to Mauritian Prime Minister Navinchandra Ramgoolam, through Mauritius, China will gain a "springboard for entry into Africa." The increased economic vulnerability of the Mauritian economy due to its general lack of natural resources and the pending end to the preferential sugar supply quotas to the EU has shifted the focus of the Mauritian government toward China to attract value-added manufacturing investments. "This agreement is of major significance to Mauritius as it marks China's commitment towards Mauritius in this period of transition" said Ramgoolam.[19]

Another important outcome from this arrangement is an increase in China's strategic presence on the Indian Ocean rim. Since Mauritius traditionally falls within India's political and commercial sphere of influence, the Indian government has paid particular attention to the Chinese SEZ announcement.

As the SEZs mature—and depending on their operational success—private Chinese firms will be motivated to enter them. As of 2008, China's commercial engagement in Africa has been politically led; Chinese investments or project participation have been carried out either by state-owned firms or the microenterprises of Chinese migrant entrepreneurs. As the Mauritian SEZ becomes more entrenched and export oriented, China's growing body of private firms will be attracted to the zone since it will provide a convenient "Chinese managed zone" for manufacturing businesses and its offshore location would circumvent acts of trade protectionism against Chinese products. Thus, the PRC's strategy of establishing international manufacturing SEZs takes into consideration the market reality of a hostile trading environment.

Tanzanian SEZ: A Logistics Hub

Following the commitment made by the PRC to establish three to five SEZs in Africa before the next FOCAC summit in late 2009, the Chinese government has formally announced two such zones in countries that are not only strategically and commercially important but also have enjoyed a long relationship of political trust with the People's Republic. One is the aforementioned Zambian SEZ. Beijing continues to hold former Zambian President Kenneth Kaunda in high regard. During his twenty-seven years in the presidency (1964–1991), Kaunda cemented a close political relationship with a number of generations of China's leadership including Mao Zedong, Zhou Enlai, and Deng Xiaoping. He visited China four times as president of Zambia.

The same long relationship was built between the PRC and Tanzania. Julius Nyerere visited China as president of Tanzania five times from 1964 to 1985 and on eight occasions as chairman of the South Commission between 1987 and 1997. Like Kaunda, Nyerere had a special relationship with China, and this contributed to China constructing the Tanzania-Zambia Railway (Tanzam Railway) in the 1970s.

Although not yet confirmed, it is most likely that the next formal SEZ will be established in Dar es Salaam. A senior delegation from the Chinese MOF-COM visited Dar es Salaam in 2007 to negotiate with the Tanzanian government. Negotiations between the two governments were at an advanced stage in mid-2008. China's potential establishment of a SEZ in Tanzania is not a unilateral initiative. The Tanzanian government has initiated its own SEZ in Dar es Salaam, one of thirty such SEZs to be set up across the country by 2020. The creation of designated preferential economic zones is designed to help Tanzania meet developmental objectives as set out under the National Development Vision 2025. Ironically, assistance for these forthcoming preferential zones has been provided by Japan. China's mining-focused SEZ in Chambishi is linked to Dar es Salaam via the Tanzam Railway. Not only is the railway the most important Chinese project in Zambia and Tanzania, but it is also one of the most prominent Chinese projects in Africa and is China's largest foreign aid project as of 2008. The 1,860-kilometer railroad runs from the Tanzanian capital of Dar es Salaam to Kapiri Mposhi in Zambia.

The origin of the initial project lay with Kaunda, who approached Nyerere, and together they first approached Britain and the United States for assistance to build the railway in 1970, only to be turned down. Next they approached the Soviet Union, which also declined to assist. Finally, China agreed to fund the project.[20] Construction began in 1970, and the railway was commissioned in July 1976. The project was financed through an interest-free loan of $500 million provided by China. China has continued to provide a series of interest-free loans and technical assistance to aid in the management and maintenance of the railway. Contrary to a claim by Zambian President Levy Mwanawasa on his return from FOCAC—that he had secured a debt cancellation in connection with the railway—a well-informed Zambian government official explained that the government must still repay the debt for Tanzam, which was a commercial loan from China to Zambia and is not included in the debt cancellation.[21]

The railway line is of high strategic importance to China, Zambia, and the East African region, and new investments can be expected to rehabilitate the railway line, which has fallen into a state of disrepair. In 2006, the Tanzanian Presidential Parastatal Sector Reform Commission and the Zambia Privatization Agency began discussions on the privatization of the jointly owned railway, which needs $25 million for locomotive repairs alone. Chinese investors are expected to receive priority in bids on a turn-around strategy; however, the process is particularly slow, and the successful contender had, by mid-2008, not been announced.[22]

The Chinese have already invested in the difficult Dar es Salaam port and in the construction of a customs building. Greater investment in the capacity of the port can be expected. The Dar es Salaam SEZ will be a logistics hub for commodities mined on the Copperbelt, and some local beneficiation will also take place. It is also envisioned that the SEZ will serve as a Chinese assembly and manufacturing hub for eastern Africa.

Moreover, since Beijing's announcement that it will establish two of its SEZs in Zambia and Mauritius, there has been rising competition among a number of African states to attract Chinese investment. Tanzania is facing competition from Liberia, Nigeria, and Cape Verde, which are courting Beijing to host the remaining SEZs. But taking into consideration the close historical relationship between China and Tanzania, it is unlikely that the Chinese will choose one of those states over Tanzania.

Nigeria as a Gateway to West Africa

With the recent strong flow of Chinese capital investment into Nigeria, a Chinese-initiated SEZ in Nigeria is also likely. Nigeria and South Africa act as the bookends of the sub-Saharan economy, with a combined population of almost 200 million people. Nigeria, the major economy in West Africa, is forecast by Goldman Sachs to become one of the world's eleven largest economies by 2050.[23]

Nigeria is a growing investment destination for Chinese companies. One of the largest foreign investments in the international arena as of 2008 is in a Nigerian energy concession, amounting to $2.27 billion. According to China's MOFCOM, the turnover of completed engineering contracts by Chinese companies in Nigeria reached $3.68 billion, and the volume of completed labor service cooperation contracts was $160 million by the end of 2006. Chinese firms have also committed over $2 billion to rehabilitate Nigeria's infrastructure.

More recently, the CDB indicated its intention to acquire a strategic equity stake in the United Bank for Africa (UBA), one of Nigeria's top four banks. According to Tony Elumelu, UBA's CEO, the agreement will give UBA access to "almost unlimited capital to plough into projects in energy and infrastructure."[24]

If one compares the CDB acquisition with the recent acquisition by the Industrial and Commercial Bank of China of a 20 percent stake in South Africa's Standard Bank, it is apparent that major Chinese banks are seeking to acquire minority, but strategic, stakes in African banking assets. However, the move by the CDB—a policy bank that is more directed by the government—to buy into UBA is a political decision, quite different from the Industrial and Commercial Bank's purchase of a minority stake in Standard Bank, which was an apolitical investment decision. Nigerian banks are poised for growth from their own domestic underserviced retail banking sector, as well as from the rapidly increasing infrastructural spending in the country. The CDB will buy into this growth.

The Nigerian SEZ will be a manufacturing and assembly operation for Chinese firms. In 2007, the establishment of a $500 million free trade zone in Nigeria's Ogun State was announced. A Memorandum of Understanding was signed between Chinese state-owned firm Guangdong Xinguang International Group, Guangdong Xinguang International China-Africa Investment Limited, UBA, First Bank, and the government of Ogun State.

When completed, the zone will house approximately 100 Chinese firms. Sun Jianxiong, the vice president of Guangdong Xinguang International Group, stated that Nigeria was chosen to host one of the official SEZs due to its large domestic market and accessibility to the West African and European marketplaces.[25] The announcement was made at the fifth Sino-Nigeria Business and Investment Forum in Guangzhou. The CDB and UBA will cofinance the SEZ project.

Manufacturing Hub in Egypt

In 2007, it was reported by both the Chinese and Egyptian press that a Chinese industrial zone was to be established in Egypt. Liao Xiaoqi, China's vice minister for commerce, announced the zone in late October. The twenty-square-kilometer zone will be located near Suez and will be expanded in phases over the next ten years.

Egypt's trade minister, Rachid Mohamed Rachid, has said that the zone aims to attract up to $2.5 billion in FDI. It will be developed and managed by the Chinese organization Tianjin Economic-Technological Development Area.[26] The Egyptian agency responsible for managing the zone is the General Authority of Investment and Free Zones, whose chairman, Assem Ragab, has stated that the first phase of the investment will attract 100 Chinese firms with an investment capital of $100 million.[27]

There are a number of factors that led the PRC to target Egypt as a strategic recipient of a SEZ:

—Egypt is one of Africa's largest economies and is linked to regional economies in the Middle East, as well as the EU. Therefore the zone will serve as a regional export hub.

—China and Egypt have a long-term political relationship, with Egypt being the first African state to establish diplomatic relations with the PRC in 1955. A bond of long-term trust exists between the two governments.

—Cairo is an influential regional player in Africa, more specifically in the Maghreb region.

—The Egyptian government is stable, and the investment environment for Chinese firms is predictable.

—Cairo is set to host and chair the next FOCAC heads of state summit in November 2009. International attention will then focus on Sino-Egyptian ties.

Setting up shop in the Suez Zone will be manufacturers of textiles, chemicals, gas and oil pipelines, and electronics and automotive components. All Chinese investment in the SEZ will be in conjunction with a local joint-venture partner, and all manufactured products will be for the export market only.

There has been some local criticism that the zone will only add to the competition that Egyptian and African manufacturers are already facing.[28] But Rachid, who seeks a "win-win" outcome, disagrees: "These are going to be Egyptian companies. Fine, they are going to be owned by Chinese companies, but they are going to be Egyptian factories, they are going to have to play by Egyptian rules. We prefer that than having shipments of goods coming from China."[29]

As of mid-2008, there were approximately 435 Chinese firms in Egypt, with a total investment of roughly $300 million. China is forecast to become Egypt's largest trading partner in the medium term, replacing the United States. This reflects a trend observed in most African economies, and the SEZ will accelerate this process.

To offset criticism of having provided too many concessions to Chinese investors, the Egyptian government has secured over a seven-year period a $200 million low-interest loan facility (at a maximum 2 percent cost) for Egyptian manufacturers to utilize when buying capital equipment from China. Egyptian law also prevents foreign companies from employing foreign workers beyond 10 percent of their payroll.

The Egyptian SEZ will be the strategic zone for Chinese business in North Africa. Rolled out under China's FOCAC commitments, the Suez SEZ will target the North African, Middle Eastern, and EU markets. In similar fashion to the Mauritian SEZ, it will concentrate on manufacturing for export. However, considering the microscale of investments by Chinese firms in the Egyptian SEZ, averaging $1 million per company, that Zone's impact may not be significant.

Bisecting the Continent

While the Tanzam line links Zambia to the east coast, the Benguela line links the Copperbelt—Zambia and the Democratic Republic of the Congo (the DRC)—to the west coast. Starting at Luanshya in Zambia and ending at the Angolan port of Lobito, that rail line is also being reconstructed by Chinese firms accessing preferential financing from China's banks. Together, the Tanzam and Benguela lines bisect sub-Saharan Africa. The strategic intent of the construction of these transportation corridors is to reduce supply side risk to Chinese mining firms engaging in resource extraction. The rail links, undergoing renovation at different stages, are designed to facilitate the movement of resources from the mining regions in Zambia and the DRC, in particular from the mining-focused SEZ in Chambishi.

The rehabilitation of these two railway lines will—for the first time—create a functioning east-west infrastructural corridor across the subcontinent. No longer dependent upon South African rail links, the transportation of commodities will be diverted from southern Africa. This fact could have repercussions for South African ports such as Richards Bay, which handles the bulk of commodities exports from the southern African region.

The reconstruction of the Tanzam corridor is thus a strategic component of China's SEZ strategy. Depending upon the success of the initial five Chinese

SEZs on the continent, there may be a proliferation of other Chinese-initiated SEZs announced at the upcoming FOCAC summit in 2009. This aggrandizement could create a new network of Chinese-funded and -constructed corridors linking resources in the hinterland to the coast, in keeping with the extractive intent of China's infrastructural expansion in Africa.

It is expected that the Chinese will also invest in Lobito's port in Angola, although it is more convenient to ship commodities out of Dar es Salaam than via Africa's west coast, which is far more energy focused. Angola is already receiving approximately $4.4 billion in funding from China's Eximbank to develop its infrastructure.

China's Grand Plan for Africa

Even Africa's numerous former colonial powers did not have the commitment to invest so substantially in the continent's infrastructure. China's rapid economic development, growing manufacturing capacity, population size, and massive resultant demand have led the PRC to craft a grand plan for Africa.

What are the strategic drivers of China's foray into Africa?

China needs commodity and energy assets. Without securing a predictable international supply chain of oil and key metals, China's economic growth will be undermined. With the possible exception of Iran, China is geostrategically excluded from the Middle East. The U.S. invasion of Iraq resulted in Beijing increasing its acquisition of African energy reserves. This is evident in Angola, the Sudan, and Nigeria, where Chinese national oil corporations have acquired a foothold in the energy sectors. Africa is thus at the center of China's movement into the international extractive industry economies.

The main strategic driver of Chinese ventures into Africa is Beijing's long-term strategy to remove its economy from international commodity markets. By acquiring commodity assets at source, negotiating prices with the recipient (African) government, and securing long-term supply contracts, China seeks to establish parallel markets that are removed from international commodity markets where prices are set in either London or New York.

The mining majors—Anglo American, BHP Billiton, Rio Tinto, and Companhia Vale do Rio Doce—will ultimately be selling to the traditional markets but will find new competition from state-owned Chinese trading firms. The market as we know it—an economic legacy of European colonialism in Africa—will be disrupted by Chinese state-owned corporate players. Its state-owned banking sector allows the Chinese state to direct capital and purchase international resource assets, employing a risk model that is different from that of private entities. Leveraging the state's resources is a key feature of Chinese state-owned enterprises' market entry into Africa's extractive industry. The long-term success of this strategy is dependent upon China building and maintaining close ties to African countries.

China's SEZ strategy is lifted from its own economic reform experience. Indeed, the Chinese learned from the European colonialists, who obtained free trade concessions in China in the nineteenth century. These capitalist enclaves became the trading hubs of the region and to this day are still the wealthiest cities in China—Hong Kong, Guangzhou, Macao, and Shanghai.

As China establishes export processing zones in Africa, it will earn revenue from the zones' increased exports and generate employment—crucial to offset criticism from civil society and political opposition groups that may be opposed to offering concessions to foreign investors. This offset is particularly relevant where Chinese investments have contended with stereotypes of poor governance and political motivation in relation to their overseas investments. Chinese MOFCOM officials may also have to be more willing to seek out local labor rather than rely on expatriate labor.

It is likely that some degree of criticism may emanate from civil society groups against the rollout of the SEZs as the terms of the negotiations have hardly been shared publicly by either the PRC or respective African governments. Objections persist despite the fact that word of the SEZs has generated a great deal of private sector interest in the African economies, including among South African corporations.

The economic stimuli that will be created by the SEZs offer an opportunity for African companies to partner with Chinese firms. It is imperative, however, that the government-to-government agreements provide for inclusion of local African private sectors through Sino-African joint ventures. Such provisions will maximize the developmental impact of the zones and also contribute to a positive public perception of Chinese capital on the ground.

The SEZs—if successful—may also encourage further investment liberalization by the host governments to attract foreign capital. Coupled with better infrastructure, the SEZs may improve the overall investment environment in the host country. Chinese "first mover" capital in the dedicated zones may well attract other foreign investors. China's commercial positivism toward African economies in general has already had the effect of motivating foreign investment in Africa across an array of sectors, particularly the extractive one.

Chinese investment in the SEZs is mostly in the manufacturing sector. This arrangement counters accusations that China's intentions are only extractive in nature, focusing on the energy and mining sectors. Investment in African manufacturing industries will be the next wave of Chinese investment on the continent. Initially, this approach will be centered on the SEZs, but it will expand to include the surrounding economy, market conditions allowing.

Beijing envisions that these SEZs, serving as hubs for Chinese economic activity in Africa, will offer a package of favorable incentives for Chinese businesses and serve to reduce investment risk on the continent, while at the same time becoming the new growth nodes of the African economy.

Notes

1. Gao Shangquan and Chi Fulin (eds.), *New Progress in China's Special Economic Zones* (Beijing, 1997), 3.

2. Ibid., 10.

3. Ibid., 3.

4. Yehua Dennis Wei and Chi Kin Leung, "Development Zones, Foreign Investment, and Global City Formation in Shanghai," *Growth and Change*, XXXVI (2005), 18.

5. Tatsuyuki Ota, "The Role of Special Economic Zones in China's Economic Development as Compared with Asian Export Processing Zones: 1979–1995," *Asia in Extenso* (2003), available at www.iae.univ-poitiers.fr/EURO-ASIE/Docs/Asia-in-Extenso-Ota-mars2003.pdf (accessed 8 February 2008).

6. Wei Ge, "Special Economic Zones and the Opening of the Chinese Economy: Some Lessons for Economic Liberalization," *World Development*, XXVII (1999), 1270.

7. Ota, "Role of Special Economic Zones," 19.

8. Ge, "Special Economic Zones," 1272.

9. Ibid., 1277.

10. See "Beijing Declaration of the Forum on China-Africa Co-operation (Draft)" (17 November 2000), available at http://test.fmprc.gov.cn/eng/wjdt/2649/t15775.htm (accessed 24 April 2008); "Programme for China-Africa Cooperation in Economic and Social Development," available at www.focac.org/eng/wjjh/hywj/t157834.htm (accessed 24 April 2008).

11. The Beijing Action Plan commitments include $3 billion in preferential loans and $2 billion in preferential buyer's credits over the next three years; the doubling of China's 2006 aid assistance by 2009; initiating a China-Africa development fund that will reach $5 billion to fund Chinese companies investing in Africa; training of 15,000 African professionals; establishment of 10 agricultural technology demonstration centers on the continent; building 30 hospitals and providing $37.5 million in grants to help fight malaria; dispatching 100 senior agricultural experts; and building 100 rural schools and increasing the number of Chinese government scholarships for Africans to study in China from 2,000 to 4,000 by 2009. See "Address by Hu Jintao at the Opening Ceremony of the Beijing Summit of the Forum on China-Africa Cooperation" (4 November 2006), available at http://english.focacsummit.org/2006-11/04/content_4978.htm (accessed 24 April 2008).

12. For case studies of this behavior in six African economies, see Christopher Burke, Lucy Corkin, and Nastasya Tay, *China's Engagement of Africa: Preliminary Scoping of African Case Studies* (Stellenbosch, 2007).

13. See "Beijing Declaration of the Forum on China-Africa Co-operation (Draft)" (17 November 2000).

14. The other countries include Cameroon, Liberia, the Sudan, Namibia, South Africa, Mozambique, and the Seychelles.

15. Martyn Davies and others, *How China Delivers Development Assistance to Africa* (Stellenbosch, 2008).

16. Ibid.

17. Interview between the author and Situmbeko Musokotwane, economic adviser to the president, Office of the President, Government of Zambia (14 June 2007).

18. Interview between the author and Chai Zhi Jing, director, Africa Division, Ministry of Commerce, People's Republic of China (22 June 2007).

19. In mid-July 2007, Prime Minister Ramgoolam led an official mission and business delegation to China to motivate Chinese investment for the island economy. Cities visited include Beijing, Shanghai, and Qingdao. See "Mauritius: Cheap Chinese Loans," *Africa Research Bulletin: Economic, Financial and Technical Series*, XLIV (2007), available at www.blackwell-synergy.com/doi/full/10.1111/j.1467-6346.2007.01108.x?cookieSet=1 (accessed 19 May 2008).

20. Interview between President Kenneth Kaunda and Chris Burke, research fellow, Centre for Chinese Studies, Stellenbosch University (16 August 2006).

21. "Zambia-China Deals on DANWEI Website," *People's Daily* (19 November 2006); interview between Chris Burke, research fellow, Centre for Chinese Studies, Stellenbosch University, and a government official, Lusaka, Zambia (16 May 2007).

22. Davies and others, *How China Delivers*, 53.

23. Goldman Sachs's N-11 (Next-Eleven) report provides a list of the top eleven emerging economies in terms of investment potential and economic growth. See Jim O'Neill and others, "How Solid Are the BRICs?" Global Economics Paper 134 (1 December 2005).

24. Matthew Green, "Nigeria Banks Seek Bigger Stage," *Financial Times* (30 October 2007), available at http://us.ft.com/ftgateway/superpage.ft?news_id=fto10302007 1819291105&page=2 (accessed 20 May 2008).

25. *This Day* (21 September 2007).

26. Andrew England, "Egypt and China in Investment Deal," *Financial Times* (30 October 2007), available at http://us.ft.com/ftgateway/superpage.ft?news_id=fto 103020071819291106 (accessed 20 May 2008).

27. Liu Baijia, "Chinese SEZ Likely in Egypt," *People's Daily* (14 November 2007), available at www.chinadaily.com.cn/bizchina/2007-11/14/content_6253381.htm (accessed 20 May 2008).

28. England, "Egypt and China."

29. Ibid.

DAVID H. SHINN

8

Military and Security Relations: China, Africa, and the Rest of the World

Chinese military and security relations with Africa have progressed from support for independence and revolutionary movements in the 1960s and 1970s to a more pragmatic relationship in the 1990s and the first decade of the twenty-first century. China's national security interests focus overwhelmingly on its periphery: South Asia, Southeast Asia, Central Asia, West Asia (including the Middle East), Russia, Japan, Mongolia, and the Koreas. China is also much concerned about the ability of the United States and Europe to project military and economic power into Asia. Africa and Latin America, however, are not a critical part of China's security policy. Africa is a security issue only in terms of China's effort to secure the energy, mineral, and timber resources used to fuel its economy. These needs translate into a strategy that encourages a desire to strengthen stability in African countries that sell or have the potential to sell China significant quantities of raw materials. Looking to the future, China may conclude that it needs a blue-water navy that no longer relies on the United States to protect the sea lanes from Africa and the Middle East that are used to transport essential imports.

In the case of those African countries where China already has a major interest in the extraction of raw materials, China supports the political status quo and existing governments. These countries include Angola (oil), the Sudan (oil), Congo-Brazzaville (oil, timber, and base metals), Equatorial Guinea (oil and timber), Libya (oil), Gabon (timber, iron ore, and manganese), Zambia (copper and base metals), Nigeria (oil), South Africa (iron ore, diamonds, base metals, platinum, manganese, copper, and aluminum), Ghana (manganese), Namibia (copper), the Democratic Republic of the

Congo (base metals), and Cameroon (timber).[1] Algeria, Chad, and Maurita-nia, which produce oil, may soon join this group. African countries that export raw materials to China are often high on Beijing's list of countries with which it has close security relationships.

Military Support to African Liberation Movements

There is a long history of Chinese military transfers to, exchanges with, and training for countries and organizations in Africa. It began with assistance and training for African liberation groups dating from the late 1950s. Some of these regimes, such as Robert Mugabe's Zimbabwe African National Union (ZANU), are still in power. China recognized Algeria's National Liberation Front (FLN) provisional government in 1958 and immediately began fur-nishing it with small arms. It provided training for rebels from Guinea-Bissau in 1960. As the Sino-Soviet split developed and the Soviets supported South Africa's African National Congress (ANC), China turned to the Pan-Africanist Congress. When the ANC prevailed, China managed to normalize relations with it in the early 1980s and promised military aid beginning in 1984. China developed considerable goodwill with those governments that remained in power and more generally in Africa through its early support of liberation movements.

China obtained agreements from Tanzania, Ghana, and Congo-Brazzaville to train freedom fighters on their territory. The training in Tanzania focused on Eduardo Mondlane's Mozambique Liberation Front (FRELIMO), whose fighters received free weapons from China and adopted Chinese tactics of guerrilla warfare. In the early 1960s, FRELIMO began sending delegations to China. ZANU forces also received Chinese training in Tanzania while China assisted the Revolutionary Committee of Mozambique in Zambia. In Ghana, Chinese arms experts trained nationalists from the Portuguese territories; the first group of five Chinese experts in guerrilla warfare arrived there in 1964. The Chinese instructors remained until Ghana experienced a coup early in 1966, which ended the program.[2] China also coordinated its military training for liberation groups with the Organization of African Unity, reportedly pro-viding the organization's liberation committee with 75 percent of all the mil-itary aid that it received from countries outside Africa during 1971 and 1972.[3] China often provided military assistance to whatever liberation group was not being aided by the Soviet Union. China even encouraged dissenters to break away from groups supported by the Soviet Union and to form their own organizations.[4]

Some of China's early military support for African revolutionary movements backfired. Although largely forgotten, China trained and supplied arms to a number of losing opposition and revolutionary groups in Africa. China initially supported the Popular Movement for the Liberation of Angola (MPLA), which ultimately formed Angola's government. As the MPLA strengthened its ties to the Soviet Union, however, China shifted its military assistance in the late 1960s to the National Union for the Total Independence of Angola (UNITA). Jonas Savimbi, UNITA's leader, received training in China. By 1973 China had focused its support on the National Front for the Liberation of Angola (FNLA) and its leader, Holden Roberto. In 1974, Beijing sent its first group of 112 Chinese instructors to Zaire to train the FNLA. While Moscow increased its support to the MPLA, China resumed modest assistance to UNITA. South African intervention in the Angolan civil war on the side of the FNLA-UNITA forces embarrassed China. More embarrassment followed when the Soviet-sponsored MPLA was victorious. The MPLA declared independence in 1975. Having failed to pick the wining team in Angola, China established diplomatic ties to the MPLA government in 1982.[5]

China regarded the Congo (then called Congo-Léopoldville and its capital, Léopoldville, now known as Kinshasa) as an important revolutionary target. In 1961, China recognized the radical government led by Antoine Gizenga based in Stanleyville, now Kisangani.[6] At the urging of the Soviets, Gizenga joined the more moderate government of Cyrille Adoula, leaving the Chinese high and dry. China continued to support armed opposition against the government in Léopoldville, providing assistance to Pierre Mulele, a former education minister in the Patrice Lumumba government, and Gaston Soumialot, a former minister of justice for Kivu Province in the Gizenga government. China quietly offered guerrilla training, including five months for Mulele, and weapons to those forces operating in the eastern Congo. Stanleyville fell to Congolese government forces late in 1964, and the Chinese-supported insurgent leaders fled to the Sudan.[7] Although China's agents failed to seize power, China managed to normalize relations in 1972 with Zaire (now the Democratic Republic of the Congo) and eventually developed a strong military relationship with its leaders.

Military Assistance in the 1960s and 1970s

China regarded Africa as an important part of its bid for international legitimacy and as part of the global struggle against Western imperialism and Soviet hegemony. In the early 1960s, China provided modest quantities of arms and some training to Zanzibar, Tanganyika, Congo-Brazzaville, rebels in the eastern Congo, Tutsis during the Rwanda-Burundi conflict, the FLN in Algeria, and insurgent nationalists in Niger and Cameroon.[8] Disappointed by the 1964 mutiny of the British-trained army in Tanganyika, President Julius Nyerere invited China to rebuild the defense forces, which it did from the ground up, including the provision of weapons.[9] Between 1967 and 1971, China supplied Africa (excluding Egypt) with 245 major weapons systems: 50 tanks and self-propelled guns, 160 artillery pieces, 20 armored personnel carriers, and 15 small naval combatants. This was, however, only about 5 percent of Africa's major weapons imports.[10]

According to the U.S. Arms Control and Disarmament Agency, Africa acquired only $42 million worth of Chinese arms from 1961 to 1971. This placed China seventh as an arms supplier to Africa (excluding Egypt) after the Soviet Union, France, the United States, Britain, West Germany, and Czechoslovakia. Tanzania received 83 percent of this total, while Algeria, Congo-Brazzaville, and Guinea received modest amounts. This represented only about 2.4 percent of Africa's military acquisitions. Deliveries by Moscow far exceeded those from Beijing. Only in Tanzania did Chinese arms deliveries surpass those of all other suppliers. They accounted for 65 percent of total Chinese deliveries, or more than four times the value of the next most important source—Canada. China replaced Canada in 1970 as Tanzania's major supplier of military assistance. During the early 1970s, China provided twenty T-59 medium and fourteen T-62 tanks, ten P6 torpedo boats and Swatow gunboats, and twelve MiG-17 fighters. It built a naval base at Dar es Salaam and a military airfield at Ngerengere outside the capital. Chinese instructors trained the Tanzanian army, navy, and air force.[11]

With experience, Chinese military cooperation avoided egregious mistakes, and China's assistance became a significant positive aspect of its diplomacy. From 1967 to 1976, China transferred $142 million in arms to Africa. China's share of the African arms market was about 2.8 percent. Congo-Brazzaville ($10 million), Tanzania ($75 million), and Zaire ($21 million) were the major recipients of Chinese arms transfers during this period. Cameroon, Egypt, Guinea, the Sudan, Tunisia, and Zambia each obtained an estimated $5 million in arms while Burundi, the Gambia, Malawi, Mali, Mozambique, and Rwanda each received about $1 million in arms.[12] Between 1955 and 1976, an estimated 2,675 African military personnel were trained in China. Tanzania headed the list with 1,025, followed by Congo-Brazzaville with 425; Guinea, 350; the Sudan, 200; Sierra Leone, 150; Cameroon, 125; Zaire, 75; Mali, Mozambique, Togo, and Zambia, about 50 each; and Algeria and Somalia, 25 each.[13]

Chinese arms transfers to Africa from 1966 to 1977 included patrol boats, tanks, and MiG-17s, -19s, and -21s to Tanzania; MiG-17s and tanks to the Sudan; tanks to Zaire; and gunboats to Cameroon, Congo-Brazzaville, Equatorial Guinea, Guinea, and Tunisia. In 1977 Beijing delivered small arms, ammunition, and antiaircraft guns to Botswana after Western states refused to arm Botswana's defense force. China airlifted military equipment and field artillery to Zaire during the 1977 Shaba emergency.[14] Beijing also put itself in a potentially compromising position by arming anti-MPLA forces in Angola in the 1970s, arming Zaire against anti-Mobutu invaders from Angola in 1977–1978, and arming Somalia against Ethiopia after 1978.[15]

Military Assistance in the 1980s

By the late 1970s, there was a fundamental shift in China's approach to arms transfers. Beijing began to focus its arms sales on new customers such as Bangladesh, Burma, Iran, Iraq, and Thailand. Sales to African countries, other than Egypt, dropped significantly. China agreed in 1982 to provide Egypt with fighter aircraft.[16] The first Romeo-class submarines that China sold to Egypt arrived in 1984 with worn-out engines.[17] Most of the weapons China transferred up to this point were relatively low-tech, consisting primarily of Chinese copies of Soviet systems from the1950s and 1960s. The T-59 tank was the Chinese version of the Soviet T-54. F-6 and F-7 fighter jets were Chinese versions of the MiG-19 and MiG-21. The Silkworm antiship missile was an improved version of the Soviet 1950s-era P-15 Styx.[18]

During the 1980s, Egypt received eighty F-7 fighters, ninety-six Hai Ying-2 surface-to-surface missiles, seven Hainan-class and six Huangfen fast attack craft, three Jianghu-class frigates, and six Romeo-class submarines. China transferred twenty T-55 armored personnel carriers to Guinea-Bissau. Zimbabwe received fifteen F-6 fighters, fifty-two F-7 fighters, thirty-five T-59 tanks, and twenty T-60 light tanks. China also began training Zimbabwean pilots in the 1980s.[19] China maintained Zaire's Chinese-built T-62 medium battle tanks and other armored vehicles and maintained the navy's Chinese-built patrol craft during the 1980s.[20] The first Chinese arms sales to the Sudan began in the late 1980s and included financing from Iran.[21]

Military Assistance in the 1990s

Africa was not a major recipient of Chinese arms in the 1990s, although transfers did increase from the 1980s. A great attraction of China's equipment was its low price. Chinese weapons reputedly were simple to operate and maintain; they were also similar to Soviet-Russian systems, which formed the basis of many African countries' arsenals. Furthermore, China was one of the few available sources of arms for states like the Sudan and Zimbabwe. Yet, China's arms' quality was generally inferior to alternative weapon suppliers. In some cases, China had a significant stock of old weapons of which it hoped to dispose, and some of this stockpile ended up in Africa.[22]

The U.S. State Department recorded $1.3 billion in Chinese weapons deliveries and agreements to Africa from 1989 through 1999. Of this total, $200 million went to North Africa, $600 million to Central Africa, and $500 million to southern Africa. Deliveries to North Africa included 10 surface naval combatants and 100 antiship missiles; deliveries to Central Africa consisted of 100 tanks, 1,270 artillery pieces, 40 armored personnel carriers, 13 surface naval combatants, 20 supersonic combat aircraft, 30 other military aircraft, and 30 surface-to-air missiles; and deliveries to Southern Africa included 40 tanks, 2 surface naval combatants, and 20 supersonic combat aircraft. China, though, was far from the most important arms supplier to Africa during the 1990s. From 1989 through 1999, U.S. military transfers to and agreements with Africa totaled $2 billion (mainly to Egypt); U.S.S.R.-Russia transfers and agreements totaled $7.6 billion.[23]

The Congressional Research Service tracks conventional arms transfers to developing nations. It includes North African nations in its Near East category. According to the Congressional Research Service, China provided 5.54 percent ($200 million) of total deliveries by value to sub-Saharan Africa from 1992 to 1995. This percentage jumped to 15.56 percent ($500 million) during 1996–1999. The United States provided less than 4 percent of deliveries to sub-Saharan Africa during both periods. Russia was the most important source of weapons to sub-Saharan Africa, accounting for almost 14 percent ($500 million) in 1992–1995 and 25 percent ($800 million) in 1996–1999.[24]

It is difficult to allocate these regional arms transfer figures to individual countries. The following military cooperation is indicative rather than complete. Chinese advisers trained the 41st Commando Brigade, a rapid intervention unit in Kisangani. In the 1990s, China sold 6 F-7M Airguard fighters; 2 Y-8 transport aircraft; 50 Z-6 troop-carrying helicopters, military trucks, 122 mm towed howitzers, T-59 tanks, 37mm anti-aircraft guns; 100 1,000-pound high-altitude bombs; and 100 antipersonnel and antitank mines to the Sudan. China also had a role in building three arms factories outside Khartoum, and a Chinese company constructed an arms factory in central Uganda in 1995. During the Ethiopian-Eritrean war of 1998–2000, China sold large quantities of military equipment to both sides; Ethiopia received ammunition, mortars, and vehicles.[25]

China transferred one Y-12 transport aircraft to Zimbabwe, six to Kenya, three to Mauritania, two to Namibia, and three to Zambia; it also transferred four Hainan-class patrol craft to Algeria and one patrol craft to Sierra Leone. Zimbabwean pilots were trained on the Chinese F-7, and from 1996 through 1998, ninety officers received training in various specialties in China. Beijing supplied large shipments of small arms to Laurent Kabila in the Congo in the late 1990s. China delivered $3 million in small arms to Algeria in 1996–1998, and $14 million to Morocco in 1998. During the 1990s, it supplied a modest amount of small arms to Cameroon, Côte d'Ivoire, the Democratic Republic of the Congo, Djibouti, Egypt, Gabon, Guinea, Madagascar, Niger, Nigeria, Rwanda, South Africa, Tanzania, Tunisia, Uganda, and Zambia. China delivered $100 million in arms to Algeria during 1996–1999.[26]

South Africa, which has its own arms export industry, is a special case. It not only purchased a modest quantity of Chinese arms in the 1990s, but in 1996–1997, South Africa sold almost $2 million in nonsensitive military equipment to China.[27] African countries also expanded their military attaché presence in Beijing during the 1990s. In 1988, only nine African countries had military attachés at their embassies in Beijing; by 1998 thirteen African countries had resident military attachés.[28]

Military Assistance in the Twenty-first Century

Chinese military cooperation with Africa in the twenty-first century suggests a loose correlation with countries that are important suppliers of energy and raw materials. The leading African exporters of oil to China in 2006 were Angola, Congo-Brazzaville, Equatorial Guinea, the Sudan, and Libya. South Africa, Gabon, and Zambia were important exporters of minerals and base metals. China's military assistance to Africa is not, however, confined to countries that provide it with raw materials. China offers at least modest quantities of military assistance or training to nearly every African country with which it has diplomatic relations. The country with which it has maintained one of the longest and strongest military connections—Tanzania—falls into this category. Dar es Salaam does provide the port and rail terminus for copper exports from Zambia, but Tanzania exports few natural resources to China. Libya, on the other hand, now a significant oil exporter to China, seems to have had no military links to Beijing. This result may be due to a continuing Libyan-Taiwanese trade connection and reports, denied by Taipei, that Taiwan was selling military equipment to Libya.[29]

China's January 2006 African policy document stated that China would promote high-level military exchanges and actively carry out military-related technological exchanges and cooperation. It added that China would help train African military personnel and support defense and army building in African countries for their own security. Finally, the document stated that China would support African Union and UN peacekeeping operations in Africa.[30] After the 2006 Forum on China-Africa Cooperation (FOCAC) summit in Beijing, forty-eight African countries and China issued a declaration that called for a new "strategic partnership" between China and Africa. The signatories agreed to enhance international cooperation to address global security threats and nontraditional security challenges.[31]

One recent analysis of global Chinese military diplomacy emphasized that the conduct of foreign military relations by the People's Liberation Army (PLA) is a strategic level activity in support of the larger foreign, diplomatic, economic, and security agenda set by China's leadership. The PLA does not engage in freestanding military initiatives conducted by military professionals for military reasons. In other words, the PLA is not an independent actor; it must coordinate its activities with the party and state bureaucracy. The PLA maintains an ambitious global program of military exchanges and training programs that include most African countries. Arms sales are also a way to make a profit, without concern for the human rights policies of the recipient. China does not, however, enter into formal military alliances with any country.[32]

The Congressional Research Service reported that, on a worldwide basis, China was the number six arms supplier from 1998 through 2001. Although China is a relatively small-scale arms provider compared to the top five, 83 percent of its transfers went to the developing world. China remained sixth for the period 2002–2005, but the percentage of its arms going to the developing world jumped to 94 percent. China was the fifth-largest supplier of arms to the developing world from 1998 to 2005, well behind the United States, Russia, France, and the United Kingdom. From 1998 to 2001, Russia provided 25 percent of all arms deliveries to sub-Saharan Africa, while China was in second place at 15 percent. From 2002 to 2005, Germany delivered the most arms ($600 million) to sub-Saharan Africa at 22 percent, while Russia and China tied at 18 percent or $500 million each. During this period, China delivered another $100 million in arms to Algeria and $400 million in arms to Egypt. By comparison, the United States delivered $5.8 billion in arms to Egypt from 2002 to 2005.[33]

China has no problem maintaining important military ties to African countries that are anathema to the West such as the Sudan and Zimbabwe. This approach coincides with its policy in other parts of the world. China has, for example, strong military links to Iran, which Beijing sees as an important supplier of oil and a geopolitical instrument to lessen U.S. influence in the Middle East. In Latin America, two of China's strongest military connections are with Cuba and Venezuela, the latter another source of petroleum.[34]

China is a major supplier of small arms and light weapons to Africa. While it does not earn a large amount of revenue from such sales, they help to underscore China's status as an international power. Chinese AK-47 assault rifles are common in national armies as well as among armed rebel groups such as those in the eastern Congo. They have also appeared in Uganda, Rwanda, and Burundi—and, more recently, in Chad and Darfur in the Sudan. France's Minister of Defense Michele Alliot-Marie complained before the upper house of the French parliament late in 2006 that Chinese arms too often appear in conflict situations in Africa, in contravention of embargoes.[35]

According to the Norwegian Initiative on Small Arms Transfers, China has transferred small quantities of small arms, valued well under $1 million, to the following African countries since 2000: Benin, Botswana, Burkina Faso, Cameroon, Djibouti, Egypt, Libya, Mozambique, and Zambia. China transferred larger amounts of small arms to Ethiopia ($8.2 million worth from 1998 to 2003), Kenya ($1 million from 2001 to 2003), Namibia ($2.3 million from 2000 to 2002), Niger ($1.2 million from 1998 to 2002), South Africa ($2.6 million from 1995 to 2004), the Sudan ($2.9 million from 1997 to 2004), Tanzania ($1.8 million from 1995 to 2003), Uganda ($2.5 million from 1996 to 2004), and Zimbabwe ($3.6 million from 1995 to 2004).[36] The Small Arms Survey lists Chinese transfers to fewer African countries and somewhat different amounts: $56,000 worth of arms to Kenya in 2003, $4.7 million to the Sudan in 2002–2004, $64,000 to Uganda in 2004, and $42,000 to Zimbabwe in 2004.[37]

African countries increased their permanent defense attaché offices in Beijing from thirteen in 1998 to eighteen in 2007. In 1985, there were nine Chinese military attaché offices in Africa; by 2006 there were at least fourteen, located in Algeria, the Democratic Republic of the Congo, Egypt, Ethiopia, Liberia, Libya, Morocco, Mozambique, Namibia, Nigeria, the Sudan, Tunisia, Zambia, and Zimbabwe. Although this list includes several important oil- and mineral-rich countries that export to China, it excludes oil and mineral suppliers, such as Angola, Equatorial Guinea, and South Africa. It also excludes Tanzania, a country with one of the longest and most important military relationships with China. Between 2001 and 2006, China held 110 bilateral security-related meetings with African countries, while Chinese military leaders visited Africa more than 30 times, often going to more than one country during each visit. However, no African states have participated in joint military exercises with China.[38]

Key Bilateral Military Relationships since 2000

A review of publicly available information on military cooperation between China and ten key African countries since 2000 provides an overview of the variety of China's military engagement with the continent. Except for information on exchange visits, Chinese sources provide relatively little data on military cooperation with other countries; most of the information comes from African sources. There are also significant differences among African countries in the availability of information on Chinese military cooperation. Former British colonies seem to be more willing to allow their material to appear in open sources. The ten African countries selected below tend to have more expansive military ties to China than do countries that are not mentioned. All forty-eight African countries that recognize Beijing probably have at least some military interaction with China. Military cooperation—especially high-level military exchanges—is an integral part of China's African policy.

Algeria

Algeria has a long military relationship with China dating back to its war of independence with France. Since 2000, China and Algeria have had numerous high-level military exchanges. The Chinese defense minister held extensive consultations with the Algerian military in 2000. According to the Stockholm International Peace Research Institute (SIPRI), Algeria received twenty-five antiship missiles valued at $35 million from China in 2000–2002. The commander of the Algerian navy visited Beijing in 2005, at which time the Chinese defense minister said the two armed forces would enhance exchanges and cooperation. China's commander of the Second Artillery Force visited Algeria in 2005 for talks on increasing military cooperation. The vice chairman of China's Central Military Commission held talks with his counterpart in Algiers in 2006, where they pledged to expand military exchanges and cooperation. In Beijing in 2006, the presidents of China and Algeria signed a strategic cooperation agreement that includes military affairs. It is similar to the agreement China has with South Africa.[39]

Angola

As China's primary source of oil in Africa, Angola is becoming a more important partner for military cooperation. The chief of the PLA's general staff received Angola's deputy minister of defense in Beijing in 2000. The Angolan defense minister met several months later with China's then vice chairman of the Central Military Commission, Hu Jintao, and with the Chinese defense minister. The deputy chief of the PLA's general staff visited Angola the following year. Angola's deputy chief of army for administration led a delegation to China in 2004, where he acknowledged the value of China's training of Angolan armed forces as well as the equipping of various military units. A high-ranking Chinese officer then visited Luanda, where he held talks on training Angolan military officers and replacing military equipment.[40]

Angola announced, in 2004, the creation of an elite tactical and operational support unit, with $6 million in financing from China for the unit's training center. Angola selected a Chinese company, Jiangsu International, to build the center. The chief of the PLA's general staff held talks in Beijing in 2005 on training and equipment supply with his Angolan counterpart. The Angolan chief of staff said the discussions were part of a military cooperation program outlined several years earlier by the two countries. China signed an agreement in 2006 for $100 million to upgrade Angola's military communication infrastructure. In 2007, a Chinese military delegation visited Angola in connection with the implementation of technical military cooperation and the signing of a technical cooperation agreement aimed at providing Chinese-supplied military equipment to the Angolan armed forces. As many as thirty Angolan military personnel receive training in China each year.[41]

Egypt

The first country on the African continent to recognize Beijing, Egypt has a well-developed, but discreet, military relationship with China. Discussions by the author with a number of Egyptians in Cairo during July 2007 left the impression that China is pursuing these military links more vigorously than Egypt is. Nevertheless, together with Pakistan and Iran, Egypt was one of the three largest recipients of arms from China in 2001–2005. China was, however, an insignificant supplier of arms to Egypt when compared to the United States.[42]

Egypt and China signed a contract valued at $347 million at the end of 1999 to export and eventually coproduce K-8E jet aircraft and provide pilot training for the Egyptian air force. China delivered the first aircraft in 2001: a two-seat advanced training jet and light air-to-ground attack aircraft. China delivered the eightieth and final aircraft to Egypt at the end of 2005. China National Aero-Technology Import and Export Corporation awarded a production certificate to Egypt's A.O.I. Aircraft Factory in 2005 for achieving production technology, quality control, and production management of the K-8E aircraft, with parts provided by China. The Egyptian company plans to build forty of the K-8E aircraft by 2010.[43]

A Chinese guided missile destroyer and supply ship passed through the Suez Canal in 2002 and docked in Alexandria during the PLA navy's first around-the-world voyage. The PLA navy has also provided training to the Egyptian navy, which was funded by the China State Shipbuilding Corporation.[44] Egypt received thirty multiple rocket launchers from China in 2004.[45] Along with South Africa, Egypt was one of only two African countries to observe a PLA military exercise in 2005.[46] That same year, the PLA's Institute of Science invited cadets from Egypt and a number of non-African countries to participate in activities at the military academy in Nanjing and visit the homes of PLA officers.[47]

The chief of the PLA's general staff received an Egyptian delegation led by the commander of the navy in 2004, and the Chinese minister of defense welcomed a delegation led by the commander in chief of the Egyptian armed forces and minister of defense the same year. The Chinese defense minister visited Egypt in 2005 for discussions on enhancing cooperation in training, armament, and exchange of information. A month later, the deputy chief of the PLA's general staff received an Egyptian military training delegation in Beijing. In Cairo in 2006, the Egyptian defense minister held talks on military cooperation with his Chinese counterpart. Also in 2006, the assistant chief of the PLA's general staff met with a visiting group of Egyptian officers, led by the commander of the northern military region. Of all African countries, Egypt has received the highest number of senior Chinese military delegations thus far during the twenty-first century.[48]

Ghana

Ghana's military ties to China are modest in terms of dollar value but are growing in their impact. China's defense minister held talks in Beijing in 2000 with his Ghanaian counterpart on developing ties to the Ghanaian armed forces. The Ghanaian defense minister returned to Beijing in 2003 for talks on upgrading military equipment and Chinese assistance for the construction of a ministry of defense office complex. Ground breaking occurred in 2007 for the $6.75 million office complex, with Ghana contributing $1.7 million and China the remainder. A Chinese company is expected to complete the project in eighteen months. Ghana signed a $30 million loan agreement with China's Eximbank in 2007 to acquire equipment and build a dedicated communications system for the police, armed forces, prison service, and other security agencies. The loan has an interest rate of 2 percent and is repayable in twenty years. ZTE Corporation of China is the project contractor.[49]

During a 2004 visit to Ghana by China's vice minister of commerce, the two countries inaugurated a combined military-police barracks at Burma Camp in Accra, financed by a $3.8 million interest-free loan. China also made available a modest grant to purchase vehicles for Ghana's armed forces. In 2005, China presented forty troop-carrying vehicles and fifteen pick-up trucks to the Ghanaian ministry of defense. Ghanaian officials said in 2006 that the armed forces would take possession of four Chinese K-8 jet aircraft and a flight simulator in exchange for Ghana's Gulfstream presidential jet and an undetermined amount of cash from the ministry of defense.[50]

Nigeria

China does not yet import a large quantity of petroleum from Nigeria, but it is engaged in a major effort to penetrate the Nigerian oil market. This endeavor coincides with growing military cooperation between Nigeria and China. The Chinese defense minister received his Nigerian counterpart in Beijing in 2001 and again in 2002 to discuss military cooperation. Nigeria's minister of defense returned in 2004 when his Chinese counterpart announced that military ties between China and Nigeria had strengthened and that China attached great importance to the development of military cooperation with Nigeria. Meeting in Beijing in 2007, the Nigerian defense minister told the Chinese defense minister and vice chairman of the Central Military Commission that Nigeria wanted to enhance its cooperation with the PLA.[51]

Poly Technology, a Chinese defense company, announced in 2004 that it was prepared to partner with the government-owned Defense Industries Corporation of Nigeria (DICON). The Nigerian government had been seeking to revive DICON, which had resumed production of small arms, grenades, and ammunition for the Nigerian army. There is no indication, however, that any Chinese company is currently partnering with DICON.[52]

China granted Nigeria $1 million in 2001 to upgrade its military facilities. Nigeria's chief of defense staff expressed appreciation at the same time for the thirty Nigerian officers taking courses at various Chinese military institutions. Nigeria negotiated a $251 million contract in 2005 with the China National Aero-Technology Import and Export Corporation to purchase twelve F-7M Airguard multipurpose combat aircraft (the Chinese version of the upgraded MiG-21) and three FT-7NI dual-seat fighter trainer aircraft. The deal included twenty PL-9 short-range air-to-air missiles, unguided rockets, bombs for antitank and runway denial missions, and training in China for twelve Nigerian pilots. A separate deal valued at more than $70 million was designed to refurbish five of the Nigerian air force's Alenia G-222 transports. China also donated to the Nigerian armed forces $3 million worth of military equipment that included vehicles, emergency runway systems, communications gear, computers, uniforms; and twenty-one Chinese experts to train Nigerian soldiers to use the equipment.[53] Nigeria ordered Chinese patrol boats to secure the swamps and creeks of the troubled Niger Delta, where Chinese technicians have been threatened and kidnapped. Nigeria's vice president complained publicly in 2006 that his country first turned to the United States for patrol boats but concluded that American help would not arrive fast enough. The United States did provide 4 old craft, but Nigeria argued as many as 200 may be required. Nigeria also ordered thirty-five smaller, high-speed patrol boats from a U.S. company, but only about half had arrived by early 2007. As of March 2007, seventeen U.S. defender class response boats had arrived in Nigeria. Deputy Assistant Secretary of Defense Theresa Whelan stated that the Nigerian navy, however, is not properly trained to use the boats and thus they sit idle in the Delta. U.S. concerns over corruption, human rights violations in Nigeria's security forces, and a low level of operational readiness in the Nigerian navy reportedly delayed American deliveries. A senior Nigerian naval officer commented that Nigeria was let down by the reluctance of the United States to offer more support and described the promise of Chinese boats as a welcome development.[54]

Chinese engineers designed, constructed, and launched Nigeria's geostationary communications satellite, known as Nigcomsat-1, in 2007. China's Eximbank provided $200 million in preferential buyer's credits for the $300 million project. The state-owned China Great Wall Industry Corporation will monitor the satellite from a ground station in China and train Nigerian engineers to operate a tracking station in Abuja. When the project was put out for bidding in 2004, Western companies showed little interest. The launch of the satellite received heavy media coverage in Nigeria and may encourage other African countries to follow Nigeria's lead in turning to China. Although the Nigerian satellite is a civilian project, China's space agency is managed by the military. The successful launch provides another important link to China's military.[55]

South Africa

China's second-largest African trading partner in 2006, South Africa, is developing a "strategic" relationship with China, although the definition seems to emphasize trade and economic ties more than military relations. South Africa sells considerable minerals to China, has more investments there than China has in South Africa, and has even sold some weapons to China. South Africa is developing a mature relationship with Beijing, which it did not even recognize until 1998. China's defense minister laid the foundation for military cooperation between the two countries in 1998 during a visit to South Africa. South Africa's defense minister returned the visit in 2000, during which then Chinese Vice President Hu Jintao said China was willing to promote cooperation between the two armed forces. Shortly thereafter, during its first-ever cruise to Africa, the Chinese navy visited the naval base outside Cape Town.[56]

During a visit to Beijing in 2001, China's defense minister told the chief of South Africa's defense forces that China was ready to strengthen cooperation between the armed forces of the two countries. In a second visit the same year by South Africa's defense minister, his Chinese counterpart commented that further development of military cooperation and exchanges would benefit both sides. During the first session of the Sino–South African Binational Commission meeting in Pretoria in 2002, the foreign ministers of China and South Africa emphasized the need to cooperate in the fight against terrorism. They said that terrorism should be confronted under the aegis of the United Nations (UN) or as an international undertaking.[57]

The first meeting of the Sino–South African Defense Committee convened in South Africa in 2003 and was followed by a visit from the chief of the PLA's general staff. The second meeting of the Defense Committee took place in Beijing in 2005, where the two countries agreed to improve exchanges and cooperation between their defense departments and armies. South Africa's defense minister said that his country attached importance to the strategic partnership with China. South Africa is the only African country that conducts regular, formal security consultations with China. In a subsequent visit to Beijing later in 2005, South Africa's deputy minister of defense noted that China and South Africa enjoyed a wide range of cooperation between their military forces.[58]

The director of the PLA's general armament department visited South Africa in 2006; the chief of South Africa's defense forces visited Beijing the same year. China's defense minister said Beijing was ready to deepen cooperation between the two armed forces. South Africa's National Assembly signed an agreement in 2006 formalizing a "strategic political partnership" with China that included military relations. The third session of the Sino–South African Defense Committee took place in Pretoria at the end of 2006. In 2007, the vice chairman of China's Central Military Commission received the South African air force chief.[59]

South Africa has a history, albeit poorly understood by outsiders, of selling arms to China. Although once a South African arms manufacturer and exporter, Armscor today is the designated acquisition agency for the defense ministry. In the 1980s, Armscor was caught pirating American missile technology and selling it to countries like China. In 1992, Denel was created from the manufacturing operations of Armscor; it is a parastatal organization controlled by the Department of Public Enterprises. Denel is now the major manufacturer of weapons systems for South Africa and acts like a for-profit private company. South Africa has actively marketed G5 and G6 artillery pieces in China. China purchased Denel's 35mm dual purpose gun; several years later a European source identified the 35mm gun on China's new self-propelled antiaircraft gun system as South African in origin. Denel also may have sold unmanned air vehicles to China.[60]

The Sudan

The Sudan is an important source of oil and the location of up to $6 billion of Chinese investment, most of it in the oil industry; however, it also poses a growing dilemma for China because the international community has put pressure on Beijing to use its influence with Khartoum to end the conflict in Darfur. This pressure has had some positive results. Although China continues to oppose sanctions against the Sudan, it played a key role in convincing Khartoum to accept a hybrid African Union (AU)–UN peacekeeping force of 26,000 troops in Darfur. China has also contributed two contingents of peacekeepers to the UN force in southern Sudan and the hybrid force in Darfur.

Liu Guijin, China's special representative for Darfur, explained that Beijing has a two-track policy to resolve the Darfur crisis. China attaches equal importance to the peacekeeping operation and the political process. Although numerous reports indicated that Chinese weapons had been used by the Sudanese government in Darfur and by rebel groups in Chad, Liu Guijin emphasized that China was doing its best to prevent its weapons from finding their way into the wrong hands.[61]

China has long been an important supplier of military equipment to the Sudan. Foreign assistance in the 1990s helped the Sudan build three arms factories outside Khartoum for ammunition, mortars, and assembling tanks based on the T-55 model and armored personnel carriers. It has become conventional wisdom that China was behind all three factories. However, the author's findings during a visit to Khartoum in July 2007 to verify China's assistance suggest a more complex situation. While China certainly played a role, Arab money and Iranian technical help were also factors. The machine tools in the assembly plant are from Germany because the Sudan had doubts about the quality of Chinese equipment. The precise involvement of China in 2007 in these factories remains shrouded in secrecy. The Sudan's defense minister announced in September 2007 that the Sudan had become self-sufficient in conventional weapons and was in the process of developing missiles. He added that the Sudan was the third most important producer of weapons in Africa after Egypt and South Africa.[62]

Accounts of Chinese activity in the Sudan tend to be exaggerated. Hale, for example, commented in 2004 that China had deployed 4,000 troops to the Sudan to protect its investment in a pipeline that transported oil from the production area to Port Sudan. Hale said he learned of these troops from South African government officials. Although widely repeated, this account has not been confirmed. A non-Sudanese source, who has traveled widely in the country over many years, suggests that the number was much smaller and consisted of Chinese military personnel in civilian clothing assigned to security duty in the oilfields when the government was fighting the Sudan People's Liberation Movement. A cease-fire took effect in 2003, and the Chinese troops are no longer present.[63]

The Sudan acquired thirty-four Shenyang jet fighters from China in 2000. Another account indicated that the Sudanese military had installed Chinese-made radar at the Juba army garrison along the White Nile River. SIPRI reported the delivery in 2003 of three A-5C Fanton FGA aircraft, noting that the number might increase to twenty. Amnesty International reported that the Sudan in 2005 imported from China $24 million in arms and ammunition and $59 million in parts and aircraft equipment. SIPRI said that the Sudan also took possession of twelve K-8 jet trainers in 2006. A separate report in 2006 indicated that the Sudan spent $100 million on Shenyang fighter planes, including twelve F-7 jets; however, this account may be a variation on the SIPRI data or even a repeat of the deal concluded in 2000. The Sudan also received a shipment of Dong Feng military trucks, and China reportedly trained fifty Sudanese pilots on helicopter gunships. While China continues to be an important supplier of military equipment to the Sudan, SIPRI statistics for conventional weapons suggest that Russia now provides much more equipment by dollar value.[64]

The Sudan's defense minister met with his counterpart in Beijing in 2000. When the Chinese government said it was satisfied with military cooperation between the two countries, the Sudan's chief of staff of the armed forces visited Beijing in 2002. The Sudan's minister of defense returned to China in 2003 to discuss the equipping and training of Sudanese armed forces. In 2005, the Sudan's chief of staff of the armed forces visited China again after a statement by his Chinese counterpart that Beijing was willing to increase exchanges and cooperation in every field between the two armed forces. China's vice chairman of the Central Military Commission and nineteen commanders visited Khartoum in 2005 and discussed a range of cooperation with the Sudanese president and defense minister. The deputy chief of the Sudan's general staff and the commander of the air force made separate visits to China the same year.[65]

The commandant of the Sudanese Higher Military Academy's Institute for Defense Affairs visited China in 2006, followed by the arrival of the Sudanese defense minister. The Chinese minister of defense told the visiting Sudanese joint chief of staff early in 2007 that China was willing to cooperate militarily in every sphere but urged Khartoum to be more flexible on the UN peace plan and to improve the security and humanitarian situation in Darfur. Sudanese officials also announced in 2007 that Khartoum had signed contracts with China and Russia for the modernization of the Sudanese air force. Both countries agreed to supply planes and train Sudanese personnel.[66]

Uganda

A minor trade partner with China and not strategically important, except that it is part of the Great Lakes region where China has long-standing interests, Uganda nevertheless has benefited from a modest military relationship with Beijing. China donated fifty-two military trucks valued at $1 million to the Uganda People's Defense Forces (UPDF) in 2002. A Chinese company funded a $4 million renovation of the country's largest military barracks and contracted to build the UPDF's first division headquarters at Kakiri in northern Uganda. China trains Ugandan military personnel, and Chinese experts manage a North Korean–built plant in Uganda that produces ammunition.[67]

The Ugandan defense minister visited Beijing in 2003 after his Chinese counterpart said that China was prepared to promote friendly cooperation between the armies. China donated twenty-four Jiefang troop carriers, two fuel trucks, two water tankers, and various spare parts to the UPDF in 2006. Following criticism in 2006 from Amnesty International that Uganda had received arms from China, Uganda's defense minister responded that his country had been dealing with China for a long time and that it would continue to accept arms from China until it developed its own capacity to manufacture weapons. A senior Chinese military officer visited Uganda in 2006 to discuss increasing the supply of arms, training Ugandan officers, and signing contracts for Chinese companies to construct additional military facilities. According to a report in the *Indian Ocean Newsletter*, Chinese military cooperation with Uganda could reach $1.5 billion over the next five years.[68]

Zambia

China and Zambia have had an important relationship dating back to China's construction of the Tanzania-Zambia Railway, which began in 1970. Zambia is China's major copper supplier. So far this century, the military relationship has consisted primarily of high-level exchange visits and aircraft sales. A senior Chinese military delegation, led by the PLA's commissar of the general department of military equipment, visited Zambia in 2000. The permanent secretary of Zambia's defense ministry reciprocated with a visit to Beijing the following year, while the chief of the PLA's general staff visited Lusaka. In 2002, the PLA's political commissar of the Beijing military area command went to Zambia, and Zambia's commander of land forces visited Beijing the same year. The Zambian minister of defense visited Beijing in 2005 and returned in 2007, at which time the two countries agreed to expand cooperation between their armed forces.[69]

In 2000, China delivered eight K-8 trainer-combat aircraft to Zambia. In 2006, the Zambian air force received five Y-12 series, twin-engine transport aircraft built by Harbin Aviation Industry and one Y-7 transport aircraft. China reportedly financed the deal with a preferential loan. Zambia planned to use the aircraft primarily for troop transport, emergency rescue operations, and the delivery of ballot boxes to remote areas. Zambia is the only foreign country to receive Chinese military medical experts. The first group arrived in 1984 at a Zambian hospital. As of early 2007, 163 PLA medical experts had worked in Zambia, treating about 10,000 Zambian soldiers and their family members. The current group consists of ten physicians working in a variety of specialties.[70]

Zimbabwe

China's long association with President Robert Mugabe, dating back to the liberation period, probably best explains China's close, continuing military ties to Zimbabwe. Except for tobacco, Zimbabwe is not an important supplier of raw materials to China. After the 2002 arms embargo on Zimbabwe by

Western countries, China became the country of choice for supplying military equipment, an opportunity that China welcomed. The commander of Zimbabwe's air force visited Beijing in 2000 after the PLA's chief of the Chinese general staff said it was prepared to raise military cooperation with Zimbabwe. Zimbabwe's acting defense minister visited Beijing in 2001and returned in 2002, and the commander of Zimbabwe's army visited China in 2005.[71]

In 2004, there was a widely believed report from Harare that Zimbabwe had plans to purchase US$240 million in arms from China, including 12 Chinese-made FC-1 fighter aircraft and 100 military vehicles. The FC-1 is a lightweight, multipurpose fighter similar to Russia's MiG-33. It reportedly would serve as a credible challenge to the JAS-39 Gripen multipurpose fighters purchased by South Africa from Sweden. This transaction caused considerable apprehension in South Africa and led to international concerns about a regional arms race. The Chinese ambassador to South Africa and China's embassy in Zimbabwe quickly denied that there was any sale of FC-1 aircraft to Zimbabwe. The aircraft do not appear to have arrived in Zimbabwe, and it would be difficult for the local air force to maintain them. However, in 2004 Zimbabwe did order US$1.6 million in arms and riot gear from China, and in 2005 Beijing provided the Zimbabwean armed forces with thirty-nine military trucks and educational and medical equipment worth more than US$3 million.[72]

Zimbabwe purchased six K-8 advanced jet trainers from China's Nanchang Aircraft Manufacturing Company in 2005, at an estimated cost of US$120 million. The K-8s replaced British Aerospace Hawk fighter jets. Upon delivery, Mugabe described the purchase as part of Zimbabwe's successful "Look East" policy.[73] Zimbabwe's Ministry of Defense announced in 2006 that it had purchased six additional K-8 aircraft from China and had made an initial payment of US$4.6 million for the estimated US$240 million package of twelve aircraft. The author has not been able to confirm delivery of the additional six K-8s. Although Zimbabwe may have intended initially to purchase the more sophisticated FC-1 aircraft from China, it would appear that it has substituted K-8s for the FC-1s.[74]

The commander of the Zimbabwean air force met in Beijing with the Chinese chief of the general staff in 2006. China donated US$1.5 million worth of machines and construction equipment to Zimbabwe's armed forces in 2006. Beginning in the 1960s, at least twenty Zimbabwean military officers were trained annually in China; in 2006–2007 Zimbabwe sent fifty-five officers to China for training. During a 2006 visit to Zimbabwe's army headquarters by a Chinese military delegation, the chief of the Zimbabwean

defense forces praised Chinese military training programs and the second-
ment of PLA army instructors to the Zimbabwe Staff College. A few months
later, Mugabe paid tribute to the Chinese PLA team at the Staff College. The
political commissar of China's air force visited Harare in 2007, at which time
Zimbabwe's defense minister expressed appreciation for China's generous
support for Zimbabwe's military effort.[75]

Chinese Policy on Arms Deliveries

China has not declared its arms exports to the UN register of conventional
arms since it withdrew from the register in 1998 to protest U.S. reporting on
exports to Taiwan. Although China gives a lot of lip service to small arms
export controls, its systems leave much to be desired. The 2000 Beijing Declaration stated that China would cooperate in stopping the illegal production,
circulation, and trafficking of small arms and light weapons (SALW) in Africa.
Chinese officials are quick to note that China has intensified cooperation with
Africa against illicit proliferation, transfer, and trafficking of SALW.[76]

Assistant Foreign Minister Zhai Jun stated in 2006 that China always takes
a cautious and accountable attitude toward the export of military equipment
to Africa. He said that China only exports military hardware to the governments of sovereign states and never exports weapons to any nonstate entity or
individual. China requires that the recipient government certify the end user
and the ultimate purpose. The recipient must promise not to transfer the
weapons to any third party. Zhai added that China strictly observes UN resolutions and does not export military equipment to countries and regions
where the Security Council has imposed arms sanctions.[77]

During the author's visit to Beijing in January 2007, Chinese officials
insisted privately that China does not sell arms to countries for use in conflict
zones, although they acknowledged that Chinese weapons have appeared in
those areas. They argued that any Chinese weapons that show up in conflict
zones were purchased on the international arms market. The officials added
that China tries to monitor these movements and insisted that China would
fine violators. They pointed out, for example, that after conflict broke out
between Cameroon and Nigeria, China stopped providing arms to both sides.
China says that it controls all exports of conventional military items, including small arms, in accordance with the Regulations on Control of Military
Product Exports. Despite these assertions and the fact that state-run companies manufacture all Chinese weapons, serious questions remain about the
control of exported military equipment, especially SALW.[78]

China issued its first publicly available export control regulations covering military equipment in 1997. It codified China's export principles and adopted some international export control standards. It failed to include, however, a list of specific military items controlled under the regulations. China revised these regulations in 2002 but again did not list specific military items. The regulations remained vague. A Chinese white paper on arms control issued in 2005 stated that international mechanisms for arms control should be maintained, further strengthened, and improved. It added that firmly combating illegal activities in the area of SALW was of great importance to maintaining regional peace, stability, and development; fighting terrorism; and cracking down on international organized crime, drug trafficking, and smuggling.[79]

Chinese officials say that they are not in the arms business to make money. However, during a 2007 discussion with the author in Beijing, one African ambassador to China whose country has purchased Chinese weapons begged to differ with this assertion. In addition, the Middle East offers one of the best rebuttals to China's claim. Israel was, at least until recently, China's second-largest arms supplier. It transferred Harpy antiradar drones, Python air-to-air missiles, and advanced technology for China's new J-10 fighter. At the same time, China sold to Iran, Israel's adversary, the HY-2, C-801, and C-802 anti-ship ballistic and cruise missiles. China is one of the principal facilitators of Iran's ballistic missile program. Such actions suggest that despite protestations to the contrary, China is willing to provide military assistance and equipment to any party whenever it will advance Chinese interests.[80]

A spokesperson from the Chinese foreign ministry pointed out in 2006 that statistics from the SIPRI indicate that from 2000 to 2004, global conventional military exports by the United States were estimated at $25.9 billion. Weapons exported by China during the same period were valued at $1.4 billion or 5 percent of the U.S. figure.[81] These figures may not include all conventional weapons transfers, nor do they include SALW. They also do not acknowledge the high percentage of China's transfers to Africa, nor do they prove that the transfers followed international guidelines.

Chinese Peacekeeping Operations in Africa

When China assumed its membership on the UN Security Council in 1971, it opposed peacekeeping operations. With the end of the Cold War, China took a more practical approach to this issue. Beginning in the early 1990s, China provided small numbers of personnel for UN peacekeeping operations. It has had as many as twenty observers in the Western Sahara since

1991. In the mid-1990s, China sent small numbers of observers to do peacekeeping in Mozambique, Liberia, and Sierra Leone. Beginning in 2000, it contributed ten observers to the UN mission along the Ethiopia-Eritrea border. Then, marking a significant increase in its support for UN peacekeeping operations, China sent a small number of observers and more than 200 troops to the Democratic Republic of the Congo in 2001, and contributed about 600 troops and police to the mission in Liberia in 2003. It sent a small number of observers to Côte d'Ivoire and Burundi in 2004. China tends to provide military observers and medical, transportation, engineering, and logistical specialists for these UN operations, rather than infantry personnel. China is also providing financial assistance to the AU for its peacekeeping missions in Darfur and elsewhere.[82]

As of April 2008, China had 1,457 military peacekeepers, observers, and police participating in 7 UN peacekeeping operations in Africa. Chinese personnel were assigned to both missions in the Sudan (613), Côte d'Ivoire (13), Liberia (581), the Democratic Republic of the Congo (234), Ethiopia-Eritrea (2), and Western Sahara (14). Globally, China was the twelfth-largest contributor to UN peacekeeping operations with 1,981 personnel. The United States ranked forty-third with 300 personnel.[83] China was in the process, in early 2008, of increasing its numbers by sending a 315-person engineering unit to the AU-UN hybrid mission in Darfur. A five-person advance team arrived in October 2007.[84] The only 2008 UN peacekeeping operation in Africa where China remains unrepresented is the UN Mission in the Central African Republic and Chad; that force had just begun in late 2007. UN Secretary General Ban Ki-moon selected a Chinese general in 2007 as the new force commander for the UN mission in the Western Sahara. This is the first time that a Chinese national has commanded a UN peacekeeping operation.[85]

China's most significant peacekeeping involvement in Africa is linked to countries where it has either a major interest in natural resources or there are special considerations. China has important mining concessions in the Democratic Republic of the Congo and major oil investments in the Sudan. Although Liberia once exported significant quantities of hardwood timber to China, it is a special case. Partly as a reward for terminating its recognition of Taiwan and restoring relations with Beijing in 2003, China sent nearly 600 engineers, medical personnel, and transportation specialists to the UN peacekeeping operation in Liberia.[86]

Beijing made support for peacekeeping operations part of its African policy statement in 2006 and backed up that rhetoric with tangible assistance. China has established bases for prospective peacekeepers in Nanjing (Jiangsu

Province) and Langfang (Hebei Province). The centers offer training in foreign languages, emergency treatment, logistical support, conflict prevention, and cooperation with peacekeepers from other countries.[87] This involvement has been welcomed by African leaders. Liberian President Ellen Johnson-Sirleaf, for example, told Chinese journalists in February 2007, before the arrival of Chinese President Hu Jintao, that "Liberia will never forget the friendship of Chinese peacekeeping soldiers."[88] At the same time, Chinese arms reached both sides of the Ethiopia-Eritrea dispute, conflicting parties in the Democratic Republic of the Congo and Sierra Leone, and both the government of the Sudan and rebels in Darfur and Chad. Although no nation can fully control the movement of small arms sold on the international market, China has been embarrassed on a number of occasions as its weapons have appeared in African conflict zones.[89]

Other Security-Related Issues

China strongly professes support for the elimination of landmines but, like the United States, has not signed the Ottawa Landmine Convention. The AU and most African states strongly back the Landmine Convention. However, China has been engaged in mine clearance in Eritrea and trained 120 Eritrean mine clearance specialists. Since 1998, it has also worked with the UN to provide training in land mine disposal and donated equipment to Mozambique, Ethiopia, Rwanda, Angola, and Eritrea. It has pledged to remain active in African demining efforts.[90]

As China's interests and presence on the ground expand in Africa, Chinese nationals have become increasingly threatened by local conflicts. Two rebel groups attacked a Chinese oil facility located between South Darfur and West Kordofan in the Sudan late in 2006.[91] Ten Chinese sailors were among those captured by pirates when the latter seized two South Korean fishing vessels off Somalia in 2007.[92] In northern Niger, Tuareg-led rebels in 2007 captured and released a Chinese uranium executive, forcing his company to suspend activities in the region.[93]

Militant groups in the Niger Delta of Nigeria have threatened Chinese interests and nationals on several occasions. A spokesperson for the militant Movement for the Emancipation of the Niger Delta criticized China for taking a $2.2 billion stake in a Niger Delta oilfield and warned the Chinese government and its oil companies to stay out of the delta. It added that the Chinese government, by investing in "stolen" crude, placed its citizens in the line of fire. Gunmen in the delta kidnapped five Chinese employees of the Sichuan Telecommunications Company early in 2007. Nigerian militants subsequently seized nine Chinese oil workers near Port Harcourt. Two other Chinese nationals were taken in Anambra State in Nigeria. The militants eventually released all of the Chinese unharmed.[94]

The most serious attack against Chinese workers in Africa occurred in the Ogaden region of Ethiopia in April 2007, at an oil exploration site operated by Sinopec's Zhongyuan Petroleum Exploration Bureau and staffed by 37 Chinese and 120 Ethiopians. The Ogaden National Liberation Front, which had earlier warned all foreign oil companies to stay out of the Ogaden, attacked the facility, killing nine Chinese and at least sixty-five Ethiopians. They also kidnapped and then released seven Chinese.[95]

A Chinese foreign ministry spokesperson said that these attacks would not deter China from investing in Africa, although it planned to increase security measures.[96] State-owned Sinopec announced that it was not pulling out of Ethiopia. At the same time, official Chinese sources in Addis Ababa told the author in July 2007 that Chinese companies have pulled out of the Ogaden and had no immediate plans to return. While these developments will not have any significant impact on China's quest for raw materials in Africa, they may cause the government to rethink the initiation of commercial operations in conflict zones and will certainly result in more host-country and Chinese security in areas where there have been threats against foreign interests or a history of rebel activity.[97] He Wenping, one of China's leading Africanists and the head of African studies at the Chinese Academy of Social Sciences, commented that Chinese companies should evaluate the security situation before starting projects abroad.[98]

At the November 2007 China-Africa Forum in Beijing, China agreed to strengthen counterterrorism cooperation with Africa, although it did not spell out how this would be done.[99] He Wenping subsequently reported that China had begun an exchange of intelligence, as well as joint counterterrorism training programs, in many African countries.[100] China has also pledged to engage in a more intensive dialogue with Africans on nontraditional security issues such as small arms trafficking, drug trafficking, and transnational economic crimes. Finally, China supports Africa's efforts to remain free of nuclear weapons and has agreed to cooperate in promoting nuclear disarmament and nonproliferation of nuclear weapons.[101]

Africa and Chinese Naval Interests

During the Ming Dynasty (1368–1644), Zheng He was the first Chinese navigator to reach the African coast. He made voyages to some thirty countries in West Asia and East Africa from 1405 to 1433, predating Christopher

Columbus, Vasco da Gama, and Ferdinand Magellan. In 2005, on the 600th anniversary of Zheng's voyages, Chinese Vice Premier Huang Ju called on the Chinese people to carry forward Zheng's spirit of scientific exploration and the expansion of friendly cooperation with peoples of other countries.[102] Two experts on Chinese naval strategy argued that China's "Zheng He diplomacy" was no longer willing to entrust its maritime interests to the U.S. Navy: China would deploy naval forces to defend its interests. It would focus its attention not just on the Pacific, but southward, along the sea lanes that convey vital commodities to China.[103]

The modern Chinese navy sent its first-ever naval fleet formation to Africa in 2000, with port calls in Tanzania and South Africa. Rear Admiral Huang Jiang, chief of the general staff of the South China Sea Fleet, joined the Shenzhen 167 guided missile destroyer, the Nancang 953 supply ship, and 480 officers and sailors during stops at Dar es Salaam and the Simonstown naval dock near Cape Town.[104] The commander of the North China Sea Fleet, Ding Yiping, accompanied a guided missile destroyer, a supply ship, and 500 crew members on China's first world cruise in 2002. After passing through the Suez Canal, the ships called at Alexandria, Egypt.[105]

While intended primarily to improve political and military relations with the host nations, those ship visits suggest that China may be serious about eventually extending its naval reach into the waters off Africa. At the same time, China is quick to note that it does not have any bases in Africa and, as a matter of national policy, does not seek traditional military alliances with other countries. Perhaps surprisingly, there have been no Chinese naval visits to Africa since the 2002 call at Alexandria.

The Chinese navy has a force of seventy-two principal ships, about fifty-eight attack submarines, some fifty medium and heavy amphibious lift vessels, and approximately forty-one coastal missile patrol craft. China is building and testing second-generation nuclear submarines: the Jin-class nuclear-powered ballistic missile submarine and the Shang-class nuclear-powered attack submarine, both of which began sea trials in 2005. The navy also operates twelve Kilo-class submarines, the newest of which are equipped with the supersonic, wire-guided, and wake-homing torpedoes. In 2006, China received the second of two Russian-made guided missile destroyers; the PLA navy's newest ship, a guided missile destroyer, is designed for antiaircraft warfare. In 2006, China also began producing its first guided missile frigate.[106]

In addition to long-range submarines, China's growing interest in developing an aircraft carrier capacity would seem to signal a naval strategy aimed at extending China's power well beyond its coastline. China first began to discuss developing an indigenous aircraft carrier in the late 1970s. It purchased two former Soviet carriers in 1998 and 2000. Although China used both of them for floating military theme parks, PLA navy engineers learned useful design information. China also purchased from Russia in 1998 a third carrier that was only 70 percent complete at the time of the collapse of the Soviet Union. Recent work on the carrier has renewed the debate about China's interest in developing a carrier capacity, although it could also be used for training purposes or even as another floating theme park. A senior Chinese general commented in 2006 that carriers are indispensable if China wants to protect its maritime interests. Estimates vary as to when China could deploy an operational aircraft carrier. Some experts say it could happen by 2015, while others believe it would be 2020 or beyond.[107]

Beijing published a white paper entitled *China's National Defense in 2006* that said that the navy "aims at gradual extension of the strategic depth for offshore defensive operations" and must guard not only coastal areas but also nearby oceans.[108] At least one expert has interpreted this reference as an intention to develop a blue-water fleet with long-range, all-weather capabilities.[109] An increasing number of analysts, including some in the Pentagon, subscribe to the belief that China is engaged in building a blue-water navy. An internal memo to former Defense Secretary Donald Rumsfeld argued that China was building up military forces and setting up bases along sea lanes to the Middle East to project its power overseas and protect its oil shipments. China is constructing a deepwater Indian Ocean port at Gwadar in Pakistan and building a container port facility at Chittagong, Bangladesh. Together with Chinese-developed ports in Cambodia and Burma, these facilities will eventually permit the Chinese navy to extend its sea power into the Indian Ocean.[110] Other experts are not convinced that China is trying to become a global military power or build a blue-water navy. David Finkelstein, director of the China Studies Center at the Center for Naval Analysis, argues that the PLA is creating a "littoral plus" force aimed at guarding the sea lanes in the near region.[111]

In 2006 testimony before the U.S.-China Economic and Security Review Commission, Cortez Cooper, director of East Asia Studies at Hicks and Associates, suggested that by 2020 Beijing hopes to focus on building Chinese military capabilities in its "greater periphery," particularly the Straits of Malacca, the Indian Ocean, and the Persian Gulf. Cooper notes this will require the development of a blue-water fleet and a strategic bomber force to protect trade in goods and natural resources. He argued that while it is not in China's interest to build a high-cost carrier navy for at least two decades, China may develop a hybrid force that has one or two carrier groups designed to provide minimum blue-water power projection. In the meantime, China is working hard to obtain access for its maritime forces in key nations along these sea lanes.

If China has embarked on or plans to build a blue-water navy, the reasons for it are clear. The Chinese economy has been growing at an extraordinary rate. To stay in power, the current leadership of the Communist Party must continue this high annual GDP growth rate. The ability of the Chinese economy to sustain a high growth rate is dependent on the importation of large quantities of raw materials, especially oil. In 2003, China became the world's second-largest consumer and third-largest (after the United States and Japan) importer of oil. While oil and gas account for only about 20 percent of China's energy requirement (coal, most of it available locally, provides the preponderance of China's energy needs), the importance of gas and oil to the economy is growing each year. China currently imports more than 40 percent of its oil, and this could rise to 80 percent by 2025. About 80 percent of China's imported oil—that which comes from the Middle East and Africa—passes through the Straits of Malacca. These sea lanes are now controlled largely by the United States. China also relies exclusively on foreign-owned tankers to transport its oil imports. This situation is not tenable over the long term for a power that has global aspirations.[112]

Most analysts connect Chinese interest in expanding security of the sea lanes to oil coming from the Middle East. While it is true that about 50 percent of China's oil imports now originate in the Middle East, this argument overlooks an important point. Because of insecurity in the Middle East, Chinese oil imports from the region have declined in recent years. China now receives about 33 percent of its oil imports from the African continent, and the percentage is expected to rise. Africa currently holds more than 9 percent of the world's proven petroleum reserves and remains largely unexplored. More oil finds are anticipated in Africa than in any other part of the world. China also imports from Africa large quantities of minerals and timber that are essential to sustaining China's booming economy.[113]

Another Chinese concern that has implications for eastern Africa and African islands in the Indian Ocean is the growing naval strength of India. China and India have good relations now and have even held joint naval maneuvers, but there is no guarantee that that situation will remain stable. Previous Chinese support for Pakistan and continuing close relations with Islamabad could pose a problem for the future. India's alignment with the United States may also give China some pause. How India defines its interests in the region and configures its military power may put additional pressure on China to match Indian naval strength. All of China's imported oil from the

Middle East and oil and minerals from Africa pass through the Indian Ocean. It may have been no coincidence that Hu Jintao included the Seychelles on his 2007 Africa tour.[114]

The Future of the China-Africa Military and Security Relationship

Chinese military and security cooperation with African countries is a corollary to Beijing's much greater use of soft power in advancing its interests on the African continent. China will continue to maximize its military and security relationship with African countries, focusing on those that export large quantities of oil and raw materials to China or have the ability to do so in the future. Consequently, China will try to expand its military cooperation with important oil producers such as Angola and Nigeria and initiate programs in countries such as Equatorial Guinea, Chad, and Libya. China will not be deterred from its close military relationship with the Sudan, in spite of international pressure to stop the provision of arms, but it will continue trying to moderate Khartoum's policies in Darfur and support the Comprehensive Peace Agreement with South Sudan.

Although China will take greater care before placing its nationals in harm's way while developing or exploiting oil and mineral deposits on the African continent, it will continue to take higher risks than Western companies or governments. When the security situation does not permit an on-the-ground presence, China will sign licensing agreements that it can draw on in the future, as it did for an oil concession in Somalia. Maintaining access to African oil, gas, minerals, and timber is so important to the fueling of China's economy both now and in the future that Beijing will make every effort to expand military-security cooperation with resource-exporting countries.

There will probably be an expansion of Chinese support for UN and AU peacekeeping operations in Africa. Such involvement provides China military access in African countries in a manner that is generally welcomed by both the Africans and the international community. The Chinese military presence provides useful experience for its forces, first-hand intelligence on particular conflict situations, and, in the case of UN peacekeeping operations, reimbursement to the Chinese government for its troop participation. Chinese troop contributions to both of the peacekeeping operations in the Sudan also allow China to deflect some of the criticism leveled against it due to the oil connection and sale of arms to the government of the Sudan.

While there is not likely to be any significant increase in Chinese military grant assistance to Africa, one can expect Chinese low-interest loans to be used increasingly to fund projects related to military infrastructure. This low-interest lending has already been used for telecommunications projects in Ghana and Angola. It has also been used for the construction of military headquarters and barracks in a number of countries. Chinese companies have shown that they can quickly complete reasonably good quality projects at low cost. This keeps the loan money in China while pleasing African governments at the same time. Chinese state-owned companies manufacture the products; the loans are transferred from one government account to another. The same concept applies to military aircraft and equipment sales.

China has a long and generally good record of training African military personnel. This is another area where there will likely be a sharp increase in cooperation, in spite of the continuing language problem. To some extent, growing Chinese involvement in African peacekeeping operations will result in increased training cooperation, especially when Chinese units serve in missions with African troops. Training is also a relatively low-cost way to maximize the military-to-military relationship. China sees a long-term benefit in these more personal ties between African and Chinese military personnel.

China currently lacks the ability to protect oil shipments on the high seas and through the Straits of Malacca. In the event of a conflict involving Taiwan, it probably fears that the United States would use its naval power to disrupt the flow of oil to China. Consequently, China will probably seek first to extend its naval capacity into the Straits of Malacca and then to the Persian Gulf and Indian Ocean, which are more essential to Beijing's energy security. Because of the African coast's greater distance from China, protecting its interests in the sea lanes around Africa will be a lower priority. For the time being, China will rely on the projection of soft power in the region. Nevertheless, China is almost certainly planning a naval force that eventually can protect the sea lanes around and from Africa. Doing so will inevitably result in closer collaboration between the PLA navy and African leaders and port facilities.

Conclusion

In the early 1990s, former Chinese leader Deng Xiaoping suggested guidelines for China's foreign and security policy that came to be known as the "24 character" strategy, which included instructions to "observe calmly; secure our position; cope with affairs calmly; hide our capacities and bide our time; be good at maintaining a low profile; and never claim leadership." The phrase "make some contributions" was added later. Senior Chinese national security officials often quote these guidelines. There has been some debate within

China's security community in recent years over this strategy, especially the relative emphasis placed upon "never claim leadership" and "make some contributions." Nevertheless, the strategy continues to guide China's short-term desire to downplay its ambitions and long-term strategy to build up China's power to maximize options for the future.[115] China is prepared to bide its time as it methodically strengthens its military and security relations with Africa.

Notes

1. Harry G. Broadman, *Africa's Silk Road: China and India's New Economic Frontier* (Washington, D.C., 2007), 120. Table 2A.4 lists, by African country, the percentage of principal exports to China.

2. Alaba Ogunsanwo, *China's Policy in Africa, 1958–1971* (London, 1974), 146–147; 172–173. The text of the protocol for sending Chinese military experts to Ghana is located on pp. 283–284. The names, specialty, and dates of service for the Chinese experts are found on p. 277. See also Ian Taylor, *China and Africa: Engagement and Compromise* (London, 2006), 94–95;110–112.

3. He Wenping, "Moving Forward with the Time: The Evolution of China's African Policy" (Hong Kong, 2006), 5.

4. Michael H. Glantz and Mohamed A. El-Khawas, "On the Liberation of African Liberation Movements," in Warren Weinstein (ed.), *Chinese and Soviet Aid to Africa* (New York, 1975), 209–210. For an excellent early analysis of how the Sino-Soviet split played out in Africa, see Richard Lowenthal, "China," in Zbigniew Brzezinski (ed.), *Africa and the Communist World* (Stanford, 1963), 142–203.

5. Taylor, *China and Africa*, 75–86; Steven F. Jackson, "China's Third World Foreign Policy: The Case of Angola and Mozambique, 1961–93," *China Quarterly*, no. 142 (1995), 396–398, 401–402, 404–411, 413–415, and 417–420.

6. Bruce D. Larkin, *China and Africa 1949–1970* (Berkeley, 1971), 55–57.

7. Emmanuel John Hevi, *The Dragon's Embrace: The Chinese Communists and Africa* (New York, 1966), 97–105; Larkin, *China and Africa*, 71–74, 179–183; Alan Hutchison, *China's African Revolution* (London, 1975), 110–114; Vidya Prakash Dutt, *China and the World: An Analysis of Communist China's Foreign Policy* (New York, 1964), 80–85; Mohamed A. El-Khawas, "China's Changing Policies in Africa," *Issue: A Journal of Opinion*, III (1973), 25; Tareq Y. Ismael, "The People's Republic of China and Africa," *Journal of Modern African Studies*, IX (December 1971), 516.

8. John K. Cooley, *East Wind over Africa: Red China's African Offensive* (New York, 1965), 51–52, 155–159; Hevi, *Dragon's Embrace*, 108–112; Larkin, *China and Africa*, 171, 183–184; Ogunsanwo, *China's Policy in Africa*, 173; Warren Weinstein, "Chinese Policy in Central Africa: 1960–73," in Warren Weinstein (ed.), *Chinese and Soviet Aid to Africa* (New York, 1975), 59–66, 70–71.

9. Ogunsanwo, *China's Policy in Africa*, 138–139, 212–213.

10. Joseph P. Smaldone, "Soviet and Chinese Military Aid and Arms Transfers to Africa: A Contextual Analysis," in Warren Weinstein and Thomas H. Henriksen (eds.), *Soviet and Chinese Aid to African Nations* (New York, 1980), 106.

11. George T. Yu, *China and Tanzania: A Study in Cooperative Interaction* (Berkeley, 1970), 62–66; Smaldone, "Soviet and Chinese Military Aid," 104–106; Martin Bailey, "Tanzania and China," *African Affairs*, LXXIV (1975), 44–45.

12. Smaldone, "Soviet and Chinese Military Aid," 105.

13. Ibid., 107.

14. Ibid., 106.

15. Lillian Craig Harris, *China's Foreign Policy toward the Third World* (Washington, D.C., 1985), 81–82.

16. Lillian Craig Harris and Robert L. Worden, *China and the Third World: Champion or Challenger?* (Dover, MA, 1986), 147.

17. Daniel L. Byman and Roger Cliff, *China's Arms Sales: Motivations and Implications* (Santa Monica, 1999), 25.

18. Ibid., 3–4.

19. Ibid., 50–53; Taylor, *China and Africa*, 119.

20. See "Zaire: Foreign Military Relations," available at http://reference.allrefer. com/country-guide-study/zaire/zaire198.html (accessed 16 December 2007). This study is part of a Library of Congress country study series. Data are as of 1993.

21. Human Security Baseline Assessment, "Arms, Oil and Darfur: The Evolution of Relations between China and Sudan," *Sudan Issue Brief*, VII (2007), 4.

22. Byman and Cliff, *China's Arms Sales*, 23–25.

23. U.S. Department of State, *World Military Expenditures and Arms Transfers* (Washington, D.C., 2003), 165–166, 187–189, available at www.state.gov/t/vci/rls/ rpt/wmeat/1999_2000/ (accessed 16 December 2007).

24. Richard F. Grimmett, "Conventional Arms Transfers to Developing Nations, 1992–1999," *CRS Report for Congress* (2000), 53, 55.

25. Human Security Baseline Assessment, "Arms, Oil and Darfur," 4–5; Mark Curtis and Claire Hickson, "Arming and Alarming? Arms Exports, Peace and Security," in Leni Wild and David Mepham (eds.), *The New Sinosphere: China in Africa* (London, 2006), 38; Chung-lian Jiang, "Oil: A New Dimension in Sino–African Relations," *African Geopolitics*, Issue 14 (2004), available at www.african-geopolitics.org/show. aspx?ArticleId=3702 (accessed 16 December 2007); Chris Alden, *China in Africa* (London, 2007), 26.

26. Grimmett, "Conventional Arms Transfers," 58; Curtis and Hickson, "Arming and Alarming?" 44; Alden, *China in Africa*, 25; Kenneth W. Allen and Eric A. McVadon, *China's Foreign Military Relations* (Washington, D.C., 1999), 22, 33.

27. Human Rights Watch, "Arms Trade in Practice," in *Question of Principle: Arms Trade and Human Rights* (October 2000), available at www.hrw.org/reports/2000/ safrica/Sarfio00-05.htm (accessed 16 December 2007).

28. Allen and McVadon, *China's Foreign Military Relations*, 95.

29. "China Demands Libya Cease Official Ties with Taiwan," Xinhua (11 May 2006); "Taiwan Defends Ties with Libya Despite Protests from China," Deutsche Presse-Agentur (11 May 2006); "Taiwan Denies Report of Arms Sales to Libya," Agence France-Presse (2 August 2006).

30. Chinese Ministry of Foreign Affairs, "China's Africa Policy" (January 2006), available at www.chinese-embassy.org.za/eng/zxxx/t230687.htm (accessed 16 December 2007).

31. Chinese Ministry of Foreign Affairs, "Declaration of the Beijing Summit of the Forum on China-Africa Cooperation" (16 November 2006), available at www.fmprc.gov.cn/zflt/eng/zxxx/t280370.htm (accessed 16 December 2007).

32. Kristen Gunness, "China's Military Diplomacy in an Era of Change" (Washington, D.C., 2006).

33. Richard F. Grimmett, "Conventional Arms Transfers to Developing Nations, 1998–2005," *CRS Report for Congress* (2006), 40, 58, 61, 63, 66.

34. June Teufel Dreyer, "The China Connection" (Miami, 2006), 3, 6.

35. "France Says Finding Too Many Chinese Arms in Africa," Reuters (14 December 2006).

36. Wild and Mepham, *The New Sinosphere,* 44.

37. *Small Arms Survey 2007* (Geneva), 102, 106–107, available at www.smallarmssurvey.org/files/sas/publications/yearb2007.html (accessed 11 June 2008).

38. Susan M. Puska, "Resources, Security and Influence: The Role of the Military in China's Africa Strategy," *China Brief,* VII (30 May 2007), available at www.jamestown.org/terrorism/news/article.php?articleid=2373435 (accessed 16 December 2007). For a current list of African military attachés in Beijing, see Beijing Military Attaché Corps, "Attaché List," available at www.bjmac.org/HTML/Attaches.htm (accessed 16 December 2007).

39. See "SIPRI Arms Transfers Database," available at http://armstrade.sipri.org (accessed 16 December 2007); "China Defense Minister Chi Haotian Concludes Algeria Visit," Xinhua (16 November 2000); "Chinese Defense Minister Meets Algerian Guests," Xinhua (30 May 2005); "PLA Senior Official Leaves Beijing on Visit to Algeria, Tunisia," Xinhua (19 November 2005); "Chinese Military Official Pledges Further Military Exchanges with Algeria," Xinhua (14 August 2006); "Chinese-Algerian Presidents Sign Statement on Strategic Cooperation," Xinhua (6 November 2006).

40. "China's Chief of General Staff Meets Angolan Guests," Xinhua (24 January 2000); "PRC's Hu Jintao Meets Angolan Defense Minister," Xinhua (8 May 2000); "Chi Haotian Meets with Angolan Defense Minister," Xinhua (8 May 2000); "Angola to Reinforce Friendly Relations with China," Xinhua (28 June 2001); "Military Cooperation between Angola and China under Discussion," Angola Press Agency (9 August 2004); "Angolan, PRC Delegations Discuss Military Cooperation," *Folha 8* (21 August 2004).

41. "Angola: Chinese Company to Build Special Forces Training Center," Panafrican News Agency (23 September 2004); "PLA Chief of Staff Holds Talks with Angolan

Counterpart," Xinhua (11 June 2005); "Angolan and Chinese Armies Strengthen Co-
Operation," Angola Press Agency (15 June 2005); "China-Angola Sign 9 Cooperation
Agreements," afrol News (7 March 2006); Loro Horta and Ian Storey, "China's Por-
tuguese Connection," *YaleGlobal Online* (22 June 2006), available at http://yale
global.yale.edu/display.article?id=7634; "Chinese Military Delegation Ends Visit to
Angola," Angola Press Agency (2 April 2007); Jonathan Holslag and others, *China's
Resources and Energy Policy in Sub–Saharan Africa: Report for the Development Com-
mittee of the European Parliament* (Brussels, 2007), 64.

42. Bjorn Hagelin, Mark Bromley, and Siemon T. Wezeman, "International Arms
Transfers," in *SIPRI Yearbook 2006: Armaments, Disarmament and International Secu-
rity* (London, 2006), 461, available at http://yearbook2006.sipri.org/ (accessed 16
December 2007).

43. "China Delivers First Batch of Jointly Produced K-8E Training Planes to Egypt,"
Xinhua (11 July 2001); "China Awards Aircraft Production License to Egyptian Manufacturer," Xinhua (29 August 2005); "Egypt Produces 80 Chinese-Designed K-8E
Aircraft in Past Five Years," Xinhua (11 December 2005). For background information
on this project, see "K-8E Karakorum in Egypt," available at www.aviationfans.com/
node/8 (accessed 16 December 2007).

44. "Chinese Military Official Hails Egyptian-Chinese Cooperation," Middle East
News Agency (15 June 2002); U.S. Navy, Office of Naval Intelligence, *China's Navy
2007*, 118, available at www.fas.org/irp/agency/oni/chinanavy2007.pdf (accessed 16
December 2007).

45. Wild and Mepham, *The New Sinosphere*, 44.

46. "Officers from 24 Countries to Observe Chinese Military Drill," Xinhua (26 September 2005).

47. "Military Academy Launches China's 1st International Cadets Week," Xinhua
(2 November 2005).

48. "Liang Guanglie Calls for Further Promoting Military Cooperation with Egypt,"
Xinhua (6 April 2004); PRC Defense Minister Cao Gangchuan Discusses Cooperation
with Egyptian Counterpart," Xinhua (20 September 2004); "Egyptian, Chinese Min-
isters Discuss Expansion of Armed Forces' Cooperation," Middle East News Agency (9
April 2005); "Chinese Defense Minister Hails Developing Sino-Egyptian Ties," Xinhua
(10 April 2005); Luo Zheng, "Zhang Li Meets with Egyptian Military Training Dele-
gation," *Jiefangjun Bao* (4 May 2005); "Egypt, China in Military Cooperation Talks,"
Middle East News Agency (10 July 2006); Zhang Shun, "Zhang Qinsheng Meets
Egyptian Guests," *Jiefangjun Bao* (7 August 2006); Puska, "Resources, Security and
Influence."

49. "Defense Minister Chi Haotian Holds Talks with Ghanaian Counterpart," Xin-
hua (27 June 2000); "Ghana: Defense Minister Leaves for Beijing to Discuss Military
Training Programs," Ghana Broadcasting Corporation Radio 1 (12 October 2003);
"China to Build Ghana Defense Ministry Offices," Ghana Broadcasting Corporation
Radio 1 (20 April 2007); "Ghana, China Sign Loan Agreement," Ghana News Agency
(26 June 2007).

50. "Chinese Funded Barracks Inaugurated in Accra," Radio Ghana (11 March 2004); "China Donates 55 Vehicles to Defense Ministry," Ghana Broadcasting Corporation Radio 1 (7 February 2005); "Ghana to Exchange Presidential Jet with Four Chinese Fighter Planes," Joy FM (Accra) (24 May 2006); "Ghana's Air Force to Take Delivery of Four Aircraft from China," TV3 (Accra) (12 October 2006).

51. "Chinese Defense Minister Chi Haotian Meets Nigerian Counterpart," Xinhua (16 July 2001); "Chi Haotian Meets Nigerian Counterpart," Xinhua (23 April 2002); "Cooperation between China and Nigeria Fruitful, Defense Minister," Xinhua (25 June 2004); "Luo Zheng, "Cao Gangchuan Holds Talks with Nigerian Defense Minister," *Jiefangjun Bao* (8 April 2007).

52. "Chinese Firm May Manage Nigeria's Defense Industries Group," Panafrican News Agency (19 September 2004). See also Michael Klare and Daniel Volman, "America, China and the Scramble for Africa's Oil," *Review of African Political Economy,* XXXIII (2006), 305.

53. "Nigeria to Buy Military Equipment Worth $251 Million from China," Radio Nigeria-Abuja (29 September 2005); "Nigeria: China Donates $3 Million Equipment to Nigerian Armed Forces," Rhythm FM (28 October 2005); Hagelin, Bromley, and Wezeman, "International Arms Transfers," 531; Alden, *China in Africa,* 26; Donovan C. Chau, *Political Warfare in Sub-Saharan Africa: U.S. Capabilities and Chinese Operations in Ethiopia, Kenya, Nigeria, and South Africa* (Washington, D.C., 2007), 2, 38, and 41–42, available at www.strategicstudiesinstitute.army.mil/pdffiles/pub766.pdf (accessed 16 December 2007).

54. Dino Mahtani, Mure Dickie, and Demetri Sevastopulo, "Nigeria Shifts to China Arms," *Financial Times* (28 February 2006); "Nigeria Let Down by U.S. Oil Aid," UPI (28 February 2006); "More Patrol Boats to Guard Coast," *Africa Energy Intelligence* (22 March 2006); Ndubisi Obiorah, "Who's Afraid of China in Africa? Towards an African Civil Society Perspective on China-Africa Relations," in Firoze Manji and Stephen Marks (eds.), *African Perspectives on China in Africa* (Cape Town, 2007), 47; "U.S. Partners on Security for Oil-Rich Delta Region," *Africa News* (15 March 2007); Jim Fisher-Thompson, "U.S. Partners with Nigeria on Security for Oil-Rich Delta Region" (15 March 2007), available at www.america.gov/st/washfile-english/2007/March/200703151535251EJrehsiF0.7514307.html (accessed 5 June 2008).

55. Jim Yardley, "Snubbed by U.S., China Finds New Space Partners," *New York Times* (24 May 2007), available at www.nytimes.com/2007/05/24/world/asia/24 satellite.html?_r=1&scp=2&sq=snubbed%20by%20US%20China%20&st=cse&oref= slogin (accessed 28 May 2008); Edward Cody, "China Builds and Launches a Satellite for Nigeria," *Washington Post* (14 May 2007), A11.

56. "China's Chi Haotian, South Africa Defense Minister Hold Talks," Xinhua (5 June 2000); "Chinese Navy Ships Begin First Ever Visit to Africa," *People's Daily* (28 July 2000). For a complete list of China–South Africa military exchanges between 1998 and 2003, see "China-South Africa Bilateral Relations: 4. Military Exchanges," *Chinadaily.com* (26 January 2007), available at www.chinadaily.com.cn/china/2007-01/26/content_793507_10.htm (accessed 16 December 2007).

57. "China's Chi Haotian Discusses Bilateral Defense Ties with South African Counterpart," Xinhua (22 August 2001); "Chinese Defense Minister Meets South African Counterpart," Xinhua (11 December 2001); "Tang Jiaxuan, South African Foreign Minister Urge International Community Not to Neglect Developing States While Fighting Terrorism," Xinhua (14 January 2002).

58. "China-South Africa Bilateral Relations: Military Relations"; Wang Qun, "South African Vice President Jacob Zuma Meets with Visiting PLA Chief of General Staff Liang Guanglie," Xinhua (7 May 2003); "China, South Africa Agree to Enhance Defense Exchanges," Xinhua (17 June 2005); "China-South Africa Defense Committee to Hold Second Meeting," Xinhua (24 June 2005); "China, South Africa to Strengthen Military Cooperation," Xinhua (21 November 2005).

59. "Senior Chinese Military Officer Leaves for Two-Nation Tour," Xinhua (31 May 2006); Zhang Shun, "Cao Gangchuan Meets with South African National Defense Force Commander," Jiefangjun Bao (2 September 2006); "South Africa, China Sign Strategic Political Partnership," South African Press Association (25 September 2006); "China-South Africa Defense Committee Holds 3rd Meeting in Pretoria," Jiefangjun Bao (7 December 2006). See also "China, South Africa Vow to Strengthen Military Ties," China View (17 July 2007), available at http://news.xinhuanet.com/english/2007-07/17/content_6388503.htm (accessed 16 December 2007).

60. Terry Crawford-Browne, "Denel: An Industry Out of Control" (19 October 2000), available at www.ecaar.org/za/Papers/denel.htm (accessed 16 December 2007); Richard Fisher, Jr., "IDEX 2007 Showcases China's Productive Weapons Sector" (26 March 2007), available at www.strategycenter.net/printVersion/print_pub.asp?pubID=152 (accessed 25 April 2008). Background on the Armscor case can be found in U.S. v. Thomas P. Jasin, appeal submitted to the U.S. district court for the eastern district of Pennsylvania on 7 December 2001. See U.S. v. Thomas P. Jasin, 280 F3d 355 (3d Cir, 5 February 2002), available at http://bulk.resource.org/courts.gov/c/F3/280/280.F3d.355.00-4185.html (accessed 28 April 2008).

61. "Vision for Darfur," Beijing Review (16 August 2007), 12; Edward Cody, "In China, a Display of Resolve on Darfur," Washington Post (16 September 2007), A14; "Beijing Says It Is Trying to Keep Chinese-Made Weapons out of Darfur," Associated Press (5 July 2007).

62. Human Security Baseline Assessment, "Arms, Oil, and Darfur," 5–6; Lindsey Hilsum, "Re-enter the Dragon: China's New Mission in Africa," Review of African Political Economy, XXXII (2005), 422; "Sudan Has Drones, Is Pursuing Missiles-State Media," Reuters (6 September 2007); Daniel T.M. Large, "Sudan-China Relations: An Historical Perspective on 'China's Outpost in Africa,'" paper presented at the International Sudan Studies Conference (Bergen, Norway, 6 April 2006), 8.

63. David Hale's expertise lies in Chinese affairs. See comments by David Hale in "Video #25—China: Commodities Consumption" (16 January 2006), available at www.pbs.org/nbr/site/research/educators/060106_25a/ (accessed 16 December 2007). See also Bill Gertz and Rowan Scarborough, "Inside the Ring," Washington Times (5

March 2004). Author's conversation with foreign expert on the Sudan (Washington, D.C., 2 October 2007).

64. Charles Smith, "UN Suspends Aid Flights to Sudan," *WorldNetDaily* (11 August 2000), available at www.worldnetdaily.com/news/article.asp?ARTICLE_ID=20626 (accessed 16 December 2007); SIPRI Arms Transfers Database"; "SPLM: Reign of Corruption and Political Stagnation," *Sudan Today* (8 November 2006), available at www.sudantribune.com/spip.php?article18550 (accessed 16 December 2007); Amnesty International, "Appeal by Amnesty International to the Chinese Government on the Occasion of the China-Africa Summit for Development and Cooperation," available at www.amnesty.org/en/report/info/AFR54/072/2006 (accessed 16 December 2007); Large, "Sudan-China Relations," 8; Amnesty International, "Sudan: Arms Continuing to Fuel Serious Human Rights Violations in Darfur" (8 May 2007), available at www.amnesty.org/en/report/info/AFR54/019/2007 (accessed 16 December 2007).

65. "Chinese Defense Minister Chi Haotian Meets Sudanese Counterpart," Xinhua (16 June 2000); "China's Fu Quanyou, Sudanese Chief of Staff of Armed Forces Discuss Relations," Xinhua (25 March 2002); "Sudan: Defense Minister to Leave for China, India on 3 December," Sudan Radio (2 December 2003); "Senior Chinese Military Leader Stresses Friendship with Sudan," Xinhua (20 July 2005); "Sudanese President Meets Chinese General, Lauds Ties with China," Sudan News Agency (31 October 2005); "CMC Vice Chairman Xu Caihou Meets Sudanese General Staff Deputy," *Jiefangjun Bao* (9 December 2005); "Chinese Chief of General Staff Meets Sudanese Air Force Commander," Xinhua (22 December 2005).

66. "PLA Deputy Chief of General Staff Zhang Li Receives Sudan Military Delegation," *Jiefangjun Bao* (14 March 2006); "China, Sudan to Promote Cooperation between Armed Forces," Xinhua (31 March 2006); "China, Sudan to Boost Exchanges between Armed Forces," Xinhua (3 April 2006); "China Raises Darfur as Boosts Ties with Sudan," Reuters (3 April 2007); Mure Dickie and Mark Turner, "China Boost for Sudan Military," *Financial Times* (3 April 2007), available at http://search.ft.com/ft Article?queryText=china+boost+for+sudan+military&y=0&aje=true&x=0&id=0704 03010399&ct=0&nclick_check=1 (accessed 28 May 2008); "Sanctioned Sudan Turns to China, Russia, Iran and North Korea for Weapons," *World Tribune* (5 September 2007), available at www.worldtribune.com/worldtribune/WTARC/2007/af_sudan_09_ 05.asp (accessed 28 May 2008).

67. "Uganda: China Donates 52 Military Trucks to Army," *New Vision* (Kampala, 1 August 2002); "Uganda: Weapons Agreements Violations?" *Financial Times Information* (1 December 2004).

68. "Chinese Defense Minister Cao Gangchuan Holds Talks with Ugandan Counterpart," Xinhua (4 September 2003); "Chinese Government Donates Trucks to Ugandan Army," Xinhua (25 March 2006); "Mbabazi Defends Arms Purchases from China," *New Vision* (Kampala, 14 June 2006); Margaret C. Lee, Henning Melber, and Sanusha Naidu, *China in Africa* (Uppsala, 2007), 33; "Chinese Officers at Work," *Indian Ocean Newsletter* (18 November 2006).

69. "Zambian President Meets PRC Military Delegation," Xinhua (3 November 2000); "Chinese Defense Minister Chi Haotian Meets Zambian Guests," Xinhua (20 August 2001); "PLA Chief of General Staff Fu Quanyou Starts Visit to Zambia," Xinhua (25 November 2001); "China, Zambia to Enhance Military Ties," Xinhua (10 June 2002); "Fu Quanyou Meets Zambian Military Delegation," Xinhua (7 August 2002); "NPC Vice Chairwoman Meets Zambian Defense Minister," Xinhua (11 July 2005); "Chinese, Zambian Defense Ministers Agree to Develop Military Cooperation," Xinhua (20 June 2007).

70. "China Exports Light, Multi-Purpose Airplanes to Zambia," Xinhua (31 July 2006); "China Delivers Two Planes to Zambia," Xinhua (18 August 2006); "SIPRI Arms Transfers Database"; "Hu Jintao Hails Contributions of PRC Military Physicians in Zambia," Xinhua (5 February 2007).

71. "PLA Chief of Staff Fu Quanyou Meets Zimbabwean Air Commander," Xinhua (15 November 2000); "PRC Chi Haotian Meets Zimbabwean Acting Defense Minister," Xinhua (12 June 2001); "Chi Haotian Holds Talks with Zimbabwean Defense Minister," Xinhua (30 October 2002); Luo Zheng, "Xiong Guangkai Holds Talks with Zimbabwe Army Commander," *Jiefangjun Bao* (1 September 2005).

72. Garth le Pere (ed.), *China in Africa: Mercantilist Predator or Partner in Development?* (Johannesburg, 2007), 193; Leon Engelbrecht, "Analysts Surprised at Zim 'Fighter Deal,'" South African Press Association (14 June 2004); "China Denies Jet Fighters Report," *Zimbabwe Independent* (25 June 2004); "China Denies Reports of Fighter Jet Sales to Zimbabwe," Xinhua (21 June 2004); "Zimbabwe Reportedly Buys Arms, Riot Gear from China," *Zim Online* (Johannesburg, 11 November 2004); "China, Zimbabwe to Strengthen Military Ties," Xinhua (31 July 2006).

73. "Zimbabwe Takes Delivery of Six Chinese-Made Trainer Jets," Agence France-Presse (14 April 2005); "Broke Government Splashes US$120 Million on Fighter Jets," *Financial Gazette* (22 April 2005); "SIPRI Arms Transfers Database"; John Garver, "Interpreting China's Grand Strategy," *China Brief*, V (5 June 2005), 10.

74. Lebo Nkatazo, "Zimbabwe Splashes on New Chinese K-8 Jets" (24 August 2006), available at http://www.newzimbabwe.com/pages/army14.14602.html; "Cash-Strapped Harare Buys More Military Jets," *Business Day* (24 August 2006); Helmoed-Romer Heitman, "Zimbabwe Set to Acquire More K-8s," *Jane's Defence Weekly*, XXXXIII (6 September 2006), 19.

75. Zhang Shun, "Liang Guanglie Meets with Zimbabwean Air Force Commander," *Jiefangjun Bao* (11 July 2006); "China, Zimbabwe to Strengthen Military Ties," Xinhua (31 July 2006); "ZDF Relations with Chinese Army Hailed," *Herald Online* (Harare, 24 October 2006), available at www.zimbabwesituation.com/oct24_2006.html#Z22 (accessed 24 May 2008); "President Presents Certificates to 57 Officers," *Herald* (Harare, 2 December 2006); Li Nu'er, "Zimbabwean Defense Minister Meets with High Level Chinese Military Delegation," *Jiefangjun Bao* (18 April 2007).

76. Curtis and Hickson, "Arming and Alarming?" 37–39.

77. Briefing by Assistant Foreign Minister Zhai Jun on 26 October 2006 at the International Press Center prior to the FOCAC Beijing Summit.

78. For additional background, see Byman and Cliff, *China's Arms Sales,* 31–41. For China's official position, see Ministry of Foreign Affairs of the People's Republic of China, "China's Non-Proliferation Policy and Measures" (21 May 2007), available at www.fmprc.gov.cn/eng/wjb/zzjg/jks/kjlc/fkswt/fkszc/t141197.htm (accessed 16 December 2007). Also see "Statement by Chinese Representative at UN Workshops on Small Arms and Light Weapons" (19 April 2005), available at www.mfa.gov.cn/eng/wjb/zzjg/jks/kjfywj/t195801.htm (accessed 16 December 2007), and "Statement by Chinese Representative at UN Workshop on Small Arms and Light Weapons" (19 April 2005), available at www.mfa.gov.cn/eng/wjb/zzjg/jks/kjfywj/t192412.htm (accessed 16 December 2007).

79. Wild and Mepham, *The New Sinosphere,* 39; Jonathan Holslag, "Friendly Giant? China's Evolving Africa Policy" (Brussels, 2007), 9.

80. Hagelin, Bromley, and Wezeman, "International Arms Transfers," 457; Office of the Secretary of Defense, *Annual Report to Congress: Military Power of the People's Republic of China 2007* (23 May 2007), 28, available at www.defenselink.mil/pubs/pdfs/070523-China-Military-Power-final.pdf (accessed 16 December 2007); Peter Brookes, "The Global Dragon," *Armed Forces Journal* (2006), 49; Jim Cooney, "Chinese Oil Dependence: Opportunities and Challenges," in Williamson Murray (ed.), *Strategic Challenges for Counterinsurgency and the Global War on Terrorism* (Carlisle, PA, 2006), 111; Ilan Berman, "The Impact of the Sino-Iranian Strategic Partnership," testimony before the U.S.-China Economic and Security Review Commission during a hearing on "China's Proliferation to North Korea and Iran, and Its Role in Addressing the Nuclear and Missile Situations in Both Nations" (14 September 2006).

81. "China Always Prudent in Arms Trade: FM Spokeswoman," Xinhua (13 June 2006).

82. Stefan Staehle, "China's Participation in the United Nations Peacekeeping Regime," MA thesis (George Washington University, 21 May 2006), 47–48 and 104–106; Elling N. Tjonneland and others, *China in Africa: Implications for Norwegian Foreign and Development Policies* (Bergen, 2006), 13–14, 42, 55; Holslag and others, *China's Resources,* 7–8; Alden, *China in Africa,* 26; Puska, "Resources, Security and Influence."

83. For UN peacekeeping data, see "UN Mission's Contributions by Country" (30 September 2007), available at www.un.org/Depts/dpko/dpko/contributors/2007/sept07_5.pdf (accessed 24 May 2008), and "Ranking of Military and Police Contributions to UN Operations" (30 September 2007), available at www.un.org/Depts/dpko/dpko/contributors/2007/sept07_2.pdf (accessed 24 May 2008).

84. Cody, "In China, a Display of Resolve"; "China Sends 5 Peacekeepers to Darfur in Advance," Xinhua (11 October 2007).

85. "Chinese Selected to Lead UN Peacekeeping Force in Western Sahara," UN News Service (27 August 2007).

86. Ministry of Foreign Affairs, People's Republic of China, *China's Foreign Affairs, 2004 Edition* (Beijing, 2004), 202–203; Alex Vines, "The Scramble for Resources: African Case Studies," *South African Journal of International Affairs,* XIII (2006), 72;

Denis M. Tull, "China's Engagement in Africa: Scope, Significance and Consequences," *Journal of Modern African Studies,* XXXXIV (2006), 475; "Liberian President Praises Ties with China," Xinhua (28 September 2006).

87. Wu Miaofa, "A Significant Change," *Beijing Review* (10 May 2007), 11.

88. "Chinese President in the Spotlight over Sudan," *Sudan Tribune* (2 February 2007); "Chinese Leader in War-Battered Liberia, under the Spotlight over Sudan," *TurkishPress.com* (1 February 2007), available at http://archive.turkishpress.com/news.asp?id=161223 (accessed 28 May 2008).

89. See for example the 18 October 2007 letter "on behalf of more than 180 faith-based, advocacy, and human rights organizations in the U.S." to President Hu Jintao from the executive director of the Save Darfur Coalition, available at http://darfur.3cdn.net/68b1507e04161d3433_8zm6bneoc.pdf (accessed 16 December 2007).

90. "Kibaki Leads Calls to Ban Landmines," *The Nation* (Kenya, 3 December 2004); "Chinese Mine-Sweeping Experts Return Home from Thailand," Xinhua (1 December 2005); "China Trains 230 Foreign Mine Clearance Personnel," Xinhua (20 December 2006); Information Office of the State Council of the People's Republic of China, "China's National Defense in 2004" (December 2004), available at http://english.peopledaily.com.cn/whitepaper/defense2004/defense2004.html (accessed 16 December 2007).

91. Edmund Sanders, "A Search for Oil Raises the Stakes in War-torn Darfur," *Los Angeles Times* (3 March 2007), A1–3.

92. "Ten Chinese among Sailors Captured Off Somalia," Associated Press (17 May 2007).

93. "Niger Rebels Free Chinese Hostage in Uranium Firm," Reuters (10 July 2007).

94. Craig Timberg, "Militants Warn China over Oil in Niger Delta," *Washington Post* (1 May 2006), available at www.washingtonpost.com/wp-dyn/content/article/2006/04/30/AR2006043001022_pf.html (accessed 28 May 2008); Qin Jize, "Gunmen Kidnap 5 Chinese in Nigeria," *China Daily* (6–7 January 2007); "Chinese Telecom Firm's Special Team Arrives in Nigeria on Hostage Rescue Mission," Xinhua (9 January 2007); "Nigerian Militants Release Five Chinese Workers," VOA News (18 January 2007); "Two More Chinese Kidnapped in Restive Southern Nigeria," Agence France-Presse (20 March 2007); Ian Taylor, "Sino-Nigerian Relations: FTZs, Textiles and Oil," *China Brief*, VII (30 May 2007), 11–13; Obiorah, "Who's Afraid of China," 51.

95. Tsegaye Tadesse, "Rebels Kill 74 in Ethiopia Oil Field Raid," Reuters (24 April 2007); Jeffrey Gettleman, "Ethiopian Rebels Kill 70 at Chinese-Run Oil Field," *New York Times* (25 April 2007), available at www.nytimes.com/2007/04/25/world/africa/25ethiopia.html?partner=rssnyt&emc=rss (accessed 28 May 2008); "Freed Chinese Oil Workers Arrive in Ethiopian Capital," *Thomson Financial* (30 April 2007).

96. Alexa Olesen, "China Says Ethiopia Attacks Will Not Stop It from Investing in Africa," Associated Press (4 April 2007).

97. "China Is No Fair-Weather Friend to Africa," Reuters (15 May 2007); Adam Wolfe, "Ethiopian Attack Is Latest Test of China's Strategy in Africa," *World Politics*

Review (1 May 2007), available at www.worldpoliticsreview.com/Article.aspx?id=745 (accessed 25 April 2008); Chris Buckley, "China Condemns Ethiopia Attack amid Oil Security Fears," Reuters (25 April 2007); "Petroleum Companies Unable to Start Work on Exploration Projects," *The Reporter* (Addis Ababa, 21 October 2007).

98. Edward Cody, "China's Expansion Puts Workers in Harm's Way," *Washington Post* (26 April 2007), available at www.washingtonpost.com/wp-dyn/content/article/2007/04/25/AR2007042500736.html (accessed 28 May 2008).

99. Forum on China-Africa Cooperation, "Beijing Action Plan (2007–2009)" (16 November 2006), available at www.fmprc.gov.cn/zflt/eng/zyzl/hywj/t280369.htm (accessed 16 December 2007).

100. He Wenping, "The Balancing Act of China's Africa Policy," *China Security*, III (2007), 25.

101. Forum on China-Africa Cooperation, "Addis Ababa Action Plan (2004–2006)," available at www.focac.org/eng/zyzl/hywj/t157710.htm (accessed 16 December 2007); "Beijing Action Plan (2007–2009)," 11–12.

102. "China Celebrates Ancient Navigator's 600th Anniversary of Navigating World," Xinhua (11 July 2005). See also the Preface to this volume.

103. James R. Holmes and Toshi Yoshihara, "Soft Power at Sea: Zheng He and Chinese Maritime Strategy," *U.S. Naval Institute Proceedings*, CXXXII (2006), 38.

104. "Chinese Navy Ships Begin First Ever Visit to Africa," *People's Daily* (28 July 2000); "Naval Ships' Head Meets Tanzanian Army Chief," *People's Daily* (29 July 2000); "Chinese Naval Task Group Begins Three-Day Visit," Xinhua (10 August 2000).

105. "Chinese Military Official Hails Egyptian-Chinese Cooperation," Middle East News Agency (15 June 2002); "Chinese Naval Fleet Ends Visit to Egypt," *People's Daily* (18 June 2002); "Chinese Ambassador to Egypt Interviewed on Naval Fleet's Visit, Strategic Ties," Xinhua (4 July 2002).

106. Office of the Secretary of Defense, *Military Power 2007*, 3–4.

107. Ibid., 4, 24. See also Staff Report, "PRC Carriers by 2010?" *Defense and Foreign Affairs Strategic Policy* (2007), 8–9; "The Long March to Be a Superpower," *Economist* (4 August 2007), 23.

108. Information Office of the State Council, People's Republic of China, *China's National Defense in 2006* (29 December 2006), available at www.fas.org/nuke/guide/china/doctrine/wp2006.html (accessed 16 December 2007).

109. Willy Lam, "China Outlines Ambitious Objectives in Its Defense White Paper," *China Brief*, VII (10 January 2007), 2–3.

110. Congressional Research Service, "China Naval Modernization: Implications for U.S. Navy Capabilities—Background and Issues for Congress" (7 February 2007), 35–38; Bill Gertz, "China Builds Up Strategic Sea Lanes," *Washington Times* (18 January 2005); Robert J. Art, "Agreeing to Agree (and Disagree)" *National Interest* (2007), 38; Brookes, "The Global Dragon," 49; "The Long March to Be a Superpower," 21; James Holmes, statement before the U.S.-China Economic and Security Review Commission on "China's Energy Consumption and Opportunities for U.S.-China

Cooperation to Address the Effects of China's Energy Use" (14 June 2007), available at www.uscc.gov/hearings/2007hearings/hr07_06_14_15.php (accessed 16 December 2007).

111. Author's notes on remarks by David M. Finkelstein on "China's Military Modernization," Senate Dirksen Office Building (23 March 2007).

112. Office of the Secretary of Defense, *Military Power 2007*, 8–9; Bang Quan Zheng, "A Rising China: Catalysts for Chinese Military Modernization," in Sujian Guo (ed.), *China's Peaceful Rise in the 21st Century: Domestic and International Conditions* (Aldershot, Britain, 2006), 197–198; Hongyan He Oliver, "Reducing China's Thirst for Foreign Oil: Moving Towards a Less Oil-Dependent Road Transport System," *Woodrow Wilson China Environment Series* (2006), 41–43; Wu Lei and Shen Qinyu, "Will China Go to War over Oil?" *Far Eastern Economic Review*, CLXIX (2006), 40; Robert E. Ebel, "China's Energy Future," unpublished paper (2006); Antoine Halff, "The Panda Menace," *National Interest* (2007), 40; Linda Jakobson and Zha Daojiong, "China and the Worldwide Search for Oil Security," *Asia-Pacific Review*, XIII (2006), 61–64.

113. Jacques de Lisle, "China Rising: Assessing China's Economic and Military Power," *Foreign Policy Research Institute Conference Report* (Philadelphia, 2007).

114. Steven J. Forsberg, "India Stretches Its Sea Legs," *U.S. Naval Institute Proceedings*, CXXXIII (2007), 42; Richard D. Fisher, Jr., "China's Submarines Pose Regional, Strategic Challenges," *Armed Forces Journal*, CXLIII (2006), 37; Scott Baldauf and Joseph J. Schatz, "Chinese Leader's Almost Triumphal Trip to Africa," *Christian Science Monitor* (9 February 2007), available at www.csmonitor.com/2007/0209/p01s04-woaf.html (accessed 28 May 2008); U.S.-China Economic and Security Review Commission, "China's Energy Consumption."

115. Office of the Secretary of Defense, *Annual Report to Congress: Military Power of the People's Republic of China 2006* (23 May 2006), available at www.dod.mil/pubs/pdfs/China%20Report%202006.pdf (accessed 16 December 2007).

DEBORAH BRAUTIGAM

9

China's Foreign Aid in Africa: What Do We Know?

Several years ago, China's foreign aid program started to emerge from the shadows where it had been operating for close to five decades. Rumors of a huge new aid program ran through Western papers and magazines. By late 2006, concern about China's role as a donor gained a place on the agendas of the major players in the global aid regime. Bilateral and multilateral agencies in Washington, Stockholm, Canada, London, and Oslo organized a number of meetings on China's aid, where participants expressed worries about debt sustainability, the lack of conditions favoring governance and human rights, and environmental impacts.

Other chapters in this volume elaborate on those concerns. This chapter provides an overview of China's aid program (context and history), separates out "aid" from the other economic instruments being used by Beijing, and explains the changing rationale for aid from the 1950s to the present. It outlines what we know about the quantity of China's aid in Africa and provides a brief comparison with Taiwan's aid program. This chapter draws on interviews with Chinese officials in Beijing and Washington (during 2007), and in several African countries, and on the author's extensive fieldwork in Africa during the 1980s and 1990s. The interviews and fieldwork are complemented by a reading of recent newspaper articles and by library research. Information is offered with caveats: much is known about China's aid, but there is still much more that is unclear, difficult to interpret, or deliberately kept hidden.

China's aid program needs to be seen in relation to China's economic engagement with the African continent as a whole, and in comparison to the size of the aid programs of the West. It is not terribly large. For example, in 2006 alone, two-way trade between China and Africa came to $55 billion, while the cumulative total of aid to Africa from 1957 to mid-2006 amounted to only $5.7 billion.[1] In 2006, China's budgeted total expenditure for foreign aid in Africa (grants, zero-interest loans, and the cost of the interest subsidy on concessional loans) was close to $500 million. Approximately a quarter of the projects funded by China's Eximbank in Africa are concessional. Although Beijing does not regularly release figures on concessional loans, Standard and Poor's reported that between 2001 and 2005, the Eximbank had funded a total of seventy-eight concessional projects worldwide for RMB 10 billion ($1.24 billion).[2] Eximbank officials revealed to World Bank officials that it had funded fifty-five concessional projects in Africa by the end of 2005 for a total of $800 million.[3]

China's Aid Program in Africa: Overview

Chinese sources date the beginning of their aid program to 1950, the year after the establishment of the People's Republic.[4] Although the initial aid transfers went to North Korea, North Vietnam, and other socialist countries in China's immediate neighborhood, China's aid program expanded quickly beyond the socialist bloc into South Asia, the Middle East, and Africa. By 1975, China had aid programs in more African countries than did the United States, and this pattern continues today.

Reports in the media on China's "return" to Africa suggest that the Chinese left after the Maoist period, turning inward to focus on their own development, but that is not the case: they remained, working quietly in all of the countries where they had wrestled diplomatic recognition away from Taiwan. In the mid-1980s, China's aid program reached worldwide an annual level of some $220 million.[5] By the 1990s, China was the largest developing country donor outside of the Organization for Petroleum Exporting Countries: more than 500,000 Chinese experts had been dispatched to more than 100 countries, working on more than 1,426 aid projects.[6] In 2006, China had ongoing aid projects in 86 developing countries and counted more than 114 countries as current or former recipients of Chinese aid.[7] Although Vietnam, North Korea, and Cambodia were China's most important early aid partners, after the 1970s, Africa received the bulk of China's aid. Table 9-1 illustrates the cumulative scope of the program, worldwide, as it stood in 1989, the last year for which the United States Central Intelligence Agency publicly provided statistics, which themselves must be regarded as rough approximations.

The largest single component of China's aid has always been infrastructure, and indeed, China's aid program is best known through two major projects:

Table 9-1. *Chinese Aid in Comparative Perspective, 1960–1989*
Millions of US$

Recipient region	Cumulative amount (estimate)
East Asia	514
Latin America	314
Middle East and South Asia	4,053
Africa	4,728
Total	9,655

Source: Central Intelligence Agency, *Handbook of Economic Statistics* (Washington, D.C., 1990).

the massive Tanzania-Zambia (Tanzam) Railway (completed in 1976), which employed some 25,000 Chinese over more than half a decade, and in Asia, the mountainous, trans-Himalayan Karakoram Highway linking China and Pakistan (completed in 1986). However, these megaprojects are the exceptions to the rule. Most of China's aid has come in the form of small and medium-size projects, such as a loan of $8.6 million to construct two administration buildings in Burkina Faso, or the launch of a $3 million irrigation project in Ghana. In scores of countries, the Chinese have implemented the construction of public buildings such as ministry office blocks, cultural centers, stadia, schools, hospitals, and clinics, as well as roads and bridges. Also significant has been China's support of light industry (factories producing bricks, textiles, paper, lumber, or cement) and particularly agro-industry (sugar refineries and grain mills). Agriculture has also been an important target of aid. In Africa, for example, more than forty-four countries have each hosted an average of three separate Chinese agricultural aid projects, many focusing on irrigated rice and vegetables. Given the urge to privatize state-owned industries across Africa, aid for state-owned enterprises is no longer common, but the Chinese have begun lending to African governments with the idea that concessional funds will be passed on to private sector firms to foster joint manufacturing ventures with Chinese firms.

From the discussion above, it is clear that China is not a new donor in Africa. The People's Republic of China extended aid in the 1950s to Algeria (1958) and Egypt (1959), and, as sub-Saharan African countries became independent in the 1960s, China established aid programs in an additional eleven African countries. In the 1970s, forty-three African countries had Chinese aid programs, and through the next three decades, China established formal diplomatic ties to all African countries except Swaziland, and established aid programs in all of them. These aid programs continue to operate (often at modest levels) in all of these countries except where the countries were wooed successfully by Taiwan.

In its breadth and scope (if not in funding), China's African aid program, thus, resembles that of the United States more than any other donor. The Scandinavians tend to focus their aid on a smaller number of countries: Tanzania and Zambia, for example. The French and other European countries frequently target their former colonies. In contrast, China operates an aid program in nearly every country in Africa, including many with per capita incomes much higher than China's: Mauritius, Botswana, and South Africa, for example. By early 2008, China had carried out more than 840 aid projects in Africa, constructing health centers, stadia, and hospitals; and teaching rice cultivation, sugar processing, and textile milling.

The Chinese Aid System, in Brief

Chinese Premier Zhou Enlai's visit to ten African countries—Egypt, Algeria, Morocco, Tunisia, Ghana, Mali, Guinea, the Sudan, Ethiopia, and Somalia—between 13 December 1963 and 5 February 1964 signaled the early importance that China placed on relations with the African continent. In a speech in Bamako, Mali, Zhou outlined eight principles that still guide China's foreign aid today.[8] China's aid is supposed to be based on equality, mutual benefit, and respect for the sovereignty of the host. Loans were to be nonconditional and interest free, with repayment easily rescheduled, and projects were designed to make the recipient self-reliant rather than dependent on China. To do so, the Chinese promised to select income-generating projects that could be constructed rapidly. Finally, China pledged to provide countries with top quality Chinese equipment and materials at international prices, accompanied by experts who would transfer fully their technical knowledge and live at the standards of their local counterparts. While similar types of commitments could be found among other aid-giving countries, the frank emphasis on mutual benefit and the pledge of noninterference continue to distinguish China's aid program from those programs operated by the West.

China offers aid in three forms: grants (which might include in-kind transfers of rice, material goods, or, rarely, cash); zero-interest loans; and, since 1995, low-interest "concessional" loans with subsidized interest rates. China's aid is coordinated by its Ministry of Commerce; within the ministry, the Department of Aid to Foreign Countries handles foreign aid policy, drafts and circulates most of the laws and regulations governing foreign aid, and puts together the budget for foreign aid from other ministries. The ministry's Bureau for International Economic Cooperation (at the same level in the Chinese hierarchy) manages the direct implementation of aid, organizes short-term training, and reviews the qualifications of Chinese firms that bid on tenders for the implementation of turnkey projects, the supply of materials for aid projects or as "in-kind" aid, and some prefeasibility studies. The Ministry of Commerce's Tendering Board for Foreign Assistance Projects holds meetings almost weekly to examine bids and establish the ground rules for bidding (that is, how many firms will be invited, or whether tendering will be wide open or limited) on each "complete plant" (turnkey) and material supply project. The Ministry of Health manages medical teams separately (although construction of clinics and other health infrastructure is handled by the Ministry of Commerce). Scholarships for Africans to study at Chinese universities are handled by the Ministry of Education. The Ministry of Agriculture helps advise on the selection of teams to implement fisheries and agricultural projects and provides technical assistance in rural areas. These projects are now increasingly subject to competitive bidding and are managed by the Ministry of Commerce.

Concessional loans are managed by the China Eximbank, one of China's three policy banks that carry out government directives and whose operations are subsidized by the government. The Eximbank coordinates with the Ministry of Commerce on the selection of projects to be financed by concessional loans. Only larger projects (minimum size of RMB 20 million, or about $2.4 million) that involve considerable use of Chinese goods (at least 50 percent) and services (that is, Chinese construction firms as contractors) can be funded with concessional loans. China also offers small amounts of multilateral aid through organizations like the Food and Agriculture Organization and the World Food Program, and it has a small, but growing, humanitarian aid program of its own, coordinated by the Ministries of Commerce, Foreign Affairs, and Defense. Finally, the China Development Bank is involved in Africa through a growing number of loans and its sponsorship of the China-Africa Development Fund (discussed below). However, it does not offer concessional loans.

Why Does China Give Aid?

Confident in its historic position as an important player on the world stage, China has used aid both as a form of exchange that resembles the ancient imperial practice of tribute, and as a very modern expression of soft power: a tool of diplomacy and an instrument to meet political, strategic, and economic goals.⁹ China's aid program enables the country to build business, cement political ties, and enhance its image at home and abroad as a rising but "responsible" power. During the 1960s and 1970s, aid served as an important component of China's foreign policy, assisting the quest for political recognition and support from other developing countries for Beijing's claim to the United Nations (UN) Security Council seat held by Taiwan from 1949 to 1971. Since China's market-oriented reforms began in 1978, aid—tied to trade—has boosted Chinese exports and foreign exchange earnings, and aid agreements have frequently led to profitable construction and management contracts for state-owned companies. Several of the state-owned firms that participated in the construction of the massive Tanzam Railway—for example, China Complete Plant Import and Export Corporation (China Complant) and China Civil Engineering and Construction Corporation—are today ranked among China's largest companies and have bid successfully on dozens of profitable infrastructural projects in Africa and elsewhere. The evolution of China's aid program over half a century shows these shifts clearly. The shift comprises four clear phases: security and socialism (1950–1963), third world leadership (1964–1977), cooperation for mutual benefit (1978–1994), and gearing up for going global (1995–present). Although elements of each phase are seen in the other periods, they differ by virtue of the role aid played in Chinese leaders' political goals.

Security and Socialism, 1950–1963

China's aid program developed during a long period of tension with both the Soviet Union and the United States. From 1949 to 1960, China established diplomatic relations with both emerging and established socialist or radical nationalist developing countries, and extended aid to many of them, as well as to most of the countries on or near its borders: North Korea, North Vietnam, Mongolia, Nepal, Cambodia, and Burma. At least eleven of the first fifteen countries to receive aid from China had socialist or radical nationalist governments. After the break with the Soviet Union, countering Russian influence guided some of the odd relationships China developed in Africa: the corrupt dictator Mobutu Sese Seko (Zaire-Congo) became one of China's largest aid recipients due to Mobutu's opposition to the Soviet-backed regime in neighboring Angola.

Third World Leadership, 1964–1977

China's ties with the Soviet Union deteriorated in the late 1950s, and in 1960 President Sergei Khrushchev cut off economic aid to China and withdrew

Soviet experts and technicians. Pushed into a position of independence, China accelerated its cultivation of other developing countries in an effort to establish a counterweight to both Soviet hegemony and capitalist imperialism, and to solidify its international position through winning the UN seat held at that time by Taiwan. From 1961 to 1971, when Beijing took its seat as one of the five permanent members of the UN Security Council, China extended aid to twenty-three new countries, sixteen of them African.

Developing countries, burdened with high-interest loans, difficult reschedulings, and donors who regularly interfered in their internal affairs and attached conditions to aid, appreciated the symbolic counterpoint provided through China's low-profile, highly concessional assistance. Chinese envoys in secret missions to African states courted African leaders who had chosen to recognize Taipei's claim to be the official China. They promised to continue Taiwan's existing aid projects and offered loans to underwrite a set of new projects. Even during the height of the chaotic Cultural Revolution in the late 1960s, China's aid program expanded: the agreement for the famous Tanzam Railway was signed in 1967.[10] By the end of the 1970s, seventy-four countries were receiving aid from China, and during that decade (a period that included overlapping commitments to the Tanzam Railway and the Karakoram Highway), Beijing appeared to be spending an average of at least $350 million a year on foreign aid.[11]

Cooperation for Mutual Benefit: 1978–1994

Between 1979 and 1982, China's aid program stalled temporarily as Chinese leaders began to feel their way toward a more market-oriented, "open-door," international economic policy. A 1987 study reported that new aid commitments announced in the media fell from $254 million in 1980 to $25 million in 1981 before recovering to $289 million in 1984.[12] The "open door" to the West; the growing demand for foreign exchange and decentralization within China; and a new concern with economic results, efficiency, and profits led to a major reshaping of China's foreign aid program, blurring the lines between foreign aid and other forms of economic relations.

Chinese leaders announced that they would undertake no new aid projects on the scale of the Tanzam Railway or the Karakoram Highway. In the early 1980s, they began to highlight "promoting joint prosperity" as a major foreign policy goal, and one that would be pursued with the use of foreign aid and other forms of economic cooperation. China would be "spending less," but "doing more."[13] In December 1982, Chinese Premier Zhao Ziyang traveled to Africa to promote South-South cooperation. During discussions with African leaders, Zhao announced that henceforth four principles—equality and mutual benefit, stress on practical results, diversity in form, and common progress—would guide China's economic and technical cooperation. "The four principles," commented Beijing Review, "are aimed at gradually switching the emphasis of China's cooperative economic and technical relations with other Third World countries from extending loans to developing cooperation which can benefit both partners."[14] By October 1983, the Chinese media announced that the new policies were working: "Once completed . . . many projects have been shifted from foreign aid to technical cooperation programs at the request of the recipient countries."[15] After China's leaders made the decision to restructure their aid program, annual aid commitments rose again over the next several years (this belies the assumption made by many that China "left" Africa during the 1980s and 1990s and only recently returned). For example, China's 1984 aid commitments of $258.9 million to Africa alone made China Africa's sixth-largest donor for that year, surpassing Japan, Norway, Sweden, and the United Kingdom.[16]

Zhao's announcement formalized a shift that had been underway for several years as Chinese organizations began to plan ways in which they could earn foreign exchange from the good contacts and relationships that they had built up through foreign aid. Economic objectives have always been a feature of China's aid. Chinese aid is almost entirely tied to the purchase of Chinese goods and services; in 1987 Beijing announced that 69 percent of China's aid funds were spent on (Chinese) equipment, the rest presumably was spent on local costs (local labor, energy, and materials) and some equipment and machinery imported from advanced industrial countries.[17] Yet economic gain for China was not originally a primary concern. Chinese officials made little effort to institutionalize a supplier relationship; to sell spare parts, additional services, or replacement equipment to earlier projects; or even to press for payments when the zero-interest loans came due. This changed with the post-Mao reforms, and those changes accelerated during the 1990s.

The shift to the market was also reflected in the variety of forms that aid began to take as Chinese aid officials were given leave to implement experiments to stretch aid money and help ensure that the projects completed by China could sustain their benefits in the difficult economic environment of the 1980s and 1990s. There were also a growing number of tripartite agreements where China itself supplied little or no funding but instead relied on funding provided by African governments, private companies, and international aid agencies. Debt-equity swaps, joint ventures, assisted sustainability, and aid-to-profit were also new elements of China's aid in this period.

TRIPARTITE COOPERATION. In one of the experimental forms of aid, tripartite cooperation, the Chinese stretched their own resources by supplying the equipment and manpower for a project, while another donor supplied the bulk of the funding, and the recipient country contributed some local support. Sometimes China's contributions to organizations, such as the UN Family Planning Association and the UN Capital Development Fund, became the seed capital for tripartite cooperation. The Chinese have supplied technicians, equipment, and management to the World Bank and financed projects such as well drilling and rice cultivation in Somalia and rice cultivation in Rwanda. Many of these latter efforts do not qualify as aid under Chinese terms (or any terms) but are simply forms of the economic "cooperation" announced in the 1983 reforms: labor and management services, contracting for construction, joint ventures in production or mineral exploration, or "tripartite cooperation."[18] Between 1976 and 1988, Chinese firms worldwide had fulfilled $6.9 billion worth of this type of profit-oriented contract; between 1989 and 2005, the value of completed contracts of this kind rose to $166.7 billion.[19]

DEBT-EQUITY SWAPS. China also undertook country-level experiments to address the problem that China's aid loans posed for debt-distressed countries. In some cases, China encouraged debt-equity swaps, allowing debtor governments to invest part of their loan debt (in local currency) in joint ventures. Zairian sources announced that during his visit to Zaire in January 1983, Zhao promised to write off a tenth of Zaire's debt in this manner.[20] Chinese companies originally established by the Ministry of Agriculture and the Ministry of Foreign Economic Relations to implement aid projects also became part owners of a sugar company in Togo and a sisal factory in Tanzania.[21]

ASSISTED SUSTAINABILITY. During the 1980s, while Western donors were emphasizing austerity and liberalization in structural adjustment policies that failed to address the fiscal and balance of payments crises caused in part by plummeting commodity prices, China emphasized direct action to maintain crumbling state assets. Countries suffering from rusting and underutilized factories, pot-holed roads, and semi-abandoned state farms (many, but not all, former Chinese aid projects) could benefit from "assisted sustainability": supplying spare parts, repairing decayed railway tracks, renovating crumbling irrigation dams, and managing sugar mills fallen into near bankruptcy. This assistance could be provided as aid or under commercial terms at very reasonable rates. The state-owned corporation China Complant sent a team to Africa in 1982 to survey fifty-two projects to determine the need for spare parts and ways to improve their supply.[22] China and Tanzania signed an agreement to renovate more than sixty former Chinese projects built over the previous two decades.[23]

FROM AID TO PROFITS. A final development occurred during this period. Chinese state-owned corporations with previous experience in Africa under foreign aid were eager to translate that experience into profit. Chinese contractors had a number of advantages over Bechtel; Louis Berger; and other well-established, U.S.-based international engineering contractors in Africa. Their labor was inexpensive, and they were willing to undertake projects for "friendly prices" to generate future contracts. In many African countries, Chinese construction teams handed over a completed office building or health center financed under Chinese foreign aid, and then they remained in the country, establishing branches of their home office and setting up shop, either independently or in a joint venture with a local partner. The proof of their competence was visible: a stadium here, an irrigation system there. More important, the Chinese practice of retaining bulldozers and heavy equipment brought over for construction, and charging only depreciation against aid project accounts, worked to give the new companies a tremendous cost advantage when bidding for commercial construction contracts in their host countries.

In such ways, China's aid in the immediate postreform period reflected an emphasis on markets, efficiency, and profits. China's shift toward market-oriented economic cooperation gave the Chinese greater control over projects that were now seen as opportunities for joint profit, not simply one-way transfers. However, the switch, whereby the same company might be implementing a Chinese aid project one month and bidding on a commercial project the next, confused observers, some of whom began to assume that every project featuring Chinese firms was foreign aid. The "diversity of forms" taken by official economic cooperation (and often by different units under the same ministry) increased the confusion over what was foreign aid, and what was not. This issue is revisited below.

Gearing Up for Going Global: 1995–Present

From 1995 to the present, China has accelerated the "win-win" cooperation of the 1980s in a drive for strategic partnerships, where aid has become one tool in an array of increasingly robust economic instruments that were first tried out in the previous decade, often on an experimental basis. Trade and access to mineral resources have played increasingly central roles in this period, but they are by no means the only purposes for aid. As with the earlier reforms of the 1980s, the new framework for foreign aid and economic cooperation particularly focused on Africa, where Chinese leaders continued to highlight the importance of their ties to the continent. Beginning in 1991, for example, Chinese Foreign Minister Qian Qichen began to visit a group of African countries each January, and this tradition has continued with each successive foreign minister.[24]

In mid-1995, after much discussion at high levels, Beijing held a large conference on further reform of China's foreign assistance programs, bringing them even more into line with the push toward economic rationality in China's domestic decisions. By the new millennium, with trade sharply expanded and Chinese companies increasing their outward investment in other developing countries, foreign aid became a smaller component of China's economic relations with other developing countries. This shift was reflected again in yet another name change in China's economic bureaucracies: the Ministry of Foreign Trade and Economic Cooperation became simply the Ministry of Commerce in the spring of 2003. At the same time, China expanded its economic and political engagement with African countries in a well-planned strategy that culminated in 2000 with the launch of the Forum on China-Africa Cooperation (FOCAC).

Although observers commonly assume that China gives aid today in Africa primarily to countries with natural resources that China needs for its rapid economic growth, there is not much evidence even now that the aid program *itself* is skewed in this direction. China continues to send health teams, operate scholarship programs, and carry out infrastructural and production projects in nearly all of the developing countries with which it has diplomatic ties. The confusion over China's aid can be traced in part to the fact that China is a socialist developmental state. The bulk of China's significant economic activities in Africa—natural resource imports, bank loans, infrastructural construction projects, and foreign investment—is carried out by government-owned banks, companies, and departments that are generally nontransparent (although this attribute is rapidly changing).

The pledges made in 2006 at the FOCAC summit in Beijing declared that Chinese leaders *over the next three years* would

—double the 2006 level of aid to Africa;

—provide $3 billion in preferential loans and $3 billion in preferential buyer's credits;

—establish a $5 billion fund to encourage Chinese investment in Africa;

—provide 4,000 university scholarships a year by 2009; build 100 rural schools, 30 hospitals, and 30 malaria prevention and treatment centers;

—build 10 agricultural technology demonstration centers staffed by 100 senior agricultural experts;

—set up 3 to 5 special economic cooperation zones for Chinese investment;

—provide some $1.4 billion in additional debt relief to low-income Africa for all overdue, zero-interest loans owed to China; and

—send 300 youth volunteers to work in Africa.[25]

Although the Chinese billed the economic cooperation measures as com-bining aid, trade, investment, and social development, some outsiders inter-preted this entire list to be foreign aid. "Beijing Pledges Aid Billions to Woo Africa," announced the *Observer*.[26] It may indeed have a positive develop-mental impact, but few would call this initiative "foreign aid." What, then, *is* China's current foreign aid, and how much are the Chinese giving to Africa?

How Much Aid Does China Give Today?

The media hype about Chinese aid in Africa has been intense. With the Chi-nese declining to give any official figures for annual aid to Africa, journalists, scholars, and even researchers at institutions like the World Bank and the International Monetary Fund (IMF) have grabbed any figures they could find and published them as hard facts. Some have reported figures as high as $9 bil-lion in "aid" for just one project in Nigeria.[27] A journalist at the *Christian Sci-ence Monitor* claimed that China's aid to Africa in 2006 was "three times the total development aid given by rich countries" (this would make it about $100 billion annually).[28] Others confuse regular loans (not aid) with concessional loans and grants (aid). For example, on 3 November 2006, two journalists cir-culated a report on Bloomberg.com, announcing that with an estimated $8.1 billion in "loans" committed to Africa for 2006, the Chinese were nearly tripling the "loans" offered by the World Bank.[29] The figure of $8.1 billion was subsequently widely circulated as a solid fact on "Chinese aid."[30]

What Is Aid?

In the West, over time and through much negotiation, a consensus has grown about what counts as "official development assistance" (ODA) in North-South flows, and those same guidelines should also be used for South-South aid like that offered by China. The Development Assistance Committee (DAC) of the Organization for Economic Cooperation and Development (OECD) has defined ODA as grants or loans that are intended primarily to foster devel-opment in the recipient country, and that have at least a 25 percent grant ele-ment.[31] Interviews in China confirm that the OECD-DAC guidelines have been closely studied by the Ministry of Commerce and the China Eximbank, and it is highly likely that the Chinese now use these same guidelines in their own calculations of foreign aid. For example, the China Eximbank reduced its already low interest rate on concessional loans in part to make them conform to international standards.

The DAC also tracks official outflows in a second category, which it calls "other official flows." These are moneys that come from governments but do not qualify as aid. It is worth focusing on this definition more closely because many of the flows that have made the headlines are in this category. Other official flows include development loans with less than a 25 percent grant element, and "official bilateral transactions, whatever their grant element, that are primarily export-facilitating in purpose. *This category includes by definition export credits extended directly to an aid recipient by an official agency or institution* [emphasis added]."[32]

Some areas of confusion and controversy arise. On the one hand, it is clear that very few of the large economic transactions between China and developing countries actually qualify as ODA (or what we call "foreign aid"). For example, few of the large sums mentioned in the November 2006 FOCAC summit should be viewed as ODA. On the other hand, the $3 billion in concessional loans over three years might qualify as ODA, although it would depend very much on the terms of the loans and their subsequent grant elements. Furthermore, the fact that they are offered by the China Eximbank could be interpreted to mean that they are "primarily export-facilitating in purpose." The projected $2 billion to be offered by the China Eximbank in preferential export credits for Africans to import Chinese equipment do not appear to be ODA by the DAC rules, even if they are low interest. The $5 billion fund for Chinese enterprises, or subsidies that allow Chinese banks to provide low-interest loans to secure business for Chinese firms, should also clearly not be counted as "aid." Indeed, as noted below, official Chinese sources do not appear to include figures like those in the external assistance budget. What do they count?

Chinese Aid: How Much Goes to Africa?

In June 2006, Chinese Premier Wen Jiabao announced that China's assistance to Africa between 1957 and 2006 had totaled RMB 44.4 billion ($5.7 billion).[33] This total is in line with the amounts estimated by Western researchers.[34] External aid in the Chinese budget includes the face value of the Ministry of Commerce's grants and zero-interest loans, and the interest subsidy (but not the face value) of the concessional loans made by the China Eximbank. The principal for Eximbank loans comes from funds raised on domestic and international capital markets. The Ministry of Commerce provides the Eximbank with a subsidy that makes up the difference between its cost of funds (say 6 percent) and the concessional interest rate that it charges borrowers (generally 2 percent). Thus, for an Eximbank concessional loan of $500 million, the annual "foreign aid" allocation (assuming a difference of 4 percent between interest rates) would be only $20 million (4 percent of $500 million). Chinese sources report that Eximbank is given a strict quota of the amount of concessional loans it can offer annually, given that they pose a cost that must be included in the national budget.

China's annual budget for foreign aid has expanded over the past ten years from around $450 million a year to an estimated $1.4 billion for 2007.[35] In 2003, Minister of Foreign Affairs Li Zhaoxing reported to the FOCAC that aid to African countries between 2000 and 2003 absorbed 44 percent of China's total aid.[36] Assuming that this figure has been a steady percentage, China's aid budget for Africa would be approximately $462 million in 2006 and $616 million in 2007. Doubling aid by 2009 as promised would bring the budget for African aid to around $1 billion a year. As noted above, however, these figures include only the interest subsidy—not the face value—of China's concessional loans.

Pushed by the "going global" policy, China's concessional loan program has been growing rapidly, at about 35 percent a year between 2001 and 2005. At the end of 2005, the Eximbank had approved "more than" 200 projects in Africa, totaling RMB 50 billion (about $6.6 billion). A World Bank study reported, however, that as of 2005, the Eximbank had funded only $800 million worth of concessional loan projects in Africa (a cumulative total of 55 projects).[37] These data suggest that much of the China Eximbank activity in Africa does not qualify as ODA. However, if we take the promise of $1 billion in concessional loans a year for three years to be ODA-qualified loans, and add it to the official figure of budgeted aid (author's estimate) of around $616 million in 2007, the figure is $1.6 billion for ODA in 2007; this amount should rise to around $2 billion in 2009.

Clearly, significant resources are available as "development finance" from China, even if not all of the figures hyped in the media actually qualify as "aid" or ODA. It is the rapid increase in these flows that raise concerns. It is here that China's official loans provide a significant challenge to Washington-based institutions such as the IMF and the World Bank, whether or not they constitute aid. Yet, whether it is counted as aid or official flows, the magnitude of Chinese finance going to Africa is still far lower than that from the OECD. In 2005 alone, OECD members committed $30.7 billion in grants to African countries, while total public and private bilateral loan commitments from OECD members amounted to $11.8 billion.[38]

China and Taiwan

Competition with Taipei for diplomatic recognition has been a long-standing battle for Beijing, and one that is extremely important to the mainland political leadership. The majority of African countries recognized Taipei as "China" at independence; some refrained from recognizing either Taipei or Beijing. Official recognition came with aid, and Taiwanese aid emphasized agricultural assistance. In 1968, for example, Taiwan's "Project Vanguard" had 1,239 agricultural experts in 27 countries, many in Africa.[39] Although Beijing won back its UN seat in 1971, the competition did not end. As Taiwan transitioned to democracy in the mid-1980s, its political leadership decided to take advantage of the shock caused by Beijing's 1989 crackdown at Tiananmen Square to reinvigorate its "dollar diplomacy."[40] Beginning in 1989, five countries reestablished relations with Taiwan (Belize, Central African Republic [CAR], Grenada, Liberia, and Lesotho). China responded by breaking diplomatic relations, in accord with its strict "one-China" policy. Within months, these five countries were enjoying generous new aid projects. Taiwan also promised to complete any unfinished Chinese projects. African countries that switched back to Taiwan over the past decade and a half also include Burkina Faso, Chad, the Gambia, Guinea-Bissau, Niger, São Tomé and Príncipe, and Senegal (CAR switched between Beijing and Taipei four times before January 1998). As of 2008, only four African countries recognized Taipei: Burkina Faso, Swaziland, São Tomé and Príncipe, and the Gambia.

Taiwan's foreign aid program was reorganized in 1989 as the International Economic Cooperation Development Fund (IECDF), and in 1996–1997 Taipei established an autonomous organization, the International Cooperation and Development Fund (ICDF). In a manner similar to Beijing, Taipei concentrates its aid on public works infrastructure, vocational training and technical education, and agriculture. The government also supports micro-, small-, and medium enterprises through credits extended to financial intermediaries, and it offers emergency recovery loans.[41] Taiwan has a youth volunteer program and, like Beijing, sends medical teams: in 2005, Burkina Faso, Chad, Malawi, and São Tomé and Príncipe hosted such teams.

Since 1988 Taipei has openly reported aid figures for its foreign loans and technical assistance programs in the annual reports and bulletins issued by the

IECDF and, later, the ICDF. Net official development assistance reported by Taipei to the OECD-DAC totaled $513 million in 2006, $483 million in 2005, and $421 million in 2004, although there was no breakdown by region.[42] According to the official aid agency (ICDF), in 2005, 42 percent of Taiwan's overseas mission expenditures went to Africa (including medical missions), but only 28 percent of technical assistance went to that continent and 12 percent of loans. The ICDF reported in 2005 that technical assistance was concentrated in four sectors where Taiwan had particular expertise: agriculture, private sector development, health, and information and communication technology.

Taiwan's overall aid program seems to be based on loans (there is no mention of grants), and the ICDF emphasizes productive projects that are sustainable, with an emphasis on cost recovery and the ability to generate income. Although it is widely understood that Beijing will break diplomatic relations with countries that recognize Taipei as "China" (and obviously, aid is only given to countries with formal diplomatic ties), government-sponsored economic cooperation for profit can continue (for both Beijing and Taipei), even that involving government-owned enterprises. For example, after Liberia switched official ties to Taipei and China broke off diplomatic relations, a private hospital managed by China's Heilongjiang Province International Economic and Technical Cooperation Corporation closed its doors. Six months later, after unspecified "renovations," the hospital resumed operations with the return of eight Chinese doctors. Likewise, Chinese firms competed for contracts in Swaziland and Malawi, even when both were staunch allies of Taipei. In 2005, for example, Chinese engineering, design, and labor supply firms earned revenues of $5.28 million and $1.09 million from contracts in Malawi and Swaziland, respectively.[43]

Conclusion

China's African aid is clearly not a new phenomenon. It has gradually changed over the past five decades, and today the program operates as one component of an array of economic relationships that have been built over time in most of the countries on the African continent. Like other major powers, China uses aid to complement other areas of soft power. The country still operates outside the global aid regime, but there is some evidence that Chinese officials are organizing their own aid system (including the aid channeled through the China Eximbank) in ways that clearly parallel the norms that have been established in the OECD.

Furthermore, China's mercantilist, state-sponsored engagement with Africa (including "aid") reflects modes of engagement that the West (and Japan) have abandoned only very gradually, and unevenly, and at income levels far above those prevailing in China today. The large sums that have aroused so much concern (to the extent they can be confirmed) are likely *not* ODA but rather forms of state-backed finance for trade. It is worth remembering that China's South-South economic ties to Africa are patterned after extremely similar North-South relationships. China's nontransparent, oil-backed loans in Angola and Nigeria, for example, are patterned after similar loans extended with much less notice by private Portuguese and London banks. China's export subsidies resemble pre–World Trade Organization programs in Japan and France. Bundling aid into nontransparent packages of finance, as China does, is a practice that used to be quite common in the "tied" aid programs of today's wealthy countries. In fact, China learned how to do so in the late 1970s, when Japan and the West first began to invest in, and give tied aid to, China.[44]

This report on China's African aid leaves many questions unanswered. Until Beijing decides to release a comprehensive account of aid (and especially until it can be formulated along the lines of the OECD-DAC), Chinese official flows will not be comparable with those from other donors. Only guesswork is possible at this stage, based on a patchwork of random, semiofficial announcements. That said, careful research and interviews can enable a robust portrait of China's aid system, its changes over time, and its organization and operation in the field.

China is likely to become more important as a source of development finance for Africa. Chinese bankers do not impose governance conditions on their lending, and they are willing to follow the borrowing government's own system for evaluating the social and environmental impact of projects. On the one hand, the Chinese option is allowing infrastructural projects to go forward, creating much-needed electrical, transportation, and telecommunications capacity. On the other, the lack of social and environmental safeguards is beginning to create resistance among African civil society groups. We can expect these pressures to continue, as African societies balance the opportunities and threats created by the sharp growth in Chinese aid.

Notes

1. He Wenping, "Africa: China's Top Priority," *Beijing Review,* XLIX (2006), 14–17. He Wenping is director of the Division of African Studies at the Institute of West Asian and African Studies, Chinese Academy of Social Sciences (CASS); Zhang Hongming,

"China Policy of Assistance Enjoys Popular Support," *People's Daily* (23 June 2006), available at http://english.peopledaily.com.cn/200606/23/eng20060623_276714.html (accessed 18 October 2007). Zhang Hongming is deputy director of the Institute of West Asian and African Studies, CASS. He Wenping confirmed Zhang Hongming's position in an interview (Beijing, July 2007).

2. Reported in Peter Bosshard, "China's Role in Financing African Infrastructure" (Berkeley, CA, 2007), 4.

3. Harry G. Broadman, *Africa's Silk Road: China and India's New Economic Frontier* (Washington, D.C., 2007), 275.

4. This section draws on Deborah Brautigam, *Chinese Aid and African Development: Exporting Green Revolution* (New York, 1998), 37–53.

5. Organization for Economic Cooperation and Development (OECD), "The Aid Programme of China" (Paris, 1987), 5. Data on the value of China's aid are difficult to obtain, as the Chinese still regard much information concerning the magnitude of their program as a state secret.

6. Brautigam, *Chinese Aid and African Development*, 44.

7. "China Aids 86 Developing Countries in 1st 11 months," Xinhua (29 December 2006).

8. People's Republic of China, "Eight Principles Guiding China's Economic and Technical Aid to Other Countries" (Beijing, 1964).

9. On "soft power," see Joseph Nye, *Soft Power: The Means to Success in World Politics* (New York, 2004).

10. George T. Yu, "Africa in Chinese Foreign Policy," *Asian Survey*, XXVIII (1988), 854.

11. OECD, "Aid Programme of China," 5; see also Wolfgang Bartke, *The Agreements of the People's Republic of China with Foreign Countries, 1949–1990* (Munich, 1992). Figure is not adjusted for inflation.

12. OECD, "Aid Programme of China," 18.

13. *Africa Confidential*, XXIII (1982), 7.

14. Li Ke, "China's Aid to Foreign Countries," *Beijing Review*, XXVI (1983), 18.

15. Foreign Broadcast Information Service–China-83 (13 October 1983), A2.

16. Brautigam, *Chinese Aid and African Development*, 47; OECD, "Aid Programme of China," 8.

17. Zhang Kewei, "Chinese Assistance to Third World," *Beijing Review*, XXX (1987), 29.

18. Xinhua (8 October 1983).

19. National Bureau of Statistics, People's Republic of China, *China Statistical Yearbook 2006* (Beijing, 2006).

20. Colin Legum (ed.), *Africa Contemporary Record: Annual Survey and Documents, 1982–1983* (New York, 1984), A99. However, it is not clear whether any joint ventures occurred in Zaire.

21. In 1982, the Ministry of Foreign Economic Relations was merged with the Ministry of Foreign Trade to become the Ministry of Foreign Economic Relations

and Trade. This ministry became the Ministry of Foreign Trade and Economic Cooperation in 1993 and was further consolidated as the Ministry of Commerce in 2003.

22. *New Liberian* (Monrovia) (4 October 1983), 5.

23. Xinhua (21 August 1986).

24. See also Li Anshan, 28 in this volume.

25. See also Stephanie Rupp, 76 in this volume.

26. Tracy McVeigh, "Beijing Pledges Aid Billions to Woo Africa," *The Observer* (5 November 2006), available at www.guardian.co.uk/china/story/0,,1939974,00.html (accessed 18 October 2007).

27. Moises Naím, "Rogue Aid," *Foreign Policy,* XCVI (2006), 96–95; Joshua Kurtlantzick, "Beijing's Safari," Carnegie Endowment for International Peace Policy Outlook 29 (Washington, D.C., 2006), 2.

28. Danna Harman, "China Takes Up Civic Work in Africa," *Christian Science Monitor* (27 June 2007), 1,13.

29. Christopher Swann and William McQuillen, "China to Surpass World Bank as Top Lender to Africa (Update2)" (3 November 2006), available at www.bloomberg.com/apps/news?pid=newsarchive&sid=afUHTifuOkR0 (accessed 6 October 2007). Compounding the error, the authors cited $2.3 billion as "loans" committed by the World Bank, whereas the correct figure of World Bank funding committed to sub-Saharan Africa in fiscal 2006 was more than double this amount at over $4.6 billion ($1.1 billion in grants, $3.5 billion in International Development Association credits, and $40 million in International Bank for Reconstruction and Development loans). See http://web.worldbank.org/WBSITE/EXTERNAL/COUNTRIES/AFRICAEXT (accessed 16 September 2007).

30. The Bloomberg.com figure was cited as China's "aid" by, among others, Howard W. French, "Commentary: China and Africa," *African Affairs,* CVI (2007), 127–132, and Mauro De Lorenzo, "China and Africa: A New Scramble?" *China Brief,* VII (2007), 3.

31. DAC, "Glossary" available at www.oecd.org/glossary/0,3414,en_2649_33721_1965693_1_1_1_1,00.html#1965586 (accessed 2 April 2007).

32. OECD, "2008 Survey on Monitoring the Paris Declaration: Glossary," available at www.oecd.org/document/19/0,3343,en_21571361_39494699_39503763_1_1_1_1,00.html (accessed 29 April 2008).

33. He, "Africa: China's Top Priority"; Zhang, "China Policy of Assistance."

34. See, for example, Bartke, *The Agreements,* 7.

35. National Bureau of Statistics, *China Statistical Yearbook* (Beijing, various years); Qi Guoqiang, "China's Foreign Aid: Policies, Structure, Practice and Trend" (Oxford, England, 2007); Qi Guoqiang, personal communication (26 July 2007).

36. Li Zhaoxing, "Report by H. E. Mr. Li Zhaoxing, Minister of Foreign Affairs of the People's Republic of China to the Second Ministerial Conference of the China-Africa Cooperation Forum" (Addis Ababa, 15 December 2003).

37. Broadman, *Africa's Silk Road,* 274.

38. World Bank, *Global Development Finance: The Development Potential of Surging Capital Flows* (Washington, D.C., 2006).

39. "Diplomacy through Aid," *Time Magazine* (18 October 1968), available at www.time.com/time/magazine/article/0,9171,902440,00.html (accessed 18 October 2007).

40. Ian Taylor, "China's Foreign Policy towards Africa in the 1990s," *Journal of Modern African Studies*, XXXVI (1998), 443–460.

41. ICDF, "Operations and Activities," available at www.icdf.org.tw/english/e_affair_invest.asp (accessed 19 September 2007). Unless otherwise noted, information on Taiwan's aid program comes from the ICDF website and annual reports accessed there.

42. OECD-DAC, "Net Official Development Assistance," available at www.oecd.org/dac (accessed 19 September 2007).

43. National Bureau of Statistics, *China Statistical Yearbook 2006*.

44. For more on this subject, see Deborah Brautigam, "China's African Aid: Transatlantic Challenges," German Marshall Fund Paper Series (Washington, D.C., 2008), and *Rogue Donor? The Real Story of Chinese Aid and Engagement in Africa* (Oxford, forthcoming).

PAUL HUBBARD

10

Chinese Concessional Loans

China's recent economic aid to Africa has the more traditional international aid donors worried. Outsiders fear that the Chinese government is giving away billions of dollars on the continent to buy political influence, thus supporting authoritarian regimes while undermining the governance and anticorruption efforts of traditional donors. But outsiders, and probably the Chinese themselves, know very little about how the Chinese aid system actually works.

China's aid program is designed to promote China's own foreign policy goals. In a recent study of China's growing soft power, Kurlantzick describes aid as an integral part of the arsenal.[1] Not surprisingly, these foreign policy goals are not aligned with those of the bilateral and multilateral donors of the developed world.

The absence of conditionality is a feature of China's soft power diplomacy—China differentiates itself from other world powers by refusing to "make demands upon other nations' sovereignty, economic models, governance or political culture."[2] Touring Africa in early 2007, President Hu Jintao highlighted the fact that China's preferential loans do not carry political conditions.[3] This difference from established Western donors led the British

The author wishes to thank Dennis De Tray and the Center for Global Development for hosting him in Washington, D.C., from May to August 2007, and for making it possible for him to attend the China in Africa conference at the John F. Kennedy School of Government. The author also thanks Sarah Rose, Kate Vyborny, Sahar Shah, Luyao Wang, Eugene Martin, Deborah Brautigam, and Carol Lancaster for providing comments on earlier drafts. For a good overview of this subject, see Carol Lancaster, *The Chinese Aid System* (Washington, D.C., 2007).

secretary of state for international development to criticize China for being willing to finance unsustainable levels of debt in Africa, while ignoring the issue of governance.[4] In congressional testimony, the commissioner of the U.S.-China Economic and Security Review Commission claimed that China is offering a wealth of assistance in building African infrastructure without concern about whether the benefits are accruing to the African people or only to corrupt leaders, and without conditions to improve governance that Western countries and organizations demand.[5]

International financial institutions are also concerned. For the International Monetary Fund, Beijing's policies risk unleashing "a new wave of hidden debt" for Africa.[6] The World Bank, under former President Paul Wolfowitz, worried that Chinese loans gave borrowers an opportunity to avoid governance safeguards.[7] Multilateral banks are "losing projects in Asia and Africa to Chinese banks because [the Chinese] 'don't bother about social or human rights conditions.'"[8]

Aside from the much publicized lack of conditionality, little is known about Chinese preferential lending. As Kurlantzick observes, "In its aid, infrastructure building, and business deals, China also demonstrates little respect for transparency and other aspects of good governance."[9] In interviews, Chinese officials have been either unwilling or unable to provide details of loans. Scholars and policymakers are left to speculate on the details of Chinese aid.[10]

Recently, a Chinese diplomat claimed to the author that Chinese aid is transparent and that details are published in Chinese language sources. This argument suggests that it is a "veil of ignorance" rather than a "lack of transparency" that frustrates Western aid analysts.

This chapter examines this proposition by reviewing China's concessional lending program, which is managed by the China Eximbank. It relies on Chinese language sources from the websites of the Ministry of Commerce, the China Eximbank, the Ministry of Foreign Affairs, and official news outlets, such as the People's Daily and Xinhua New Agency. Using these sources, rather than English language sources, makes it possible to find more details on the recipients, sectors, and amounts of Chinese concessional lending.

How Does the Concessional Loan Program Work?

Since its founding in 1994, the China Eximbank has provided concessional loans (also known as preferential or low-interest loans) to developing countries on behalf of the Chinese government. The concessional lending program is separate from the bank's other activities and is also managed separately from its sizable commercial lending facilities.

Figure 10-1.

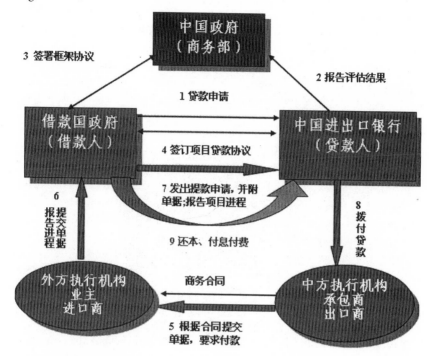

Source: China Eximbank, "Project Cycle," available at www.eximbank.gov.cn/yewu/duiwaiyh.jsp (accessed 27 October 2007).

Explanation of numbered items is based on the author's translation:

1. The government of the borrowing country submits an application to the China Eximbank.
2. The China Eximbank reports the evaluation to the Ministry of Commerce.
3. The Chinese government signs a framework agreement with the borrowing country.
4. The borrowing government signs a project agreement with the China Eximbank.
5. According to the contractual terms, the Chinese contractors and exporters invoice the foreign executing agency requesting payment.
6. The foreign executing agency submits the invoice and progress report to the borrowing country government.
7. The foreign government submits a drawing application, invoice, and progress report to the China Eximbank.
8. The China Eximbank then disburses the funds to the exporter.
9. The foreign government pays interest and fees and loan repayments to the China Eximbank.

The China Eximbank website explains, in English, Chinese, and French, the policy and procedures behind the Chinese Government Concessional Loan.[11] Not surprisingly, most information is provided in Chinese. Even the schematic diagram on the Chinese language site is much more comprehensive than the English version. The Chinese version illustrates the life-cycle of a concessional loan, as shown in figure 10-1.

As the diagram shows, a concessional loan agreement depends on at least two acts of state. A bilateral framework agreement is signed between the borrowing country and the People's Republic of China. Then a loan agreement is made between the China Eximbank and a representative of the borrowing country's government. Those agreements are signed by high-ranking government ministers and a president or vice president of the China Eximbank. Each agreement, therefore, provides an opportunity for a high-profile official signing ceremony.

These signing ceremonies are often reported in Chinese and announced on an official government website. A review of reports on the ceremonies and recent lists of bilateral treaties with the People's Republic of China reveals some information about China's lending program. These announcements do not provide details of loan disbursement, interest payments, or when loans are repaid or forgiven. They do, however, provide an authoritative starting point from which to track particular projects.

Since the borrower tends to be a developing country with little media capacity, the most comprehensive reports usually appear only on the Chinese side. For example, although the newswire Reuters did carry a report of China's 2006 concessional loan to Eritrea, the story did not provide project details other than a quote from the Eritrean information minister, Ali Abdu, that the $23 million loan would be "for the development of infrastructure for both fixed and mobile telephones."[12]

On the Chinese side, the websites of the Ministry of Commerce, the Ministry of Foreign Affairs, and China Central Television carried much more detailed information in Chinese. While the terms of the loan are not reported, the size of the loan is confirmed (RMB 166 million, [$23 million]), and some details are given about the eighteen-month fixed and wireless network projects for which the loan is provided. The project's aim is to increase telephone subscription in Eritrea from 1.5 to 6.5 percent.[13]

Who Is Borrowing from the China Eximbank?

In 1997, *China Daily* reported that since 1995 the Eximbank had provided RMB 1 billion ($138 million) in concessional loans to fund fifteen projects in ten countries. Botswana, Côte d'Ivoire, Equatorial Guinea, Gabon, Kenya, and the Sudan were identified as six of the ten recipients. In 1998, *China Daily* reported that "nearly 30 projects" had been funded by concessional loans, also indicating that Cameroon, Guyana, and Papua New Guinea had been recipients.[14] *People's Daily* in 2001 reported that there were seventy-two concessional

Table 10-1.   *Chinese Treaties with the Phrase "Concessional Loan Framework Agreement" in the Title, 2004–2006*

Treaty number	Date signed	Country	Signing location
24	18 February 2004	Jamaica	Beijing
29	24 February 2004	Suriname	Beijing
42	18 March 2004	Laos	Vientiane
51	28 March 2004	Maldives	Male
63	20 April 2004	Cambodia	Beijing
111	22 June 2004	Syria	Beijing
113	24 June 2004	Togo	Kara
7	29 January 2005	Venezuela	La Paz
9	31 January 2005	Trinidad and Tobago	Port of Spain
30	7 April 2005	Bangladesh	Dhaka
54	25 May 2005	Mongolia	Ulan Bator
95	18 July 2005	Vietnam	Beijing
106	3 August 2005	Togo	Lomé
116	17 August 2005	Kenya	Beijing
37	3 April 2006	Tajikistan	Beijing
44	4 April 2006	Fiji	Suva
42	4 April 2006	Philippines	Manila
55	6 April 2006	Yemen	Beijing
129	10 July 2006	Zambia	Lusaka
165	7 September 2006	Congo-Kinshasa	Kinshasa
218	30 November 2006	Benin	Cotonou

Source: People's Republic of China, Ministry of Foreign Affairs (www.fmprc.gov.cn/chn/wjb/zzjg/tyfls/tfsckzlk/zgywgsbtyylb), various years.

loan projects in thirty-six states. By the end of 2002, the Chinese claimed ninety projects in more than forty-one states.[15]

Lending activity from 2002 to 2006 can be partially identified through the Ministry of Foreign Affairs's annual table of bilateral agreements. Many of these agreements are called "economic cooperation agreements" or "development loan agreements," which may or may not contain terms for concessional lending. There are twenty-one bilateral agreements within these tables that are explicitly named "concessional loan framework agreements."

Taking them at face value, twenty additional recipient countries can be positively identified from twenty-one bilateral agreements with this title (table 10-1). The caveat is that while a framework agreement makes it possible to borrow under the concessional scheme, the existence of a framework agreement does not guarantee that a loan is actually disbursed by the Eximbank.

The framework agreement sets the broad parameters for the Eximbank to extend a loan, but the framework agreement expires if the loan is not finalized within a fixed period.[16]

How Much Is Being Borrowed?

By aggregating these data with Chinese government source information detailing when the China Eximbank loan agreements have been signed, it is possible to identify at least forty-nine states that have framework agreements or have already received concessional loans. The list in table 10-2 is incomplete, but it gives a good idea of the geographical range of borrowers. It shows agreements with countries of which traditional donors are wary, such as Angola, Equatorial Guinea, and Zimbabwe. It also shows concessional loan agreements with richer countries, such as Botswana and Mauritius.

Using official Chinese reports of concessional loan signing ceremonies between recipient governments and representatives of the China Eximbank, it is possible to identify twenty-eight separate concessional lending agreements. Those reports typically contain details of the signing ceremony, identifying who signed for each party, the size of the loan, and the sector in which the concessional loan was being provided (table 10-3). Sometimes the Chinese exporter for the project is also identified.

This process has identified loans worth RMB 5.9 billion ($773 million) made between 1998 and 2007. The mean loan size is RMB 213 million ($28 million). This suggests that the scale of the China Eximbank concessional lending has increased significantly since 2000, when the mean loan size per project (based on the last available figures) was RMB 67.8 million ($8.2 million).[17]

Although the Chinese like to pledge billions of dollars worth of aid, those modest loan sizes suggest that the actual volume of loans disbursed is significantly lower than that. The estimate that annual lending approaches $10 billion can be safely rejected, given that this amount would require the Chinese to sign a separate loan agreement almost every day of the year. It is unlikely that the Chinese aid apparatus has such a capacity. Beijing's pledges are large enough to capture headlines, but as with traditional donors, actual disbursements have trouble keeping up with the rhetoric.[18]

Is This Official Development Assistance?

Kurlantzick argues that when assessing Chinese assistance, we need to look beyond traditional definitions of aid.[19] The Chinese do use the term "conces-

Table 10-2. *Potential Recipients of Chinese Concessional Loans,*
by Geographical Region[a]

Africa	*Asia*	*Western Asia and North Africa*
Angola	Bangladesh	Egypt
Benin	Cambodia	Morocco
Botswana	Indonesia	Sudan
Cameroon	Laos	Tunisia
Congo-Brazzaville	Maldives	Yemen
Congo-Kinshasa	Mongolia	
Côte d'Ivoire	Pakistan	*North America and Oceania*
Djibouti	Philippines	Fiji
Equatorial Guinea	Vietnam	Papua New Guinea
Eritrea		Samoa
Ethiopia		Tonga
Gabon		
Ghana		*Latin America*
Kenya		Guyana
Liberia		Jamaica
Mali		Suriname
Mauritius		Trinidad and Tobago
Mozambique		Venezuela
Nigeria		
Tanzania		*Europe and Central Asia*
Togo		Tajikistan
Zambia		Turkmenistan
Zimbabwe		Uzbekistan

Source: Ministry of Foreign Affairs, People's Republic of China, available at www.fmprc.gov.
cn/eng.
a. Regional classification according to the Ministry of Foreign Affairs.

sional loan" (*youhui daikuan*), but this does not mean that the lending would qualify as official development assistance (ODA) and therefore be directly comparable to other international donor practices.[20]

Qualification as ODA primarily depends on the specific terms of the loan. In the Chinese case, these terms are routinely omitted in reports about the Eximbank loans. The bilateral framework agreement that authorizes the loan does, however, set the broad parameters for the loan. Although these details also do not tend to be reported, electronic copies of six of these framework agreements appear on a provincial open government information website.[21]

Table 10-3. *China Eximbank Concessional Lending Agreements, 1995–2007*
Units as indicated

Borrower	Loan amount^a Millions of RMB	Millions of dollars^b	Year	Sector
Equatorial Guinea	48	5.75	1995	Forestry
Morocco	150	18.12	1998	Health
Laos	290	35.04	1999	Cement
Congo-Brazzaville	200	24.16	2000	Cement
Congo-Kinshasa	80	9.66	2000	Telecommunications
Jamaica	100	12.08	2000	Water
Mali	150	18.12	2000	Cement
Mauritius	150	18.12	2000	Sewage
Uzbekistan	100	12.08	2001	Agricultural machinery
Zimbabwe	62	7.45	2001	Local infrastructure
Mauritius	100	12.07	2002	Housing
Morocco	50	6.03	2002	Dam
Pakistan	481	58.09	2002	Port
Djibouti	99	12.00	2003	Telecommunications
Vietnam	336	40.56	2003	Mining
Vietnam	710	85.64	2003	Electricity
Botswana	200	24.13	2004	Housing
Tunisia	140	16.89	2004	Telecommunications
Botswana	150	18.29	2005	Road
Egypt	130	15.85	2005	Textiles
Vietnam	550	67.05	2005	Railway
Vietnam	530	64.61	2005	Railway
Eritrea	166	20.80	2006	Telecommunications
Kenya	161	20.17	2006	Electricity
Kenya	239	29.94	2006	Telecommunications
Tunisia	50	6.26	2006	Telecommunications
Zimbabwe	200	25.06	2006	Agricultural machinery
Eritrea	350	45.28	2007	Cement

Source: Various Chinese-language websites of People's Republic of China Ministry of Commerce, Ministry of Foreign Affairs, and *People's Daily*.
a. Not adjusted for inflation.
b. Exchange rate is average for loan year. For 2007, US$1 = RMB 7.73.

Table 10-4. *Basic Details of Six Chinese Concessional Loan Agreements,*
2001–2003
Units as indicated

Borrowing country	Date signed	Maximum loan term (years)	Interest rate (percent per year)
Tanzania	14 May 2002	15	2.0
Tonga	30 March 2001	15	2.5
Turkmenistan	18 February 2003	10	3.0
Venezuela	17 April 2001	15	3.0
Vietnam	27 February 2002	12	3.0
Zambia	25 June 2001	12	3.0

Source: See note 20.

These agreements, listed in table 10-4, were signed between 2001 and 2003, and show a maximum loan term (including any grace period) of between ten and fifteen years. The per annum interest rate is set between 2 and 3 percent.

While the loans are on concessional terms, whether the grant element is large enough to qualify technically as ODA remains an open question.[22] But even if the terms are strictly concessional, they would only count as ODA if the main (though not necessarily the sole) objective is the "promotion of economic development and welfare."[23] Here it is interesting to consider an article published in Chinese that appeared in *Market Daily* (a publication of the *People's Daily*). This article was part of a series on trade and investment in Africa aimed at Chinese enterprises.

The article begins by advising Chinese firms that "in order to support and assist Chinese firms doing trade and business in Africa to overcome the problem of insufficient funding, the Chinese government has already signed reduced interest concessional loan framework agreements with 26 African countries." The funds are tied to certain conditions: a Chinese firm should "purchase and import from China as much equipment, technology and services as possible"; the host site should have "plentiful local resources, a vast market for goods, favorable economic prospects."[24]

The advice does note that the project must be "capable of promoting the host country's economic development," and the consent of the host government is required before the project can go ahead.[25] Nevertheless, the loans retain a strong commercial flavor, suggesting that China is indeed following the earlier Japanese model of providing development aid to promote its own domestic export-led growth.[26] The requirement that "the government of the host country will need good credit and be capable of servicing the debt" is a further indication that the Chinese government is not currently planning to forgive those debts.[27]

Conclusion

The apparent lack of transparency in China's aid program is not driven by a deliberate policy of secrecy. In the last decade, China has adopted and has been attempting to implement a policy of open government information. Because of this approach, most of the source material upon which this chapter has relied has been readily available on various official websites. The fact that most of this material is not accessible to non-Chinese readers is not the result of Chinese obfuscation.

Although Chinese language sources are vital in providing some of these details that might otherwise be missed, they are incomplete. They do not report all, or even the majority, of concessional loans that are made. Nevertheless, the information that is available, if not complete and systematic, does at least allow us to understand better how the Chinese aid system works and to reject some of the more outlandish estimates of the size of China's aid program.

Between 1997 and 2004, the Chinese government sporadically released, via the press, details of the number of projects, countries, and approximate size of the concessional lending program. To build confidence internationally and to provide a clearer picture of China's development policies, the Chinese government should begin regular publication of these statistics in the annual report of the China Eximbank.

Likewise, it would not be difficult for the Ministry of Foreign Affairs to publish a list of countries with which China has a concessional loan framework agreement, and for the China Eximbank to publish a list of project agreements signed with recipient governments. Given that the Chinese government already has shown a willingness to publish this kind of information, there is no barrier to it being released on a regular basis as a complete set.

However, there remains information that the Chinese government has so far been unwilling to provide publicly. This information includes the precise terms of loans and information on actual financial flows. These data are important for the analysis of official aid flows and for other donors to coordinate their own developmental assistance. What is unclear is whether China, for political reasons, prefers to maintain strict confidentiality or whether it is simply unable at this stage effectively to monitor its own lending program.

One plausible reason for the China Eximbank's reluctance to reveal details of its concessional loans is a desire to protect the commercial confidentiality of Chinese exporters. The advice given to exporters on applying for concessional loans suggests that the primary purpose is to provide capital to Chinese exports. The economic development of a recipient country is a condition of the loan but not its dominant purpose. In this case, the exporting firm has a competitive commercial incentive not to reveal the terms of its financing. Likewise, the Chinese government may give greater weight to the particular domestic commercial interests of its firms than to the international public interest in transparency. The problem for China is that this approach bolsters suspicions that China is only in Africa for commercial exploitation.

An alternative explanation is that the loans would not technically qualify as ODA when compared against the guidelines of DAC donors. By maintaining some ambiguity, the Chinese government may be attempting to generate goodwill as an aid donor.

For China to establish its credentials as a responsible donor, it will need to embrace major donor lending norms relating to the regular and systematic release of information concerning aid flows. Transparency does not need to change the character of Chinese lending. Indeed, the Chinese model, by harnessing the self-interest of Chinese firms in developing loan projects, appears to enjoy the virtue of supply-side sustainability. But to create sustainable demand for Chinese development capital, China will need to reassure the developing world of its good intentions. Greater transparency will provide some of this reassurance.

Notes

1. Joshua Kurlantzick, *Charm Offensive: How China's Soft Power Is Transforming the World* (New Haven, 2007), 84.

2. Ibid., 44.

3. "China Announces $3 Billion Loan Plan for Africa," *New York Times* (30 January 2007), available at www.nytimes.com/2007/01/30/world/africa/30fbrief-china andafrica.html (accessed 20 May 2008).

4. "Benn: China's Aid Could Harm Africa," *Guardian* (8 February 2007), 19.

5. U.S. House of Representatives, Committee on International Relations, "China's Influence in Africa," hearing before the subcommittee on Africa, Global Human Rights and International Operations, 109th Cong. 1st sess. (Washington, D.C., 28 July 2005), 45–46.

6. Alan Beattie and Eoin Callan, "China Lends Where the World Bank Fears to Tread," *Financial Times* (8 December 2006), 6.

7. Francoise Crouigneau and Richard Hiault, "Wolfowitz Slams China Banks on Africa Lending," *Financial Times* (24 December 2006), 13.

8. Beattie and Callan, "China Lends," 6.

9. Kurlantzick, *Charm Offensive*, 165.

10. See Deborah Brautigam, chapter 9 in this volume; Carol Lancaster, *The Chinese Aid System* (Washington, D.C., 2007), 1.

11. China Eximbank, "Chinese Government Concessional Loan," available at http://english.eximbank.gov.cn/business/government.jsp (accessed 30 April 2008); www.eximbank.gov.cn/yewu/duiwaiyh.jsp (accessed 27 October 2007).

12. Ed Harris, "Eritrea Signs Phone Loan from China," Reuters (12 April 2006), available at www.alenalki.net/content/view/115/2/ (accessed 30 April 2008).

13. Based on author's translation of the Chinese language report, available at www.gov.cn/zwjw/2006-04/13/content_253071.htm (accessed 27 October 2007).

14. "Bank Broaches Concessional Loan Rethink," *China Daily* (18 May 1998); "Eximbank to Finance Equipment Exports," *China Daily* (4 August 1997).

15. "The Economic and Cultural Wave" (author's translation), *People's Daily Overseas Edition* (26 February 2001), available at www.people.com.cn/GB/paper39/2771/394354.html (accessed 20 May 2008); "China Eximbank Already Providing Finance to More Than Forty-One Developing Countries" (author's translation), *People's Daily* (28 December 2002), available at www.people.com.cn/GB/paper464/8102/766909.html (accessed 20 May 2008).

16. See, for example, People's Republic of China, "The Government of the People's Republic of China and the Government of the Kingdom of Tonga Framework Agreement Concerning Preferential Loans Extended by China to Tonga" (30 March 2001), available at www.gsfzb.gov.cn/law-1/news/view.asp?id=27562 (accessed 27 October 2007).

17. "Eximbank Provides Loans for Vietnam," Xinhua (23 October 2000). This assumes that the total of RMB 4.678 billion reported here for sixty-nine projects does not include nonconcessional lending.

18. "China Announces $3 Billion Loan"; Avinash Persaud, "Hypocrisy in the Criticism of China's Loans to Africa," *Financial Times* (6 February 2007), 14. See also Brautigam, 199.

19. Kurlantzick, *Charm Offensive*, 97.

20. According to the terms of the Organization for Economic Cooperation and Development's (OECD) Development Assistance Committee (DAC).

21. Electronic copies of concessional loan framework agreements between the People's Republic of China and the following six countries were accessed through the Governmental Legislative Information of Gansu Province website: Tanzania, available at www.gsfzb.gov.cn/law-1/news/view.asp?id=27573; Tonga, available at www.gsfzb.gov.cn/law-1/news/view.asp?id=27562; Turkmenistan, available at www.gsfzb.

gov.cn/law-1/news/view.asp?id=27611; Venezuela, available at www.gsfzb.gov.cn/law-1/news/view.asp?id=26883; Vietnam, available at www.gsfzb.gov.cn/law-1/news/view.asp?id=26988; Zambia, available at www.gsfzb.gov.cn/law-1/news/view.asp?id=27489 (all accessed 27 October 2007).

22. See Helmut Reisen, "Is China Actually Helping Improve Debt Sustainability in Africa?" preliminary draft presented at International Conference "Emerging Powers in Global Governance" (Paris, 6–7 July 2007), 4, available at www.iddri.org/Activites/Conferences-internationales/070706_PaperReisen_confpaysemergents.pdf (accessed 28 October 2007).

23. See DAC, "Glossary," available at www.oecd.org/glossary/0,3414,en_2649_33721_1965693_1_1_1_1,00.html#1965586 (accessed 28 October 2007).

24. See Huang Zequan, "How to Apply for a Concessional Loan (Invest in Africa)," *Market Daily* (22 October 2004) (based on author's translation), available at www.people.com.cn/GB/paper53/13217/1185583.html (accessed 20 May 2008).

25. Ibid.

26. Lancaster, *Chinese Aid System*, 4.

27. Huang, "How to Apply for a Concessional Loan."

JOSHUA EISENMAN

11 China's Political Outreach to Africa

Over the last three decades the People's Republic of China (PRC) has implemented an international outreach campaign designed to build lasting ties to African political parties and organizations. In the pursuit of improved official state-to-state relations and in support of Chinese domestic economic development, the Communist Party of China's (CPC) International Department (CPC-ID) and its affiliated organizations have used their deep pockets and admirable diplomatic adroitness to engage African political parties.[1] Parliamentary delegations from the National People's Congress (NPC) have also been a part of these efforts, albeit to a lesser degree.

CPC-ID and NPC delegations are valuable teams that work with African counterparts to lay the foundations for commercial and diplomatic cooperation, provide opportunities for interactions among Chinese and African political elites, and follow up to ensure that policies are implemented in accordance with the CPC's strategic objectives. Despite the success of its political outreach, however, the CPC-ID remains among the "least well understood organs of China's foreign policy system."[2]

Birth of Political Outreach in Africa:
Revolutionary Ideology to Soviet Hegemony

CPC ties to African political groups before 1978 were based on anticolonial revolutionary ideology and then gradually adapted to counter the Soviet threat. In the 1950s and 1960s, Beijing's primary motivation in Africa was the affirmation of its own brand of communism and support for various revolutionary and anticolonial liberation movements. CPC efforts to develop relations with African political parties led the Chinese to diversify ties and deal with a range of factions at the same time. In Angola, for instance, at separate times—and sometimes at the same time—the CPC supported the ruling Popular Movement for the Liberation of Angola, as well as its rivals, the National Liberation Front of Angola and the National Union for the Total Independence of Angola (UNITA).[3] Beijing and UNITA leader Jonas Savimbi capitalized on the latter's ties to South Africa, even using that racist regime as a transit point for weapons supplies to UNITA fighters.[4] This collaboration did not, however, prevent the CPC from supporting the Pan Africanist Congress and, to a lesser degree, the African National Congress in their efforts to topple apartheid in South Africa.

Party-to-party contacts were less formal during this early revolutionary period than they are today. Many African political parties (and the CPC) were headed by revolutionary leaderships focused almost entirely on domestic developments. As a result, between 1950 and 1970, few African political parties visited China and no CPC delegations traveled to Africa.[5] Those political contacts that did occur in Africa were either with the military or with so-called *subordinate* CPC groups known as "mass organizations" (*qunzhong zuzhi*) and "people's organizations" (*mingjian tuanti*).[6] The lingering influence of the colonial powers and the extension of Cold War tensions on the continent preoccupied Beijing's engagement and limited it almost entirely to militant revolutionary ideology and small arms shipments.

Beijing aided any African revolutionary force fighting a guerrilla war—a hallmark of the Chinese style—by hastening "the development of [African] political opposition groups and guiding them towards conceptions of action closely akin to her own."[7] China's state-run press portrayed the CPC as shepherd of a flock of African parties moving toward a new democratic revolution. Premier Zhou Enlai nurtured the idea that Africa was engulfed in a wave of revolutionary zeal. At the November 1960 Moscow summit of communist parties, China's state-run press reported that African parties were "studying Mao's works and using Chinese guerilla methods."[8]

The CPC laid claim to the moral high ground by condemning vestiges of Western colonialism. Chinese speeches, editorials, and publications stressed the role of "Mao Zedong Thought" and the scope of armed struggles.[9] By asserting that anticolonial conflicts in Africa and elsewhere were proletarian revolutions, the CPC exaggerated its influence among African revolutionary groups. Calls for armed struggle did not cost much, so if an indigenous group chose rebellion, the CPC might support it with subversive rhetoric and modest arms shipments.[10] Yet while many African leaders were steeped in Maoist revolutionary thought and liberation politics, their direct contacts with the CPC remained limited.[11]

The CPC's ideology of a continuous proletarian revolution was gradually altered in favor of antihegemony. This change paralleled the party leaders' shift from dogmatism to pragmatism, a domestic development that was catalyzed by widespread cynicism as the Cultural Revolution's most turbulent days subsided. The largely disillusioned CPC leadership, weary of ideological fervor and fearful of Soviet aggression, turned to geopolitical realism rooted in self-preservation to propel policymaking. Beijing began to support only those revolutionary movements that fought against imperialist forces—a term synonymous with groups supported by Moscow and, to a lesser extent, Washington. Indeed, the CPC's willingness to place geopolitical objectives before ideological consistency grew apace with the Soviet threat. The result was a strategy designed to preoccupy Soviet resources in far-off conflicts—particularly in Africa.[12]

The CPC's turn from ideology to pragmatism reflected the organization's gradual transformation from a revolutionary party to a ruling party. The resulting changes in institutions and priorities were reflected in the CPC's outreach to African political parties. The CPC became willing "to grant ideological autonomy, and when African countries seemed to embark on a policy closely akin to Chinese thinking, Peking refrained from claiming that the Africans were following a Maoist path."[13] In this way, the gradual removal of ideology from China's foreign policy cleared the way for the CPC to build ties to African ruling parties across the entire political spectrum. In 1977, the CPC formally began to work toward this goal and undertook a full reconstruction of the CPC-ID.[14]

PRC's Modern-Era Political Outreach in Africa

Since the Third Plenary Session of the Eleventh CPC Central Committee held in 1978, the CPC-ID has emerged as the department primarily "responsible for the party's international exchanges and communications with foreign political parties and organizations."[15] Deng Xiaoping, the exiled four-time party boss, supported a new CPC-ID strategy to cultivate contacts with various parties on the basis of "four principles of party-to-party relations: independence, complete equality, mutual respect, and noninterference in each others internal affairs."[16] The CPC-ID was also given four main responsibilities: implementing the CPC Central Committee's principles and policies, researching foreign developments and key global issues, providing briefings and policy proposals to the Central Committee, and carrying out CPC exchanges with foreign political parties and organizations.[17]

From these four principles and four responsibilities, the CPC-ID derived seven guidelines to govern its interaction with foreign political parties. These were laid out in 2001 in a speech by the CPC-ID Vice Minister Cai Wu:

—"Establish a new type of relations between parties—new, sound and friendly relations."

—"Every party should decide its own country's affairs independently."

—"No party should judge the achievements and mistakes of foreign parties on the basis of its own experience."

—"All parties should be completely equal; they should respect each other and not interfere in each other's internal affairs."

—"Ideological differences should not be obstacles to establishing a new type of party-to-party relations. When developing exchanges and cooperation with foreign parties, parties in the various countries should proceed from the spirit of seeking common ground while reserving differences."

—"The purpose of exchanges and cooperation with foreign parties should be to promote the development of state-to-state relations."

—"In their relations with foreign parties, all parties should look to the future and forget old scores."[18] This "complete concept for establishing a new type of party-to-party relations" served to operationalize CPC strategy and stands as a useful guide to understanding CPC political outreach in the modern era.[19]

This approach to political outreach has been gradually developed to engage African ruling parties and cultivate long-standing and stable relationships that underpin and augment official ties, regardless of ideology (in accordance with the fifth guideline listed above).[20] As a result of its success, between 1978 and 1990, the CPC-ID established ties to dozens of African political parties. The vast majority, over thirty parties, were governing parties (*guozhengdang*), while only two were opposition parties (*fanduidang*). Between 1978 and 1990, the CPC-ID conducted over 300 exchanges with these political parties, underwrote the travel costs for dozens of African delegations, and helped facilitate meetings with the CPC cadre, administrators of Chinese state-run companies, and government officials.[21] This period was the beginning of the PRC's political outreach, when Sino-African commercial ties were still at low levels. Throughout the 1980s, Sino-African trade, for instance, averaged only $1 billion annually according to the Chinese General Administration of Customs.[22]

Between 1991 and 1996, the growing number of African political parties (approximately 1,800 by 1997), political power sharing in some countries, and turnover in older African parties undermined CPC efforts.[23] Meanwhile, in 1992 Deng Xiaoping went to southern China to inaugurate the country's first Special Economic Zones, thereby giving the CPC leadership's full blessing to market reforms. Development was now unquestionably placed at the forefront, and Chinese people were told to get rich, leading many to turn to trade with extensive Chinese communities in the West to make their fortunes. As a result, attention was drawn away from Africa, and in terms of prestige, funding, and personnel, African programs at China's state-run research institutions played subordinate roles to their counterparts in American, European, and Asian studies.[24]

In the early 1990s, this contraction of PRC political outreach in Africa and some well-targeted financial incentives enabled the Republic of China (Taiwan) to establish formal relations with several African countries at the PRC's expense.[25] Senegal, a longtime ally of Beijing and one of West Africa's most important states, switched sides. For nearly thirty years, the PRC had cooperated with Senegal, helping to build hospitals and even a huge national stadium. Taipei also used its financial resources to woo the Gambia and Niger, providing the former roughly $35 million in assistance and helping the latter pay civil service salaries.[26] In the years since, however, the PRC's resurgent political outreach campaign—led by the CPC-ID—plus economic incentives and growing international influence have combined to win over all but four African states that still maintain official relations with Taiwan.[27]

Lead by CPC Chairman Jiang Zemin, the so-called third generation of CPC leadership gave international political outreach a strategic and methodological makeover in the mid- to late-1990s. The CPC's increasingly technocratic elite continued Deng's efforts to address economic challenges. Reforms were designed to foster economic growth and integrate the country into the global economy, and this objective required the CPC to develop political relationships to support such goals. These new international efforts coupled with a receding Soviet (and later Russian) influence gave the CPC an opportunity to extend cooperation with African political parties. Meanwhile, the durability of ruling parties in key African states, such as Egypt, Ethiopia, South Africa, the Sudan, Zambia, and Zimbabwe, provided a ready group of potential CPC partner organizations. Timely developments in both China and Africa combined to push Sino-African political ties toward a new era of cooperation.[28]

Under current CPC Chairman Hu Jintao and the party's fourth generation leadership, China's surging need for energy and minerals to power its impressive economic growth has increased the value of political capital with resource-rich Africa states and, in turn, the importance that the CPC attaches to its political outreach efforts on the continent. The CPC's willingness to share its newly acquired wealth with its African counterparts has also helped to improve party-to-party ties. In the run-up to Zambia's 2006 presidential elections, for instance, the CPC supported the ruling Movement for Multi-party Democracy (MMD) party.[29] Rumors about the amount of CPC financial support for the MMD abound, but what is known for certain is that then Chinese Ambassador Li Baodong gave the ruling MMD strong diplomatic support when he threatened that Beijing would "have nothing to do with Zambia if Sata wins the elections."[30] Michael Sata, head of the Patriotic Front and the leading opposition candidate, responded by accusing Li of acting as a "MMD cadre" and "openly campaigning for the MMD."[31]

In the 1990s, China's grants, loans, and low-cost infrastructural projects came largely in response to Taiwan's dollar diplomacy victories, but over the last decade their expansion and refinement reflects a long-term strategy to court African political elites. By any calculation these efforts have yielded impressive results. Between 1997 and 2006, there have been more than 200 exchanges with political parties in 40 sub-Saharan African countries. As of 2006, the CPC had established ties to at least sixty sub-Saharan African political parties.[32] The CPC continues to expand ties to African ruling parties and parties included in ruling coalitions, and, when appropriate, the CPC develops new lines of communication with opposition parties.

Methods of PRC Political Outreach with African Political Parties

The CPC now cultivates ties to dozens of African political parties. Although the details of each relationship are unique, there are crosscutting consistencies in the PRC's approach. Through an examination of these consistencies, this section identifies and describes five primary methods: hospitality, party cadre training, information management, opposition party outreach, and interparliamentary exchanges.

Hospitality

The CPC's expanding political outreach activities can be seen in terms of the frequency of visits and the level of the visitor. Between 1997 and 2006, for instance, the CPC-ID feted over sixty African party chiefs.[33] During these meetings, African party leaders and their Chinese counterparts looked to translate party ties into long-term bilateral cooperation on issues of mutual interest and concern. The meetings themselves provided a forum for the exchange of views, coordination of policies, provision of economic assistance, and voicing of grievances. Leaders of China's state-controlled firms depend on the CPC-ID and its related liaison organizations (like the Chinese Association of International Understanding [CAFIU]) to arrange appropriate meetings and social activities with African delegations. On the other side, African party leaders rely on their CPC-ID hosts to ensure access to relevant Chinese political and business leaders.[34]

Visits from African political party delegations give the CPC-ID an opportunity to practice its intoxicating mix of contemporary and traditional hospitality. CPC-ID hosting techniques are derived from centuries of Chinese tradition and can be traced back to the teachings of Confucius.[35] According to Solomon, "The most distinctive characteristic of Chinese negotiating behavior is an effort to develop and manipulate strong interpersonal relationships with foreign officials [and] feelings of good will, obligation, guilt or dependence to achieve their negotiating objectives."[36] Hosting, according to the report, allows the Chinese "to carry out negotiations on their own turf and by their own rules while maximizing [the visitor's] sense of gratitude, awe and helplessness."[37] This may help to explain why the CPC hosts many more delegations then it sends to Africa.

The CPC's rhetoric of equality, mutual respect, and noninterference, coupled with first-class hospitality, has won over African elites from across the political spectrum. While delegations looking to visit the United States, for instance, are subject to an endless array of security procedures and red tape, Beijing has simplified procedures and supported delegations led by African political leaders. One former African ambassador to China recounted his own experience: "When I was arriving at my post, I was scheduled for a brief meeting and photo with President and CPC Chairman Jiang Zemin. Instead, we spoke for nearly an hour. President Jiang not only had a broad continental view of Africa, but I was also very impressed with his detailed knowledge of African issues and how close they were to his heart."[38]

Anecdotal information suggests that there is also a more nefarious side to the CPC-ID's hospitality. It is assumed, although hard evidence is lacking to substantiate, "that ID attachés work closely with Ministry of State Security (undercover) personnel abroad for the purpose of intelligence collection and agent recruitment."[39] Hostesses can be employed to entertain foreign visitors and solidify relationships and agreements with African elites. In the long term, however, evidence of such liaisons can be leveraged. The latter scenario, often called a "honey trap," is a common method utilized by clandestine Chinese operatives.[40] According to one retired senior African diplomat who served extensively in China, these methods are common, although, he said, differing attitudes toward sexuality within Chinese and some African cultures may undermine this strategy's effectiveness.[41]

Cadre Training

The Chinese government has sponsored the training of hundreds of African personnel in areas of diplomacy, economic management, national defense, agriculture, science, technology, and medical treatment.[42] Among these programs are CPC initiatives to educate African party officials through political cadre training sessions. Between 1998 and 2006, the CPC brought to China, for political training, party officials from more than ten African governing parties. The CPC has also been requested by some African parties to help set up their own party schools.[43] Senior CPC cadre and specialists in areas such as party development and structure teach roughly two-week-long training programs and help to encourage African political parties to coordinate international policies with the CPC.[44]

According to one CPC-ID official attached to an embassy in Africa, CPC-ID cadre training programs are based on "equality" and "mutual respect."[45] The increasingly influential CPC uses rhetoric to invoke the relative equality of the past and to avoid directly confronting growing power asymmetries in the bilateral relationship. This rhetoric is used in contrast to what CPC and African party officials perceived as the more heavy-handed and unequal Soviet political training of the past. For this reason, according to the CPC-ID official, "CPC-ID cadre training programs are conducted only at the request of African political parties, who are asked to submit specific requests about their party's particular needs. African political parties' demands for CPC-ID cadre training programs have enhanced the understanding, friendship, and cooperation between these parties and CPC."[46]

The CPC naturally seeks to partner with like-minded African parties and uses cadre training and party management courses to develop interpersonal ties and influence future generations of African political leaders. CPC cadre training, however, varies dramatically among African political parties. Where long-standing CPC relationships exist, like with Tanzania's ruling Party of the Revolution (Chama Cha Mapinduzi), Uganda's National Resistance Movement, and South Africa's Communist Party, CPC instructors have conducted training sessions on diverse topics, ranging from internal party governance to CPC Chairman Jiang Zemin's theory of the "Three Represents."[47] In Angola, conversely, the strong party structure and decades of Soviet training of the

Popular Movement for the Liberation of Angola make CPC cadre training unnecessary.[48] According to Li Chengwen, Chinese ambassador to the Sudan, CPC cadre training courses can contain about twenty participants from one African country or several.[49]

Information Management

The CPC also transmits information back to China about African host countries. These efforts range from normal embassy functions and general reporting about domestic politics to more covert information collection.[50] Even determining if a particular African embassy has a CPC-ID envoy can be a difficult task. Foreign attachés "do not openly identify themselves as such, usually identifying themselves simply as Foreign Ministry personnel."[51] For instance, one CPC-ID official posted to an African embassy carried three business cards: one from his CPC-ID bureau, another as PRC embassy staff, and yet another as a research fellow at CAFIU.[52] Another CPC-ID attaché posted to a different African embassy identified himself as an embassy official until further enquiries clarified his CPC-ID affiliation. Indeed, informational obstacles make it uniquely difficult to identify confidently those African countries that have CPC-ID attachés and those that do not.[53] Generally speaking, the CPC-ID tends to be more active in developing states dominated by one party; however, it also works to keep relations with opposition parties temperate in case of a switch in political power.

The CPC seeks to improve its image and influence public sentiment through its relations with African political parties. According to one report, the United Front Work Department, a CPC international outreach organization tasked with "perception management," was singled out in March 2007 to receive a portion of the more than $3 billion budget that the party allocated for "exerting more international influence through diplomacy and national image-lifting."[54] CPC delegations are part of this public relations offensive, which entails the provision of "facts" (*shishi*), "statistics" (*xuju*), and "materials" (*cailiao*) designed to "help African parties better understand CPC policies and China's national condition."[55] One such publication, *China and Africa*, was released in September 2006 for distribution by PRC embassies. It contains a variety of Chinese government statistics, as well as a chapter called "Cooperation and Support between China and Africa in the Political Arena." *China and Africa* promotes the "frequent association between the Chinese National People's Congress and its counterparts in African countries, as well as contacts between political parties."[56]

Opposition Party Outreach

Information collection has been expanded through the CPC's increased outreach to opposition parties. Shambaugh describes this practice: "By maintaining ties with nonruling parties, the ID [CPC-ID] has been able to keep track of domestic politics in various nations and to establish contacts with a wide range of politicians and experts who subsequently staff governments after they come to power."[57] Opposition party outreach, however, remains a secondary priority in Africa and is not appropriate in all cases. Ties to opposition political figures in one-party dominated African states, in particular, could open the CPC to accusations of interference in internal affairs.[58] In Angola, Egypt, Ethiopia, Zambia, and Zimbabwe, among China's most important African partners, the CPC maintains ties only to ruling parties.

Political outreach to African opposition parties remains in its infancy and is regularly subordinated if it jeopardizes CPC relations with the ruling party.[59] However, Africa expert Liu Naiya and others see opposition party outreach as an important growth area for the CPC-ID in Africa.[60] Since CPC-ID opposition outreach is still relatively new and can be politically sensitive, links have been quite limited and are particularly hard to trace. However, two relations—with the Sudan and South Africa—reveal the increasingly flexible nature of the CPC-ID's political outreach to opposition groups.

Since 2002 the CPC has developed a close party-to-party relationship with the Sudan's Islamist National Congress Party (NCP), and until 2005 it had no contacts with opposition political parties, including the Sudanese Communist Party.[61] After the signing of the Comprehensive Peace Agreement (CPA) between the NCP and the opposition Sudan People's Liberation Movement (SPLM) in 2005, the two have joined to form a tenuous government of national unity. The CPA legitimized the SPLM and opened the door for the gradual expansion of SPLM-CPC political relations. The first outreach took place in March 2005, when then SPLM chief commander Salva Kiir Mayardit was delegated by then party leader John Garang to head a SPLM delegation to China to "hold talks on economic cooperation between the two parties."[62]

After the untimely death of Garang in July 2005, the CPC and SPLM did not hold meetings in 2006.[63] In 2007, however, CPC and SPLM party-to-party relations expanded considerably. In February, while visiting Khartoum, President Hu Jintao met again with Kiir, now Sudan's first vice president, and invited him to return to China.[64] Six months later, on 17 July, Kiir touched down in Beijing. After meeting again with Chairman Hu, Kiir held a press conference where he said that they "discussed the cooperation between the SPLM and the Chinese Communist Party."[65] Indeed, it is certainly likely that SPLM-CPC party-to-party ties were also discussed when Kiir held talks with Wang Jiarui, head of the CPC-ID.[66] Notably, the CPC-ID's website posting about this meeting reflects the sensitivity of gatherings with African opposition party leaders. As usual, for instance, the posting mentions China's support for the Sudan's "peace, unification and development," but unlike in most official CPC-ID announcements, the name of Kiir's party, the SPLM, is not mentioned.[67]

Before conducting opposition party outreach, the CPC-ID must pay particular attention to domestic political tensions in each African capital. In the case of Khartoum, any expansion of SPLM-CPC ties must take place within the framework of the Sudan's government of national unity and the CPA. For this reason, during his July 2007 China trip, Kiir was also obliged to affirm the "strength of the partnership between the National Congress and the Sudan Liberation Movement (SPLM)."[68]

The CPC's ties to the SPLM, and to opposition parties in general, are part of a hedging strategy. In the case of the Sudan, the CPC continues to develop extensive and public ties to the NCP, while taking advantage of opportunities to ensure its influence in southern Sudan through expanding ties to the SPLM. To this end, in August 2007, an official Chinese delegation, invited by Kiir, arrived in Juba, the capital of South Sudan, to gather "more information about southern Sudan."[69] As the case of the Sudan suggests, the CPC does conduct exchanges with opposition parties, but those contacts are subjugated to ties to the ruling party and are conducted in a less public fashion or behind a veil of state-to-state relations.

This pattern prevails in South Africa, where the CPC has been able to maintain its relations with the South African Communist Party (SACP) as part of the ANC's ruling coalition. In July 2007, for instance, Wang Dongming, deputy head of the CPC's Department of Organization and member of the CPC Central Committee, led a CPC delegation to South Africa to address the SACP's Twelfth National Party Congress.[70] But the CPC has also reached out to the opposition Democratic Alliance (DA) party. In April 2005, CAFIU hosted a week-long visit to Beijing, Shanghai, and the Three Gorges Dam for a DA delegation headed by then party leader Tony Leon.[71]

To develop relations with opposition parties like the DA, the CPC-ID and the NPC work together to conduct Beijing's political outreach. In September 2006, for instance, the NPC was the first national legislature to sign a Memorandum of Understanding establishing a regular mechanism for exchanges with the parliament of South Africa.[72] As part of this mechanism, Fu Zhihuan, chairman of the NPC's Finance and Economic Committee, led a delegation to South Africa in March 2007 to strengthen financial cooperation between the NPC and South African parliament.[73] NPC delegations have become increasingly important tools for aiding CPC outreach to nonruling parties.

NPC Interparliamentary Exchanges

Although the CPC-ID conducts the lion's share of PRC political outreach in Africa, interparliamentary exchanges via the NPC are also part of this effort. The NPC works at "strengthening and improving the mechanism for regular exchanges with other parliaments and congresses."[74] But because foreign relations are only one of the NPC's official responsibilities, it remains an important but junior partner in relation to the CPC-ID.

The NPC conducts exchanges with foreign parliaments, including over a dozen in Africa.[75] As is the case with the CPC-ID, the NPC's current political outreach strategy was defined in the post-1978 period. In the intervening years, "the NPC has proactively developed exchanges and cooperation with foreign parliaments and international parliamentary organizations."[76] In 2006, the NPC received a total of ninety delegations from fifty-six countries, and NPC delegations visited thirty countries and regions.[77] This political outreach, like that of the CPC-ID, is intended to "inject fresh vitality into the development of state-to-state relations" and "strengthen mutual trust in the political arena and promote mutually beneficial cooperation."[78]

Unlike the CPC-ID, however, which is purely a party organ, the NPC nominally includes a mix of government and political party influence. Nearly all countries' top legislative bodies include a mix of government and party influence, but, unlike in democratic countries, one party—the CPC—dominates the Chinese legislative body. Thus, while the NPC's Foreign Affairs Committee and Bilateral Friendship Groups are officially state organizations, they are dominated by and accountable to the CPC. Wu Bangguo, chairman of the Standing Committee of the NPC, explained this relationship: "We must uphold the Party's leadership. The CPC is the leadership core for the cause of socialism with Chinese characteristics. Upholding the Party's leadership is a basic prerequisite and fundamental guarantee for success in the work of people's congresses. All the work of people's congresses must contribute to improving the Party's leadership, consolidating the Party's position as the governing party and ensuring implementation of the Party's line, principles and policies."[79]

The NPC's international outreach efforts serve to complement the work of the CPC-ID. This cooperation is not surprising since the two organizations not only share policy objectives, they also share tactics and sometimes leaders. Wu Bangguo, for instance, is also a member of the Standing Committee of the Political Bureau of the CPC; CPC-ID Vice Minister Ma Wenpu is also a vice chairman of the NPC's Foreign Affairs Committee; and between 1998 and 2002, Jiang Enzhu, the current NPC Foreign Affairs Committee chairman, served simultaneously as the Foreign Affairs Committee's vice chairman and as a member of the CPC Central Committee.[80]

Tactically, the NPC and CPC-ID work in tandem to balance Beijing's international political outreach. While the CPC-ID's mandate to increase exchanges with ruling African parties is quite clearly defined, the NPC's international exchanges in Africa are fewer in number but can be more diverse in character. NPC leaders can take on a range of commercial and ceremonial roles, from leading a delegation of 200 Chinese businessmen to Cairo, to representing President Hu Jintao for the inauguration of Senegalese President Abdoulaye Wade.[81]

The political outreach efforts of the NPC and CPC-ID can overlap during visits by African party leaders who are also legislators. In African states where legislatures (like China's) are controlled by a single ruling party, the NPC sometimes assists the CPC-ID in hosting African political party delegations. In March 2007, for instance, a ZANU-PF party delegation led by Kumbirai Manyika Kangai—secretary for external relations for the political bureau of Zimbabwe's ruling party as well as deputy speaker of Zimbabwe's house of assembly—was hosted by the CPC-ID for meetings with NPC interlocutors led by He Luli, vice chairwoman of the NPC Standing Committee.[82]

In the Sudan's case, party-to-party and NPC political outreach efforts also overlap considerably. In March 2007, for instance, Nafi'a Ali Nafi'a, deputy president of the Sudan's ruling NCP, arrived in Beijing as a CPC-ID guest.[83] He met with Wu Bangguo who, in his NPC capacity as "China's top legislator," said that the "CPC would like to expand exchanges and cooperation with the NCP."[84] This statement underscores the tandem efforts of the CPC-ID and the NPC.

Conclusion

The CPC-ID and the NPC have collaborated to extend PRC relations with political parties throughout Africa. In the 1960s and 1970s, these efforts were intended to spread revolutionary ideology; in the 1980s, they were altered to oppose hegemony; and as of 2008, they support CPC development objectives. As discussed above, PRC political outreach activities are well funded, targeted at governing elites, and, to a lesser degree, engage opposition parties.

They include a menu of well-developed techniques including hospitality, party cadre training, information management, opposition party outreach, and interparliamentary exchanges. Taken together, these elements constitute a unique approach to developing relations with African political elites that remains largely unexplored by Western political parties, which remain almost entirely focused on winning domestic elections. The PRC's international political outreach strategy in Africa has been largely successful in cultivating the personal relationships intended to open new opportunities for Chinese foreign policymakers and state-run firms.

Notes

1. The International Department of the Central Committee of the Communist Party, the functional organ of the Central Committee responsible for the party's outreach work, was originally founded in 1951 as the Liaison Department. On 12 January 2007, the author accompanied Ambassador David H. Shinn to a meeting with Vice Minister Ma Wenpu at the CPC-ID headquarters in Beijing to discuss the CPC's relations with African political parties. That meeting and those that preceded it took place with the support of the Chinese Association of International Understanding.

2. The CPC's desire to keep its political outreach activities out of the headlines makes "many things that one would like to know simply not knowable." David Shambaugh, "China's 'Quiet Diplomacy': The International Department of the Chinese Communist Party," *China: An International Journal*, V (2007), 26–27. While press reports about the CPC's political outreach in Africa are scarce, it is the websites of these organizations that provide some of the most useful information about their histories, objectives, activities, strategies, and methods.

3. Interview between author and Isaias Samakuva, president of UNITA, Luanda, Angola (14 August 2007).

4. Ibid.

5. Li Liqing, "Zhongguo yu heifeizhou zhengdang jiaoyu de lishi yu xianzhuang" ("Chinese Communist Party's Contacts with [Black] African Political Parties: A History and Status Quo"), *West Asia and Africa*, III (2006), 16–19.

6. Ibid., 16.

7. Bruce D. Larkin, *China in Africa 1949–1970: The Foreign Policy of the Peoples' Republic of China* (Berkeley, 1971), 157.

8. New China News Agency (8 November 1960), as quoted in W. A. C. Adie, "Chinese Policy towards Africa," in Sven Hamrell and Carl Gösta Widstrand (eds.), *The Soviet Bloc, China and Africa* (Uppsala, 1964), 53.

9. Adie "Chinese Policy towards Africa," 53.

10. Larkin, *China in Africa 1949–1970*, 156; Shambaugh, "China's 'Quiet Diplomacy,'" 27.

11. Patrick Tyler, *A Great Wall* (New York, 1999), 204; Li, "Chinese Communist Party's Contacts," 16.

12. Richard Lowenthal, "The Sino-Soviet Split and Its Repercussions in Africa," in Hamrell and Widstrand, *The Soviet Bloc, China and Africa,* 132.

13. Eugene K. Lawson, "China's Policy in Ethiopia and Angola," in Warren Weinstein and Thomas H. Henriksen (eds.), *Soviet and Chinese Aid to African Nations* (New York, 1980), 172.

14. Shambaugh, "China's 'Quiet Diplomacy,'" 38.

15. International Department of the Central Committee of the CPC, "Welcome Message from the Minister" (26 December 2003), available at www.idcpc.org.cn/english/profile/message.htm (accessed 13 January 2008). The CPC-ID is divided into fourteen functional offices, of which eight are regional bureaus. Bureau III (West Asian and North African Affairs) and Bureau IV (African Affairs) are relevant to this chapter's examination; however, a full explanation of all CPC-ID offices is available at its website. See also International Department of the Central Committee of the CPC, "Office Lineup," available at www.idcpc.org.cn/english/profile/office.htm (accessed 15 January 2008).

16. Quoted from Cai Wu, vice minister of the International Department of the Central Committee of the CPC, "A Review of and Reflections on the 80 Years of Foreign Contacts of the Communist Party of China (CPC)," broadcast on China Radio International, *Interviews with Public Figures* (1 July 2001), available at www.idcpc.org.cn/english/article/20010701.htm (accessed on 13 January 2008).

17. Posted on the CPC-ID website under "Functional Features," available at www.idcpc.org.cn/english/profile/features.htm (accessed 13 January 2008).

18. Cai, "A Review of and Reflections."

19. Ibid.

20. These efforts are based entirely on mutual interests and allow, for instance, the secular CPC to develop close ties to the Sudan's ruling Islamist National Congress Party (NCP) while forgoing all relations with the Communist Party of the Sudan.

21. Li, "Chinese Communist Party's Contacts," 17.

22. Yao Guimei, "Reinforcing Sino-African Trade and Economic Cooperation Opening up the Development Space," in Kinfe Abraham (ed.), *China Comes to Africa: The Political Economy and Diplomatic History of China's Relation with Africa* (Addis Ababa, 2005), 96.

23. Li, "Chinese Communist Party's Contacts," 17.

24. Interview between author and He Wenping, director of African Studies Section, Institute of West Asian and African Studies, Chinese Academy of Social Sciences (23 October 2007). Anecdotal information was also mentioned independently during interviews conducted by the author at the China Institute of Contemporary International Relations, Chinese Association of Social Sciences, and China Institute of International Studies, Beijing (January 2007).

25. Li, "Chinese Communist Party's Contacts," 18.

26. Howard French, "Taiwan Competes with China to Win African Hearts," *New York Times* (24 January 1996), A3.

27. The Gambia, Burkina Faso, Swaziland, and São Tomé and Príncipe recognize the Republic of China or Taiwan.

28. Li, "Chinese Communist Party's Contacts," 17.

29. In September 2005, for instance, Yu Zhengsheng of the political bureau of the central committee of the CPC led a delegation to Lusaka, Zambia. While there, the CPC delegation met with Information Minister Vernon Mwaanga, Defense Minister Wamundila Muliokela, and MMD National Secretary Katele Kalumba. The MMD national secretary hailed the growth in the CPC-MMD relationship and assured the delegation that his party was committed to ensuring that it won the 2006 elections. "China Lauds State for Economic Gains," *Times of Zambia* (Ndola) (14 September 2005), available at http://allafrica.com/stories/printable/200509140091.html (accessed 15 January 2008).

30. Dickson Jere, "China Issues Warning over Opposition Leader's Remarks," *Agence France-Presse* (5 September 2006).

31. "Zambia: Chinese Envoy Is Being Childish—Sata," *The Post* (Lusaka) (6 September 2006), available at http://allafrica.com/stories/200609061078.html (accessed 5 June 2008).

32. Li, "Chinese Communist Party's Contacts," 17.

33. Ibid., 17–18.

34. Ibid., 18. In May 2006, after returning from an eight-day visit to China, Nafi'a Ali Nafi'a, deputy chairman for political affairs of the Sudan's ruling party, gave a press conference in which he described the types and objectives of meetings organized by his CPC-ID hosts. Nafi'a said the delegation had meetings "with a number of Chinese ministers, leaderships of the Chinese Communist Party, and the officials of the Chinese companies operating in Sudan." Those "meetings affirmed the importance of boosting further the joint cooperation in the economic and commercial fields and coordinating the political stances in the various regional and international forums." See "Sudan and China Sign Agreements," *Sudan Tribune* (22 May 2006), available at www.sudantribune.com/spip.php?article15796 (accessed 20 January 2008). Nafi'a returned to Beijing in March 2007, again as a guest of the CPC-ID; see "China to Expand Friendly Relations with Sudan," *Xinhua* (29 March 2007), available at www.sudantribune.com/spip.php?article21053 (accessed 20 January 2008).

35. In his *Analects,* Confucius wrote: "It is a pleasure to welcome friends from afar!" This connection that Confucius made was also made by Dr. Tao Zhan, president of Shandong University, in "While Friends Coming from Afar" (18 December 2007), available at www.president.sdu.edu.cn/news/news/jqyj/2007-12-18/1197960071.html (accessed 5 June 2008).

36. Richard H. Solomon, *Chinese Political Negotiating Behavior: A Briefing Analysis* (Santa Monica, 1985). Solomon is now president of the U.S. Institute of Peace. He served as director of policy planning at the Department of State, a senior staff

member of the National Security Council, professor of political science at the University of Michigan, and head of the political science department at the RAND Corporation.

37. Ibid.

38. Interview between the author and Phillip Idro, former Ugandan ambassador to China, in Johannesburg, South Africa (11 September 2007).

39. Shambaugh, "China's 'Quiet Diplomacy,'" 45. Parentheses in original text.

40. In 2006, a Japanese diplomat in Shanghai committed suicide after he was black-mailed by Chinese intelligence about an affair he had with an operative working at a karaoke bar. Hiroko Nakata, "China Slammed over Cryptographer Honey Trap Suicide," *Japan Times* (1 April 2006), available at http://search.japantimes.co.jp/cgi-bin/nn20060401a2.html (accessed 21 January 2008). In another example of "a classic honey trap," Katrina Leung, a Los Angeles businesswoman and FBI informant, had a sexual relationship with two senior FBI counterintelligence agents while providing intelligence to the Chinese government. See the comments of Joel Brenner, head of the U.S. Office of National Counterintelligence, in "China Says Military Transparent and Not a Threat," *Agence France-Presse* (6 March 2007), available at www.spacewar.com/reports/China_Says_Military_Transparent_And_Not_A_Threat_999.html (accessed 15 January 2008).

41. Interview between author and a former senior African diplomat who served in China (fall 2007).

42. "Focus Is on Aid and Support for Africa," *Business Day* (1 October 2004).

43. Li, "Chinese Communist Party's Contacts," 18.

44. Ibid. Also, interview between author and Li Chengwen, Chinese ambassador to the Sudan (8 July 2007).

45. Interview between author and Zhang Jianwei, first secretary and CPC-ID representative at the PRC embassy in Cairo, Egypt (15 July 2007).

46. Ibid.

47. Li, "Chinese Communist Party's Contacts," 18.

48. Interview between author and Paulo T. Jorge, secretary of the Political Bureau for International Affairs, and Francisca Amelia N'Gonga, chief of the American Division, MPLA Headquarters, and former foreign minister (15 August 2007).

49. Interview between author and Li Chengwen, Chinese ambassador to the Sudan (8 July 2007).

50. Shambaugh, "China's 'Quiet Diplomacy,'" 45.

51. Ibid.

52. According to CAFIU's constitution (Chapter II: Tasks, article 5), the organization "establishes and develops friendly relations of cooperation with various NGOs, social and political organizations, research institutes and personages of various circles throughout the world," available at www.cafiu.org.cn/english/Column.asp?Column Id=22 (accessed 15 January 2007).

53. According to interviews with embassy staff and CPC-ID members, as of August 2007, there are CPC-ID attachés in Egypt, Ethiopia, South Africa, and Namibia. There

are no attachés in the Sudan, Nigeria, or Angola. The presence of attachés in all other African countries remains undetermined.

54. "China Budgets $3 billion for 'Perception' Ops," *World Tribune* (23 March 2007).

55. Li, "Chinese Communist Party's Contacts," 19.

56. This publication was provided by Chinese embassy personnel in South Africa and by personnel at China's Mission to the United Nations in New York. Yuan Wu, *China and Africa* (Beijing, 2006), 33.

57. Shambaugh, "China's 'Quiet Diplomacy,'" 32.

58. Interview between author and Li Chengwen, Chinese ambassador to the Sudan (8 July 2007).

59. Ibid.

60. Interview between author and Liu Naiya, party secretary at the Institute of West Asian and African Studies, Chinese Academy of Social Sciences, Los Angeles (23 October 2007).

61. Interview between author and Li Chengwen, the Chinese ambassador to the Sudan (8 July 2007). See also "Chinese Communists to Promote Ties with Sudanese Ruling Party," Xinhua (17 May 2006).

62. "Delegation of Sudanese Former Southern Rebels Leaves for China," *Al-Sahafah* (in Arabic) (17 March 2007). Accompanying Kiir on this delegation were SPLM economic section head Akwal Manak, chairman of SPLM external relations Niyal Dheng, and SPLM spokesmen Samson Kwaje and Pagan Amum. Interestingly, this delegation does not appear on the CPC-ID's website nor in any Xinhua or other Chinese press reports. The delegation is also mentioned by the *Sudan Tribune* in "President Hu Invites Sudan's Salva Kiir to Visit China," *Sudan Tribune* (3 February 2007), available at www.sudantribune.com/spip.php?article20078 (accessed 21 January 2008).

63. Extensive searches and interviews yielded no results.

64. "President Hu Invites."

65. "Sudan, China Share Identical Views on Darfur Issue," Sudanese News Agency (19 July 2007), available at www.reliefweb.int/rw/rwb.nsf/db900SID/YSAR-75AMBQ ?OpenDocument&RSS20=02-P (accessed 21 January 2008).

66. International Department of the Central Committee of the CPC, "Sudan Expects China's Continuous Support" (18 July 2007), available at www.idcpc.org. cn/english/news/070718.htm (accessed 14 January 2008).

67. Ibid.

68. "Sudan, China Share Identical Views."

69. "Sudan: Chinese Delegation Begins Visit to Southern Region," Sudanese Media Center (25 August 2007).

70. Blade Nzimande, "The SACP 12th National Congress: A Highly Successful Gathering of South African Communists" (18 July 2007), available at www.sacp.org. za/main.php?include=pubs/umsebenzi/2007/vol6-13.html (accessed 14 January 2008); "CPC Delegation Leaves for Three African Countries," *People's Daily* (9 July 2007), available at http://english.peopledaily.com.cn/90001/90776/6211273.html (accessed 14 January 2008).

On this trip, Wang's CPC delegation also made stops in Zimbabwe to meet with President Robert Mugabe and Ethiopia to meet with Prime Minister Meles Zenawai. See International Department of the Central Committee of the CPC, "China Becomes Zimbabwe's Top Priority Cooperation Partner: President" (19 July 2007), available at www.idcpc.org.cn/english/news/070719.htm; International Department of the Central Committee of the CPC, "Ethiopian PM Speaks Highly of China's Peaceful Rise" (20 July 2007), available at www.idcpc.org.cn/english/news/070720.htm (both accessed 14 January 2008).

71. Democratic Alliance, "Leon Leads DA Delegation to China" (17 April 2005), available at www.da.org.za/da/Site/Eng/News/print-article.asp?id=5135 (accessed 14 January 2008).

72. Consulate-General of the PRC in Cape Town, "China's NCP and SA Parliament Strengthen Financial Cooperation" (2007), available at http://capetown.china-consulate.org/eng/xwdt/t306944.htm (accessed 14 January 2008).

73. Ibid.

74. Wu Bangguo, "Work Report of NPC Standing Committee" (12 March 2007), available at http://english.peopledaily.com.cn/200703/12/eng20070312_356460.html (accessed 14 January 2008).

75. As of 14 January 2008, the NPC had bilateral friendship groups coordinate exchanges with Benin, Cameroon, Central African Republic, Côte d'Ivoire, Djibouti, Egypt, Ethiopia, Gabon, Kenya, Mali, Mauritania, Morocco, South Africa, and Tunisia. See "Bilateral Friendship Groups," available at www.npc.gov.cn/englishnpc/Organization/node_2863.htm (accessed 14 January 2008).

76. See NPC, "NPC's Foreign Contacts," available at www.npc.gov.cn/english-npc/about/2007-11/20/content_1373256.htm (accessed 14 January 2008). Wu describes how the NPC uses interparliamentary exchanges to achieve its objectives: "During the exchanges, the two sides conducted a thorough exchange of views on bilateral relations and major international and regional issues of common concern, drew up general plans for multilevel exchanges and cooperation in various areas, and discussed ways and means to promote cooperation in practical matters." Wu, "Work Report of NPC Standing Committee."

77. Wu, "Work Report of NPC Standing Committee."

78. Ibid.

79. Ibid.

80. "China's Top Legislator Pledges Friendly Relations with Sudan," *People's Daily* (16 May 2006), available at http://english.peopledaily.com.cn/200605/16/eng2006 0516_265916.html (accessed 21 January 2008). Comparisons were conducted among the members of the Foreign Affairs Committee of the Tenth National People's Congress, as listed on the NPC's website, available at www.npc.gov.cn/englishnpc/Organization/2007-11/20/content_1373179.htm (accessed 15 January 2008). See also China Vitae website biographies of Jiang Enzhu, available at www.chinavitae.org/biography/Jiang_Enzhu, and Ma Wenpu, available at http://chinavitae.com/biography/Ma_Wenpu (accessed 15 January 2008).

81. In April 2007, Han Qide, vice chairman of the NPC Standing Committee, representing President Hu Jintao, attended the inauguration of Senegalese President Abdoulaye Wade. "Chinese Envoy Arrives in Senegal to Attend Presidential Inauguration Ceremony," Xinhua (3 April 2007). In July 2007, the chairman of the NPC Standing Committee, Wu Bangguo, headed a delegation of about 200 businessmen to Cairo, Egypt, to help implement Chinese commitments from the November 2006 Forum on China-Africa Cooperation (FOCAC) summit. See "Egypt Values Implementation of FOCAC Beijing Summit Commitments," Xinhua (9 July 2007).

82. "He Luli Meets Zimbabwean Guest," Xinhua (19 March 2007), available at www.idcpc.org.cn/english/news/070319-3.htm (accessed 14 January 2008).

83. In a press statement released after his return, Nafi'a mentions the CPC-ID's strategy to boost "cooperation in the economic and commercial fields and coordinate political stances" and describes his meetings with "Chinese ministers, leaderships of the Chinese Communist Party and the officials of the Chinese companies operating in Sudan." See "Sudan and China Sign Agreements."

84. "China to Expand Friendly Relations with Sudan."

12

China's Role in Human Rights Abuses in Africa: Clarifying Issues of Culpability

As other chapters in this volume demonstrate, China has extensive and rapidly increasing economic involvement in African countries, including trade, investment, and aid. How should one assess that involvement?

The authors of this chapter do not share many analysts' and commentators' alarm concerning China's economic relations with Africa. Too much of the literature tends to enumerate individual Chinese investments in or agreements with African countries without situating them within a broader comparative context, assuming, rather than demonstrating, that they are significant. Why is China's investment in an oil refinery in Nigeria a concern per se? To measure the impact of such an investment, one would need to know the capacity of that particular refinery relative to the total refining capacity of Nigeria.

All too often, the specter of Chinese expansion is invoked, especially by sensationalistic and even sinophobic media, without working out the actual effects of China's economic activities. On the other hand, the authors of this chapter consider the assumption that China acts out of developing world or anticolonial solidarity to be naïve. China's activities in Africa, like those of other non-African countries, are motivated primarily by its own economic and security, as well as diplomatic, interests.

The authors wish to thank Myriam Hebabi for excellent research assistance and those who commented on draft versions of this chapter. Stephen Brown gratefully acknowledges funding from the Social Sciences and Humanities Research Council of Canada. Chandra Lekha Sriram gratefully acknowledges funding from the Nuffield Foundation under SGS/01159/G for research in the Sudan, which informed the discussion of that country.

China permits African countries to circumvent the conditions upon which assistance from the West and international financial institutions is predicated. China thus challenges the West's monopoly of financing and policy agenda setting. This approach poses no problems per se under international law. The main legal concern, rather, is the issue of human rights. Many policymakers and human rights advocates have criticized China's activities because several African countries in which China or Chinese-owned companies are involved have extremely poor human rights records.

This chapter argues that it is important to be clear about the extent to which China might bear responsibility for abuses in certain African states, and it does so by clarifying for which acts China may be legally responsible rather than just morally culpable. Moral arguments are not irrelevant. Certainly the following discussion should not be taken as an apology for Chinese actions, but the chapter focuses on legal, not moral, responsibility for two main reasons. First, legal codes are far more precise than moral codes and have bodies established to adjudicate disputes. It is thus much easier to make a culpability argument that could be concretely supported in court. Second, if this chapter were to assess China's moral responsibility, such a focus would exclude other international actors in Africa, and that would make little sense. Companies from a wide range of Western and non-Western (mainly Asian) countries have business relationships, especially in extractive industries, with numerous African governments that commit or fail to prevent grave human rights abuses.

This chapter examines the impact of China's involvement in two countries subject to significant international scrutiny and criticism: the Sudan and Zimbabwe. These two case studies were selected because in few African countries does the occurrence of abuses match the extent of those occurring in the Sudan and, to a lesser degree, Zimbabwe. Moreover, international sanctions have been applied to both countries (albeit much stronger in the case of the Sudan), and nowhere else in Africa has the growing economic role of one international partner—China—received such attention.[1] We considered a few other African countries, but set them aside. For instance, the United States government and U.S.-based oil companies are closely involved with the authoritarian regime of Equatorial Guinea's Teodoro Obiang Nguema, among the worst violators of human rights on the continent. One could not justify focusing solely on China's involvement there. Similarly, governments and oil companies from many countries have close ties to the government of Angola, often condemned for its disregard for human rights, especially in the oil-producing enclave of Cabinda. It is hard to argue that China bears particular

responsibility when it is only one among many international actors supporting the Angolan government.

Documenting small-scale human rights abuses in African countries, especially in countries with better human rights records, would overly dilute the
focus of this chapter. For example, the treatment of workers of one Chinese-
run copper mining operation in Zambia, where unsafe and inhumane working conditions have been reported, is better framed as the nonapplication of
domestic labor laws. Moreover, one would also need to investigate the conditions in other foreign-operated mines and industries to determine if Chinese
practices were any worse than those of other countries. The same logic applies
to the violation of local environmental protection and anticorruption laws.
Instead, the authors' interest is in China's collusion with and possible culpability for large-scale human rights abuses under international law. The Sudan
and Zimbabwe make excellent case studies for this purpose as they constitute
"worst-case scenarios," where it might actually be possible to assess specific
Chinese legal culpability. If a case is to be made anywhere in Africa regarding
Chinese responsibility, the Sudan and Zimbabwe are the best places to look.

China and Human Rights

As with its economic activities in Africa, China's position on human rights, in
particular its foreign policy in relation to human rights, has been the subject
of increased discussion.[2] The government of the People's Republic of China
has maintained for some time that human rights are a Western creation and
are inappropriate for China or indeed Asia—a position also championed by
former Prime Minister Lee Kuan Yew of Singapore. The so-called Asian values argument holds that Asian countries value community and family over
individuality and thus do not require international human rights guarantees
that emphasize individual civil and political rights.[3] China further makes the
claim that civil and political rights should not be given primacy over economic, social, and cultural rights, and that China was committed to promoting the latter.

China refrained from joining international human rights conventions until
the 1990s. Following the crackdown on dissidents in Tiananmen Square in
1989 and the international criticism that it provoked, China began to engage
with the international human rights architecture.[4] In 1991, the Chinese government issued the first of many white papers on China's human rights policy.[5]
This paper, like the ones that followed, emphasized China's commitment to
human rights but carefully circumscribed that commitment by emphasizing

national conditions and national views. The white papers present a rosy account of the protection of human rights in China but are notably lacking in discussions of many civil and political rights, such as freedom of expression and association, or protection against torture or genocide.[6] Instead, discussion of protection of human rights begins, in the two most recent white papers, with accounts of improvement in crime prevention.[7]

A close reading of what the white papers do and do not discuss suggests that China has a very limited view of what constitutes human rights protection, far narrower than the language of the international conventions that it has signed. As Human Rights Watch has pointed out, the papers "whitewash" China's human rights record, making no reference to crackdowns on scholars and members of the Falun Gong spiritual group.[8] Further, while recognizing "human rights," China has adamantly insisted that promotion of human rights must not impede on state sovereignty and be used as a political tool to interfere in the internal affairs of states. While this position was staked out in significant part to prevent criticism of China's own domestic human rights record, it also explains China's wariness of censuring African governments for their own abuses.

Chinese Responsibility? Legal Accountability of States for Violations by Other States

It is important to be clear about the circumstances under which China (or any other state) is responsible for abuses committed in another state. To that end, the authors consider here whether states might be legally (rather than morally) responsible for abuses in another state—for it is not the case that any state is legally responsible for all actions taken by another state with which it trades. There nonetheless might be moral reasons to encourage a state such as China, which engages extensively with abusive regimes in Africa, to use its leverage over such regimes to encourage them to change their behavior. Here, the authors consider a number of ways in which China might be culpable for abuses committed by or in another state through passive support for abuses, active support for abuses, commission of abuses by Chinese agents, and shielding of the abusive government. States and other international actors can passively support the commission of human rights abuses and atrocities and may be held responsible for them. If a first state's action assists a second state (or nonstate actor) in committing such abuses, and it could be reasonably expected to have known that those abuses would take place, then the first state is responsible. This principle has been clearly established in the International Law Commission's

2001 Draft Articles on Responsibility of States for Internationally Wrongful Acts.[9] While the articles are not in themselves binding international law, they are viewed as reflecting custom. Article 16 states that "A State which aids or assists another state in the commission of an internationally wrongful act by the latter is internationally responsible for doing so if: (a) That State does so with the knowledge of the circumstances of the internationally wrongful act; and (b) The Act would be internationally wrongful if committed by that State."[10]

The principle of complicity liability has been affirmed in a series of civil suits in the United States filed under the Alien Tort Claims Act (ATCA), where companies ranging from Unocal to Coca-Cola (discussed below) have faced charges, not of direct commission of human rights abuses, but of complicity with state or parastatal actors.[11]

Of course, such engagement may involve more than passive support; it may also involve active support to the commission of human rights violations. Passive support—where a state is not directly promoting the violation of rights by another state but rather facilitating them, such as through the sale of arms to an abusive regime—might be a violation by that state as well.[12] However, even if passive support to a country with a very poor human rights record creates responsibility, it must foreseeably generate abuses. In short, foreign aid, contracts, and direct investment by China in another country do not automatically mean that China is responsible for that state's abuses, although it might morally deserve blame. Thus, arms sales to states whose military would foreseeably use them to target civilians would implicate China in those activities, whereas general development assistance would not. Similarly, investment in or contracts with an abusive state would only implicate China if the associated activities were directly related to abuses.

Where the Chinese government or government-owned and -regulated corporations contract with a state for services, such as security, they may be responsible for the behavior of those state actors. Thus, if security forces attack civilians or displace people to facilitate Chinese operations, China would also be responsible. The articles on state responsibility, mentioned above, make this clear. Case law in the United States under the ATCA reinforces this argument. For example, Unocal, a California-based oil company, was found to be liable for massacres of Burmese villagers by the Burmese military, with whom it had contracted for security while laying an oil pipeline. The company was found to be liable because it knew or should have known that the Burmese military and state-owned corporation with which it worked would commit violations. Likewise, Coca-Cola faced a lawsuit for its payments to paramilitaries in Colombia who were hired to protect its factories but also engaged in campaigns of terror against civilians and killed several labor organizers.[13] Where China engages the services of the state apparatus, it bears part of the blame for the latter's foreseeable abuses. It might also be to blame for provision of goods (including roads or other infrastructure) that the host government uses to engage in abuses.

The Chinese government is clearly responsible for acts by its own agents, whether employees of the government or of state-owned and -run enterprises. These might include the direct commission of abuses, such as extrajudicial killing, torture, massacres, or use of slave labor, any or all of which might be undertaken in support of economic enterprises, such as oil exploration and exploitation. However, to date, there are no significant allegations by human rights advocacy and monitoring groups that such direct abuses have occurred, with a few exceptions noted in the Sudan case study below. This is not unusual: in conflict-prone countries, many non-Chinese companies have hired the host state's military or private security companies, as illustrated by the two examples above, but direct abuses are relatively rare.

China's position as one of only five states with a permanent seat on the United Nations (UN) Security Council gives it the power to veto resolutions that might condemn client states or authorize actions against them, such as sanctions or intervention. It can and has delayed and narrowed resolutions by threatening to veto them. Thus, regimes may feel free to engage in massacres, torture, enforced disappearances, and even genocide, with the promise that China will shield them from the international community's response. Where such vetoes or threats of veto result in a delay, watering down, or halting of a resolution, many lives may be lost or irreparably harmed. However, though it may be morally responsible, it is not at all clear that China is legally responsible for the acts of the abusive state—although it may fall foul of obligations to punish or prevent genocide and torture.[14] As discussed below, there are calls for China to use its considerable power and influence on the Security Council and in Africa to pressure abusive regimes to change, rather than to shield them.

The authors have sought thus far to parse responsibility for distinct acts and omissions, but of course, in many countries the situation is considerably more complex. Many countries of interest are embroiled in vicious cycles of conflict and abuse of human rights. Thus, investment, contracting, or operations in many countries carry a very high risk of aiding human rights abuses or the commission of war crimes, genocide, or crimes against humanity. In countries engaged in vicious internal conflict, the sale of arms to any party will foreseeably result in harm to civilians. Where countries have poor human rights records, this is even more likely to be the case.[15] That is not to say that China should cease all external involvement in countries experiencing conflict or serious human rights abuses; most other states in the international system do not terminate their activities, save for the implementation of UN or regional sanctions. However, with involvement comes risk, and it is for this reason that some Western companies have withdrawn from conflict situations rife with human rights abuses, in part clearing the way for Chinese corporations. This was the case with Talisman Energy, a Canadian oil company operating in the Sudan, which withdrew its operations when it became the subject of an ATCA lawsuit and suffered severe damage to its reputation because of public pressure campaigns.[16]

Country Cases

The African countries where human rights abuses are frequent and Chinese engagement is significant are the Sudan and Zimbabwe. Angola and Equatorial Guinea could constitute other possible cases, but in both instances, Western companies—especially oil companies based in the United States—play a similar role to Chinese companies, and it is therefore difficult to make any meaningful distinctions between China's and other countries' roles. Moreover, documentation is not as widely available, and in the case of Angola, state abuse is far less extensive than in the countries examined here. For those reasons, we focus below on Zimbabwe and the Sudan.

The Sudan

China's activities in the Sudan predate the Darfur crisis. China's rapid growth relies upon oil, and it extracts a significant amount in the Sudan, with most operations being conducted by the state-owned and -run Chinese National Petroleum Company (CNPC).[17] However, while CNPC exploration has been extensive, the Chinese-owned company partnered with the Canadian company Talisman and Malaysian company Petronas, so much of any responsibility attributable to CNPC and therefore China would also be attributable to Canada and Malaysia, where those states owned or exercised significant control over those companies. Nonetheless, Chinese interest in Sudanese oil is undeniable, and to ensure continued access to that oil, China has been a staunch supporter of the Sudanese government.[18] As a result, China has been the subject of significant international criticism, with advocates either blaming it for the abuses perpetrated in Darfur by the janjaweed militias, with the support of the Sudanese armed forces, or demanding that it place pressure upon the Sudanese government to refrain from or curtail abuses and permit a significant international peacekeeping force. However, China—like any other country investing or carrying out commercial activities abroad—cannot be held to account for every violation committed by a host state. Rather, any analysis must be clear about the nature of activities by the Chinese government or state-operated corporations that may directly or indirectly facilitate abuses. These include China's direct supply of arms to the Sudan's military—both before and after the imposition of a UN arms embargo on the sale of weapons to the Sudan destined for Darfur—and direct support to or facilitation of rights abuses through the construction of roads and the hiring of the Sudanese military for security. China may be responsible in some moral, but not legal, sense for its failure to restrain the actions of the Sudanese government, over which it has or might be presumed to have some influence.

China has engaged in extensive arms sales to the Sudanese government, selling it some $100 million in arms between 1996 and 2003 alone. These weapons included jets and helicopter gunships, reportedly used for the repression of civilians in the South as part of the now terminated North-South conflict. The weaponry, which China sold to the Sudan throughout the 1990s, helped the government target villages in the South during the long-running conflict with the Sudan People's Liberation Army.[19] In particular, such targeting resulted in massive civilian casualties and forced displacement. The depopulation of certain areas such as Unity State was not incidental; the government removed populations from areas targeted for oil exploration by the CNPC. Violence has arisen since the 2005 North-South peace agreement in parts of the South where Petrodar, a consortium involving Chinese and Malaysian companies, is conducting exploration. There has been significant displacement of the civilian population (particularly Dinka) and environmental damage, with tensions leading to civilians killing the Petrodar team leader in January 2006.[20]

China's arms sales clearly facilitated gross abuses by the Sudanese government, but the sales themselves did not violate international law. While the United States imposed sanctions and the European Union (EU) imposed an arms embargo, China was bound by neither. However, if China knowingly sold weapons that were used for abuses, then it might be complicit. Given the record of the Sudanese government, it was certainly foreseeable that weaponry provided could be used to attack civilians.

China actively resisted the imposition of international sanctions that would prevent it from selling arms to the Sudan, as did Russia, another significant supplier of arms to the Sudan. Until the passage of UN Security

Council Resolution 1591 in 2005, which bars sales to all parties involved in the conflict in Darfur (on which China abstained), such sales were not illegal. However, arms sales made by both Russia and China since the passage of this resolution do appear to violate the embargo.[21] While both governments insist that they are not selling arms destined for Darfur, Amnesty International has reported that small arms and aircraft supplied by China and Russia have been sighted in Darfur and that such aircraft have been used by the Sudanese military to support janjaweed attacks on civilians.[22] The UN has further found that the government has painted aircraft white and even stenciled UN or African Union (AU) logos on them to mislead civilians into believing them to be aid aircraft.[23]

Evidence for the *direct* commission of human rights abuses by Chinese agents is limited. China has acknowledged bringing some 10,000 Chinese laborers to work in oilfields before 1999. In southern Sudan, there were rumors that China used or intended to use its own prisoners as laborers, but these have not been substantiated.[24] The Chinese-owned oil corporation that engaged in oil exploration in South Sudan during the long-running North-South conflict did not seek to restrain abuses by Sudanese forces but rather has benefited from and facilitated them. Using weapons provided by China, among others, the Sudanese government attacked civilian populations on the ground and from the air. The Chinese government helped to build a road, meant to facilitate access to oilfields, which also permitted attacks on civilians by the government. The Sudanese army provided "security" to the CNPC to facilitate access to and transport of oil; there are allegations of significant abuses by these forces.[25] Clearly, abuses committed by Chinese agents or by Sudanese forces in Chinese employ could be attributed to China, much as abuses by the Burmese military were attributed to Unocal. It is more difficult, however, to pin responsibility for the facilitation of abuses, such as through the construction of the road. Nonetheless, if China constructed a road with the knowledge that it would be used to displace civilians, then it might bear responsibility for this outcome.[26] If past patterns hold, there is good reason for concern that China could commit or facilitate abuses in Darfur as part of its oil exploration and exploitation activities. China holds the concession for vast parts of the Sudan, ranging from West Kordofan to some sections of Darfur. However, other external actors may yet be more significant in Darfur, as companies such as HiTech (United States) and Qahtani (Saudi Arabia) hold significant concessions in the region.[27]

Western oil companies that are based in countries that place human rights and conflict conditionalities upon investments abroad potentially face civil lawsuits for the commissioning of or complicity with human rights abuses. This risk does not apply, however, in states where no such international or domestic legal restraints exist. Such was the case with China's activities in the Sudan until the expansion of the UN's arms embargo. Thus, while Western companies withdrew from the Sudan, Chinese (and to a lesser degree Russian) companies seized the opportunity and took their place. Both countries engaged in significant oil exploration and arms sales to the government of the Sudan, in spite of the North-South conflict and its associated human rights abuses, and now despite the conflict in Darfur. China has been widely criticized for its failure to restrain the Sudanese government, which has defied pressure by the UN, the AU, and many powerful states.

While it is argued above that China or any other state is not automatically legally responsible for the abuses of the Sudanese state, this does not mean that China should not or could not seek to restrain that state's excesses. The prospects for China imposing such constraints on the Sudan are considered at the conclusion of this chapter. It would appear, however, that prospects are somewhat limited, given China's use of its veto power to shield Sudanese officials from action by the UN Security Council. China resisted for some time—and threatened to veto—specific sanctions on four named individuals, the expansion of the mandate of the UN mission in the Sudan to include Darfur, and an arms embargo covering imports to the Sudanese government. While China eventually relented and abstained from the vote in these instances, its objections delayed action while the situation in Darfur worsened. Again, saying so does not render China legally responsible for the actions of the Sudanese government, but its behavior may well be regarded as morally reprehensible.

Chinese activities have clearly facilitated many abuses by the Sudanese government. Still, it is important to distinguish those for which it is clearly responsible from those that one might merely wish it to constrain or prevent. China is clearly responsible for the current delivery of weapons that are known to be used by parties to the conflict in Darfur and are in violation of the UN embargo. It can also be said to be complicit in abuses by the Sudanese government in oil exploitation in the late 1990s in Unity State, where it also knew the ends to which its weapons and road construction would be used. China can further be found responsible where abuses were committed by Sudanese forces that it hired for security, and if its oil exploration involved harm to the Chinese laborers (whether prisoners or not) that it used in southern Sudan. These acts should be clearly distinguished from action or inaction for which China is frequently criticized, such as investing or engaging in oil exploration and exploitation in the Sudan more generally or for failing to restrain that government more specifically.

Zimbabwe

China began supporting the Zimbabwe African National Union (ZANU, the core of the current ruling party) in the 1970s, during the latter's liberation war against the white-based Rhodesian government. It did so to counterbalance the Soviet Union's support for ZANU's rival, the Zimbabwe African People's Union (ZAPU). After independence, Chinese support "cooled" and the ZANU-dominated government drew assistance from a broad range of international actors, including Britain and Sweden.[28]

President Robert Mugabe's government committed its first large-scale human rights abuses soon after independence. By then, Chinese support was no longer significant. After unrest in Matabeleland, the region from which ZAPU mainly drew its support, the army targeted presumed ZAPU supporters there. Operation Gukurahundi, as it was designated (a Shona word that roughly translates as "the early rain that washes away the chaff"), resulted in the death of an estimated 20,000 people between 1981 and 1984 and ended when ZANU absorbed ZAPU and formed the ZANU-PF (Patriotic Front) in 1987. The Fifth Brigade, used in this operation, had been trained by North Korea.

The next decade was relatively peaceful, though characterized by "quiet" repression and coercion, especially during election campaigns. Opposition movements periodically emerged, but less than free and fair polls ensured that they could not win. A major shift, however, occurred in 2000, after the ruling party lost a referendum that, among other things, would have amended the constitution to concentrate power in the hands of the president. This was ZANU-PF's first defeat in two decades in power. Worried about the possible loss of parliamentary elections to the opposition Movement for Democratic Change (MDC), in spite of all the advantages of incumbency (including a slanted playing field and a plethora of irregular practices at its disposal), ZANU-PF reacted very strongly. After so-called war veterans (of the 1970s liberation war) mobilized to obtain pensions and other benefits from the government, the government quickly co-opted them, encouraging them to seize farms owned by whites, who were seen as key supporters of the MDC. One by one, various social and ethnic groups seen as pro-opposition were targeted by the war veterans (some of whom were visibly too young to have been actual combatants in the 1970s). The workers on white-owned farms were attacked and often chased away, while the rural poor were intimidated by the control of food rationing during a period of drought and shortages. The 2002 presidential elections, in which fifty opposition supporters were killed, were widely considered seriously flawed.[29]

During this period, the government increased its repression. In 2001–2002, it created ZANU-PF youth militias and used them to intimidate and attack opposition supporters. Also, not long after the March 2005 parliamentary elections, the army launched Operation Murambatsvina ("Drive Out the Trash" or "Restore Order"), which demolished shanty towns—generally considered pro-MDC—with less than twenty-four hours' notice given to residents. According to a UN report, approximately 700,000 people lost their dwellings or the sources of their livelihood.[30] Further repression followed, and the government took additional steps to gain access to assets that it could use for patronage purposes, including more farm seizures and the nationalization of controlling shares in internationally held companies.

Beginning in 2000, and to a greater degree after the 2002 elections, Western countries imposed a series of punitive measures. These included the drastic reduction of nonhumanitarian foreign aid, suspending Zimbabwe from the Commonwealth, putting in place an arms embargo, and imposing "smart sanctions," notably freezing regime elites' bank accounts and banning their travel to the EU and the United States. The World Bank and the International Monetary Fund also ceased assistance. Faced with increased international isolation and an economic crisis reaching epic proportions, President Mugabe in 2005 announced a new "Look East" policy. Henceforth, Zimbabwe would turn its back on the West and turn to Asia, especially China, for trade, investment, and loans. This made official a practice that was already in place. With the Western economic withdrawal, China had already become an economic partner of growing importance.

In recent years, Chinese companies have invested in mining and farming, as well as building roads.[31] In exchange for mining concessions, China has also reportedly become the largest importer of Zimbabwean tobacco, as well as an important supplier of cell phones, televisions, and radios.[32] Chinese firms have provided agricultural equipment and helped with electricity generation.[33] China is farming 1,000 km^2 of farmland seized from white commercial farmers, while China Aviation Industry has provided 3 airplanes to Air Zimbabwe, and First Automobile Works of China has sold some 1,000 buses.[34] China has also sold light arms to Zimbabwe and even built a weapons factory.[35] In 2005, China sold Zimbabwe 6 jets for its air force, soon followed by 12 jet fighters and 100 military vehicles, valued at about US$240 million, at a time when 1 million Zimbabweans were at risk of starvation.[36] Beijing is also supplying tanks, artillery, armored vehicles, and antiaircraft batteries.[37] China might also have provided the Zimbabwean government with riot control gear and radio-jamming equipment.[38] In addition, China has reportedly provided equipment to monitor electronic communications and has planned to provide assistance in the area of law enforcement and prison management.[39]

China also has given Zimbabwe political support at the international level. As a permanent member of the UN Security Council, it can block UN condemnations of Mugabe's government and binding sanctions. Among non-African countries, only China endorsed the 2005 elections. It also publicly supported Operation Murambatsvina.[40]

Still, Chinese support has not been as strong as Mugabe had hoped. In 2005, he traveled to Beijing to request additional assistance and received only US$6 million for grain imports.[41] The Chinese government is reported to be "suspicious of Mugabe's tactics—notably his willingness to literally starve his opposition and destroy the Zimbabwean economy."[42] Attempts to secure a US$2 billion loan in 2006 were unsuccessful. Faced with insufficiency of Chinese support, Zimbabwe has attempted to obtain financing elsewhere, including Libya, which at one time provided most of Zimbabwe's oil.

In fact, China never seemed as keen about its relationship with Zimbabwe as Zimbabwe was about China. As early as 2002, even before Mugabe launched the "Look East" policy, China expressed concern about the possible negative impact of factory invasions and chaotic land reform policies on Chinese economic interests.[43] Though Zimbabwe has among the most important platinum deposits in the world, as well as over forty other minerals, many of these resources are as yet unexploited and require significant investment to do so (unlike tobacco, which is more easily cultivated).[44] The return on such investments was unknown, especially when there were "arrangements with local government elites that inhibit profit making."[45] China grew increasingly worried about whether its loans would ever be repaid, a concern that increased when the Zimbabwean government failed to meet some of its obligations. As the government nationalized an increasing number of foreign assets, fears of eventual expropriation also dampened Chinese interest.[46] In fact, many large-scale projects never made it beyond the announcement stage.[47] In 2007, further motivated by the Zimbabwean government's renewed crackdown on the opposition, China recognized that Zimbabwe was increasingly becoming an economic and diplomatic liability.[48] In August, Chinese officials signaled their government's intent to limit future involvement to humanitarian assistance, such as food aid.

Though it is reasonably clear that the Zimbabwean government has committed large-scale violations of its citizens' human rights, what responsibility can be attributed to China? There are no allegations of Chinese agents directly committing abuses or of China actively supporting violations. It is likely that the Zimbabwean security forces have used Chinese-supplied light arms in individual acts of repression. However, for China to bear any legal responsibility, one would have to demonstrate either that Zimbabwean forces were acting on behalf of the Chinese, which has never been alleged, or that China knew or should reasonably have known that the weapons would be used to violate human rights at the time of the sale, which is difficult to establish. Unlike its Sudanese counterpart, the Zimbabwean government has not used Chinese weaponry to bomb villages or forcibly displace their entire population. Although the origin of the tractors used in Operation Murambatsvina is unknown, tractors had not been used previously as weapons in Zimbabwe (unlike the case of Israel in the Gaza Strip [see note 12]), and it would not be possible to impute responsibility to the weapons' or tractors' supplier or country of origin. As the Chinese-supplied jets have not been used against Zimbabwean civilians, it would be even harder to establish that China should have expected the Zimbabwean government to use them to commit abuses.

Though no strong case can be made for China's passive support of human rights *abuses,* it can be accused of passive support for *abusers.* Indeed, as mentioned above, China has shielded Mugabe's regime from international opprobrium, including potentially binding UN sanctions. However, only a weak case can be made that China is benefitting from Zimbabwean abuses, based on Chinese contracts for farmland previously held by white commercial farmers. One could argue that China, through its provision of financial and diplomatic support, has facilitated the survival of the Mugabe regime and that it has failed to restrain the government's abuses. However, that assumes that China's support was key in keeping the regime in power and that China actually had the power to alter Zimbabwean policy. The fact that China is currently disengaging from Zimbabwean affairs with no discernible effect on the Mugabe regime suggests that actual Chinese influence was not particularly strong.

Conclusion

China is a natural "alternative partner of 'pariah states,'" and the Sudan and Zimbabwe are viewed by many as pariahs.[49] In places where Western countries and companies refrain from involvement in or withdraw from countries with poor human rights records, China can easily position itself profitably. For instance, when Talisman Energy and other Western oil companies were pressured to divest from the Sudan, the Chinese took their place, as did to a lesser extent Indian, Malaysian, and Qatari companies.[50] Under such circumstances, Western business opportunities are lost to Asian countries, without any concomitant improvement in the behavior of the abusive regime. For some, the moral high ground is worth the financial sacrifice. The unintended consequence of human rights lobbying that led to the withdrawal of Talisman and other companies may well have been the engagement of companies with less concern (and less legal obligation) to respect human rights.

While an ethical analysis of behavior is important, the goal of this chapter is to focus on legal culpability. The authors agree with Taylor that Chinese "discourse in Africa effectively legitimizes human rights abuses and undemocratic practices under the guise of state sovereignty and 'noninterference'" and that "China *is* undermining emergent international regimes."[51] In particular, China's involvement in Africa is undermining not only human rights but also principles of good governance, transparency, and accountability to which African countries themselves have subscribed via the AU, the New Partnership for Africa's Development, and the Extractive Industries Transparency Initiative, among others. What this chapter determines is to what degree Chinese activities are permissible or prohibited under international law.

In the Sudan and Zimbabwe—the two worst-case scenarios in which particularly abusive regimes are associated with China—some clear legal responsibility can be argued. In the Sudan, China's supply of weapons used in Darfur is in apparent violation of the UN embargo. One could maintain that China is complicit with the government's abuses in Unity State, where it supplied the government with weapons and built roads that it should have known would be used to commit large-scale human rights violations. Some culpability could also be attributed to China for abuses committed by the Sudanese forces in its employ. China cannot be held accountable, however, for more general activities in the oil sector or for failing to pressure the government to refrain from committing abuses.

In Zimbabwe, there is less evidence of legal culpability. There is very weak evidence to suggest that the Chinese government should have known that the weapons it provided would have been used to violate rights. Likewise, the fact that Chinese companies are using some land seized from white commercial farmers does not make for a very strong case. As discussed in the context of the Sudan, China, likewise, cannot be held legally culpable for shielding the Mugabe regime from international sanctions or for not preventing abuses.

Thus, even in the two worst cases—that is, where the states have clearly committed large-scale human rights abuses and also have significant relations with China—very few and limited instances of Chinese legal culpability can be found. One can therefore reasonably conclude that it is even less likely that a great degree of legal responsibility for significant violations can be identified elsewhere in Africa. This does not mean that China bears no moral responsibility in the Sudan and Zimbabwe, where it was an important international partner, or elsewhere. However, any assessment of moral responsibility in other countries, such as Angola or Equatorial Guinea, should also consider the involvement of all international actors, not only Chinese ones. In such cases, moral culpability is likely to be broadly shared.

China's actions in Africa appear to be based on weighing the trade-off between political and economic considerations on a country-by-country basis. On one hand, it has become increasingly embarrassing for China to be associated with 'pariah states.' On the other hand, access to natural resources is required to sustain China's exceptional economic growth rate. Are the economic benefits that accrue from engaging with an abusive regime worth the cost on the international political level? At a time when China seeks international respectability, an increased emphasis is being placed on the political side of the equation, but that does not necessarily trump economic interests.

A clear impediment to any Chinese role in limiting human rights abuses in African countries is China's firm stand on the nonuniversality of human rights, in particular its resistance to the imposition of international human rights standards on its own behavior and on the behavior of countries in which it is active. Nonetheless, even if China does not adhere to those international norms, its active opposition to their application in Africa incurs a political and sometimes economic cost. As long as China has a significant economic and strategic interest in African countries that are prone to human rights abuses, it is unlikely to sacrifice that interest to follow standards to which it does not subscribe, unless the cost of noncompliance increases to the point where it becomes damaging economically—for instance, as a result of "naming and shaming."

In the case of Zimbabwe, the trade-off between political and economic interests has virtually disappeared. As the Mugabe government's human rights record worsens, the political costs of continued Chinese support rise. As the economy continues in its downward descent, economic benefits for China have all but evaporated. Indeed, the lack of economic benefits alone provides a convincing argument for China to pursue its economic interests elsewhere. The fundamental cause behind China's growing disenchantment with Zimbabwe though remains unclear. If political interests, in fact, outweigh the financial calculus, China might actually, as a next step, stop using its influence to protect Zimbabwe from more aggressive international pressure.

In the Sudan, there is some potential for China to play a positive role, including pressuring the government to stop the fighting and gross violations of human rights in Darfur. In light of the intransigence of the Sudanese government, it is not surprising that some countries are turning to China to exercise leverage. Even the United States has apparently asked China to pressure the Sudan.[52] While China's record in the Sudan is appalling, the outlook is not entirely negative. China's willingness to pressure the Sudanese government— and to do so openly rather than through quiet diplomacy—was increasing in late 2007.

Such policy changes may well be attributed to China's eagerness to improve its international reputation, especially prior to hosting the 2008 Olympics. Human rights advocates have increased pressure on China, with some having dubbed the Beijing games the "Genocide Olympics" in the hopes of encouraging China to use its leverage on Khartoum.[53] On the positive side, China encouraged the Sudan to accept a UN peacekeeping mission and did not veto UN Security Council Resolution 1706—the expansion of the existing AU force to a hybrid AU-UN force. It did not veto the UN Security Council resolution expanding the arms embargo or the resolution referring the situation in Darfur to the International Criminal Court. It may well have significant leverage in the Sudan because of its investments there. It may also enjoy additional credibility, precisely because of its criticism of so-called Western human rights. China has claimed that it has raised concerns about Darfur in discussions with the Sudan, including at the presidential level, and China appointed a special envoy for the crisis in Darfur in 2007.[54] However, both China and Russia have resisted attempts to expand the arms embargo and to place travel and assets sanctions on four specific individual leaders in the Darfur conflict.[55] It further seems unlikely, given Chinese economic interests and the potential for Russian investors to replace the Chinese, that China will be prepared to place significantly more pressure upon the Sudan.

However, China's efforts to apply pressure on the Sudanese government, in spite of its strong economic interests there, suggest that China might prove more willing to uphold international norms than was previously believed possible. It remains to be seen whether this is the start of a significant new trend or was merely an attempt at developing positive public relations before the 2008 Beijing Olympics. It does nonetheless demonstrate that China is not immune to public pressure and that it may yet be convinced to do more to uphold principles of human rights abroad, even if it is reluctant to apply them at home.

Notes

1. China is indeed an important trading partner of the Sudan: figures are unreliable and sometimes vary widely, but somewhere between 32 and 71 percent of Sudanese exports went to China in 2005 and 2006, while 18–21 percent of imports were from China. For Zimbabwe, however, Chinese trade is far less important: China accounted for about 8–9 percent of Zimbabwean exports and 4–6 percent of imports during the same years. Compare this to the 40–45 percent of Zimbabwean trade that was with South Africa. See Economist Intelligence Unit reports for the Sudan and Zimbabwe, available at www.eiu.com (accessed 19 December 2007); International Monetary Fund, "Direction of Trade Statistics," available at www.imfstatistics.org/dot (accessed 19 December 2007); Bank of Sudan, "Economic Indicators," available at www.cbos.gov.sd/english/econe.htm (accessed 19 December 2007).

2. Ann Kent, *China, the United Nations, and Human Rights: The Limits of Compliance* (Philadelphia, 1999); Kent, "China's Growth Treadmill: Globalization, Human Rights, and International Relations," in Ronald C. Keith (ed.), *China as a Rising World Power and Its Response to "Globalization"* (London, 2005), 18–37; Andrew J. Nathan, "Human Rights in Chinese Foreign Policy," *China Quarterly*, CXXXIX (1994), 622–643.

3. Fareed Zakaria, "Culture Is Destiny: A Conversation with Lee Kuan Yew," *Foreign Affairs*, LXXIII (1994), 109–126; Bangkok Declaration on Human Rights (1993), available at www.regency.org/human_rights/bangkok_declaration.pdf (accessed 19 December 2007); Kishore Mahbubani, *Can Asians Think? Understanding the Divide between East and West* (Hanover, NH, 2001).

4. Dingding Chen, "Understanding China's Human Rights Policy: The Limits of International Norms" (n.d.), available at http://cosa.uchicago.edu/dingdingchen3.htm (accessed 19 December 2007).

5. See Information Office of the State Council, People's Republic of China, "Human Rights in China" (November 1991), available at www.china.org.cn/e-white/7/index.htm (accessed 19 December 2007).

6. The 2004 white paper contains a brief reference to legal protections for freedom of information, speech, and the press, but proceeds to refer to state spokespersons and news conferences as evidence of such protections. See Information Office of the State Council, People's Republic of China, "White Paper: Progress in China's Human Rights Cause in 2003" (16 April 2004), available at www.china-un.ch/eng/bjzl/t85082.htm (accessed 19 December 2007).

7. Ibid.; Information Office of the State Council, "China's Progress in Human Rights in 2004" (April 2005), available at www.china.org.cn/e-white/20050418 (accessed 19 December 2007). See also Nathan, "Human Rights," 624–628.

8. Human Rights Watch, "China: White Paper a 'Whitewash'" (10 April 2001), available at http://hrw.org/english/docs/2001/04/10/china242.htm (accessed 19 December 2007).

9. International Law Commission, "Draft Articles on Responsibility of States for Internationally Wrongful Acts" (November 2001), available at www.kentlaw.edu/faculty/bbrown/classes/IntlLawFall2007/CourseDocs/DraftArticlesonStateResponsibility(ILC).pdf (accessed 19 December 2007). This issue was also squarely presented by the decision of the International Court of Justice in the *Case Concerning United States Diplomatic and Consular Staff in Tehran* (*United States of America* v. *Iran*), 1980 ICJ 3 (24 May 1980).

10. "Draft Articles on State Responsibility," article 16.

11. See Chandra Lekha Sriram, *Globalizing Justice for Mass Atrocities: A Revolution in Accountability* (London, 2005), 61–78.

12. This issue is hotly contested. In *Corrie* v. *Caterpillar*, a civil case in the United States, heavy equipment manufacturer Caterpillar was sued for damages, including death and loss of property, arising from the Israeli government's use of its bulldozers in the Gaza Strip. The case was dismissed. See *Cynthia Corrie et al.* v. *Caterpillar, Inc.*, C05-5192FDB, U.S. Court of Appeals for the Ninth Circuit (November 2005), available at http://ccrjustice.org/files/Corrie_decision_11_05_0.pdf (accessed 19 December 2007).

13. These cases are discussed in Sriram, *Globalizing Justice*, 61–78.

14. Office of the High Commissioner for Human Rights, "Convention on the Prevention and Punishment of the Crime of Genocide" (9 December 1948), available at www2.ohchr.org/english/bodies/ratification/1.htm (ratified by China in 1983) (accessed 19 December 2007), and "Convention against Torture and Other Cruel, Inhuman or Degrading Treatment or Punishment" (19 December 1984), available at www2.ohchr.org/english/bodies/ratification/9.htm (ratified by China in 1988) (accessed 19 December 2007).

15. For a discussion of these dynamics, see Human Security Centre, *Human Security Report 2005: War and Peace in the Twenty-First Century* (New York, 2005).

16. *Presbyterian Church of Sudan, et al.* v. *Talisman Energy Inc.*, 244 F. Supp. 2d 289 (S.D.N.Y. 2003).

17. See, generally, Ian Taylor, "China's Oil Diplomacy in Africa," *International Affairs*, LXXXV (2006), 937–959.

18. As Daniel Large has reminded the authors, China's interest in the Sudan is political as well as oil driven, and its activities in oil exploration peaked in 2002 (personal communication, 8 November 2007).

19. Jemera Rone, *Sudan, Oil, and Human Rights* (New York, 2003), 605–621, reproduced in Human Rights Watch, "China's Involvement in Sudan: Arms and Oil" (November 2003), available at www.hrw.org (accessed 19 December 2007).

20. European Coalition on Oil in Sudan, "Oil Development in Northern Upper Nile, Sudan" (May 2006), available at www.ecosonline.org/back/pdf_reports/2006/

ECOS%20Melut%20Report%202006/ECOS%20Melut%20Report%20final-DEF.pdf (accessed 19 December 2007).

21. UN Security Council Resolution 1591 (29 March 2005), UN Doc. S/RES/1591. See Amnesty International, "Sudan: Arms Continuing to Fuel Serious Human Rights Violations in Darfur" (8 May 2007), available at www.amnesty.org/en/library/info/ AFR54/019/2007 (accessed 19 December 2007).

22. "China, Russia, Deny Weapons Breach," BBC (8 May 2007), available at http:// news.bbc.co.uk/2/hi/africa/6632959.stm (accessed 19 December 2007).

23. Amnesty International, "Sudan: Arms."

24. Human Rights Watch, "China's Involvement in Sudan."

25. Amnesty International, "Appeal by Amnesty International to the Chinese Government on the Occasion of the China-Africa Summit for Development and Cooperation" (1 November 2006), available at www.amnesty.org/en/library/info/AFR54/ 072/2006 (accessed 19 December 2007).

26. Chandra Lekha Sriram, "China, Human Rights, and the Sudan" (30 January 2007), available at http://jurist.law.pitt.edu/forumy/2007/01/china-human-rights-and-sudan.php (accessed 19 December 2007).

27. Daniel Large drew our attention to these concessions in Darfur (personal communication, 8 November 2007).

28. See Jeremy Youde, "Why Look East? Zimbabwean Foreign Policy and China," *Africa Today*, LIII (2007), 8.

29. While the authors did not consult this source, further discussion of the situation in Zimbabwe can be found in Robert I. Rotberg, "Winning the African Prize for Repression: Zimbabwe," in Robert I. Rotberg (ed.), *Worst of the Worst: Dealing with Repressive and Rogue Nations* (Washington, D.C., 2007), 166–192.

30. Anna Kajumulo Tibaijuka, "Report of the Fact-Finding Mission to Zimbabwe to Assess the Scope and Impact of Operation Murambatsvina by the UN Special Envoy on Human Settlements Issues in Zimbabwe" (18 July 2005), available at www. unhabitat.org/downloads/docs/1664_96507_ZimbabweReport.pdf (accessed 19 December 2007), 7.

31. Raphael Kaplinsky, Dorothy McCormick, and Mike Morris, "The Impact of China on Sub-Saharan Africa" (November 2007), available at www.ids.ac.uk/ids/ bookshop/wp/wp291.pdf (accessed 19 December 2007); also see details in John Blessings Karumbidza, "Win-Win Economic Cooperation: Can China Save Zimbabwe's Economy?" in Firoze Manji and Stephen Marks (eds.), *African Perspectives on China in Africa* (Cape Town, 2007), 93–94.

32. Youde, "Why Look East?" 11. See also "Zimbabwe: China's Lifeline," *Africa Research Bulletin*, XLIII (2006), 17002; "Zimbabwe: Sanctions Remain," *Africa Research Bulletin*, XLIV (2007), 17288.

33. Joshua Eisenman and Joshua Kurlantzick, "China's Africa Strategy," *Current History*, CV (2006), 223.

34. Michael Wines, "From Shoes to Aircraft to Investment, Zimbabwe Pursues a Made-in-China Future," *New York Times* (24 July 2005), A10.

35. Michal Meidan, "China's Africa Policy: Business Now, Politics Later," *Asian Perspective*, XXX (2006), 84; Valérie Niquet, "La stratégie africaine de la Chine," *Politique étrangère* (2006), 364–365.

36. Eisenman and Kurlantzick, "China's Africa Strategy," 222; "Zimbabwe: Chinese Purchases," *Africa Research Bulletin*, XLIII (2006), 16766.

37. Niquet, "La stratégie africaine," 365.

38. Eisenman and Kurlantzick, "China's Africa Strategy," 223.

39. Sophie Richardson, "China Can Help the People of Zimbabwe and Sudan," *Human Rights Watch Commentary* (3 November 2006), available at http://hrw.org/english/docs/2006/11/03/china14509.htm (accessed 19 December 2007); *International Herald Tribune* (25 July 2005).

40. Youde, "Why Look East?" 10–11.

41. Dennis M. Tull, "China's Engagement in Africa: Scope, Significance, and Consequences," *Journal of Modern African Studies*, XLIV (2006), 473.

42. Richardson, "China Can Help."

43. "Zimbabwe: China Adds Pressure," *Africa Research Bulletin*, XXIX (2002), 14906.

44. Eisenman and Kurlantzick, "China's Africa Strategy," 220.

45. Chris Alden, "China in Africa," *Survival*, XLVII (2005), 154.

46. "Zimbabwe: China's Lifeline."

47. Stephanie Kleine-Ahlbrandt and Andrew Small, "Beijing cools on Mugabe," *International Herald Tribune* (3 May 2007), available at www.iht.com/articles/2007/05/03/opinion/edkleine.php (accessed 16 May 2008); "African Development Bank: Annual Meetings (Shanghai)," *Africa Research Bulletin*, XLIV (2007), 17358.

48. Ibid.

49. Tull, "China's Engagement," 468. See also Rui P. Pereira, "A nova política da China em África," *Relações Internacionais*, X (2006), 34. As Daniel Large has pointed out, different sectors of the U.S. government view the Sudan simultaneously as a pariah for political reasons and as an important ally in the "global war on terror" (personal communication, 8 November 2007).

50. Thus, while CNPC sought Talisman's share in joint exploration, when the latter withdrew, it was granted to Indian company ONGC Videsh Limited instead (Daniel Large, personal communication, 8 November 2007).

51. Taylor, "China's Oil Diplomacy," 958. Italics in original.

52. Human Rights Watch, "Letter to China on the Crisis in Darfur" (29 January 2007), available at http://hrw.org/english/docs/2007/01/29/sudan15189.htm (accessed 19 December 2007); Richardson, "China Can Help"; "China-Africa Summit: Focus on Human Rights, Not Just Trade" (2 November 2006), available at http://hrw.org/english/docs/2006/11/02/china14498.htm (accessed 19 December 2007); "Africa-China: Beijing Summit," *Africa Research Bulletin*, XLIII (2006), 17135–17137.

53. "China and Darfur: The Genocide Olympics?" *Washington Post* (14 December 2006), A30, available at www.washingtonpost.com/wp-dyn/content/article/2006/12/13/AR2006121302008.html (accessed 19 December 2007).

54. Howard W. French, "Chinese Leader to Visit Sudan for Talks on Darfur Conflict," *New York Times* (25 January 2007), A6; "Sudan: UN Force?" *Africa Research Bulletin,* XLIV (2007), 17056–17058; "Sudan: China Reviews Stance," *Africa Research Bulletin,* XLIV (2007), 17090; Steve Bloomfield, "Chinese Envoy to Put Pressure on Sudan over Darfur," *Independent* (11 May 2007), available at www.independent.co.uk/news/world/africa/chinese-envoy-to-put-pressure-on-sudan-over-darfur-448342.html (accessed 19 December 2007); "China's Darfur Envoy Hits Back at Campaigners," *Agence France-Presse* (8 September 2007).

55. "Sudan: Deadline Diplomacy Is Failing," *Africa Research Bulletin,* XLIV (2007), 16622–16624.

NDUBISI OBIORAH, DARREN KEW, AND YUSUF TANKO

13

"Peaceful Rise" and Human Rights: China's Expanding Relations with Nigeria

The rapidly evolving Chinese-African relationship presents opportunities and challenges for Africa. Some African countries are benefiting from higher commodity prices, arising from China's immense demand for natural resources for its manufacturing industries. Chinese trade, investment, and infrastructural aid are fundamentally reshaping Africa's economies to the benefit of local consumers and businesses in some countries but also to the primary benefit of ruling elites in others, especially those with extraction-based economies.

Nigeria, as Africa's sociopolitical giant, should have a leading role in shaping China's involvement on the continent. In addition, Nigeria's relative wealth and complexity should give it greater leverage than smaller African countries in its relationship with China. So far, however, the pattern is similar to that throughout the rest of sub-Saharan Africa: the Chinese government is building extensive relationships with the Nigerian government and elites through billions of dollars in oil investments and unconditional development aid. Meanwhile, a growing Chinese diaspora is immigrating to Nigeria and playing a greater role in local markets, and an unregulated flood of cheap Chinese commodities is driving out the few remaining small Nigerian manufacturers. So far, this impact has gone largely unmarked by the Nigerian public. If these trends continue, will Nigerians lash out at the immigrant Chinese presence as have Zambians and other African host populaces?

The authors wish to thank Frank Ihedoro and John Lewis Moore for their assistance in conducting and compiling survey research.

To prevent this backlash, civil society actors in Nigeria and Africa as a whole must work to ensure that the public's economic and political interests, and not the usual interests of elites, are central to their governments' engagements with China. The Chinese government's emergence as a potential competitor with U.S. and European interests also offers African governments an opportunity to return the continent to center stage in global politics. Africa's governments should seek to maximize the benefits of a potential strategic partnership with China, while actively working to avoid the perpetuation of an asymmetrical relationship akin to Africa's current trade and political relations with the West.

Nigeria over the next five years will pose an important test case in this regard. What footprint has Chinese trade with and immigration to Nigeria left so far, and to what direction does this point for the future of the Chinese-Nigerian relationship and for China's role on the continent overall?

How Africa Discovered China

The evolution of the Chinese-African relationship has not been based on one-way traffic, with a passive Africa responding to Chinese overtures; on the contrary, African individuals and governments have initiated contact and sought relations with China since before independence. African liberation movements sought assistance from China, and the international liaison section of the Chinese Communist Party has contacts with political parties and movements in Africa both dating from the 1950s. Postindependence leaders such as Julius Nyerere of Tanzania and Kenneth Kaunda of Zambia looked to China for models of political and socioeconomic nation building in the 1960s. Furthermore, there are long-standing personal and commercial links between Africa and China, Hong Kong, Taiwan, and the overseas Chinese diaspora. Taiwan and Hong Kong were widely known across Africa by the early 1970s as sources for imports of cheap textiles and consumer goods, with African traders visiting regularly to place orders and negotiate deals with the Chinese. For instance, traders from southeastern Nigeria established extensive commercial networks, often based on personal relationships, with Hong Kong and Taiwanese manufacturers and traders as well as with overseas Chinese communities in Southeast Asia. Hong Kong and Taiwanese traders began to establish representative offices and trading outposts in African countries in the late 1970s and eventually began to invest in manufacturing and other operations in Africa. By the late 1980s, there was a visible increase in Chinese residents and Chinese-owned businesses in many sub-Saharan African countries.

In the late 1990s, the introduction by the U.S. government of preferential textile quotas for Africa further encouraged Chinese firms to establish operations
in African countries.

The increased popularity of China in the 1970s led to greater awareness of
Chinese history and culture among ordinary Africans. Some Africans who visited China as students, traders, or employees of Chinese businesses eventually
stayed on and settled in China. In recent years, some Chinese companies, universities, and schools have recruited employees, including academics and foreign language teachers, from the African diaspora in Europe and North
America. The number of African residents in China is growing and may soon
be of political significance.

As China refocused its relations with Africa from ideological to trade in the
1990s, the dominant image of China in Africa also changed from that of an
ideological ally against colonialism, apartheid, and Western domination to a
business partner and emerging economic colossus. The Chinese doctor or
technical aid worker traded places with the Chinese entrepreneur or state
corporation. Trade between China and Africa has expanded rapidly, from an
approximate $12 million in the early 1950s to about $18.55 billion in 2003.
Chinese government figures estimate the number of Chinese companies operating in Africa in 2004 at 674 (Lyman puts this number at 800), with a total
investment of $1.509 billion.[1] Chinese state-owned and private businesses
operating in Africa have invested in diverse sectors of African economies
including mining, agriculture, fisheries, tropical hardwoods, manufacturing,
telecommunications, construction, entertainment, leisure, and hospitality.[2]
China has canceled billions of dollars of the debt that it is owed by African
states and has offered further debt relief and additional aid to many African
countries.[3]

China's Booming Relationship with Nigeria

China sent its first trade delegation to Nigeria in 1961, one year after the
country gained independence from Britain. In 1960, bilateral trade volume
between the two countries was below $1 million. By 1996, the volume of trade
between Nigeria and China had risen to $178 million. Trade rose sharply
under President Olusegun Obasanjo, reaching $570 million by 1999, $860
million in 2000, and $1.14 billion in 2001. Between 2002 and 2005 alone, the
two-way trade increased by $3 billion. In the first 9 months of 2007, the trade
value was $870 million, a 50 percent increase over the same period in 2006.

More than thirty Chinese companies and consortia are actively engaged in construction, oil and gas exploitation, technology, services, and education.[4]
Obasanjo visited China twice, in 2001 and 2005, and President Umaru Yar'Adua visited in 2008. Chinese President Hu Jintao reciprocated, visiting Nigeria in 2006 and 2007. High-level ministerial and parliamentary visits have also taken place between the two countries. During all of these visits, many bilateral and trade agreements between the two countries were signed. During President Obasanjo's 2001 visit, both leaders signed agreements on trade and on investment promotion and protection.[5] Supporting agreements on sincere friendship, mutual trust, mutual economic benefit and common development, and enhanced consultation and mutual support were also signed. The same year, Obasanjo agreed to sell China 50,000 barrels of crude oil per day (bbl/d).

In November 2001, the China Trade Exhibition, the largest fair ever held in Africa by the China Council for the Promotion of International Trade (CCPIT), was held in Lagos at the invitation of the Nigerian Association of Chambers of Commerce, Industry, Mines, and Agriculture. The trade exhibition was organized by CCPIT and the China Chamber of International Commerce. Forty-eight Chinese companies attended. Exhibits included motorcycles and parts, auto parts, bicycle parts, tires, agricultural machines, weaving machines, cookware, air conditioners, color televisions, refrigerators, small household electrical appliances, electronics, diesel engines, and power generators.[6] In 2003, the China Civil Engineering Construction Corporation constructed the Abuja Sports Complex and the head office of the Nigerian Communications Commission.[7]

When Obasanjo visited China in April 2005, the two countries signed four bilateral agreements to promote economic and trade relations, including
—investment cooperation,
—technical cooperation,
—a Memorandum of Understanding (MOU) for the Nigerian Telephony Project, and
—cooperation with Huawei Technologies investment in Nigeria.[8]
The telecom plants owned by Huawei and Zhong Xing Telecommunication Equipment Company were expected to go into production in Abuja by the end of 2005. As of mid-2008, however, the project was still incomplete, even though $5.3 billion for the second phase of the project and 75 percent of the counterpart funding had been paid.[9] The intended areas of close cooperation between the two countries were in oil and gas exploitation, power generation

and energy, railway development and modernization, agriculture, communications, manufacturing, tourism, military and defense, increased trade and investments, an overseas development assistance program, and improving financial relationships. On 13 October 2005, Nigeria and China signed a contract agreement for the construction of 598 artesian wells for 18 states and the Federal Capital Territory, Abuja, at the cost of N695 million ($5.8 million).[10]

During President Hu's visit to Nigeria in April 2006, Nigeria and China signed an additional four agreements and three MOUs on a range of programs to enhance their economic ties, including

—a financing agreement of N8.36 billion ($500 million) in concessionary export grants through the China Eximbank to support infrastructural development,

—provision of about N670 million ($5.6 million) for the training of fifty Nigerian officials and medical personnel on comprehensive malaria prevention and control,

—the supply of antimalarial drugs worth N83.6 million ($696,000) in support of the Roll Back Malaria Partnership,

—establishment of a team of experts for a Nigeria-China cultural friendship project,

—provision by Huawei Technologies of a National Information Communication Technology Infrastructure Backbone to the Federal Ministry of Science and Technology, and

—support for Nigeria's railway modernization project.

On 28 November 2006, former President Obasanjo laid the foundation for the project in Kajola, Ogun State. The contract was awarded to the China Civil Engineering Construction Corporation at a cost of $8.3 billion. Some of the railway routes it covers are Lagos-Ibadan (181 kilometers), Ibadan-Ilorin (200 kilometers), Ilorin-Minna (270 kilometers), Minna-Abuja-Kaduna (360 kilometers), and Kaduna-Kano (305 kilometers).[11] The Eximbank, at the commencement of the project, offered the Nigerian federal government a loan of $2.5 billion for the project, of which $500 million was concessional. The annual interest rate on the loan is only 3 percent.[12]

China has also increased its volume of agricultural imports from Nigeria. By mid-2006, 80,000 tons of cassava chips were exported to China, and Nigeria had already received an order from China to supply another 102,000 tons in a period of 10 months. Within the same ten-month period, China had bought sesame seeds and had indicated a willingness to buy additional agricultural produce. By 2007, there were over 400 Chinese agricultural experts in Nigeria, constructing small earthen dams.[13]

Another major area of trade is textiles and fabrics. Due to both trade concessions and smuggling, Chinese businesses have flooded Nigeria with very cheap versions of these commodities. Chinese businesses also export pharmaceuticals in large quantities to Nigeria.

Nigerian military officials have occasionally accused traditional Western suppliers of reluctance to supply them with weapons and are increasingly turning to China, particularly to fight the insurgency in the Niger Delta. In 2003, Nigeria purchased fifteen F-7NI and FT-7NI Chinese multirole combat-trainer aircraft to boost defense operations, while the Nigerian air force purchased twelve Chinese-made versions of the upgraded MiG-21 jet fighter. The Nigerian navy has also bought boats to patrol the swamps and creeks of the Niger Delta.

In 2007, China cooperated with Nigeria to launch NIGERCOMSAT 1, Nigeria's and Africa's first communication satellite. A Chinese consortium was awarded the contract to design, build, and launch the satellite, and 100 Nigerian engineers are currently receiving advanced technology training to support the satellite, at a cost to China of about $5.5 million.[14]

The trade value between the two countries in 2007 accounted for more than 14 percent of the trade between China and sub-Saharan Africa as a whole, making Nigeria the second-largest trading partner for China, after South Africa. China has made enormous direct investments in oil and gas, iron and steel, machine manufacturing, cement, electronics, motorcycle assembly, fishing, pharmaceuticals, and telecommunications. The trade balance between the two countries as of 2008 is estimated at 1.7 percent in favor of China, and China is among Nigeria's top ten trading partners in the world. China supplies 11 percent of Nigerian imports, surpassing the United States, which provides just over 8 percent. China has committed to investing or offering billions of dollars in loans in the oil, railway, and road sectors.[15]

Chinese demand for West African crude oil increased to a record high in 2006 as China's refiners struggled to replenish declining stockpiles. China bought 919,000 bbl/d of mainly Nigerian and Angolan crude for loading in December 2006, an increase of 159,000 bbl/d from the previous month. This was a match only for China's record demand of March 2006. China's buying power helped boost overall Asian demand for West African crude to 1.23 million bbl/d as of November 2006, up 60,000 bbl/d. Due to the oil windfalls resulting from China's patronage, Nigeria was able to put $6 billion on the table to clear interest and past arrears as part of a 2005 deal to eliminate some $18 billion in Paris Club debt.

In early 2006, the state-owned Chinese energy company China National Offshore Oil Corporation (CNOOC) bought a 45 percent stake in the Akpo offshore oilfield in Nigeria for $2.27 billion. The oilfield is due to start pumping in 2008. Around the same time, CNOOC bought a 35 percent interest in a license to explore for oil in the OPL 229 block off the Nigerian shore.[16]

Also in 2006, China signed contracts worth over N4 billion ($32 million) with Nigeria on a concessionary basis to explore four Nigerian oil blocks in exchange for a commitment to invest $4 billion in infrastructure in a deal signed by President Hu. The oil deal was the largest of seven bilateral agreements signed by the two countries. Under the oil deal, Nigeria gave the first right of refusal to state-run China National Petroleum Corporation for four oil exploration blocks at auction. Part of the agreement was that China bought a controlling stake in Nigeria's 110,000 bbl/d Kaduna oil refinery and engaged in substantial infrastructural development by promising to build a power-generating station to support Nigeria's woefully low electricity output. As of this writing, CNOOC is also negotiating to buy interests in two Nigerian offshore blocks from Shell Petroleum Development Corporation, worth up to $900 million each.[17]

In November 2007, Reofield Industries Limited of Hong Kong signed a $300 million agreement with the Kebbi State government in northwest Nigeria for the establishment of a sugar processing facility, hydroelectric power generating plants, and a solid minerals processing and exploration operation. The sugar processing project entails development of 10,000 hectares of sugar cane farms, enabling Nigeria to start exporting sugar in 2010.[18]

China's Eximbank is partly funding five thermal power stations in Nigeria (in Ughelli, Geregu, Papalanto, Alaoji, and Omotosho) through a $500 million export credit facility, repayable in twelve years. China has also contracted to develop, through financial and technical support, two new hydropower plants at Zungeru and Mambilla in northern Nigeria. The Mambilla power project is planned to generate 2,500 megawatts of electricity upon completion.[19]

China has offered an array of assistance beyond the loans and grants facilitating trade and investment. In 2002, the Chinese government donated anti-malarial drugs and treated mosquito nets worth about N400 million in support of Nigeria's Roll Back Malaria Program. In addition, China trained fifty Nigerian officials and medical personnel for comprehensive malaria prevention and control. Just two months after the outbreak of bird flu in Nigeria in 2006, the Chinese government donated avian influenza support materials. This gesture was repeated in November 2007, leading to an agreement between the Chinese and Nigeria, for the latter's fight against malaria and bird flu. This new partnership also included cooperation in commercial livestock development, including microcredit financing and technology acquisition.[20]

Several Nigerian educational institutions have established pedagogical and cultural links to China. One federal polytechnic college, for instance, has organized exhibitions on the Chinese culture and landscape and hosts frequent exchanges of cultural troupes and students. The Chinese government also funds the teaching of Mandarin Chinese to staff from the Nnamdi Azikiwe University in Anambra State.[21]

Signs of Growing Nigerian Resentment

While the warming intergovernmental relationship between Abuja and Beijing has produced tremendous leaps in trade and investment, local Nigerian manufacturers have suffered. Years of neglect under rapacious military rule in the 1990s had already devastated Nigeria's fragile manufacturing sector— 75 percent of Kano's manufacturers closed shop in the 1990s—but competition from Chinese imports dealt them a death blow during the Obasanjo years.

Low-cost imports from China have largely devastated the textile and other consumer product industries of Kano and Kaduna, resulting in additional unemployment, particularly among restive youths in those volatile cities. Six of Kaduna's seven textile manufacturers closed down by 2006, in part due to their inability to compete with cheap Chinese textiles and fabrics, which had benefited from concessionary trade terms or had entered Nigeria through outright smuggling. In other parts of the country, textile factories, such as Western Textile Mills, Enpee, Aba Textiles, Gaskiya Textiles, and Atlantic Textile Mills have also closed. Kaduna's last textile company, United Nigeria Textile (UNTL), closed its operations in October 2007, sending its 4,000 employees into the already saturated unemployment pool.[22] At a press conference to announce the closure of the company, Senator Walid Jibrin, the vice president of the Manufacturers Association of Nigeria and trustee of the Nigeria Textile Manufacturers Association, said:

> The cost of sourcing for black oil continues to soar. The cost of funds from the banks still remains exorbitant. It is not possible to pass on these costs to our consumer because of their weak purchasing power. As a result of all these problems the company has recorded huge losses. The company has decided to suspend operations until the situation improves. . . . We have already lost N660 million in the first quarter. By this third quarter that we are going into, we are certain of losing over N700 million. We don't want to reach a situation where shareholders' fund[s] would be affected. In 2006 we lost N700 million and for the past three years we have not declared any dividends for our shareholders.[23]

In the 1980s, Nigeria had about 175 textile plants with a total of 250,000 employees, second only to the federal civil service as an employer of labor. In the 1990s, the number of textile plants was reduced to 60, with a work force of only 30,000. The closure of UNTL left 26 textile mills in operation as of October 2007, employing 24,000 people. At that point, the Manufacturers Association of Nigeria estimated that only six textile mills would survive through April 2008 if measures were not taken by the government to salvage the situation. As president, Obasanjo had promised to raise N50 billion in loans for the textile industry and N20 billion for the cotton subsector, but no such action was taken before he left office in 2007.[24]

Beyond textiles, Chinese trading practices have begun to spark other pockets of criticism in Nigeria. In February 2006, the Nigerian Customs Department decried the "gross violation of Nigeria's import and export regulations by Chinese traders in various towns." The customs department also cited a case of thirty trailer loads of contraband goods imported into the country under mysterious circumstances by Chinese businesses and their Nigerian collaborators. The affected local markets were closed, and the key Chinese businesspeople involved were detained: a sign that the smuggling of such large quantities of goods through Nigeria's borders is increasingly viewed as a threat to Nigerian security.[25] A growing number of illegal Chinese business activities in pirated video and audio CD production have also been documented. Within a period of six weeks in 2004, for example, two plants in Lagos were shut down and their Chinese owners arrested for the illegal production of optical musical and video discs; thousands of discs, stamps, and personal computers were seized by the authorities.

Chinese business practices in Nigeria have also raised questions regarding labor relations. Chinese companies have been increasingly accused of engaging in poor labor practices, harsh treatment of employees, low wages, and poor standards of corporate governance.

Resentment has also risen over the use of Chinese laborers in construction projects, as well as regarding the increasing takeover of Nigerian markets by Chinese traders. These responses reflect a deeper concern among Nigerians regarding the growing Chinese immigrant community in Nigeria. In 2001, the Chinese embassy in Nigeria estimated the number of Chinese immigrants at 20,000, but this figure did not include the many Chinese not registered by the embassy; if Taiwanese immigrants are included, the estimate reaches more than 30,000.[26] The Chinese ambassador remarked, "We can only provide the number of those registered and working for well-known companies. There are so many others who are businessmen and women that are not registered with the embassy."[27] The Ohio University database estimated the Chinese population in Nigeria to be 50,000 in 2005.[28]

The burgeoning Chinese interests in Nigerian oil are also attracting increasing scrutiny from Nigerians. Abductions targeting Chinese in the Niger Delta region are increasing. In early 2007, for instance, militants in the region abducted five Chinese workers, releasing them later for a hefty ransom. Niger Delta militants also issued threats against Chinese interests and nationals after the signing of new oil and gas deals during President Hu's April 2006 visit to Nigeria.[29] In an e-mail to news organizations, a spokesman for the militant group, the Movement for the Emancipation of the Niger Delta (which had previously kidnapped Western oil workers and detonated two car bombs in the oil cities of Warri and Port Harcourt), criticized China for grabbing a $2.2 billion stake in a Niger Delta oilfield in 2006 and stated, "We wish to warn the Chinese government and its oil companies to steer well clear of the Niger Delta. . . . Chinese citizens found in oil installations will be treated as thieves. The Chinese government by investing in stolen crude places its citizens in our line of fire."[30]

Nigerian Reactions in Lagos

Given the recent nature of the influx of Chinese investment and immigration into Nigeria, its overall impact on Nigerian sentiments remains difficult to gauge. In light of the catastrophic impact that cheap Chinese imports have had on the textile and other manufacturing sectors, and the growing impact of Chinese immigrants in local markets, are Nigerians overall growing increasingly frustrated with China? So far, there have been no demonstrations or public mobilizations for policy change against the Chinese, as have taken place in other parts of Africa, but anecdotal evidence of public concern and resentment is growing.

In order to begin to assess this relationship, the Centre for Law and Social Action in Lagos conducted a series of interviews in the massive Oshodi and Madillas markets in Lagos with both Chinese businesspeople and Nigerian traders in December 2007 and January 2008.[31] The sample size is small—twenty-three Nigerian and eight Chinese respondents in all—but the interviews raised interesting questions.[32]

Chinese respondents proved particularly difficult to approach, since many of the individuals working in or near the Lagos markets in question did not speak sufficient English to respond to the survey. This demonstrates, however, an important barrier for communication between the two communities that could pose a problem as the Chinese role in Nigerian markets grows.

Figure 13-1. *Chinese Businesspeople: How Are Your Relationships with Other Nigerian Businesspeople, with Nigerian Customers, and with the Local Community?*

Percent responding

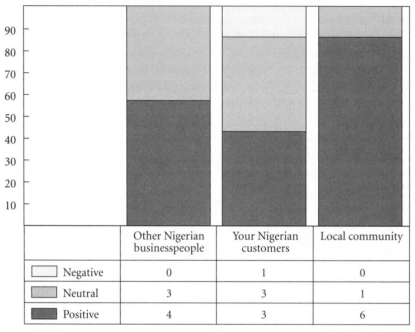

	Other Nigerian businesspeople	Your Nigerian customers	Local community
Negative	0	1	0
Neutral	3	3	1
Positive	4	3	6

Source: Survey performed by the Centre for Law and Social Action, Lagos, December 2007 and January 2008.

Most interesting is the finding that both communities have overall positive impressions of each other. The Chinese sampling, although small, showed six out of seven respondents had positive relations with the Nigerian community in Lagos, and positive to neutral relationships with Nigerian businesspeople (four positive, three neutral) and with their Nigerian customers (three positive, three neutral). Only one Chinese businessperson reported negative relations with his Nigerian customers (see figure 13-1), describing his encounters in mild terms as "problematic at times."

Not surprisingly, Chinese businesspeople complained about the same infrastructural and security problems that irritate Nigerians (figure 13-2). Five out of eight reported difficulties with electrical power supplies, and six out of eight cited Lagos's massive transportation woes as a problem, including traffic jams

Figure 13-2. *Chinese Businesspeople: What Sort of Difficulties Have You Had in Doing Business in Lagos?*

Number responding

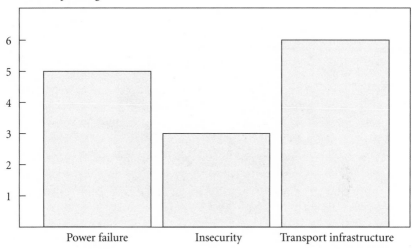

Source: See note to figure 13-1.

and poor transportation modes. Three respondents worried about "insecurity" and the "security problem" in Lagos, referring to the growing criminality in the megacity as well as to occasional political unrest.

Another important clue toward a fuller understanding of the Chinese community in Lagos came in response to a question about how and why Chinese businesspeople decided to come to Nigeria. Personal ties seem to be the dominant link through which the Chinese are coming to work in Lagos: four of the eight indicated that family members had brought them to Nigeria, while an additional two said that friends had persuaded them to come. Perhaps indicative of the immigrants overall, one individual remarked that his brother had convinced him to come to Nigeria "for greener pastures." Interestingly, three respondents added that information from the Internet had also influenced their decision to move to Nigeria.

The Nigerians, for their part, also report positive impressions of the Chinese in Lagos. Out of twenty Nigerian responses to this question, fourteen had positive impressions of the Chinese, six had neutral feelings, and no one reported a negative impression of the Chinese in Lagos (see figure 13-3). Nigerian traders commented that they had "very good," "good," "cool" (as in

Figure 13-3. *Nigerian Traders: What Sort of Impact Do You See the Chinese Having on Your Community?*

Number responding

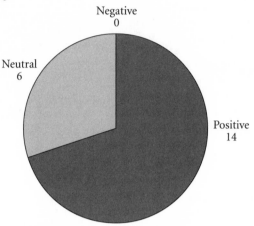

Source: See note to figure 13-1.

the American slang), and similar impressions of the Chinese doing business in Lagos, and that they had a "great impact" overall.

Figure 13-4 shows that the Nigerians report that the Chinese are predominantly (seventeen out of twenty-three responses) engaged in clothing and textiles, selling suits, jeans, shoes, sewing materials, and so on. Four Nigerian traders said that the Chinese were engaged in the electronics trade, particularly cellular phones. One trader reported that he saw Chinese engaged in business in "windows, doors, and cotton," while another one added sewing machines to his list and another simply said, "They are everywhere."

The Nigerian traders also agreed overwhelmingly that the Chinese role in the Lagos economy would expand in years to come. Seventeen respondents saw an increasing role for the Chinese in the future, only four saw their role staying the same, and no one felt that the Chinese presence would diminish (figure 13-5).

In addition, most of the Nigerian characterizations of this future role for the Chinese included comments that it was "great" or "fair," such as one respondent who remarked, "They do well and will continue to grow." One trader commented sympathetically, "I think they are great, and we are hoping that our Nigerian government policy will not affect them."

Figure 13-4. *Nigerian Traders: What Business Sectors Do You See the Chinese Active in?*

Number responding

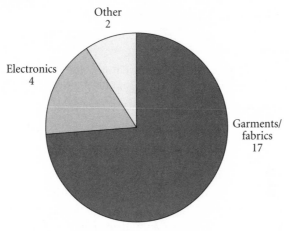

Source: See note to figure 13-1.

Figure 13-5. *Nigerian Traders: How Do You See the Chinese Community Developing over the Next Few Years?*

Number responding

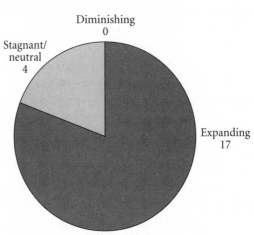

Source: See note to figure 13-1.

Two issues stand out from the comments of the Nigerian traders that may prove problematic for the Chinese immigrant community. The first is that in listing in what business sectors the Chinese are active, six of the twenty-three Nigerian traders added that the particular product that the Chinese are selling is of substandard or poor quality. One Nigerian trader complained to our researcher that "they bring substandard products. . . . Our government should insist on standards."

Second and more worrisome for the Chinese were several responses when Nigerians were asked how the Chinese could improve their relationships with local communities. Six of the twenty-three respondents remarked that the Chinese are "very cunning" and "always suspicious of people" and that they "need to improve on this." These comments indicate a perception that the Chinese community is insular, but they also suggest some growing negative stereotypes of the Chinese in Lagos. Such stereotypes are often pivotal elements in mobilizing and targeting minority and immigrant communities during violent episodes, and as such should be monitored with concern. To prevent such outcomes, the Nigerian traders in our sample advise the Chinese businesspeople to "be more friendly," "to be open," and perhaps with a note of self-interest, to "trust their close Nigerian partners."

Given the small sample, the authors can only say that these interviews suggest larger Nigerian public concerns regarding the growing Chinese presence in their country. Moreover, the Nigerians questioned for the survey were all market traders who may have had a stronger economic interest than most other Nigerians in accessing inexpensive Chinese products. At the same time, a growing Chinese immigrant community engaged in trade in Nigeria also poses a rising threat of direct competition for Nigerian traders.

So far, however, the Nigerian traders the authors reached did not perceive the Chinese as competition—rather, to some, as providers of substandard goods. Overall, in fact, the Nigerians offered a positive and welcoming view of the Chinese presence in the Lagos markets, including a sense of respect for Chinese business acumen. The Chinese also expressed generally positive views of their Nigerian neighbors, although there were an equal number of neutral views reported, suggesting Chinese reserve toward their hosts.

The notable presence of negative Chinese stereotypes among over a quarter of our Nigerian respondents, however, raises concerns that the seeds of future clashes are being sown by a lack of positive social interaction between the two communities outside the marketplace. Much of this intercultural misunderstanding may be the outcome of the natural insularity that new immigrant communities have when a significant number of their members do not speak the local language. Bridging these gaps becomes even more important in light of the finding that most of the Nigerian traders see the Chinese role in their markets as expanding. If local competition grows in intensity, these stereotypes could provide ample fuel for angry public incidents or a backlash.

The strong role of family and friendship ties in bringing the Chinese to Nigeria to live and do business also raises the potential for exponential growth in the size of the Chinese immigrant community. Once the initial "bridgehead" is established, the pioneer generation of immigrants can call on extended family and friendship networks to respond to growing business opportunities. With anywhere from 20,000 to 50,000 Chinese now in Nigeria, that bridgehead is clearly established, and our respondents indicate that a strong prevalence for family recruiting is already underway.

Making Policy: A China Model for Africa?

This initial evidence from the Lagos survey seems to suggest a fairly calm, positive relationship between the Chinese community and its Nigerian hosts, although the negative stereotypes held by some of the Nigerians and the Chinese neutrality present in the responses point to a growing sense that a reevaluation is underway. Given that all signs point toward an expanding Chinese role in Nigeria, what direction can policymakers in Nigeria take to prevent a souring of and backlash in the Nigerian-Chinese relationship?

Clearly, China's emergence as a major economic power is of great interest for Nigeria, and overall for Africa's rulers and ruled. The vexing picture of China as an "alternative" political and economic model for Africa, or as some exemplar of development *sans* democracy, warrants concern. For some of Africa's contemporary rulers, China offers evidence beyond reproach of "successful" alternatives to Western political and economic models. Furthermore, China is perceived as an ally that can help African governments escape the governance and economic preconditions imposed by Western donors and international finance institutions.

Since the early 1960s, advocates of the one-party state and "African socialism" in postcolonial Africa have contended that Western models of liberal democracy and capitalism were not viable given the socioeconomic conditions and resource constraints prevailing in Africa. Vigorous debate over appropriate development models consumed much intellectual and political energy in Africa through the 1970s and 1980s. Disillusionment induced by the collapse of the Soviet Union at the end of the Cold War and the seeming global triumph of the Washington Consensus led to a cessation of the debate in the 1990s.

The ensuing period was characterized by structural adjustment, poverty reduction, and other economic reform programs imposed on African governments by Western donors and international finance institutions. Many Africans, including intellectuals and civil society actors, perceive that their governments' adoption of the Washington Consensus has failed to deliver both bread and freedom. African rulers learned that they could successfully engage in a sleight of hand by adopting the barest minimum in political and economic reforms, which would permit bureaucracies to continue aid flows to their countries, while vigorously resisting substantive change. Furthermore, many Africans became disillusioned with economic reforms, such as they were, because their benefits did not trickle down to those at the bottom rung. In particular, "jobless growth" in Nigeria resulted in widespread popular disillusionment with structural adjustment and half-hearted poverty reduction policies, thus leading many to question the viability and efficacy of Western political and economic models in Africa.[33]

In contrast, China's spectacular success in lifting over 400 million of its citizens from dire poverty within two decades, while enhancing living conditions for several hundred millions more, has commanded great interest in Africa. Many in African intellectual and political circles are impressed by China's seeming geometric economic progress since Deng Xiaoping initiated economic reforms in China in the 1980s. This success, often attributed to China's state-led development model, has rekindled the debate in Africa over appropriate paths to development and encouraged many Africans to look to East Asia for political and economic models. Many in Africa question the wisdom of remaining wedded to the Washington Consensus and ask if indeed bread does not count more than the vote, and if human rights and democracy are not really of secondary concern to attaining political stability and economic progress.

The debate in Africa over the China model is not, however, based on a romantic vision. Admiration among the Nigerian media for China's economic success is often balanced with acute recognition of its social costs and the lack of political freedoms. Consequently, commentators often distinguish between China as an "economic model" and "political model." The *Daily Trust* newspaper, for instance, calls on Nigeria's leadership to draw lessons from China's experience with economic reform, rejecting Nigeria's adoption of World Bank and the International Monetary Fund approaches in favor of China's.[34] In contrast, an editorial in the Nigerian *New Age* noted that "the Chinese people have had to pay a heavy price in political repression and environmental degradation."[35]

Among Africa's political leaders, there are also those who recognize the trade-off between China's "peaceful rise" and democratic development. Nigerian Senate President Ken Nnamani, in a welcome address for President Hu's April 2006 visit to Nigeria, commended China's "outstanding [economic] performance exclusive of western democracy" as "the paradox of development and democracy." According to Nnamani,

> China [had] become . . . a good model for Nigeria in its quest for an authentic and stable development ideology. . . . China [was] a lesson to Nigeria on the enormous good that a focused and patriotic leadership can do to realise the dreams of prosperity and security for the citizens. . . . [I]n embracing China . . . it should not only be in the field of economic prosperity since . . . [China's] steady and gradual democratisation confirms the lesson that no nation can sustain economic development in the long run without democracy.[36]

China, Africa, and the Balance of Power

China's emergence as a global power is welcomed among many African intellectuals who hope that it may herald a return to a multipolar world in which Africa will have a greater role on the global stage. Bolaji Akinyemi, the former Nigerian foreign minister and scholar of Africa's international relations, welcomes "strategic cooperation" between China and Nigeria, noting that stronger ties between the Asian and African heavyweights were long overdue, and argues that "China is an emerging world power with a booming economy. She needs oil. Nigeria needs as much investment as possible, and to diversify the sources of its investment. In the Middle East, the United States regards China's incursion with alarm, but Nigeria is more virgin territory for suitors and Washington should not be too worried. It insulates Nigeria from influence by one power."[37]

China's enhanced presence in Africa has generated fears that Chinese trade, political, and security cooperation may enable repressive regimes in Africa to avoid even the relatively limited constraints on their conduct imposed by Western donor conditionalities. Since the late 1980s, African nongovernmental organizations (NGOs) have often collaborated with Western NGOs to pressure Western governments to demand political liberalization from African governments as a precondition for further developmental assistance. However, many African civil society actors are deeply conflicted over the external origins of donor preconditions, which often reinforce notions of powerlessness and irrelevance.

China's renewed engagement in Africa has had the effect of bringing Africa to the foreground for Western leaders and has also spurred India to intensify its economic diplomacy in Africa.[38] A meeting of experts and diplomats, convened by the African Union (AU) in Addis Ababa in September 2006, warned against the Chinese-African relationship slipping into and repeating the historical trajectory of Africa's relations with the West. While the AU experts appreciated that Chinese investment gave Africa new leverage, they noted criticisms that China was making "no serious effort" to "transfer skills and knowledge to Africa" and urged China to relocate some of its industries to Africa "as a reflection of a true spirit of partnership."[39] In April 2007, the Nigerian government convened a meeting of African foreign policy scholars and diplomats in Abuja on the theme "The New Scramble for Africa"; speakers at the conference expressed fears of Africa being caught up in a new Cold War between China and the West, with African resources as the bone of contention.

There are also critical voices among Africa's rulers. South African President Thabo Mbeki and former Nigerian President Obasanjo both criticized Chinese companies for violating labor and safety standards. Mbeki has warned against a new Chinese colonialism in Africa.

Human Security

Human rights NGOs in Africa and beyond increasingly perceive China's relations with African governments as problematic for governance and human rights in Africa. This view does not mean that African activists have adopted a wholly critical attitude toward China's enhanced role; many in Africa's civil society value the significance of the new trade and investment opportunities as well as the strategic leverage against the West that China offers.

Yet civil society groups in Africa are also concerned about the potential loss of a major source of leverage in dealing with their own governments. Over the last two decades, transnational NGO networks and enhanced cooperation between African and Western NGOs have served to put pressure on Western governments and businesses in relation to human rights abuses and democratization in Africa. African human rights activists have relied on colleagues in Western countries to mobilize pressure on their governments to demand the release of opposition figures and respect for human rights as preconditions for further aid flows. Indeed, such Western responses have served as informal life insurance for many African activists. With many African governments turning to China for political and economic cooperation without the "strings" of human rights and democracy often attached by Western governments, African activists will lose leverage.

Human rights concerns also extend to the role of the Chinese private sector in Africa and may acquire even greater significance than concerns arising from the activities of the Chinese government or its state-owned enterprises in Africa. In Nigeria,

> some Chinese private companies . . . have been accused by NGOs of violating health and safety standards as well [as] employment and environmental rights in the communities where they operate. NGOs in Nigeria have accused the Chinese logging company WEMPCO of discharging untreated effluents into the Cross River in southeastern Nigeria, thereby damaging the health and livelihoods of local fisher folk. The company is also accused of colluding with local officials and law enforcement to suppress protests by the local community. The Chinese metalworking firm, WAHUM operating in Lagos, Nigeria, has also been accused by NGOs of discharging noxious substances into the air and systematic violations of occupational safety and health standards.[40]

In the presence of conflict and instability, which in turn arise from the lack of democracy and human rights, Chinese business activities in Nigeria and across Africa face increasing risks. There is significant potential for violence directed at Chinese businesses and nationals by African insurgent groups and rebel movements, who regard China as an ally of the local repressive regime, as has happened in the Niger Delta. Thus, China would do well to reexamine its security cooperation with some African governments. In the Beijing Declaration issued at the first Forum on China-Africa Cooperation (FOCAC) summit in October 2000, the Chinese government committed itself, along with African governments, to strengthen their cooperation in stopping the illegal production, circulation, and trafficking of small arms and light weapons in Africa.

It may be possible that as Chinese capitalism matures and global branding becomes more important to Chinese companies, they become vulnerable to brand pressure, including the "naming-and-shaming" tactics adopted by NGOs in Western consumer markets. African NGOs can also work with their Western colleagues to invoke threats to mobilize mass boycotts of Chinese-made consumer goods in Western markets in order to protest China's arms exports to repressive governments in Africa. As Chinese investors move beyond resource extraction to investments of a long-term nature, perhaps they will put pressure on their government to avoid actions or policies likely to exacerbate instability or conflict, or to connect them with human rights abuses and repressive regimes in Africa.

Initial evidence suggests that Nigerians have a watchful acceptance and positive impression of China's growing impact on their country, but public perceptions of the Chinese presence could turn negative if the Nigerian government, like other African governments, manages the relationship poorly. If the catastrophic impact that cheap Chinese imports have had on Nigeria's weak manufacturing base, particularly in textiles, spreads to other sectors of the economy, it could provoke a public backlash against the growing Chinese immigrant community. The negative stereotypes of Chinese immigrants expressed by some of our Nigerian respondents are a worrisome sign of poor communication and social integration between the two groups that could exacerbate any potential conflicts that may develop. China has promised billions of dollars in loans and assistance for Nigeria's crumbling infrastructure, which could spur some job creation and economic development over time, but the lack of substantial progress on these projects thus far has raised fears that much of the money has disappeared into Nigeria's notoriously corrupt political machines.

Yet China's disparate impact on different sectors in Nigeria and other African countries suggests that a coherent Nigerian response is unlikely, much less a coordinated African one. Commodity, resource, and oil exporters may gain in the short term, but manufacturing industries, which produce the most jobs, may lose. African elites may gain from opaque deals for the extraction of natural resources, but the African poor may suffer as a result of job losses, greater corruption, and political repression. Similarly, African workers and small business owners who have lost out due to importation of cheap Chinese consumer goods may adopt a situational perspective: as consumers, they benefit from imports of cheap consumer goods, but as workers or businesspeople who have lost jobs or businesses, they may resent Chinese imports. In addition, unemployed African youths may resent Chinese companies that import labor from China.

Africa can derive important lessons from China's success in liberating itself from absolute poverty. The challenge is for African policymakers and civil society to identify the appropriate lessons from China's experience and to adapt them to the specific circumstances of their respective African countries. Given the sad trajectory of economic decline and political repression in much of Africa since 1960, China's success in economic management has appeal, especially public-private partnership and a home-grown economic reform agenda. African advocates of liberal democracy and human rights, while encouraging their governments to learn and adapt from China's economic success, must vigorously resist attempts by some African governments to invoke China's economic success as a rationalization for avoiding political liberalization. While African governments, and the Nigerian government in particular, succumb to the lure of tremendously lucrative Chinese investment, resource extraction, and development aid, they must still fulfill their commitments to human rights standards and broad-based employment.

More can also be done to build bridges between the Chinese community in Nigeria and their local neighbors. Responsibility lies locally with both Chinese and Nigerian community associations, and nationally with the Nigerian and Chinese governments. The Chinese immigrant community is still largely outside mainstream Nigerian society. The Chinese can do more to invest in their neighborhoods in terms of social and economic infrastructure and to foster greater intercultural understanding. Nigerian communities and civil society groups, for their part, can provide additional incentives for Chinese immigrants to take part in local social life and can build social relationships that can open greater channels for communication between Nigerians and the Chinese. Last, Abuja and Beijing can be proactive about managing trade decisions in a manner that includes the substantive involvement of Nigerian business associations, trade unions, rights advocates, and community associations, as well as leaders from the growing Chinese community in Nigeria.

Nigeria's great size and the relatively small and recent presence of the Chinese there make projections on the future of their relationship difficult. What is certain, however, is that China's role in Africa is growing and that Nigeria will be a central player in determining the nature and scope of that role. If China's rise is to be a peaceful one, careful management on all sides will be necessary to ensure that China's growth spurs equitable and rights-respecting development in Africa, and that it does not come at the expense of Africans.

Notes

1. Moyiga Nduru, "China and Africa in an Ever-Closer—Sometimes Thornier—Embrace," Inter Press Service News Agency (Johannesburg) (8 December 2004), available at www.africanewssearch.com/olink.php?ARG1=http://www.ipsnews.net/africa/interna.asp?idnews=26591&ARG2=105099 (accessed 25 May 2006); Terry Fitzpatrick, "Chinese Investments Are Taking the Lead in Africa," Voice of America (16 November 2007), available at www.voanews.com/english/archive/2007-11/2007-11-16-voa20.cfm?CFID=236705961&CFTOKEN=92263682 (accessed 18 March 2008).

Fitzpatrick cites Princeton Lyman of the Council on Foreign Relations as estimating the number of Chinese companies in Africa to be 800, with a total investment of nearly $12 billion.

2. Stephen Marks, "China in Africa—the New Imperialism?" *Pambazuka* (2 March 2006), available at www.pambazuka.org/en/category/features/32432 (accessed 25 May 2006).

3. Chris Melville and Olly Owen, "China and Africa: A New Era of 'South-South Cooperation'" (8 July 2005), available at www.opendemocracy.net/globalization-G8/south_2658.jsp (accessed 25 May 2006).

4. Embassy of the People's Republic of China in the Federal Republic of Nigeria, "China-Nigeria Relations" (8 July 2004), available at ng.china-embassy.org/eng/zngx/t142490.htm (accessed 17 March 2008).

5. Ibid.

6. Ndubisi Obiorah, "Who's Afraid of China in Africa? Towards an African Civil Society Perspective on China-Africa Relations," in Firoze Manji and Stephen Marks (eds.), *African Perspectives on China in Africa* (Nairobi, 2007), 35–56.

7. "Nigeria-China Relations in Perspective: 1999–2006" (15 May 2006), available at www.nigeriafirst.org/cgi-bin/artman/exec/view.cgi?archive=1&num=5899&printer=1 (accessed 20 March 2008).

8. Ibid.

9. *Daily Trust* (18 April 2008).

10. Ibid.

11. *Daily Trust* (11 November 2007).

12. "Nigeria-China Relations in Perspective: 1999–2006."

13. Obiorah, "Who's Afraid of China in Africa?"

14. "Nigeria-China Relations in Perspective: 1999–2006."

15. Embassy of the People's Republic of China, "China-Nigeria Relations."

16. Obiorah, "Who's Afraid of China in Africa?"

17. Ibid.

18. Onvebuchi Ezigbo, "Textile Industry: Labour Seeks Government's Intervention," *Thisday* (19 October 2007).

19. "Nigeria-China Relations in Perspective: 1999–2006."

20. Obiorah, "Who's Afraid of China in Africa?"

21. Ibid.

22. Ezigbo, "Textile Industry."

23. Ibid.

24. Ibid.

25. "Issues in Nigeria-China Relations" (1 May 2006), available at www.tmcnet.com/usubmit/2006/05/01/1628253.htm (accessed 5 November 2007).

26. Embassy of the People's Republic of China, "China-Nigeria Relations."

27. Ibid.

28. Center for International Collections Databank, Ohio University Libraries, Shao Center, "Distribution of the Ethnic Chinese Population around the World," available at http://cicdatabank.library.ohiou.edu/opac/index.php (accessed 12 November 2007).

29. "Nigerian Militants Claim Bomb Attack," *International Herald Tribune* (30 April 2006), available at www.iht.com/articles/2006/04/30/africa/web.0430nigeria.php (accessed 5 July 2008).

30. Ibid.

31. Chinese businesspeople were asked the following questions: How are your relationships with other Nigerian businesspeople? With your Nigerian customers? With the local community? What sort of difficulties have you had in doing business in Lagos?

Nigerian traders were asked three questions: What sort of impact do you see the Chinese having on your community? What business sectors do you see the Chinese active in? How do you see the Chinese community developing over the next few years?

32. Our researchers asked all the respondents the same sets of questions: the researchers then wrote down the subjects' responses verbatim and anonymously on a questionnaire. All quotes in this section are taken from the responses on these questionnaires. Note that one participant did not respond directly to the questions asked but instead preferred to give some general comments that are not reflected in the data.

33. "The Widening Gap," *Daily Trust* (24 April 2006).

34. Ibid.

35. *New Age* (31 March 2006); Embassy of the People's Republic of China, "China-Nigeria Relations."

36. Nnamani, "China: A Partner and Example of Development and Democracy," as quoted in *Thisday* (28 April 2006).

37. *Nigeria2Day*, daily e-mail bulletin (28 April 2006).

38. Howard French, "China Wages Classroom Struggle to Win Friends in Africa," *New York Times* (20 November 2005), available at www.howardwfrench.com/archives/2005/11/20/china_wages_classroom_struggle_to_win_friends_in_africa/ (accessed 25 May 2006).

39. Akwe Amosu, "China in Africa: It's (Still) the Governance, Stupid," Foreign Policy in Focus discussion paper (Washington, D.C., 9 March 2007), available at www.fpif.org/fpiftxt/4068 (accessed 29 April 2007).

40. Obiorah, "Who's Afraid of China in Africa?"

CHIN-HAO HUANG

14

China's Renewed Partnership with Africa: Implications for the United States

China's expansive political, economic, and military engagement in Africa reflects an increasingly dynamic and accommodating approach toward the continent.[1] Launched at the November 2006 Forum on China-Africa Cooperation (FOCAC) summit, China's renewed partnership with Africa marks a historic watershed in Chinese-African relations. Chinese activity in Africa promises future gains that benefit Africa in significant, constructive ways; at the same time, challenges are fast emerging as Beijing seeks to translate its vision of a strategic partnership with Africa into a sustainable reality.

This chapter illuminates the motivations and decisionmaking processes driving China's evolving foreign and security policy in Africa, provides an overview of China's expansive engagement in Africa and the key emergent challenges, and assesses the inherent implications of China's expansive engagement in Africa for U.S. interests in Africa and around the world, as well as for U.S.-Chinese relations. The chapter concludes by offering policy recommendations for strategically managing Chinese-African-U.S. relations in the future.

China's Evolving Approach in Africa

Beijing's proactive engagement with Africa is grounded in several key factors that undergird the new Chinese approach.[2] First, China's quest to build a strategic partnership with Africa fits squarely within Beijing's global foreign

This chapter includes previous and ongoing research on Chinese-African-U.S. relations carried out with Bates Gill and J. Stephen Morrison. The author is grateful for their support and guidance.

policy strategy and its vision of the evolving international system. Africa is seen as integral to Beijing's strategic ambition to advance a "new security concept" that can ensure China's peaceful rise as a global power and strengthen relations with key neighbors and regions. More specifically, through its overarching global approach, the leadership in Beijing seeks to sustain China's internal development and political stability at home; legitimize within the international community the historic benefits of China's rise; and achieve its longer-term goal of a more multipolar, equitable, and "democratic" international system.

As such, China's hard national interests and strategic needs bind it increasingly to the African continent. In earlier decades, expressions of political solidarity and altruism dominated Chinese discussions of Africa. These expressions are still relevant today but take a back seat to hard national and economic interests and priorities. In December 2007, the Chinese Ministry of Commerce announced that two-way trade with Africa had reached $65.9 billion for the first eleven months and was expected to total $70 billion for 2007. This puts China on par with the 2006 total trade volume between the United States and sub-Saharan Africa (based on the latest official figures available).[3] While the number pales in comparison to China's trade figures with the European Union, United States, Japan, and Southeast Asia, the International Monetary Fund (IMF) indicated that China has rapidly emerged as Africa's second-largest trading partner. More important, China signed new labor contracts worth $18.4 billion and achieved a business volume of nearly $8 billion in Africa, representing over a third of the total value of all new Chinese labor contracts overseas and a quarter of the total business volume in 2007.[4] China is already making steady progress in realizing its goal to expand two-way trade to $100 billion by 2010. It increasingly turns to Africa for resources to fuel China's development goals, for markets to sustain its growing economy, and for political alliances to support its aspirations to a peaceful rise on the global stage.

Second, the historical amity and linkages between China and Africa continue to be important factors. China's history of friendly, respectful, and helpful political ties to Africa appears to provide a durable foundation for a future strategic partnership. The Chinese leadership is often heard touting the fact that over the past fifty years Beijing has established a legacy of political solidarity and developmental assistance in partnership with Africa, at a time when China was internationally isolated, impoverished, and beset by major internal challenges. Reflecting principles dating from the Bandung Conference in 1955, Beijing staunchly supports the inviolability of African state sovereignty, noninterference in internal affairs, and the need for postcolonial nations to stand up to external "bullying" and "hegemonism." Chinese leaders also recognize that China's relationship with Africa has earned it significant diplomatic dividends. Beijing has not forgotten that Africa's support in the early 1970s was vital to China gaining its seat in the United Nations (UN). Today, in an effort to increase Taiwan's isolation in the international community, Beijing assiduously courts those remaining African countries that continue formally to recognize Taiwan.

Beijing also believes that China's history compares favorably with the poor political and security legacy left to Africa by the U.S.-Soviet rivalry of the Cold War-era. It stoked wars in places like Angola, Mozambique, and Ethiopia and created alliances with corrupt regimes and leaders.

Third, Chinese leaders and strategists believe that China's historical experience and development model resonate powerfully with African counterparts. China emerged from colonial encroachment, internal chaos, and economic destitution to achieve spectacular economic growth and infrastructural development. In the past two decades, its achievements have lifted more than 200 million Chinese citizens out of poverty. In the meantime, China can claim that it has achieved political stability and increasing international clout. Such a national narrative, it is asserted, resonates powerfully in Africa. In Beijing's view, the West's historical experiences in achieving development are too remote from the African experience and offer fewer transferable lessons. China asserts that the Western economic model has generated few dramatic success stories in Africa. In stark contrast to the West's moralizing and its conditional developmental approaches, Beijing unabashedly claims to provide aid with little to no "political strings attached" and with greater emphases on political stability and economic development.

Fourth, Chinese strategists maintain that Africa is on the verge of developmental takeoff—another idea that is well received on the continent—creating an opportunity for a more expansive Chinese role. According to this view, Africa has realized a period of relative stability and calm as compared to the dark days of the 1990s when protracted conflicts raged in more than a dozen countries. Chinese interlocutors recognize that while pockets of conflict still persist and require close international engagement—such as in Darfur, the Sudan as a whole, Somalia, the Democratic Republic of the Congo, and Côte d'Ivoire—the broader Chinese view is that Africa, by and large, has emerged as a continent of relative peace and stability, poised to make major developmental gains. Given this assessment, Beijing is keen to be an integral part of Africa's impending political and economic transformation.

Fifth, China's policymakers are also confident that a state-centric approach to Africa will build strategically on Beijing's core advantages and align China with the stated preferences of African countries. China's African policy is not complicated by private, domestic constituencies and interest groups, allowing for quicker and more decisive action. China's largest economic and business activities in Africa are dominated by state-owned and state-influenced companies, giving official Beijing another advantage in the political and economic competition for Africa. China lacks well-developed, independent business and civil society sectors, which leaves to state leaders and official diplomats the full responsibility for carrying forward its vision.

Sixth, Beijing has an interest in engaging third parties in Africa, but it will proceed cautiously, and with serious reservations. Chinese senior officials have indicated their openness to collaboration with the United States, and Chinese scholars and experts on Africa further acknowledge the value of drawing on U.S. and other Western expertise, including engagement with African civil society, business partners, and regional organizations.

China remains wary of and highly sensitive to U.S. discussion of China's approach in Africa, however, reflecting Beijing's continuing concern with perceived U.S. hegemony and the related fear that Washington's long-term intention is to contain China's ambitions to become a global power and competitor. Such thinking is rooted in Chinese nationalism that bridles against overreaching American power and influence, and U.S. sermonizing in Africa and elsewhere. The defeat of the China National Offshore Oil Company's bid for the U.S.-owned energy firm Unocal in 2005 is a relevant case in point. Chinese analysts have asserted that it was a further indication of U.S. determination to prevent the rise of a Chinese global energy firm and that the outcome of that bid directly prompted Chinese authorities to intensify their push for a strategic partnership in Africa.[5]

China's Expansive Engagement and Emergent Challenges in Africa

China's emergence as a rising global power, and the activities and intentions of its expansive foreign policy, has garnered increasing attention. While much of this attention focuses on China's growing clout in Asia, China's increasingly active economic, political, and diplomatic activities in Africa and other parts of the world are also coming under greater scrutiny.

China's engagement in Africa is not new. Beijing supported many liberation movements and other insurgencies in sub-Saharan Africa and was quick to establish diplomatic ties to, and supportive economic relations with, newly independent states as they emerged from the colonial era. Indeed, for more than half a century, the Chinese systematically cultivated solidarity and working relations with a range of African states. It was a profitable diplomatic investment that persisted into the post–Cold War era, even as Western powers were more inclined to scale back their presence.[6]

China's Africa policy is more complex, multidimensional, ambitious, and ultimately higher risk. China's increasing economic engagement is tied to conspicuously strategic goals, centered on access to energy and other scarce high-value commodities. On the diplomatic front, Beijing has shown a new determination to eliminate completely any bilateral ties between Taiwan and a dwindling number of African capitals, and to use its accelerating entry into Africa to consolidate global allegiances and Beijing's putative leadership in the developing world. Beijing has also taken on a more active role in the security sphere. China's contributions of soldiers and police to UN peace operations, especially in Africa, have increased tenfold since 2001, albeit from a low base. As of early 2008, China provided more than 1,900 troops, military observers, and civilian police to current UN peacekeeping operations worldwide. Nearly three-fourths of Chinese peacekeeping forces are supporting UN missions in Africa (primarily Liberia, the Sudan, and the Democratic Republic of the Congo).[7]

Since the November 2006 FOCAC summit, Beijing has taken steps to follow through with these commitments.[8] China announced that it has already canceled $1.42 billion of African debt, and it canceled another $1 billion as of mid-2007.[9] In 2007, China captured international attention when it hosted the annual African Development Bank conference in Shanghai. China pledged an additional $20 billion for infrastructural development in Africa over the next three years. Chinese policy in many instances is tied to ambitious commitments to revitalize depleted critical infrastructures and strengthen human skills. It is not only official China that provides direct economic and diplomatic support. Chinese companies also have become far more active as both importers of African energy and raw material resources and exporters of Chinese goods and services.

The China International Poverty Alleviation Center, established in mid-2005 to strengthen international exchanges and collaboration, has hosted two fifteen-day training courses, bringing in visiting African officials to gain a firsthand understanding of China's poverty reduction programs in some of its poorest provinces. The Ministry of Commerce and the Ministry of Agriculture also jointly sent five working groups to more than a dozen African countries to plan the establishment of agricultural technology demonstration centers to enhance collaboration on seed production, water-saving, and biological technologies in agriculture; food security; and animal health and plant protection.[10]

China has also deepened its commitments to help African nations tackle public health problems. In May 2007, at the Sixtieth Annual World Health Organization (WHO) meeting in Geneva, then Minister of Health Gao Qiang announced that Beijing would donate $8 million to the WHO to build African countries' capacity and response mechanisms to respond to public health emergencies. Gao also called on other member states to increase their aid to strengthen public health systems in Africa and other developing countries.[11]

The payoffs to China financially and politically may ultimately be significant and alter the understanding of what kinds of interventions can produce durable results. But multiple risks also attend China's expansive engagement in Africa. Business calculations on major investments are murky, and many will likely turn out badly. The bet that China can transform Africa's infrastructures where others have failed awaits proof of success.

The expectation that China can have significant sway politically and displace the influence of others must take into account Africa's sensitivity to anything that echoes neocolonialism, and how callous and indifferent "petropowers" in Africa have become as global energy markets tighten. In selecting energy-rich Angola and Nigeria as preferred partners, and in choosing to support Zimbabwe closely, China selected three of the most corrupt and difficult environments. In the Sudan, Beijing finds a partner embedded in enormous political and moral controversies of its own making. In South Africa, it has engaged a country acutely sensitive to issues of sovereignty.[12] Beijing is beginning to encounter serious challenges, such as criticism by a Zambian presidential candidate during the 2006 elections that China engaged in unfair mine labor practices, and South African trade union opposition to the flooding of South African markets with Chinese textiles. Some adjustments in approach, such as voluntary textile export quotas for South Africa, have since been set in place.[13]

As China deepens its economic and corporate engagement in Africa, it is beginning to experience increasing tensions and competing interests among its various government agencies, including the Ministry of Commerce, the Ministry of Foreign Affairs, the State-owned Assets Supervision and Administration Commission, and provincial governments.[14] Different government actors bring diverse interests and leverage points to the Africa policy debate, as well as varying capacities to see those interests served within China and Africa. For example, increasingly market-oriented Chinese foreign enterprises—and their state-related shareholders in China—are primarily interested in making a profit. While understandable, it is unclear how these enterprises will proceed if their pursuit of profits complicates or contradicts broader Chinese government policy in Africa. In short, the complex web of internal decisionmaking processes, the stovepiped nature of the Chinese bureaucracy, and the government's limited capabilities to dampen the "reputational risks" posed by the Chinese diaspora business community all reflect the increasing difficulties faced by the central government when trying to coordinate and implement official policies.

In addition, China will need to work assiduously to overcome obstacles tied to language, culture, religion, and racial bias. Because Chinese is not commonly spoken in Africa, Chinese diplomats, businessmen, technicians, doctors, peacekeepers, and other "cultural ambassadors" must learn the languages of Africa—such as English and French—in order to be effective. Similarly, future Chinese engagement in Africa will need to take into greater account the exceptional religiosity of African societies and develop an official approach, which largely has been absent, of engaging religious leaders. Religious organizations, Muslim and Christian, provide a broad and widening range of social services, especially in education and health, have extensive linkages with their counterparts outside Africa, and possess a strong public voice. The Protestant and Catholic communities in Africa are the fastest growing in membership and participation. Africa's 300 million Muslims constitute highly complex, dynamic, and variegated communities.

There are also increasing pressures on China to embrace greater transparency and do more to harmonize its donor activity in Africa with ongoing international assistance, especially with respect to debt. The Chinese practice of tying loans to African commodity exports contradicts existing lending practices set forth in Organization for Economic Cooperation and Development agreements. In late 2006, the European Investment Bank and the IMF warned that China's emergence as a major creditor was creating a wave of new debt for African countries.[15] The question of debt sustainability was also raised in 2006 by then World Bank President Paul Wolfowitz.[16] Washington is particularly concerned with Africa's borrowing patterns and the impact that they may have on the long-term effectiveness of the Heavily Indebted Poor Countries debt relief initiative and the related $31 billion debt relief package for Nigeria, concluded at the time of the 2005 Group of Eight Summit in Gleneagles, Scotland. Most dramatic, the U.S. Department of the Treasury, in 2006, reportedly labeled China as a "rogue creditor" practicing "opportunistic lending."[17]

A large part of Western concerns over Chinese lending practices stems from the fact that there is, as of 2008, no systematic sharing of data by Chinese ministries with international and bilateral donors deeply invested in Africa, or with African participants in the emerging strategic partnership launched in Beijing. Effective bilateral or multilateral mechanisms have yet to be established at a broad international level or country level for integrating assistance and avoiding duplication. China's approach makes little reference to how its efforts will relate to those of the Extractive Industries Transparency Initiative, the IMF, the World Bank, and other international assistance organizations. There is mounting concern that Chinese lending practices undermine the debt relief strategies that have reduced dramatically levels of debt in Africa over the past decade in cooperation with African states and regional bodies. The fear is that Chinese lending practices may encourage the rapid recurrence of unsustainable debt in Africa.

Implications for the United States

Like China, the United States is in the midst of an expansive phase of engagement in Africa, and it is now widely acknowledged that U.S. national interests in Africa have burgeoned to include substantial global energy stakes; regional security and counterterrorism concerns; public health; and intensifying competition with China, India, South Korea, and other Asian countries that have significantly enlarged their involvement in Africa.[18]

U.S. foreign assistance levels to Africa more than tripled during the Bush administration. Signature White House initiatives have been launched that have had a predominant focus on Africa: the five-year, $15 billion President's Emergency Plan for AIDS Relief, which could see further expansion with President Bush's pledge to double this commitment to $30 billion over ten years; the $1.2 billion President's Malaria Initiative; and the Millennium Challenge Corporation, which seeks to reward states that are well governed and performing well economically with substantial new aid compacts that will accelerate economic growth. Private sector engagement is steadily rising, concentrated in the energy field, and the latest official data at the end of 2007 indicated that annual two-way trade reached $71.3 billion in 2006, up 17.6 percent from 2005.[19]

Since 11 September 2001, U.S. military engagement in Africa has been expanded substantially through the Trans-Sahara Counterterrorism Initiative, a Gulf of Guinea maritime security initiative under development in late 2007, and an ambitious Horn of Africa counterterror program. The Combined Joint

Task Force–Horn of Africa, based in Djibouti, is in place, and could be expanded. After the Ethiopian military's intervention in Somalia in late 2006, which routed the Union of Islamic Courts government, the United States became directly involved in early 2007 by attacking fleeing convoys suspected of transporting "hard target" terrorists tied to the August 1998 al Qaeda attacks on the U.S. embassies in Kenya and Tanzania, and the subsequent attacks on Israeli tourists in Mombasa, Kenya, in November 2002. In addition, it was announced in February 2007 that a dedicated, new U.S. Africa Command (AFRICOM) would be established to oversee and coordinate U.S. military-related activities on the continent. Such activities had previously been divided among three commands: the Europe Command, the Central Command, and the Pacific Command.

This shift has called into question whether the United States has adequate personnel, resources, and internal coordinating mechanisms to manage its rising interests. It has also called into question whether these relatively "harder" interests will conflict with existing, long-standing commitments to the promotion of democracy and human rights, poverty alleviation, and conflict resolution. In the Bush years, a significant, sustained, high-level commitment had been made to ending the Sudan's North-South war and, more recently, to ending the genocide in the Sudan's western region, Darfur. The events leading up to the toppling of the Union of Islamic Courts in Somalia and the postconflict reconstruction since then have also demanded high-level U.S. foreign policy attention.

While these developments advanced, the clock on the Bush administration was ticking ever louder. In particular, the hangover effects of Iraq on U.S. credibility and legitimacy at times constrained U.S. engagement in areas like the Sudan. The American response to China's engagement in Africa will also be shaped by the overall U.S.-Chinese relationship. Broadly speaking, while U.S.-Chinese relations are generally stable, the American public, members of Congress, and executive branch officials are uncertain at best about the future with China, and at worst see China as an economic and security threat. This view may inevitably limit the ability of forward-looking policymakers to build more productive relationships for American interests together with the Chinese in Africa.

The U.S. understanding of how Chinese policies toward Africa are motivated, formulated, and executed is scant at best.[20] Likewise, U.S. understanding of evolving African sentiments toward China's expansive engagement is limited. There is a tendency on the part of the United States and China to mirror one another. U.S. critics often narrowly focus on China's pursuit of energy as the best explanation for China's policies in Africa. Yet, in the Sudan, for example, oil is important but no longer the sole strategic factor in China's foreign policy calculus.[21] Progressives in the Chinese policymaking elite argue that the Sudan's oil assets are not worth pursuing in the long run, and they have suggested scaling back relations with Khartoum in an attempt to burnish China's image and international reputation. Inversely, there is a tendency among Chinese conservatives to argue that the United States and other Western countries are merely trying to force China out of the Sudan to get its oil.[22] The Chinese critics are also quick to point out that the United States—by closely dealing with such countries as Equatorial Guinea—is just as likely to embrace autocratic, corrupt, and unstable regimes.[23]

U.S. insistence on bringing a new peacekeeping force into Darfur under a sweeping UN mandate without Khartoum's consent is seen by Beijing as a violation of the Sudan's sovereignty that raises the risk that a UN force might be used to apprehend high-ranking Sudanese officials indicted by the International Criminal Court. Those actions run counter to the long-held Chinese principle of "noninterference" and thus partially explain China's cautious approach toward the Sudan.[24] To relieve this impasse, the looming humanitarian crisis in Darfur should be given priority on the U.S.-Chinese agenda. Washington should work harder with Beijing to test Khartoum's willingness to honor a ceasefire, oversee disarmament, protect humanitarian corridors, and develop an internal Darfur dialogue. It should also explore concrete ways for China to contribute to the hybrid UN-African Union (AU) operation more significantly.[25]

U.S. knowledge of African opinion on China's expansive presence is lacking. At a minimum, American approaches need to be sensitive to the many and long-standing, positive legacies and images of the Chinese in various parts of Africa—particularly in comparison to past practices of colonial and Western powers. There is a dearth of informed analysis on China's multiple impacts in those places in Africa where China has made its greatest incursions, and American writings often lack an estimation of how U.S. influence can effectively shape Chinese approaches.

In the long list of priorities in the U.S.-Chinese relationship, engagement in Africa has second-tier status. Other pressing issues for Washington—from Iran to North Korea, from East Asian stability to fending off China's economic challenge at home (especially during the 2008 election year)—will consume more time and energy in the formulation of China policy. Unfortunately, this reality also means that in return for Chinese cooperation on such issues, Washington may be less willing or able to expend the necessary political capital to gain greater cooperation from China in places such as the Sudan.

In the absence of a better formed and informed American official response to China generally, and to Chinese-African relations in particular, more provocative voices fill the void. Some Americans argue that Chinese engagement in Africa is predominantly a form of crude mercantilism and political interventionism that directly threatens U.S. interests and hence calls for confrontation, condemnation, and containment.

An array of human rights advocacy groups and nongovernmental organizations, for example, maintain intense pressure on the U.S. government to take decisive, punitive measures in response to the situation in Darfur, including calls for forced humanitarian intervention. Although the Sudanese accepted the 16 November 2006 Addis Ababa agreement (the "Annan plan") committing Khartoum to a ceasefire and three-phase expansion of a hybrid UN-AU force in Darfur, the Sudan's President Omar al-Bashir has obstructed its implementation. With the humanitarian situation worsening in Darfur, American activist groups have intensified their efforts, which include harsh criticism of China as a partner of the Sudan. Since 2006, there have been subtle, symbolic shifts in Beijing's approach toward Darfur.[26] Diplomatically, Beijing has perceived a political need to increase its commitment to work with the international community in moving the Annan plan forward. At this early stage, however, there is no guarantee for success with Beijing's approach. While Khartoum has expressed compliance, its commitment to follow through is uncertain, and thus Beijing remains vulnerable to continued criticisms for enabling Khartoum's intransigence.

Looking Ahead

At the official level, the United States and China in 2005 began to take steps to discuss their increasingly complex and interdependent relationship. This effort, known as the Senior Dialogue, was led on the U.S. side by then Deputy Secretary of State Robert Zoellick, who called for China to join the United States in becoming a "responsible stakeholder" in the international system.[27] Both sides agreed to hold bilateral subdialogues on key regional issues. The door was thus opened in Washington to begin an effective U.S. strategy for engaging China on Africa.

Several rounds of bilateral dialogue on Africa between U.S. and Chinese policymakers have been held since then. In early March 2007, for example, U.S. Assistant Secretary of State for African Affairs Jendayi Frazer and her Chinese counterpart, Assistant Minister Zhai Jun, focused on the specific issues of debt sustainability, peacekeeping operations, Chinese companies' reputational risks in Africa, and transparency in the extractive industries. On the Sudan, the Chinese reportedly acknowledged the need for the international community to step up efforts and become more active in leveraging their respective influences in Darfur.[28]

At the fourth round of the U.S.-China Senior Dialogue, in June 2007, U.S. Deputy Secretary of State John Negroponte and Chinese Vice Foreign Minister Dai Bingguo covered a range of key bilateral and global issues, including Darfur. Constructive developments resulted from this meeting. First, the State Department's official statement at the end of the dialogue acknowledged the Chinese characterization of Darfur as a "humanitarian crisis" (as opposed to genocide). Second, the two sides agreed that the various subdialogues, including that on Africa, should continue in order to deepen mutual understanding and enhance collaboration in areas of common concern.[29]

Greater consensus has been achieved in the last few rounds of bilateral dialogue on Africa, in part because the United States is beginning to understand that China has real interests in Africa and will be engaged on the continent for the foreseeable future. Continuing to see China's economic, political, or diplomatic activities in Africa as a zero-sum game is therefore counterproductive. This emerging viewpoint is an encouraging sign; the challenge is for Washington to make a strong commitment, at a high diplomatic level, toward understanding the Chinese perspective and then to continue to test China's intentions systematically.

There will continue to be critical voices and distractions in Washington that may impede the near-term official formulation of an integrated, coherent U.S. strategy that might leverage areas of common U.S.-Chinese interests, while mitigating those areas where U.S. national interests and values are in conflict with Chinese approaches. Regardless, the trend line for China's expanding presence in Africa—and the challenges and opportunities it presents to American interests—demands greater U.S. attention and action. Critical work needs to be done to generate new, longer-range thinking and greater intellectual content to help create effective U.S. policies to engage China productively in Africa.

On the multilateral level, there remain ample opportunities for further collaboration among China, Africa, and the United States. The principles of sovereignty and nonintervention form the bedrock of Chinese foreign policy, but if an international consensus emerges, legitimated by the UN or the AU, Beijing will be more supportive of potential interventions, while still keeping a relatively low profile. On issues such as good governance, human rights, poverty alleviation, and building health care capacities, a concerted international effort seeking Chinese endorsement of principles already adopted by the AU (more specifically, the African Charter on Human and People's Rights, which was implemented in 1986) would be an important step forward. Washington should also solicit Beijing's participation in multilateral donor discussions on Africa in such venues and institutions as the Group of Eight, the Organization for Economic Cooperation and Development, and the World Bank. China's involvement would help harmonize ongoing donor activity and promote responsible lending to ensure that African countries reap the benefits of coordinated aid and debt relief while avoiding a new buildup of unsustainable debt.

On the bilateral level between Washington and Beijing, there should also be an increase in ongoing consultations to address the immediate and emergent challenges in Africa. Immediate attention is needed on the destabilizing situation in the Horn of Africa, especially regarding developments in the arc stretching from the coastal part of the Horn inland: Somalia, Ethiopia, the Sudan, and Chad. Consultations and joint solutions also should be fostered to address security and political challenges emerging in the Niger Delta, Angola, and Zimbabwe, and regarding the maritime security of energy and raw material shipments along the east coast of Africa.

Moreover, military-to-military consultations regarding Africa should be explored further. Such consultations could expand to include other key players, such as the AU and European countries. China and other crucial players are looking to augment the role of their militaries to assist in addressing security challenges in many parts of Africa. China has dramatically increased its peacekeeping forces since 2000 and is now one of the largest contributors of peacekeepers to the UN. China has peacekeepers operating in seven of the eight current UN missions in Africa.[30] As the international community contemplates increasing its presence in such locations as the Darfur region of the Sudan, and with the possibility that additional UN peacekeepers will be needed elsewhere, the United States, China, the AU, and other interested parties will need to intensify their consultations in response. The reasoning behind the forthcoming establishment of the new U.S. AFRICOM, reflective of increasing U.S concerns about stability, failed states, and terrorism in Africa, is one point of departure for U.S. and Chinese discussions about security on the continent.

In addition, civil society and nongovernmental organizations can become important facilitators for future China-Africa-U.S. collaboration. China's expansive engagement in Africa thus far has not tapped into Africa's burgeoning civil society organizations. Working with civil society organizations operating in Africa, both domestic and international, will prove an effective means to gain a better understanding of local developments and accurately gauge local reactions to China's expanding role. Governments, corporations, foundations, and philanthropies should consider ways to bring China's nascent civil society organizations into contact with their counterparts in Africa. Such interactions would include delegations of scholars and policy analysts to meet on issues of common research interest, observation of grassroots elections, cooperative activities to support environmental protection or worker safety, and other civil society activities related to good governance, religious practices, community health, and rights of women and girls.

Much more can also be done to deepen the level of Chinese scholarly understanding of contemporary Africa. Philanthropies concerned with international relations should consider support for Chinese academics and policy analysts to take up studies, fellowships, and other research and training opportunities in the United States, as well as in Europe and in Africa. This could emulate the Ford Foundation programs of the 1990s, which helped ground Chinese scholars in serious graduate-level African studies at leading American universities. Another option is to provide modest support to facilitate the participation of Chinese scholars in major academic meetings, such as university-based conferences or the annual meeting of the African Studies Association, or to support joint research projects involving U.S., Chinese, and African scholars.

In sum, any future U.S. strategy or policy option regarding Africa will require both a far greater understanding of evolving African opinions and approaches toward China's growing presence in Africa and the world, as well as a far more sophisticated understanding of the complexities of Chinese motivations and decisionmaking vis-à-vis Africa.

Notes

1. For the latest literature on the topic, see Bates Gill, Chin-Hao Huang, and J. Stephen Morrison, *China's Expanding Role in Africa: Implications for the United States* (Washington, D.C., 2007); Princeton Lyman and J. Stephen Morrison, *More Than Humanitarianism: A Strategic U.S. Approach toward Africa* (New York, 2006); Alex Vines, "China in Africa: A Mixed Blessing?" *Current History,* CVI (2007), 213–219; Harry Broadman, *Africa's Silk Road: China and India's New Economic Frontier* (Washington, D.C., 2007); Andrea Goldstein and others, *The Rise of China and India: What's in It for Africa?* (Paris, 2006); Chris Alden, "China in Africa," *Survival,* XLVII (2005), 147–164; Garth le Pere, *China in Africa: Mercantilist Predator, or Partner in Development?* (Johannesburg, 2006).

310   CHIN-HAO HUANG

2. The following points draw from Gill, Huang, and Morrison, *China's Expanding Role in Africa*, 6–13.

3. "China Becomes Africa's Second Largest Trading Partner," Beijing Zhongguo Xinwen She (27 December 2007); "China's Foreign Policy and 'Soft Power' in South America, Asia, and Africa," A Study Prepared for the Committee on Foreign Relations, United States Senate by the Congressional Research Service, Library of Congress (April 2008), 120, available at http://biden.senate.gov/imo/media/doc/CRSChina Report.pdf (accessed 29 May 2008).

4. "China Becomes Africa's Second Largest Trading Partner," Zhongguo Xinwen She [China News Service] (27 December 2007).

5. Interview between author and Chinese officials (November 2007).

6. George T. Yu, "Africa in Chinese Foreign Policy," *Asian Survey*, XXVIII (1988), 849–862.

7. For a specific breakdown of the Chinese contribution to various UN peacekeeping missions, see UN Department of Peacekeeping Operations, "Monthly Summary of Contributors of Military and Civilian Police Personnel," available at www.un. org/Depts/dpko/dpko/contributors/ (accessed 10 February 2008). As of 2008, China had contributed more than 1,400 personnel to peacekeeping missions in Africa.

8. For greater details and content of the various official statements, documents, and declarations, see "Beijing Summit and Third Ministerial Conference of the Forum on China-Africa Cooperation" (November 2006), available at http://english.focacsummit. org/documents.htm (accessed 5 December 2007).

9. William Wallis and Geoff Dyer, "Wen Calls for More Access for Africa," *Financial Times* (17 May 2007), available at www.ft.com/cms/s/34e52c64-0365-11dc-a023-000b5df10621,dwp_uuid=5cdb1d20-feea-11db-aff2-000b5df10621.html (accessed 17 May 2007).

10. "African Officials Taking Poverty Reduction Training Visit China's West," Xinhua (30 June 2007).

11. "China Donates 8 Million Dollars to WHO to Help African Countries," Xinhua (16 May 2007).

12. South African President Thabo Mbeki delivered a stern warning to China in a public speech in January 2007, describing its approach to Africa as the threat of a new colonialism that would lock Africa in underdevelopment. That warning did not go unnoticed in Beijing, and during President Hu Jintao's speech in Pretoria in February 2007, he went out of his way to assure his audience that China would create new balances in trade relations as one demonstration of its sensitivity to African interests and opinion. See "China Faces Charges of Colonialism," *International Herald Tribune* (28 January 2007), available at www.iht.com/articles/2007/01/28/news/sudan.php (accessed 10 October 2007), and "Enhance China-Africa Unity and Cooperation to Build a Harmonious World," speech by Chinese President Hu Jintao at University of Pretoria (7 February 2007), available at www.dfa.gov.za/docs/speeches/2007/jintao 0207.htm (accessed 15 March 2007).

13. See Stephanie Rupp, 66, 70–71, 72, 76 in this volume.

14. Bates Gill and James Reilly, "The Tenuous Hold of China Inc. in Africa," *Washington Quarterly,* XXX (2007), 37–52.

15. See George Parker and Alan Beattie, "EIB Accuses China of Unscrupulous Loans," *Financial Times* (28 November 2006), available at www.ft.com/cms/s/added3c2-7f4e-11db-b193-0000779e2340.html (accessed 28 November 2006); Alan Beattie and Eoin Callan, "China Loans Create 'New Wave of Africa Debt,'" *Financial Times* (7 December 2006), available at www.ft.com/cms/s/640a5986-863a-11db-86d5-0000779e2340.html (accessed 7 December 2006).

16. "World Bank President Criticizes China's Banks over Africa Lending," *International Herald Tribune* (23 October 2006), available at www.iht.com/articles/ap/2006/10/24/asia/AS_FIN_China_World_Bank_Africa.php (accessed 12 December 2006).

17. Michael M. Phillips, "G-7 to Warn China over Costly Loans to Poor Countries," *Wall Street Journal* (15 September 2006), available at http://online.wsj.com/article/SB115826807563263495.html (accessed 15 September 2006).

18. For the latest literature on the growing importance of Africa to U.S. strategic interests, see Lyman and Morrison, *More Than Humanitarianism.*

19. See "U.S.-African Trade Profile," Department of Commerce, available at www.agoa.gov/resources/US-African%20Trade%20Profile%202008%20-%20Final.pdf (accessed 20 May 2008).

20. On 8 February 2007, Deputy Assistant Secretary of State James C. Swan noted that it is important to see China's role on the continent within the broader context of China's global foreign policy strategy and a vision of the evolving international system. For the report that resulted from this transcript, see Center for Strategic and International Studies, "China's Expanding Role in Africa: Implications for the United States," available at www.csis.org/media/csis/events/070208_china_africa_transcript.pdf (accessed 11 May 2008).

21. See J. Stephen Morrison and Bates Gill, "China and Sudan," testimony submitted to the House Foreign Affairs Committee (8 February 2007).

22. Simon Robinson, "Time Running Out," *Time* (10 September 2006), available at www.time.com/time/magazine/article/0,9171,901060918-1533376,00.html (accessed 15 September 2006).

23. See Stephen Brown and Chandra Lekha Sriram, 251 in this volume.

24. China has exercised much prudence and caution in a series of UN Security Council resolutions targeting the Sudan. The concepts of "noninterference" and "national sovereignty" are important bedrocks of Chinese foreign policy and have been the basis for its conservative posture toward sanctions or other punitive measures against Khartoum since discussions in the Security Council on Darfur began in mid-2004. China's abstentions have allowed the Security Council to adopt Resolutions 1591, 1593, and 1706, targeting the Sudan.

25. J. Stephen Morrison and Chester A. Crocker, "Time to Focus on Real Choices in Darfur," *Washington Post* (7 November 2006), available at www.washingtonpost.

com/wp-dyn/content/article/2006/11/06/AR2006110600813.html (accessed 15 November 2006).

26. See J. Stephen Morrison, testimony before the Committee on Financial Services, House Subcommittee on Domestic and International Monetary Policy, Trade, and Technology (20 March 2007).

27. "Whither China: From Membership to Responsibility?" remarks by Robert B. Zoellick, former deputy secretary of state, before the National Committee on U.S.-China Relations (New York, 21 September 2005), available at http://usinfo.state.gov/eap/Archive/2005/Sep/22-290478.html (accessed 8 December 2006).

28. Interview between the author and Chinese officials shortly after the sub-dialogues.

29. "The U.S.-China Senior Dialogue: Building a Strong Framework for Mutual Trust," provided by the State Department Bureau of Public Affairs, available at www.state.gov/r/pa/scp/87166.htm (accessed 15 November 2007).

30. As of early 2008, China contributed peacekeepers to UN missions in the Western Sahara, the Democratic Republic of the Congo, Ethiopia and Eritrea, Liberia, the Sudan (in the south and in Darfur), and Côte d'Ivoire.

Contributors

Deborah Brautigam teaches in the International Development Program at American University's School of International Service in Washington, D.C. She has lived in China and several African countries, and is the author of *Chinese Aid and African Development: Exporting Green Revolution* (1998), *Aid Dependence and Governance* (2000), and coeditor of *Taxation and State-Building in Developing Countries: Capacity and Consent* (2008). She is working on a new book on Chinese aid.

Harry Broadman is economic adviser for the Africa Region at the World Bank in Washington, D.C. Previously he served as lead economist for Eastern Europe and the former Soviet Union, and as senior economist for China. Before joining the World Bank, Broadman served as chief of staff and senior economist for the president's Council of Economic Advisers; assistant United States trade representative for services, international investment, and science and technology; chief economist of the U.S. Senate Committee on Governmental Affairs; and assistant director of Resources for the Future. He is the author of *Africa's Silk Road: China and India's New Economic Frontier* (2006).

Stephen Brown is associate professor of political science at the University of Ottawa. His main research interests are democratization, foreign aid, political violence, conflict prevention, and peacebuilding, mainly in relation to Africa, as well as Canadian development policy. He is currently working on a research project on transitional violence in Angola, Kenya, Mozambique, and Zimbabwe (jointly with Marie-Joëlle Zahar, Université de Montréal), as well as a book chapter on justice and the rule of law in post-genocide Rwanda for Chandra Lekha Sriram's project on rule of law in Africa.

Martyn J. Davies is executive director of the Centre for Chinese Studies at the University of Stellenbosch, which was established under the South Africa–China Bi-National Commission at the vice presidential level. He is also a senior lecturer within the Department of Political Science at Stellenbosch, and he teaches at the University's Business School. He is writing a book on China's commercial engagement with Africa.

Joshua Eisenman is a fellow in Asia Studies at the American Foreign Policy Council in Washington, D.C., and is pursuing his Ph.D. in political science at the University of California, Los Angeles. Before joining the Policy Council, Eisenman worked as a professional policy analyst on the staff of the congressionally mandated U.S.-China Economic and Security Review Commission. He is coeditor of *China and the Developing World: Beijing's Strategy for the 21st Century* (2007). Eisenman and David H. Shinn are working on a coauthored book on Chinese-African relations.

Chin-Hao Huang is a research associate with the Stockholm International Peace Research Institute, Sweden. Previously he was a research assistant with the Freeman Chair in China Studies at the Center for Strategic and International Studies (CSIS) in Washington, D.C. Huang helped to coordinate the CSIS China-Africa project, a multiyear initiative examining Chinese intentions, policies, and practices in Africa and their implications for U.S. strategic interests. Before joining the CSIS, he served as executive director for the Georgetown International Relations Association, a nonprofit organization based in Washington, D.C. He is the coauthor of two reports on China-Africa-U.S. relations: *China's Expansive Role in Africa: Implications for the United States* (2007), and *Assessing China's Growing Influence in Africa* (2007).

Paul Hubbard is a graduate student at the Maxwell School, Syracuse University. An Australian, Hubbard was awarded a Fulbright grant to undertake a master of arts in international relations with a geographical focus on China and East Asia, studying links between transparency and development. He is on leave from the Australian Department of the Treasury.

Wenran Jiang is associate professor of political science and acting director of the China Institute at the University of Alberta. He is a senior fellow at the Asia

Pacific Foundation of Canada, vice president of the Canadian Consortium on Asia Pacific Security, board member of the Canadian Association of Asian Studies, leader of the energy and environment research group of Canada's Emerging Dynamic Global Economies Network, special advisor on China to the U.S.- and Canada-based Energy Council, and a *BusinessWeek* on-line columnist. He is a major contributor to the Jamestown Foundation's biweekly *China Brief.*

Darren Kew is assistant professor of dispute resolution at the University of Massachusetts, Boston. Kew studies the relationship between transformative conflict resolution methods and democratic development, particularly in terms of democratic institution building in Africa. Kew has worked with the Council on Foreign Relations Center for Preventive Action to provide analysis and blueprints for preventing conflicts in numerous areas around the world, including Nigeria, Central Africa, and Kosovo. He has also been a consultant to the United Nations, United States Agency for International Development, and the U.S. State Department.

Henry Lee is lecturer in public policy, the Jassim M. Jaidah Family Director of the Environment and Natural Resources Program at the Belfer Center for Science and International Affairs, and cochair of the Kennedy School's Program on Infrastructure in a Market Economy. Before joining the Belfer Center, he spent nine years in Massachusetts state government. His research interests focus on environmental management, energy policy, geopolitics of oil and gas, and public infrastructural projects in developing countries.

Li Anshan is a professor at the School of International Studies at Peking University. He has been a visiting professor at Menlo College and at the Center for African Studies, Stanford University. Li is the author of *A History of Chinese Overseas in Africa* (2000), and *British Rule and Rural Protest in Southern Ghana* (2002).

Ndubisi Obiorah is the executive director of the Centre for Law and Social Action in Nigeria. He holds master of law degrees from Harvard University and the University of Essex. He has been a visiting fellow and researcher at Harvard University, the National Endowment for Democracy, and Human Rights Watch, and has also served as project consultant to the International Centre for the Legal Protection of Human Rights.

Robert I. Rotberg is director of the Program on Intrastate Conflict and Conflict Resolution, Kennedy School of Government, Harvard University, and president of the World Peace Foundation. He was professor of political science and history, MIT; academic vice president, Tufts University; and president, Lafayette College. He is the author and editor of *Worst of the Worst: Dealing with Repressive and Rogue Nations* (2007), *Building a New Afghanistan* (2006), *A Leadership for Peace: How Edwin Ginn Tried to Change the World* (2006), *Battling Terrorism in the Horn of Africa* (2005), *When States Fail: Causes and Consequences* (2004), *State Failure and State Weakness in a Time of Terror* (2003), *Ending Autocracy, Enabling Democracy: The Tribulations of Southern Africa 1960–2000* (2002), *Peacekeeping and Peace Enforcement in Africa: Methods of Conflict Prevention* (2001), and *Truth v. Justice: The Morality of Truth Commissions* (2000).

Stephanie Rupp is assistant professor of anthropology, Lehman College, City University of New York. She was a joint research fellow with the Program on Intrastate Conflict and the International Security Program at the Belfer Center, Kennedy School of Government, Harvard University. Her ethnographical research focuses on the politics of everyday engagement between Africans and Chinese. Previously Rupp was assistant professor of sociology at the National University of Singapore.

Dan A. Shalmon served as a research associate in the Kennedy School's Environment and Natural Resources Program. He is a graduate student in the Security Studies Program at Georgetown University's Edmund A. Walsh School of Foreign Service. Shalmon is also a senior analyst in the Future Concepts and Analysis Division of Lincoln Group, LLC, a Virginia-based company supporting cross-cultural communication and understanding for public and private-sector clients operating in the Middle East, Africa, and the Pacific rim.

David Shinn served for thirty-seven years in the U.S. Foreign Service with overseas assignments in Lebanon, Kenya, Tanzania, Mauritania, Cameroon, and the Sudan. He was ambassador to Burkina Faso in the late 1980s and ambassador to Ethiopia in the late 1990s. His chapter "Ethiopia: Governance and Terrorism" appeared in *Battling Terrorism in the Horn of Africa* (2005). Shinn has been an adjunct professor in the Elliott School of International Affairs at George Washington University since 2001. He is working on a major study of Chinese-African relations.

Chandra Lekha Sriram is professor of human rights and director of the Centre on Human Rights in Conflict, University of East London. Her book, *Peace as Governance? Power-Sharing, Armed Groups, and Contemporary Peace Negotiations* (2008), involved field research in Sri Lanka, the Sudan, and Colombia.

Yusuf Atang Tanko is a graduate student in dispute resolution at the University of Massachusetts, Boston. Tanko served on the Human Rights Violations Investigation Commission and as special assistant to the chairman of the ruling political party in Nigeria, as well as the facilitator for the presidential initiative on the reconciliation of Shell and the Ogoni people in the Niger Delta.

Index

Anambra State, Nigeria, 179
Anglo American (mining company),
151
Angola, 6, 7, 51, 53–54, 80–81; arms
transfers and, 9, 164–65, 183–84;
Benguela railway and, 150–51; cadre
training and, 237–38; civil war in,
117–19, 308; corruption in, 301; geographic concentration and, 100; high
payments to, 123; human rights and,
13, 251–52, 256, 265; infrastructure
and, 74; investment and, 117, 213;
labor and, 11, 122; landmines and,
178; MPLA and, 157, 159; national
security and, 155; oil and, 4–5, 109,
112, 115, 277; oil futures and,
121–22; political outreach to, 28,
231; SEZs and, 151; transparency
and, 124; USSR and, 202
Annan, Kofi, 129–30, 306
Apartheid, 231; China's ideology and,
274
Apparel, 103–04, 106–07; Chinese
traders and, 284. *See also* textiles
Argentina, 51
Arms, 183–85; aid for, 157–61; Angola
and, 231; bilateral assistance and,
164–66, 169–70, 172–75; during
Cold War, 231; deliveries of, 175–76;
human rights abuses and, 254–55,
257; liberation movements and,
156–57; navy and, 179–83; Nigeria
and, 167–69, 277; Sudan and,
170–72, 257–59, 266; twenty-first
century and, 161–64; Zimbabwe and,
261–64. *See also* military
Armscor (arms manufacturer), 170
Asia, 87–88, 94–95, 97–98, 261, 264,
299; development and, 144; export
composition to, 96; FDI and, 104–05;
human rights abuses and, 251; oil
dependence and, 110; product diver-

sification and, 101; trade with Africa,
273; United States and, 303; values
argument and, 252; variability in,
107
Aung San Suu Kyi, 13
Authoritarian regimes, 217
Avian influenza, 278

Balance of power, 273, 289–90, 297
Bandung Conference, 297
Bangladesh, 71, 159, 181
Ban Ki-Moon, 13, 177
Banks: freezing accounts and, 261;
funding from, 279; government
management and, 114; loan condi-
tions and, 218. *See also* concessional
loans; specific banks
Bechtel Corporation, 206
Beijing Action Plan (BAP) (2007–09),
142
Beijing Consensus, 82
Beijing Declaration, 142, 175, 291
Beijing Review (journal), 204
Belarus, 5
Belgium, 40
Belize, 211
Benguela railway, 6–7, 150–51
Benin, 6; arms transfers and, 9, 163;
Chinese medical teams in, 27; geo-
graphic concentration and, 100
Benitiu province, Sudan, 126
BHP Billiton (mining company), 151
Bilateralism, 34
Block 18, 122
Bloomberg.com, 208
Blue-water navy, 155, 181–82. *See also*
naval strategy
Borrowers, 220–24; geographic range of,
222–23. *See also* banks; concessional
loans
Botswana, 27–28, 159, 200; arms trans-
fers to, 163